Hank Stram's Pro Football Scouting Report
1991 Edition

Hank Stram's Pro Football Scouting Report
1991 Edition

Player Ratings and In-Depth Analysis
on More Than 600 NFL Players and Draft Picks

Hank Stram
and
J. David Miller

Bonus Books, Inc., Chicago

©1991 by Bonus Books, Inc.
All rights reserved

Except for appropriate use in critical reviews or works of scholarship, the reproduction or use of this work in any form or by any electronic, mechanical or other means now known or hereafter invented, including photocopying and recording, and in any information storage and retrieval system is forbidden without the written permission of the publisher.

95 94 93 92 91   5 4 3 2 1

Library of Congress Catalog Card Number: 91-73572

International Standard Book Number: 0-929387-33-3

Bonus Books, Inc.
160 East Illinois Street
Chicago, Illinois 60611

Printed in the United States of America

To my high school coaches, Chuck Baer and Richard Polk; my college coaches, Elmer Burnham, Cecil Isbell, and Stu Holcomb; my friend, Stu Pritchard; Terry Brennan at Notre Dame; Matty Bell and Woody Woodard at SMU; Andy Gustafson at the University of Miami; and Lamar Hunt from Kansas City, all of whom had a great influence on my development and growth as a coach and a person.

HS

To my former coach and current New York Knights' defensive coordinator Joe Haering, who taught me to bullshit a little less, work a little harder, and when times are tough, more than ever, stick together. Joe is the last of a dying breed of rebels, who during times of adversity, *never* let the bastards get him down.

JDM

Contents

Acknowledgments ix
Introduction xi
Hank's Rankings for Each Position xiii
Quarterbacks 1
Tailbacks 29
Fullbacks 42
Wide Receivers 57
Tight Ends 84
Offensive Linemen 93
Defensive Ends 137
Defensive Tackles 154
Nose Tackles 163
Outside Linebackers 172
Inside Linebackers 189
Cornerbacks 202
Safeties 217
Best of the 1991 Rookie Class 236
1990 Individual Statistics 245
1990 Team Statistics 264

Acknowledgments

Such an extensive project would not have been possible without dedicated assistance and countless favors from numerous friends throughout the National Football League. First, a special thanks to the dozens of PR directors and assistants whom we constantly harrassed for every type of statistic imaginable. And, of course, thanks to the many scouts, personnel directors, coaches, and general managers who contributed their personal expertise to this project.

HS/JDM

I'd like to express my own personal gratitude to several people. First, to John Butler, Buffalo director of scouting, who in my opinion has few, if any, peers. Thanks to Mouse, Beverly and Brad Davis, whose motivation and friendship serve as a constant source of strength. Also Houston Oilers strength coach Steve Watterson, for his undying loyalty and support. And thanks to Atlanta coaches Jerry Glanville and June Jones, who add a little humor and reality to a business that sorely needs it.

A special thanks to Bruce Allen and all my friends at GBA Sportsworld. Bruce survived a very tough time after his father, NFL legend George Allen, passed away in January. I thought about Bruce and his father often during the writing of this book, and can't help but think that somewhere in eternity, a whirring projector is rattling into the night and God is taking notes on how to run the ball against the Dallas Flex.

Many thanks to my research staff—Dean M. Dalton, Greg Thomas, Charlie German, and Mark Lane—for their countless hours of work.

Sincere thanks to Brian Zevnik, whose loyalty and dedication puts him in a class by himself. Without Brian, this book would never have become a reality.

JDM

Introduction

Is Joe Montana still the best quarterback in the National Football League? And if O.J. Anderson is good enough to be the Super Bowl's Most Valuable Player, then why did the Giants put him on the Plan B unprotected list two years in a row?

Few sources of reference exist for the die-hard NFL fan to find answers to such questions. Football's past is filled with great men, tough men, each with his own contribution to the sport. But every fresh season offers a new stage for tomorrow's champions. Which is the very reason why this first edition of *Hank Stram's Pro Football Scouting Report*, the only in-depth analysis available of current and prospective NFL players, has been published. Inside you will find answers to virtually any question about the top, and some not so close to the top, players in the game.

What follows on these pages are our projections for the top players at each position, including evaluations of the strengths and weaknesses of more than 600 NFL players and draft picks. And in order to give you a wide overview, we have supplemented our opinions with the views of dozens of scouts and coaches from around the NFL.

We have supplied you with individual scouting reports on the players, breaking them out by position. A "Who's Missing" section follows each position grouping. We included this section because for some players there was such a wide variety of opinions, or special circumstances—injuries, great potential/weak performance—that we felt we should omit them from our rankings. But you will note from Hank's Ratings that we consider some of these players worthy of high rankings. (Example: We give Bob Golic a AA, but some scouts question whether injuries or some up-and-coming players on the Raiders will keep him out of the starting lineup.) We have also included brief analysis on who we consider to be the top available Plan B players at each position. (A player on Plan B is automatically excluded from the position rankings.)

Near the back of the book is the "Best of the 1991 Rookie Class" section. Here we have ranked the top five players at each position (we only ranked four tight ends, so we included an extra wide receiver). Once again, you may find a few surprises—our rankings don't always match the order in which the players were drafted.

Remember as you read this book that players can't be judged on one good or bad year alone—some names, and their rankings, might surprise you. But their selection came only after we spent dozens of hours watching film and interviewing coaches, scouts, and players.

Don't look for pretty boys to rate highly, either. While the typical criteria—height, weight, and 40 times—certainly is important, each nominee was judged mainly on how he performs on the football field in game situations. Players who hunt, chase, and hit or make the tough catch in the big game get the nod here. Some analysts, citing their scientific surveys and endless statistics, would lead you to believe that football has become a game of finesse and style. But the players who headline their positions in *Hank Stram's Pro Football Scouting Report* survived for simple reasons: Toughness. Attitude. And, of course, production.

Here is sampling of some of the questions we attempt to answer:
— Is a player productive at his given position?
— Does he create his own breaks?
— Is he a team player?
— Is he consistent?
— Does his team look to him for leadership?
— Is he injury prone?
— What is his potential for improvement?

Following the scouting report for each player is Hank's Rating. Each player is given a final letter grade which projects the player's role on his team and his future in the NFL. The letter grades equate as follows:

AAA — As good as they get
AA — A team force
A — A definite starter
B — A contributor
C — Average
D — Suspect

So now that you understand the book—read and enjoy. Agree and disagree. But most of all, enjoy the game.

Hank and David

Hank's Rankings

Quarterbacks

1. Joe Montana
2. Dan Marino
3. Warren Moon
4. Jim Kelly
5. Boomer Esiason
6. Randall Cunningham
7. John Elway
8. Phil Simms
9. Bernie Kosar
10. Jim Everett
11. Troy Aikman
12. Steve Young
13. Jay Schroeder
14. Steve DeBerg
15. Jeff George
16. Bobby Hebert
17. Don Majkowski
18. Wade Wilson
19. Timm Rosenbach
20. Mark Rypien
21. Jeff Hostetler
22. Vinny Testaverde
23. Chris Miller
24. Bubby Brister
25. Ken O'Brien
26. Jim Harbaugh
27. Dave Krieg
28. Billy Joe Tolliver
29. Anthony Dilweg
30. Frank Reich
31. Cody Carlson
32. Tommy Hodson

Who's Missing
1. Rodney Peete
2. Jack Trudeau
3. Steve Walsh
4. Rich Gannon
5. Gary Kubiak
6. Peter Tom Willis
7. Erik Wilhelm
8. Gilbert Renfroe
9. Andre Ware

Best of Plan B
1. Bob Gagliano
2. Mark Vlasic
3. Hugh Millen
4. Mike Tomczak
5. Todd Philcox

Hank's Rankings

Tailbacks

1. Barry Sanders
2. Thurman Thomas
3. James Brooks
4. Neal Anderson
5. Marcus Allen
6. Eric Dickerson
7. Marion Butts
8. Dalton Hilliard
9. Emmitt Smith
10. Herschel Walker
11. Gary Anderson
12. Johnny Johnson
13. Bobby Humphrey
14. Earnest Byner
15. Eric Metcalf
16. Derrick Fenner
17. Blair Thomas
18. Mike Rozier
19. Sammie Smith
20. Cleveland Gary
21. Barry Word
22. Ottis Anderson
23. Lorenzo White
24. Tim Stephens
25. Heath Sherman
26. Tim Worley
27. Dexter Carter

Fullbacks

1. Albert Bentley
2. John L. Williams
3. Craig Heyward
4. Kevin Mack
5. Merril Hoge
6. Gerald Riggs
7. Tom Rathman
8. Alonzo Highsmith
9. Anthony Toney
10. Christian Okoye
11. Brad Muster
12. Tony Paige
13. Ickey Woods
14. Rod Bernstine
15. Michael Haddix
16. Reggie Cobb
17. Anthony Thompson
18. Brad Baxter
19. Rick Fenney
20. Maurice Carthon
21. Jamie Mueller
22. Steve Smith

Who's Missing
1. Bo Jackson
2. Keith Byars
3. Rodney Hampton
4. Dave Meggett
5. Harold Green
6. Rueben Mayes
7. Steve Broussard
8. Marcus DuPree

Best of Plan B
1. Roger Craig
2. John Settle
3. Don Smith
4. Joe Morris

Hank's Rankings

Wide Receivers

1. Jerry Rice
2. Al Toon
3. Andre Rison
4. Anthony Carter
5. John Taylor
6. Willie Gault
7. Andre Reed
8. Flipper Anderson
9. Henry Ellard
10. Art Monk
11. Mervyn Fernandez
12. Sterling Sharpe
13. Webster Slaughter
14. Drew Hill
15. Mark Duper
16. Eric Martin
17. Haywood Jeffires
18. Gary Clark
19. Anthony Miller
20. Curtis Duncan
21. Tim McGee
22. Ernest Givins
23. Ricky Proehl
24. Rob Moore
25. Stephone Paige
26. James Lofton
27. Louis Lipps
28. Wendell Davis
29. Mark Jackson
30. Mark Carrier
31. Fred Barnett
32. Bill Brooks
33. Vance Johnson
34. Stephen Baker
35. Ernie Jones
36. Mark Ingram
37. Shawn Collins
38. Hassan Jones
39. Jessie Hester
40. Calvin Williams
41. Reggie Langhorne
42. Brian Blades
43. Ricky Sanders
44. Kelvin Martin
45. Irving Fryar
46. Perry Kemp
47. Tommy Kane
48. Bruce Hill

Who's Missing

1. Eddie Brown
2. Hart Lee Dykes
3. Emile Harry
4. Mark Clayton
5. Brian Brennan
6. Michael Irvin
7. Clarence Verdin
8. Brett Perriman
9. Ronnie Harmon
10. Robb Thomas
11. Robert Clark

Best of Plan B

1. Richard Johnson
2. James Milling
3. Jason Phillips

Hank's Rankings

Tight Ends

1. Keith Jackson
2. Rodney Holman
3. Eric Green
4. Steve Jordan
5. Ferrell Edmunds
6. Mark Bavaro
7. Keith McKellar
8. Jay Novacek
9. Brent Jones
10. Ed West
11. Arthur Cox
12. Marv Cook
13. Ron Hall
14. Walter Reeves
15. Clarence Kay

Who's Missing

1. James Thornton
2. Don Warren
3. Bob Mrosko
4. Mark Boyer
5. Gary Wilkins
6. Ethan Horton

Best of Plan B

1. Pete Holohan
2. Eric Sievers

Hank's Rankings

Tackles

1. Anthony Munoz
2. Jim Lachey
3. Paul Gruber
4. John Elliott
5. John Alt
6. Jackie Slater
7. Chris Hinton
8. Richmond Webb
9. Nate Newton
10. Jimbo Covert
11. Bruce Armstrong
12. Gary Zimmerman
13. Joe Walter
14. Will Wolford
15. Mark Tuinei
16. Stan Brock
17. Tunch Ilkin
18. Harris Barton
19. Ron Heller
20. Harvey Salem
21. Ken Lanier
22. Irv Pankey
23. Ken Ruettgers
24. Mike Kenn
25. Keith Van Horne
26. Lomas Brown
27. Bubba Paris
28. Dean Steinkuhler
29. Howard Ballard
30. Tim Irwin
31. Ron Mattes
32. Irv Eatman
33. Luis Sharpe
34. Kevin Call
35. Doug Reisenberg
36. Rory Graves
37. David Williams
38. Andy Heck
39. John Jackson
40. Ed Simmons
41. Steve Wright
42. Matt Darwin
43. Leo Goeas
44. David Viaene
45. Mark Dennis
46. Paul Farren
47. Tootie Robbins
48. Tony Jones
49. Kevin Haverdink
50. Tony Mandarich
51. Zefross Moss

Best of Plan B
1. John Rienstra
2. Harry Swayne

Hank's Rankings

Guards

1. Randall McDaniel
2. Mike Munchak
3. Bill Fralic
4. Tom Newberry
5. Sean Farrell
6. Max Montoya
7. Steve Wisniewski
8. Keith Sims
9. Mark Stepnoski
10. Ron Solt
11. Bruce Collie
12. Edwin Bailey
13. Jim Ritcher
14. Ron Hallstrom
15. Guy McIntyre
16. Harry Galbreath
17. Raleigh McKenzie
18. Mark Bortz
19. Tom Thayer
20. Rich Moran
21. Jim Dombrowski
22. Eric Andolsek
23. Bruce Reimers
24. Frank Cornish
25. Mark Schlereth
26. Houston Hoover
27. John Davis
28. Don Maggs
29. Terry Long
30. Steve Trapilo
31. David Richards
32. Dave Lutz
33. Jim Juriga
34. William Roberts
35. Brian Blados
36. Doug Widell
37. Eric Moore
38. Mike Schad
39. Paul Fairchild
40. Bryan Millard
41. Derek Kennard
42. Lance Smith
43. Ian Beckles
44. Dave Zawatson
45. Todd Kalis
46. Joe Milnichik
47. Randy Dixon
48. Rich Baldinger
49. Dave Cadigan
50. Brian Baldinger
51. Mike Utley
52. Gregg Rakoczy
53. Ralph Tamm

Best of Plan B
1. Roy Foster
2. Mark May

Hank's Rankings

Centers

1. Bruce Matthews
2. Courtney Hall
3. Don Mosebar
4. Jay Hilgenberg
5. Kent Hull
6. Doug Smith
7. Ray Donaldson
8. Jeff Bostic
9. Jim Sweeney
10. Bart Oates
11. David Alexander
12. Jeff Uhlenhake
13. Kirk Lowdermilk
14. Joel Hilgenberg
15. Bruce Kozerski
16. Jamie Dukes
17. Blair Bush
18. Bill Lewis
19. Danny Villa
20. Jessie Sapolu
21. Kevin Glover
22. Randy Grimes
23. Keith Kartz
24. Grant Feasel
25. Tim Grunhard
26. Mike Baab
27. Dermontti Dawson

Hank's Rankings

Defensive Ends

1. Reggie White
2. Bruce Smith
3. Chris Doleman
4. Leslie O'Neal
5. Charles Haley
6. Lee Williams
7. Charles Mann
8. Richard Dent
9. Pierce Holt
10. Leonard Marshall
11. Jacob Green
12. Greg Townsend
13. Burt Grossman
14. Trace Armstrong
15. Sean Jones
16. Kevin Greene
17. Leon Seals
18. Neil Smith
19. Renaldo Turnbull
20. Mike Gann
21. Tony Woods
22. Danny Noonan
23. Jon Hand
24. David Grant
25. Wayne Martin
26. Brent Williams
27. Ray Agnew
28. Reuben Davis
29. Jeff Cross
30. William Fuller
31. Nate Tuatagaloa
32. Marvin Washington
33. Alphonso Carreker
34. Daniel Stubbs
35. Keith Willis
36. Dan Owens
37. Bill Maas
38. Al Noga
39. Robert Brown
40. Eric Dorsey
41. Tim Green
42. Jeff Lageman
43. Darrell Davis
44. Shawn Patterson
45. Rod Saddler
46. Matt Brock
47. Sam Clancy
48. Dexter Manley

Who's Missing

1. Jim Jeffcoat
2. Jim Skow
3. Keith McCants
4. Donald Evans
5. Anthony Smith

Hank's Rankings

Defensive Tackles

1. Ray Childress
2. Keith Millard
3. Jerome Brown
4. Dennis Byrd
5. Kevin Fagan
6. Clyde Simmons
7. Howie Long
8. William Perry
9. Fred Stokes
10. Scott Davis
11. Dean Hamel
12. Steve McMichael
13. Jeff Bryant
14. Darryl Grant
15. Tony Tolbert
16. Doug Smith
17. Tim Johnson
18. Danny Noonan
19. Cortez Kennedy
20. Jimmie Jones
21. Joe Nash
22. Harvey Armstrong
23. Mark Spindler
24. Rick Bryan
25. Mike Fox

Who's Missing
1. Ken Clarke
2. Bob Buczkowski

Best of Plan B
1. Bill Pickel

Nose Tackles

1. Michael Dean Perry
2. Michael Carter
3. Henry Thomas
4. Jerry Ball
5. Dan Saleaumua
6. Erik Howard
7. Brian Sochia
8. Kevin Kragen
9. Tory Epps
10. Tim Krumrie
11. Scott Mersereau
12. Tony Casillas
13. Gerald Williams
14. Jeff Wright
15. Tim Goad
16. Bob Nelson

Who's Missing
1. Bob Golic

Hank's Rankings

Outside Linebackers

1. Lawrence Taylor
2. Derrick Thomas
3. Darryl Talley
4. Pat Swilling
5. James Francis
6. Cornelius Bennett
7. Carl Banks
8. Tim Harris
9. Rickey Jackson
10. Jesse Tuggle
11. Ken Harvey
12. Simon Fletcher
13. Junior Seau
14. Mike Cofer
15. Andre Tippett
16. Karl Mecklenburg
17. Chip Banks
18. Clay Matthews
19. Kevin Greene
20. Andre Collins
21. Aaron Wallace
22. Mike Merriweather
23. Duane Bickett
24. Ken Norton, Jr.
25. David Griggs
26. Ron Riveria
27. Hugh Green
28. Lamar Lathon
29. Wilber Marshall
30. Darion Conner
31. David Wyman
32. Darrin Comeaux
33. Greg Lloyd
34. Seth Joyner
35. Jerry Robinson
36. Bill Romanowski
37. John Roper
38. Jesse Small
39. Rufus Porter
40. Chris Martin
41. Leon White
42. Johnny Meads
43. Larry Kelm
44. Fred Strickland
45. Broderick Thomas
46. Dennis Gibson
47. Ray Berry
48. George Jamison
49. Kevin Murphy
50. Scott Stephen
51. Frank Stams
52. Chris Singleton
53. Anthony Bell

Who's Missing

1. Freddie Joe Nunn
2. Tony Bennett
3. Aundray Bruce

Best of Plan B

1. Jim Morrissey
2. O'Brien Alston

Hank's Rankings

Inside Linebackers

1. Vaughan Johnson
2. John Offerdahl
3. Pepper Johnson
4. Chris Spielman
5. Mike Singletary
6. Gary Plummer
7. Sam Mills
8. David Little
9. Billy Ray Smith
10. Dino Hackett
11. Shane Conlan
12. Mike Johnson
13. Hardy Nickerson
14. Jack Del Rio
15. Riki Ellison
16. John Rade
17. Jeff Herrod
18. Kurt Gouveia
19. Johnny Holland
20. Eugene Seale
21. Keith DeLong
22. Percy Snow
23. Byron Evans
24. Al Smith
25. Eugene Marve
26. Johnny Rembert
27. Ed Reynolds
28. Burnell Dent
29. Eric Hill
30. Ervin Randle
31. Robert Lyles

Who's Missing
1. Brian Noble
2. Carl Zander

Best of Plan B
1. Matt Millen

Hank's Rankings

Cornerbacks

1. Rod Woodson
2. Deion Sanders
3. Kevin Ross
4. Wayne Haddix
5. Albert Lewis
6. Isaac Holt
7. Don Griffin
8. Mark Collins
9. Carl Lee
10. Everson Walls
11. Nate Odomes
12. Darrell Green
13. Gill Byrd
14. Terry McDaniel
15. Eric Allen
16. J.B. Brown
17. Mark Lee
18. Eric Davis
19. Darryl Pollard
20. Reggie Rutland
21. Richard Johnson
22. Patrick Hunter
23. Eugene Daniel
24. Cris Dishman
25. Kirby Jackson
26. Ben Smith
27. Donnell Woolford
28. Ronnie Lippett
29. Cedric Mack
30. Frank Minnifield
31. Garry Lewis
32. Marcus Turner
33. Jerry Holmes
34. Toi Cook
35. Alan Grant
36. Robert Massey
37. Ray Crockett
38. Dwayne Harper
39. David Johnson
40. Jerry Gray
41. Lemuel Stinson
42. Martin Mayhew
43. Sam Seale
44. Tony Stargell
45. James Hasty
46. Vince Buck
47. Raymond Clayborn

Who's Missing

1. Eric Thomas
2. Lewis Billups
3. Darryl Henley
4. Tim McKyer
5. Bobby Butler
6. James Williams

Hank's Rankings

Safeties

1. David Fulcher
2. Joey Browner
3. Steve Atwater
4. Bubba McDowell
5. Scott Case
6. Louis Oliver
7. Mark Carrier
8. Carnell Lake
9. Mark Murphy
10. Eddie Anderson
11. Jarvis Williams
12. Erik McMillan
13. Dennis Smith
14. William White
15. Mark Kelso
16. Tim McDonald
17. Barney Bussey
18. Leonard Smith
19. Bennie Blades
20. Brian Jordan
21. Todd Bowles
22. Shawn Gayle
23. Mark Robinson
24. Lloyd Burruss
25. Mike Harden
26. Thomas Everett
27. Nesby Glasgow
28. Terry Kinard
29. Deron Cherry
30. Keith Taylor
31. Harry Hamilton
32. Vince Albritton
33. Alvin Walton
34. Tiger Greene
35. Eugene Robinson
36. James Washington
37. Wes Hopkins
38. Fred Marion
39. Gene Atkins
40. Myron Guyton
41. Brett Maxie
42. Vince Newsome
43. Johnny Jackson
44. Greg Jackson
45. Mike Prior
46. Michael Ball
47. Thane Gash

Who's Missing
1. Dave Waymer

Best of Plan B
1. Ronnie Lott
2. Jeff Donaldson
3. Felix Wright
4. William Frizzell
5. Terry Hoage

Hank's Rankings

1991 Rookie Class

Quarterbacks
1. Brett Favre
2. Browning Nagle
3. Craig Erickson
4. Dan McGuire
5. Todd Marinovich

Running Backs
1. Harvey Williams
2. Nick Bell
3. Eric Bieniemy
4. Jarrod Bunch
5. Leonard Russell

Wide Receivers
1. Alvin Harper
2. Randall Hill
3. Mike Pritchard
4. Willie Jake Reed
5. Reggie Barrett
6. Derek Russell

Tight Ends
1. Reggie Johnson
2. Chris Smith
3. Adrian Cooper
4. Jerry Evans

Offensive Linemen
1. Charles McRae
2. Pat Harlow
3. Antone Davis
4. Stan Thomas
5. Eugene Williams

Defensive Linemen
1. Ted Washington
2. Russell Maryland
3. Huey Richardson
4. Bobby Wilson
5. Eric Swann

Linebackers
1. Mike Croel
2. Dixon Edwards
3. Alfred Williams
4. Roman Phifer
5. Keith Traylor

Defensive Backs
1. Todd Lyght
2. Bruce Pickens
3. Eric Turner
4. Jesse Campbell
5. Henry Jones

Quarterbacks

Joe Montana

Birthdate: June 11, 1956
College: Notre Dame
Height: 6-2
Weight: 195
How Acquired: Drafted in third round, 1979
Final 1990 Team: San Francisco 49ers

PRODUCTIVITY

It will be years after Montana retires before fans appreciate—or understand—what they have in Super Joe. Montana never had size (6-2, 195) or great speed, but two things have made him the premier quarterback in the *history* of the game: uncanny field vision and toughness.

Montana's innate ability to *anticipate* passing lanes, long before his receivers break open, sets him apart from his peers. He throws a soft, catchable ball—but defensive backs have noticed that Montana's tightropes have slowed significantly in recent years. But the bottom line is Montana's four Super Bowl rings.

TOUGHNESS

Nobody is tougher, physically or in the crunch. Ask the Eagles—in 1989, they punished Montana with *eight* sacks and led 28–17 at the end of three. But Montana, with both elbows bleeding and limping with a bum knee, still threw 3 fourth-quarter touchdowns to cap a 38–28 victory. Last year, stepping up into the teeth of a ferocious Atlanta Falcon blitz, Montana threw for 5 touchdowns. "We beat the hell out of him," says Jerry Glanville, "and we were lucky they didn't score 100."

Montana is now thirty-four years old, and he has paid a severe price for his success. He has suffered a broken collarbone, three concussions, torn knee cartilage, elbow surgery, tendonitis, a sprained knuckle, a torn hamstring, a wrenched right shoulder, a sprained ankle, a broken little finger, two broken ribs, thrice-bruised ribs, and, of course, the now-famous ruptured disc in his spine. He now suffers from arthritis in his back. Montana's body has withstood five major operations, and doctors wonder how long this walking miracle will keep it up. "The man loves football," says backup quarterback Steve Young. "He plays his heart out every week. He is the epitome of what we all want to be."

CONSISTENCY

Montana has no peers. In his twelfth NFL season, Montana threw for a team-record 3,944 yards and threw 26 touchdowns. He also victimized a half dozen teams last year with fourth-quarter comebacks, and more than once was able to engineer a critical, clock-killing first down that kept opponents from getting another chance. When it comes to crunch time, he's the best.

LEADERSHIP

Montana's quiet, just-get-it-done attitude motivates his teammates. "He has a way of making you want to produce," says former 49er Randy Cross. "He wants to win so bad, and is so good at what he does, that you feel bad if you don't perform at the same level." In other words, Montana walks it, not talks it.

SUMMARY

When it's all over, the Montana name will be synonymous with greatness, like the Ruths, Thorpes, Mantles, and Granges before him. Nobody does it better.

HANK'S RATING: AAA

Dan Marino

Birthdate: September 15, 1961
College: Pittsburgh
Height: 6-4
Weight: 224
How Acquired: Drafted in first round, 1983
Final 1990 Team: Miami Dolphins

PRODUCTIVITY

Eight years. Two-hundred-forty-one touchdown strikes to twenty-three different receivers, ranked second among active quarterbacks to only Joe Montana, who has been in the league five years longer. Tack on 31,416 yards passing, reaching 30,000 yards sixteen games sooner than any other quarterback in history.

"Dan makes quick decisions, and once he's made a decision the ball gets there quicker than anyone who's ever gotten it there before," says Dolphin head coach Don Shula. "He has done things in his first eight years that no one has ever come close to. If you project that pace over the next five years, he'll own all the NFL records."

TOUGHNESS

Starting with the 1984 season, Marino has started 108 of the Dolphins' last 111 games. The only games he missed were Miami's three replacement games in 1987. He is one of only six NFL quarterbacks to have started 100 or more straight games. Marino is battle-proven—last year against Buffalo, he suffered three crushing sacks, but never left the game.

CONSISTENCY

Marino has great awareness of where pressure is coming from, which enables him to get rid of the ball instead of taking the sack. The Dolphins routinely have less sacks per passing attempts than any other team in the NFL. "The offense is designed to take advantage of his abilities," says Shula. In every one of Marino's eight NFL seasons, he's thrown for at least 20 touchdowns; it took Johnny Unitas eighteen years to accomplish the same feat. In 1984, Marino threw 56 (counting the playoffs) touchdowns, another record. He's also the only NFL quarterback to throw for 30-plus touchdowns in three different seasons—and he did it consecutively, from 1984 to 1986.

LEADERSHIP

"Marino has the responsibility of leading us," says Shula. Indeed. Marino has played in forty career games without throwing an interception, and the Dolphins are 31–9 in those games. Miami has made the playoffs four of his eight seasons.

SUMMARY

In the late 1980s, the patchwork Dolphins fell prey to the improving young sharks of the AFC East. But Miami's problems centered around inferior talent and a decimated offensive line. Those problems withstanding, after Montana, Marino is still the best. "Marino," says an NFC East personnel director, "is still the quickest release I've ever seen. He has great arm strength to throw the ball deep and drive it into narrow passing lanes."

HANK'S RATING: AA

Warren Moon

Birthdate: November 18, 1956
College: Washington
Height: 6-3
Weight: 210
How Acquired: Free Agent, 1984
Final 1990 Team: Houston Oilers

PRODUCTIVITY

Warren Moon had such an incredible year in 1990 that he broke George Blanda's long-held Houston club record for career passing yards without fanfare. After Moon blistered Kansas City for 527 yards and 3 touchdowns last December 15, disbelieving Chiefs linebacker Derrick Thomas ran out of adjectives. "It was one of the most unbelievable, incredible, awesome displays any quarterback ever put on. Warren is the best quarterback I've *ever* seen." When Moon's season ended with 4,689 yards and 33 touchdowns, many others agreed. Moon's had up and down years, but one constant throughout his career—he always produces, and he gets better every year.

TOUGHNESS

Some NFL defensive players have questioned Moon's ability to stand in against a heavy rush. Moon took himself out of 1989 shellackings by Cincinnati and Kansas City, and appeared to fold up in 1990 against Atlanta. "Warren just has great judgement," says a teammate. "He plays his ass off, but he's not going to risk injury by staying in a game that's pointless. That's not fear, that's intelligence." Fans are still wondering why coaches left Moon in the game in 1990 against Cincinnati in a no-win situation, when the Pro Bowler suffered a broken thumb very late in the game, long after the game had been decided.

CONSISTENCY

In 1978, he took the Washington Huskies to the Rose Bowl and was selected the game's MVP. After being spurned by the NFL, he took his game to Canada, where he won five consecutive Canadian Football League titles. In 1983, he broke the CFL records for a single season in touchdowns, yards, and completion percentage. He's marched the Oilers to the playoffs for four consecutive years. "We've been in the playoffs four times," he says. "Now it's a matter of winning the big one. I think that's where the great quarterbacks are judged, by getting to championship games and winning them."

LEADERSHIP

There's no question that as Moon goes, so go the Oilers. Although backup Cody Carlson led the Oilers to an impressive triumph over the Steelers in the 1990 season finale, only Moon has been able to consistently motivate the multiple personalities on this club. In fact, when Moon and Glanville fell out of favor with each other in 1989, it was Glanville who eventually packed his bags.

Moon's leadership style is one of performance and consistency, not one of hoops and hollers. When Moon had a chance to break the NFL record against Kansas City for most yards passing in a game, he chose instead to call successive running plays. "I wasn't going to throw the ball just to get the record," Moon said. "Records aren't that important. The key is to win." After the Oilers destroyed arch-rival Cincinnati 48–17, Moon oozed maturity. "We had the chance to rub it in," he said, "but that's not necessary. We're all professionals here."

SUMMARY

"God gave Warren a lot of gifts, including great athleticism and intelligence," says Houston offensive coordinator Kevin Gillbride. "But what impresses me the most about him is that he's still as hungry to learn and improve as he was when he came into the league." We couldn't say it any better.

HANK'S RATING: AA

Jim Kelly

Birthdate: February 14, 1960
College: Miami
Height: 6-3
Weight: 218
How Acquired: Drafted in first round, 1983
Final 1990 Team: Buffalo Bills

PRODUCTIVITY

When the Bills crushed the Raiders during the 1990 AFC playoffs, it was a paradox of Jim Kelly's seven-year career. "Nobody, including myself, thought we could score 51 points against these guys," said the Buffalo quarterback. "But when you've got as many weapons as I do and the time to throw, we can be awfully difficult." That has been the story since Kelly splashed into the professional ranks with the now defunct-USFL's Houston Gamblers in 1983: Give him time to throw, and he'll kill you. Dating back to his rookie season, when he passed for a professional record 5,219 yards (and 44 touchdowns), Kelly has long been one of pro football's most productive quarterbacks. In 1990, Kelly completed 63.3 percent of his passes for 2,829 yards, with 24 touchdowns against just 9 interceptions. "I think Jim Kelly experienced the best year of his professional career last year," says Bills head coach Marv Levy.

TOUGHNESS

Kelly's playing style is a throwback to when great quarterbacks were measured by touchdowns and toughness, not by the number of their endorsements. In the USFL, Kelly's toughness was legendary: Once when one of his receivers was hit late out of bounds by a linebacker, Kelly sprinted thirty yards downfield, stood screaming chest-to-chest against the oversized culprit, then slapped him in the head.

No stranger to injuries, Kelly's resilience puts him in the same class with Montana. His senior year at Miami, he rebounded from a separated right shoulder that some doctors said would end his career. In the USFL, he played with broken bones and stretched knee ligaments. In 1990, he shrugged off a knee that had sidelined him for three weeks to lead the Bills to touchdowns on their first five possessions against Miami in the first round of the playoffs. Despite his bad leg, he rushed 5 times for 37 yards in that game.

CONSISTENCY

Under Kelly, the NFL's highest-rated quarterback in 1990 (101.2), Buffalo is 12–0 at home dating back to 1990. If Kelly has a weakness, it's his commitment to the deep pass and taking *too much* responsibility. "Kelly commits too early to the deep pass," says a scout. "He doesn't recognize the underneath stuff quickly enough." In the Bills' 20–19 loss to the Giants in Super Bowl XXV, Kelly tried to win the game himself, despite the fact that Thurman Thomas was having tremendous success on the ground. "Jim can still learn to make better use of everyone around him," says a Houston player.

LEADERSHIP

There are numerous examples, but perhaps the best came on October 18, 1990, when Jim Kelly connected with fullback Jamie Mueller for a 14-yard touchdown with nineteen seconds left to defeat the New York Jets, 30–27. Kelly, who passed for 297 yards and 4 touchdowns, drove Buffalo 71 yards for the winning score in the final seconds. "With Jim in the huddle," says Mueller, "you never believe you're out of the game. He definitely runs the show." Kelly's pointed criticism, however, sometimes angers teammates.

SUMMARY

It took Kelly seven years to develop the field maturity to go with his incredible God-given skills. "Kelly's fearlessness makes him special," says Atlanta's Jerry Glanville. "The kid takes on linebackers, defensive backs, everybody. Even when he makes a bad decision, with his arm, he can still force the ball in there and make things happen." Put Kelly in that special class of players—with the likes of Montana and Marino—and bet that he'll be "making it happen" for at least another five years.

HANK'S RATING: AA

Boomer Esiason

Birthdate: April 17, 1961
College: Maryland
Height: 6-5
Weight: 215

How Acquired: Drafted in second round, 1984
Final 1990 Team: Cincinnati Bengals

PRODUCTIVITY

Boomer Esiason has become a consummate quarterback, in spite of the sometimes demanding offensive schemes of the Cincinnati Bengals. Though his 22 interceptions in 1990 led the NFL, he also fired 24 touchdowns. Boomer's numbers reflect the up and down Bengal offense: When it worked, as it did in both games against Pittsburgh, it was awesome. When it didn't, as against Indianapolis, Atlanta, Houston and Seattle, it was not pretty.

Some peers say Esiason is successful *in spite* of the offense. "He has so much to remember, it's unbelievable," says an AFC Central player. But the Bengals offense is not as complicated as perceived. They have two different approaches for their offense—huddle or no huddle. From the no huddle, the Bengals can run every play in their playbook, and can go with either a 2-minute, hurry-up pace, or a normal pace. A new play is signaled in to the quarterback from Wyche immediately after a play has ended—while the players are unpiling. The team also gathers on the sideline during TV timeouts. And Esiason, who threw for 3,031 yards in 1990, has good rapport with head coach Sam Wyche and knows the system.

Esiason won the AFC passing championship in 1989 for the second consecutive time, gunning for 3,525 yards and 28 touchdowns. Esiason has everything required of an NFL quarterback: charisma, a quick release, quick feet, and a quick mind. "He has one of the best arms in the game," says Wyche. "He's also accurate and has great mobility."

TOUGHNESS

Boomer is dirt-tough. After leaving a game two years ago with a severe ankle sprain, he limped back onto the field when his backup was injured. After suffering a bruised lung against the Los Angeles Raiders in 1989, he still played the next week against Houston. In 1990, he gamely played against the Raiders despite a severe groin pull. "Mental toughness is still the most important thing for an NFL quarterback," says Esiason. "In this league, everybody plays hurt."

CONSISTENCY

Since his rookie season in 1984, Esiason has never completed less than 50 percent of his passes, and has a career completion average of 56 percent. Only twice in his career have his interceptions outnumbered his touchdowns. Kansas City coach Marty Schottenheimer says preparing for Esiason is the NFL equivalent of preparing for Michael Jordon, "because he can do so many things with the ball."

LEADERSHIP

The local media and fans are charmed by Esiason's politeness, as he patiently takes the time to answer questions and sign autographs. His fiery competitiveness has also earned the respect of his teammates. Against the Rams in 1990, he single-handedly took control of the game; late in overtime, he completed five consecutive passes for 63 yards to set up the winning field goal. He finished with 471 yards and 3 touchdowns.

Esiason's leadership extends beyond the field: He discusses all phases of each game with other players (offense, defense, special teams), and attends film and strategy meetings with the offensive line. "Boomer is a student of the game who can help others because of his exceptional overview," says All-Pro tackle Anthony Munoz.

SUMMARY

Esiason wins hands down as the league's most cerebral quarterback. The offense depends upon Boomer's last-second adjustments at the line, and virtually every play in the Bengals' repertoire has dozens of line-change options.

"If Boomer makes sound on-the-field decisions and plays with an accurate arm, our team will be ranked high in the offensive statistics again," says Wyche. "But Boomer's task this year is to be an exceptional leader, to bring his team to a Super Bowl championship and not just a statistical lead in the offensive categories."

HANK'S RATING: AA

Randall Cunningham

Birthdate: March 27, 1963
College: UNLV
Height: 6-4
Weight: 203
How Acquired: Drafted in second round, 1985
Final 1990 Team: Philadelphia Eagles

PRODUCTIVITY

Randall Cunningham was the NFC's second-rated quarterback (91.6) in 1990, completing 58.3 percent of his passes for 3,466 yards and 30 touchdowns, with just 13 interceptions. Against New England, he rushed for 124 yards and threw 4 touchdowns. Against the Giants, he passed for 229 yards and 2 touchdowns and rushed for 66 yards and a touchdown. "Randall's in a world of his own," says Washington cornerback Darrell Green. "Even other top quarterbacks like Simms and Montana have to stand in awe of what Randall can do."

Cunningham's greatest virtue is his mobility. He finished fourth in his conference in rushing (942 yards) in 1990, ahead of such notables as Herschel Walker, Emmitt Smith, Ottis Anderson and Johnny Johnson. Cunningham is the first quarterback in modern NFL history to lead his team in rushing four straight years. His eight-yards-per-carry average is nearly double the average of any other *running* back in the Top 10. "Randall's a great athlete," says former Philadelphia coach Buddy Ryan. "He's too great an athlete for the Eagles not to continue to let him create big plays as a runner. It's those types of plays that scare the hell out of the defense."

TOUGHNESS

For all his circus-style antics, Cunningham's durability is outstanding. He hurdles tacklers, runs head-on into linebackers, yet seems to have the resiliency of a rubber ball. Cunningham has also proved his toughness in the pocket; in the Eagles' playoff loss to the Redskins, he was brutally sacked five times, but continued to battle back throughout the contest. "Our coaching staff worked really hard preparing us for everything they did offensively—except, of course, for Cunningham," says Washington linebacker Monte Coleman. "He just kept getting up off the ground and kept coming at us."

CONSISTENCY

Cunningham is consistently amazing. In week 8 of the 1990 season, trailing the Cowboys 20–14 with a minute remaining, Cunningham marched the Eagles on an 85-yard drive—capped by a 10-yard touchdown pass to rookie wide receiver Calvin Williams with forty-four seconds to play. He rallied the Eagles again two weeks later for two fourth-quarter touchdowns to beat Atlanta, 24–23. Against Green Bay, Cunningham scrambled seventeen yards for a touchdown—and hurdled cornerback Mark Lee for the final three yards in order to get into the end zone. "He does amazing things," says offensive tackle Ron Heller. "He plays so hard that it forces all of us to work harder and play better."

LEADERSHIP

Either due to his youth or his team's inconsistent performances, Cunningham is still perceived by NFL scouts as a superior athlete who has yet to mature into the complete leader he's capable of being. The Eagles are a talent-laden team that has floundered against lesser opponents, and Cunningham's frustration when things go bad is often visible from the stands. Perhaps the change to Rich Kotite—a quarterback-friendly coach—will help him in 1991.

SUMMARY

He is perhaps the greatest athlete to ever play quarterback, and certainly a gifted passer in his own right. But before he becomes the "Quarterback of the '90s," as he was once billed by a novel magazine, he must acquire all the mental tools that have made technicians of the game's other great quarterbacks: Patience, consistency, and poise. "Cunningham has been tremendous for Philadelphia," says Washington head coach Joe Gibbs. "He wins games on his athletic ability and sheer determination. But it takes more than that to win in the playoffs." Exactly, coach.

HANK'S RATING: AA

John Elway

Birthdate: June 28, 1960
College: Stanford
Height: 6-3
Weight: 210
How Acquired: Trade, 1983
Final 1990 Team: Denver Broncos

PRODUCTIVITY

In John Elway's last seven seasons, he has directed his team to 65 regular-season victories (69 overall), more than any other NFL quarterback. He is the only quarterback in history to pass for more than 3,000 yards and rush for over 200 yards in six consecutive seasons.

But his three Super Bowl defeats have become the Achilles' heel of his storybook career, a soft spot that frequently attracts media wolves who find it easy prey. Yet Elway has been reserved and polished in rebutting his frequent attackers, choosing to let his actions speak louder than words. "What separates John from most quarterbacks," says Denver head coach Dan Reeves, "is that he gives you the feeling that you're never really out of it." For the understated Reeves, such mild praise is the equivalent of a standing ovation.

TOUGHNESS

No season is more indicative of Elway's toughness than in 1988, when he suffered injuries to both shoulders, both ankles, both knees, his throwing elbow and assorted other bumps and bruises. Against Atlanta, he suffered a sprained ankle and sprained knee. Two weeks later, playing hurt against the Rams, he still threw 3 touchdowns, including a 1-yard rushing touchdown set up by a his own hobbling 21-yard run. The next week against the Raiders, he completed 29 of 49 for 324 yards and 2 touchdowns. He finished the year with 3,309 yards. "Nobody," says Reeves, "questions John's toughness."

CONSISTENCY

Seventeen times in eight years Elway has marched the Broncos to victory in the final minutes, including a 98-yard drive that tied Cleveland in the 1987 AFC title game (Bengals winning in overtime). Only Montana, Denver's Super Bowl nemesis, has had more last-second success among active quarterbacks. Few quarterbacks have been better in the playoffs: Elway has started seven postseason games, winning three AFC championships.

LEADERSHIP

Elway's trademark, say teammates and coaches, is his seemingly innate ability to lead his team back from certain defeat. "Elway's best if it looks impossible," screamed one Denver headline, the morning after Elway marched his team to victory in the last two minutes against Kansas City earlier this season.

"With leadership, somebody doesn't just say, 'OK, you're a leader,'" says Reeves. "John has earned it on the field, coming through in the clutch, knowing that he's the guy that can win it in the last second. You develop leadership by going into battle and coming out ahead."

SUMMARY

Until John Elway wins the Super Bowl, the city of Denver will keep a loaded gun poised at his forehead. Fierce criticism from media and fans has made him more sensitive and withdrawn; he is not the vocal leader he once was. But critics forget that Elway's number of interceptions have *always* been high. But so is his career completion average, touchdowns, and victories. Elway by himself is worth five wins a year to the Broncos. "Criticism hurts, but it's something you can't control," Elway says. "Those things are going to happen. When you're a quarterback, and you're playing in the Super Bowl, people are going to give you a tough time. Especially when you have guys like Terry Bradshaw, who always want attention and don't know the situation. But I just consider the source."

HANK'S RATING: AA

Phil Simms

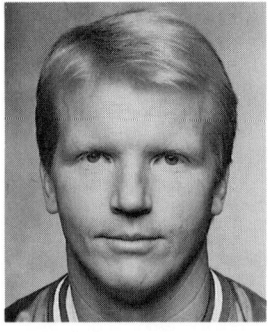

Birthdate: November 3, 1956
College: Morehead State

Height: 6-3
Weight: 214
How Acquired: Drafted in first round, 1979
Final 1990 Team: New York Giants

PRODUCTIVITY

Few quarterbacks with Phil Simms' numbers have suffered the criticism he's endured over his thirteen seasons. As backup Jeff Hostetler rode to victory in Super Bowl XXV, Simms—injured for New York's last two 1990 regular-season games—watched quietly as another player was given credit for a successful season that was largely due to his production. Simms completed 59.2 percent of his passes for 2,284 yards, including 15 touchdowns against just 4 interceptions.

TOUGHNESS

In 1989, Simms was sacked forty times. But despite the punishment he's suffered, and despite the knock that he's a brittle quarterback, Simms has missed just 7 games in the Giants' last 115 outings. And early in his career, he suffered injuries that would have put most quarterbacks down for the count: In 1980, he missed three games with a shoulder separation; in 1981, he separated his other shoulder and missed five games. In 1982, he missed the entire season with torn knee ligaments. In 1983, he missed fourteen games with a broken thumb.

Simms went down in week 15 in 1990 with a severely sprained foot. Keeping his history of serious injuries in perspective, don't expect Simms to just give up his starting job.

CONSISTENCY

Since 1984, Simms has thrown 132 touchdowns. He already owns fourteen all-time club passing records, and has been an MVP in both the Super Bowl and Pro Bowl. Dating back to his rookie season, when he won six of the first eight games he started, Simms has been a winner. His 92.7 passing rating in 1990 was the second time in three years his rating was over 90, and his 4 interceptions tied Steve DeBerg for the league's lowest total. And it was Simms twelfth season as a pro—don't tell him he's thirty-five years old.

LEADERSHIP

In 1990, during a critical four-week stretch against NFC East rivals, Simms threw 8 touchdowns against the likes of Dallas, Washington (twice), and Phoenix—all four of them victories. Simms' patience, attitude, and consistency reflect the work habits of the New York Giants. They win quietly, often without fireworks, but they win. Simms is a team player, a confident leader, and seldom makes mistakes.

SUMMARY

Simms, now entering his fourteenth season, has seen all there is to see in an NFL career. And while Simms has been repeatedly overlooked for postseason honors, he has quietly out-performed—and outlasted—many, many players. His arm isn't as live as it once was, but his courage, determination and experience give him an edge few quarterbacks can claim. But it wouldn't be a big surprise if the Giants open the season with Jeff Hostetler as their starter and Simms as a very capable backup.

HANK'S RATING: AA

Bernie Kosar

Birthdate: November 25, 1963
College: Miami
Height: 6-5
Weight: 210
How Acquired: Chosen in supplemental draft, 1985
Final 1990 Team: Cleveland Browns

PRODUCTIVITY

Bernie Kosar had the worst season of his career in 1990, and opposing coaches are openly wondering if the once-great technician has anything left. Granted, Kosar's woeful year—2,562 yards, 10 touchdowns, 15 interceptions—reflected the horrible season suffered by Cleveland's front office and ownership. But Kosar has suffered physical abuse over the past three years that he may never recover from. It was also the first time in his brilliant career that he threw more picks than touchdowns. His 65.7 rating was also a career low.

TOUGHNESS

It's hard to argue with Kosar's toughness, but the question is how much can one body take? The 1990 season was the third consecutive year Kosar suffered serious injuries during his six-year career. He missed the final two games when he suffered a chip fracture and ligament sprain of his right (throwing) thumb. At the time, the team was on a record pace for sacks and quarterback knockdowns. Atlanta and the Rams sacked him four times apiece, San Francisco crushed him three times, and Pittsburgh sacked him seven times. Kosar has been sacked seventy-one times in the past two years, and knocked down at least that many times.

CONSISTENCY

Kosar had his most inconsistent season in 1990, but again, he was not alone in mediocrity. Many experts feel the Brown's offensive design was the problem, and that even a healthy Kosar could not have made it work. But NFL scouts also point out that Kosar's timing repeatedly appeared to be a split second off, and what little zip he once had on his passes appeared to be gone. He still possesses nice touch and reads defenses well, but the arm that carried him to 16,450 career passing yards in six years appears to be waning.

LEADERSHIP

Through the Browns miserable season of 1990, Kosar was fairly quiet. "I'm really not sure what to say, other than it was a nightmare out there, and the whole season was a nightmare," he says. Although he's never been a terribly vocal leader, Kosar became invisible. For someone who has rewritten virtually all the Browns passing records in just six years, Kosar appears openly frustrated at the juggling that has taken place with management—four head coaches in four years.

SUMMARY

No quarterback can match Kosar's accomplishments at his age. Kosar entered the league in 1985, two years ahead of Vinny Testaverde, his successor at Miami. And Kosar is twelve days *younger* than Testaverde. Kosar has also played in three AFC championship games. Yet, at twenty-six, his mobility has been slowed and health questions hang over his head. But with Bill Belichick taking over and bringing in a new offense (he once worked under Ted Marchibroda), look for Kosar to find his game again if healthy.

HANK'S RATING: A

Jim Everett

Birthdate: January 3, 1963
College: Purdue
Height: 6-5
Weight: 212
How Acquired: Trade, 1986
Final 1990 Team: Los Angeles Rams

PRODUCTIVITY

For the past three seasons, Jim Everett has excelled in moderate anonymity. In 1990, he threw for 3,989, with 23 touchdowns and 17 interceptions for a 55.4 completion percentage, good for sixth in the NFC. In 1989, he led the NFL for the second straight year in touchdowns (29) while throwing for a club record 4,310 yards.

TOUGHNESS

Although Everett played much of the 1989 season with a bad back and a hip pointer, he didn't miss a game. "Jim gives us an emotional lift," says head coach John Robinson. "He's an aggressive person. I love that about him. I like his attitude." But Everett does have a reputation around the league for being a great quarterback when he's ahead, "but when he's behind, he's a different guy," says an AFC Pro Bowl defensive player. "In my opinion, he definitely can be physically intimidated." And this intimidation often leads to Everett throwing interceptions.

CONSISTENCY

How valuable is Everett? Since becoming the starter as a rookie in 1986, the Rams have reached double figures in scoring every game. Except for his rookie season, he has consistently thrown for more touchdowns than interceptions, and in 1988, he set five club records, then broke four of them again in 1989. When he's good, he's great; but when he's off, he's terrible. Proof of that in 1990: Everett was brilliant in routing Atlanta (302 yards, 3 touchdowns), but was pitiful in a 41–10 loss to Pittsburgh, when he threw two first-half interceptions that led to quick Steeler scores.

LEADERSHIP

Everett has handled the glitz of Los Angeles with relative ease, and it is reflected in his hands-on, steady management style. He is quick to praise teammates, as well as criticize them, and has earned their respect. "One thing about Jim," says Robinson, "is he plays. We've had good seasons, we've had bad seasons. Jim comes to play every week."

SUMMARY

Everett is a strong role player on a run-oriented team, and excels in that scheme. Scouts believe that on more pass-dependent teams, such as Miami or San Francisco, Everett wouldn't be as productive. "With his height and strength, he's perfect for what the Rams do," says a scout. "But he lacks the consistency of other quarterbacks in the Top 10."

HANK'S RATING: A

Troy Aikman

Birthdate: November 21, 1966
College: UCLA
Height: 6-4

Weight: 216
How Acquired: Drafted in first round, 1989
Final 1990 Team: Dallas Cowboys

PRODUCTIVITY

Regarded as "The Franchise" around Dallas, youngster Troy Aikman posted a respectable completion percentage (56.6) for the 1990 season, and despite a nagging shoulder injury that kept him out of the season's final games, he still threw for 2,579 yards. He directed winning touchdown drives against San Diego and Tampa Bay, and led the Cowboys to a 7–7 record before his injury.

TOUGHNESS

Ask Atlanta Falcons head coach Jerry Glanville about Troy Aikman's toughness. In Aikman's final preseason game as a rookie, Glanville called a safety blitz thirty-six times, and Aikman was hammered to the turf play after play. When it was over, Aikman had directed the game-winning drive and thrown for 300-plus yards, in spite of a split lip, busted chin, and assorted bruises. "He's a tough kid," says Glanville. "He'll be fine in this league." Aikman also survived a nine-sack day against the Redskins last year. He hasn't been particularly injury prone, and, to his credit, many of the offensive breakdowns can be shared by the five guys in front of the Cowboys young quarterback.

CONSISTENCY

Though showing great improvement over his rookie year, Aikman still threw 18 interceptions against just 11 touchdowns. And although the Cowboys are still building and adding key skill players almost daily, Aikman will still have to make better decisions in the heat of battle. But he did display flashes of excellence that are an exciting sign of things to come for the young Cowboys. And the expected new changes to the offense will bring out Aikman's talents even more.

LEADERSHIP

With the Cowboys seemingly out of the hunt with a 3–7 record, Aikman led them to four consecutive victories to put them back in the thick of the playoff race. After the Aikman-led Cowboys trampled the Cardinals, Phoenix head coach Joe Bugel was impressed with what he witnessed. "When you have a quarterback like Aikman, you've got a chance to win every time you play," he said. The Cowboys clearly agree.

SUMMARY

There was little doubt in Big D that, had Aikman played in the final two games, the Cowboys would've made the playoffs. "I don't wonder 'what if', I know 'what if'," says Dallas head coach Jimmy Johnson. "If Troy Aikman is healthy, we win both games and ride six straight wins into the playoffs." Aikman has endured a lot in his first two NFL seasons—both criticism and praise—but one fact is clear: As he matures and develops consistency, he will emerge a star.

HANK'S RATING: A

Steve Young

Birthdate: October 11, 1961
College: BYU
Height: 6-2
Weight: 200
How Acquired: Trade, 1987
Final 1990 Team: San Francisco 49ers

PRODUCTIVITY

With Joe Montana ending the 1990 season with another major injury and postseason operation, it seems unlikely that the San Francisco organization will honor Young's requests to be traded. Montana was so healthy throughout the fall of 1990 that Young made few appearances and just one start, throwing just 62 passes and rushing 15 times, all lows for his eight-year pro career. When called on, he completed 61.3 percent of his passes for 427 yards and 2 touchdowns.

TOUGHNESS

Young's career has been relatively injury free, ironic in that his style of play is hardly a cautious one. In an era of quarterback hook-slides, Young is an intelligent halfback taking snaps. He plays with minor bruises, but somehow avoids the major lumps, except for a lone knee injury that plagued him in 1985 with the USFL's Los Angeles Express.

CONSISTENCY

Steve Young established a 49ers' team record by completing 11 of 12 passing attempts on two different occasions. In his only start, he threw for 208 yards and rushed for 102 yards, yet fumbled four times in a 13–10 loss to the New Orleans Saints. Young is a career 56 percent passer, throwing for 9,997 yards in two different leagues (two years in the defunct USFL). He has a 50–49 touchdown-interception ratio, but his risky passing is offset by his running ability. Young has an incredible 6.2 yards per carry average over his career, for 2,200 yards and 19 touchdowns.

LEADERSHIP

After Young replaced Montana in 1990 against Minnesota, he rallied San Francisco to a 20–17 victory, throwing for 205 yards and 2 touchdowns and rushing for 59 yards. He fired the game-winning touchdown with 29 seconds to play. "Steve didn't miss a beat," says wide receiver John Taylor, who caught the winning score. "We knew we were going to win."

SUMMARY

San Francisco covets its backup quarterback, and thus far have turned down trade offers. "We certainly want Steve Young to be a part of this team," says head coach George Siefert. "He's an integral part of our offensive plans." When you hear football people say, "he could start on a lot of teams," Young is one backup that really could.

HANK'S RATING: A

Jay Schroeder

Birthdate: June 28, 1961
College: UCLA
Height: 6-4
Weight: 215
How Acquired: Trade, 1988
Final 1990 Team: Los Angeles Raiders

PRODUCTIVITY

After Al Davis handpicked Jay Schroeder as his "quarterback of the future," when he traded for him in 1988, the quarterback suffered two average, injury-marred seasons. Then he burst back to reasonable success in 1990, leading the Raiders to a 12–4 mark and division title before being annihilated 51-3 by the Buffalo Bills in the playoffs.

Schroeder completed 54.5 of his passes for 2,849 yards, the second-best season of his career. It improved his career completion percentage to just over 50 percent, and was his highest-yardage total since 1986, when he set the Redskins' season record with 4,109.

TOUGHNESS

Throughout his career, Schroeder's toughness problems haven't been physical, but mental. For the most part, he's avoided injury and has never refused to play with minor health problems. But when Washington coach Joe Gibbs showed displeasure with his young quarterback, Schroeder publicly pouted and became a distraction to the team. Schroeder, who played minor league baseball for four years, is laden with athletic ability. His attitude was largely the reason Washington agreed to trade him.

CONSISTENCY

Schroeder thrived under assistant coach Mike White's offense, which featured the long ball and a "no egos allowed" approach. After compiling a career interception-touchdown ratio of 1 to 1, Schroeder threw 19 touchdowns and just 9 interceptions in 1990—including a streak of ten games without an interception. His 1990 season was the most consistent of his career—since entering the NFL in 1985, Schroeder has thrown 69 touchdowns against 72 interceptions.

LEADERSHIP

Schroeder's ability to be a natural leader has often been questioned. But, after being generally regarded by his Washington coaches and teammates as having a bad attitude, Schroeder has consciously worked on his leadership abilities in Los Angeles. For the first time in his career, he has been called a "team player" in Los Angeles. Prior to the 1990 season, he told Raiders owner Al Davis, "I'm not a million-dollar player," and offered to split $200,000 off his $1 million salary. The two split the difference. That move endeared him to his teammates, who were shocked at his selflessness.

SUMMARY

When the running game was successful, Schroeder performed well. When it didn't—Kansas City (twice), Green Bay, and Buffalo in the playoffs—Schroeder's arm couldn't carry the Raiders. He threw 5 interceptions agains the Bills in the playoffs. Scouts still see him as a solid quarterback "when he plays within the system." But Schroeder still looks deep too often, and hurries his throws under pressure —resulting in interceptions.

No matter what the scouts say, Schroeder showed great improvement in 1990. Look for Schroeder to build on 1990 and have his finest season in 1991.

HANK'S RATING: A

Steve DeBerg

Birthdate: January 9, 1954
College: San Jose State
Height: 6-3
Weight: 214
How Acquired: Trade, 1988
Final 1990 Team: Kansas City Chiefs

PRODUCTIVITY

Steve DeBerg, in his fourteenth and best all-around season, finished 1990 with 3,444 yards and 23 touchdowns as he led the upstart Chiefs to an 11–5 record and a playoff berth. Pretty heady stuff for a thirty-six-year-old quarterback, who many assumed had run out of chances. DeBerg compiled a streak of seven games without an interception. "Steve was the biggest reason for our success," says wide receiver Emile Harry.

For Kansas City coach Marty Schottenheimer, the playoff berth was a chance to prove that his reign in Cleveland was no fluke. For DeBerg, it was a chance to redeem himself, after being upstaged four times during his career by young guns. In San Francisco, he was replaced by Joe Montana; in Denver, John Elway; and twice in Tampa Bay, by Steve Young and Vinny Testaverde. "My goal is to try not to have the number-one pick in the NFL draft come play in Kansas City," says DeBerg, jokingly. "I've waited all my life for this, and I'm going to enjoy it."

TOUGHNESS

A national television audience grimaced December 15, 1990, as rejuvenated quarterback Steve DeBerg suffered a broken little finger on his left hand against the Houston Oilers. With several million aghast viewers watching through their fingers, DeBerg braced himself, then writhed in pain as trainers popped the finger back in place and secured the injury with tape. DeBerg then shocked his own team doctors by leading the Chiefs to a 24–21 victory over San Diego the next week—while visibly wincing as every snap slammed into his broken hand.

CONSISTENCY

DeBerg's career passing percentage with four different teams nears 60 percent. Despite flashes of inconsistency (which typically reflected a lack of talent around him), DeBerg has also shown signs of greatness everywhere he's been. He's had 3,000-yard seasons with three different clubs. In San Francisco, he set then-NFL records with 347 completions in 578 attempts. In Denver, he set an NFL record by completing 18-straight passes against two different teams. At Tampa Bay, he tied for the sixth-most accurate passing game (86.2 percent) in NFL history, with a 25 of 29 performance against Detroit. And this year in Kansas City, DeBerg threw the fewest interceptions of all NFL quarterbacks who played in sixteen games (4 in 444 attempts).

LEADERSHIP

How could a younger player not respond to DeBerg? He is the ultimate opportunist, the consummate overcomer. A tenth-round pick of the Dallas Cowboys in 1977, DeBerg was waived before signing with San Francisco. In 1980, he suffered a vicious hit to the throat that took away his voice. No problem. DeBerg started nine games and played in eleven using a voice amplifier under his shoulder pads; during that span, he threw 12 touchdowns, including a career-record 93-yard scoring strike to Freddie Soloman.

SUMMARY

Although critics waited until last year to jump aboard the DeBerg bandwagon, consider this: Only once in his career (1978) has he completed less than 50 percent of his passes. The knock on DeBerg is that his lack of escapability hurts him. But as Joe Montana said, "Steve taught me to love the game. When Steve left here, he ended up with teams that haven't had too good of records, but he's always the same. He's always up, loving the game, loving the competition. He might get down a little when he's losing, but he loves the game." We couldn't have said it any better.

HANK'S RATING: A

Jeff George

Birthdate: December 8, 1967
College: Illinois
Height: 6-4
Weight: 221
How Acquired: Drafted in first round, 1990
Final 1990 Team: Indianapolis Colts

PRODUCTIVITY

Boy wonder Jeff George guided the Colts to a 5–7 record in his rookie season, including a 5–3 record over the second half of the year. He finished with 2,152 yards, 16 touchdowns and 13 interceptions, making him just the eighth of thirty-four starting rookie quarterbacks in the NFL since 1961 to throw more touchdowns than interceptions.

TOUGHNESS

This has been George's biggest question mark, though he answered some critics in 1990 when he bounced back from thirty-seven sacks, two concussions, bruised ribs, and assorted other nicks and bruises. Because of the knock against him, however, teams will continue to punish him more than others, in an effort to test his fortitude. George has yet to prove he can stand in and take a beating for four quarters like a Kelly, Esiason, or Montana.

CONSISTENCY

After a very inconsistent college career, George had a modest rookie year. He completed more than 50 percent of his passes in nine of his thirteen games, and finished with a 54.2 percent completion average overall. George also set a pattern for success: He is 4–2 in his starts without interceptions; in his seven losses, he threw 11 interceptions. Consistency, obviously, is the hardest thing for a young quarterback to learn, but down the final eight-game stretch of the season, George threw 14 touchdowns against 7 touchdowns.

LEADERSHIP

George's best game as a rookie, in the opinion of several teammates, was against Cincinnati. Showing outstanding poise, he completed 70 percent of his passes for 253 yards and fired 3 touchdowns en route to an upset victory over the Bengals. He also had a similar day against Washington, throwing for 252 yards and three scores. But the key to success in the NFL is spreading those flashes of brilliance over sixteen games. "He'll be a much more productive player [in 1991] because of the experience he has gone through," says Colts head coach Ron Meyer. "His body clock has been acclimatized to pro football."

SUMMARY

Jeff George is still an enigma. After one decent college season and one great workout in Indy, he rocketed to the top of the 1990 draft. But he has yet to prove anywhere that he can be consistent, take punishment, and show the poise that it takes to win in the NFL. His lack of movement makes him vulnerable to big hits. Those are the negatives; the positives, however, suggest George has an incredible future. "He's the most accurate passer I've ever worked out," says Atlanta offensive coordinator June Jones. "He has great velocity, but he still throws a very catchable ball with unbelievable accuracy, especially deep."

HANK'S RATING: A

Bobby Hebert

Birthdate: August 19, 1960
College: Northwestern LA
Height: 6-4
Weight: 215
How Acquired: Free Agent, 1985
Final 1990 Team: Did Not Play

PRODUCTIVITY

In 1989, Bobby Hebert completed a higher percentage of his passes (62.9) than every NFL quarterback other than Joe Montana. But when he struggled late in the year, head coach Jim Mora yanked him in favor of journeyman John Fourcade (who would quickly play himself out of the job in 1990). Hebert skipped all of last season in a contract dispute, and several teams who coveted his services lost interest when the Saints demanded two number-one picks in exchange.

Make no mistake: Hebert is a starting NFL quarterback with an accurate right arm. Apparently, Hebert will grudgingly return to a team that he publicly berated, where he has just one year remaining on his contract. In his last season (1989), Hebert completed 62 percent of his passes for 2,686 yards, 15 touchdowns, and 15 interceptions. After the Saints stumbled into the playoffs last year at 8–8, they made no bones about where their problem lies: Quarterback. "There have never been any bridges burned as far as I'm concerned," says Mora. "We'd welcome Bobby back."

TOUGHNESS

Hebert proved his toughness in the United States Football League, where he was one of the defunct league's first "homegrown" stars. Hebert has played with bruised ribs, bad knees, concussions, and dozens of other injury problems. Only severe injuries—like a broken foot in 1986—have forced him out of the lineup. A tough, big, pocket passer who cannot be physically intimidated.

CONSISTENCY

Simply put, the Saints conservative, ball-control system restricts Hebert. Hebert, who would rather run a to-hell-with-it-I'm-going-deep offense, was still the highest-rated Saints quarterback in history in 1988. His 15-touchdown seasons in 1988 and 1989 were the most since Archie Manning in 1980. But his five-year totals in New Orleans —9,667 yards, 57 touchdowns—are embarrassing next to his *three* USFL seasons: 11,137 yards passing and 81 touchdowns, numbers that led New Orleans to offer him $800,000 a year when the spring league folded in 1985.

Hebert led USFL teams to two title games in three years, where he split wins with Jim Mora. "In the USFL," says Hebert, "we went deep a lot. In New Orleans, it's more patient. I like to throw the long ball, but in this offense, I have to take what they give me."

LEADERSHIP

"Hebert is a bright guy," says fullback Craig Heyward. "On this club, Bobby's the sergeant. He may not always look brilliant, but he gets it done." If anything, his teammates quietly support him in his confrontation with the front office. "Bobby stood up for his rights," says one. "We respect what he had to do. And compared to what we had, we'll be thrilled to have Bobby back."

SUMMARY

Hebert is a great passer against man-to-man coverage. If you blitz him, or leave a receiver isolated, he'll find him. He has nice touch and throws a beautiful deep pass. "But against the Saints offense," says a division coach, "if you drop everybody off in a deep zone and force him to be patient, and if you prevent him from going up top, he'll make mistakes."

HANK'S RATING: A

Don Majkowski

Birthdate: February 25, 1964
College: Virginia
Height: 6-2
Weight: 197
How Acquired: Drafted in tenth round, 1987
Final 1990 Team: Green Bay Packers

PRODUCTIVITY

Majkowski's 4,318 yards passing and 27 touchdowns in 1989 were the second-highest in club history. Perhaps more impressive was Majkowski's sheer determination; his refusal to admit defeat, even in the closing seconds, allowed the Pack to pull out several critical victories. But Majkowski's inability last year to recover from a rotator cuff injury—suffered November 18, 1990, against Phoenix—has baffled team doctors and frustrated Packer backers.

In Majkowski's 1990 injury-shortened year, the quarterback missed the last six games and threw for just 1,925 yards. He threw 10 touchdowns against 12 interceptions, and left a giant question mark for 1991. "For us to be effective as a football team, we need somebody to step forward, to take charge," says head coach Lindy Infante. "Don does that. But we need him healthy."

TOUGHNESS

While questions abound about Majkowski's consistency, when it comes to toughness, the Majik Man has answered the bell more than once. In 1988 against the 49ers, Majkowski shrugged off knee and rib injuries to score two rushing touchdowns in a come-from-behind effort to upset the NFL champions. A fierce competitor, Majkowski made five tackles during the course of the 1988 season, including one against vaunted Detroit linebacker Chris Spielman, who had recovered a teammate's fumble. In 1987, Majkowski impressed Saints fans with a thunderous tackle of Saints linebacker Pat Swilling after an interception.

CONSISTENCY

This is Majkowski's biggest question mark. After his charmed 1989 season, Majkowski renegotiated his contract, missed the first game of the 1990 season due to his holdout, then missed the final six games due to injury. His three previous years, despite flashes of brilliance, were marred with lack of playing time, inconsistency, and interceptions. "If Don could take the next step in his development, throw fewer interceptions, be more instinctive at times, he can be a better player," says Infante. "There's still a lot of things he does that he can do better."

LEADERSHIP

The second 4,000-yard passer in team history (Lynn Dickey was the first), Majkowski became the "Majik Man" for his series of 1989 comebacks which produced five come-from-behind victories. Behind Majkowski, Green Bay rallied to beat the world champion 49ers, swept Chicago in two games and tallied *four* one-point victories, an NFL record.

SUMMARY

Majkowski is an intense competitor, is highly mobile, and has the arm strength and savvy to carry a pro team. But until he physically proves his ability to rebound from his serious injury, as well as proves that he can be consistent year in and year out, NFL scouts will continue to rate him below his potential.

HANK'S RATING: A

Wade Wilson

Birthdate: February 1, 1959
College: East Texas State
Height: 6-3
Weight: 208
How Acquired: Drafted in eighth round, 1981
Final 1990 Team: Minnesota Vikings

PRODUCTIVITY

Wade Wilson's injury-marred career has at times produced incredible numbers worthy of a starting quarterback. But at other times, Wilson has failed to live up to his ability, and it's reflected in his rollercoaster career numbers. In 1990, Wilson completed 82 of 146 passes—56.2 percent—for 1,155 yards, 9 touchdowns, and 8 interceptions. Wilson's touchdowns—and interceptions—come in bunches. He has yet to prove he can play a sixteen-game schedule and consistently win.

TOUGHNESS

Separated shoulder in 1988. Fractured knuckle in 1989. Torn ligaments on the thumb of his passing hand in 1990. Like Tommy Kramer before him, Wilson can't seem to stay healthy long enough to develop consistency. But in Wilson's defense, these are not injuries that you can play through. But like Phil Simms, who also was injury-prone early in his career, Wilson must find a way to play more than he sits.

CONSISTENCY

Wilson, while splitting time with long-gone Tommy Kramer in 1988, was the NFC's leading passer. He followed that with back-to-back injury-marred and interception-plagued seasons (12 interceptions in 1989). The bottom line: He can't be counted on for a full season. And when young Rich Gannon faltered in 1990, it left the Vikings floundering.

LEADERSHIP

Wilson's arm strength and mobility remain intact. The key element is the mental part of his game. In 1989, he had horrible disagreements with the offensive coordinator and lost his confidence. In 1990, he had new offensive coordinator Tom Moore, but injuries felled him again.

SUMMARY

In 1988, he had a 91.5 rating—the NFC's highest. In 1989, he had a 70.5 rating. In 1990, he had a 79.6 rating—twenty-first in the NFC. When he's on, he's among the top three quarterbacks in the NFL. His problem is he hasn't been "on" enough lately. "This position is a problem," says head coach Jerry Burns. "And somehow we have to get this problem solved."

HANK'S RATING: A

Timm Rosenbach

Birthdate: October 27, 1966
College: Washington State
Height: 6-2
Weight: 210
How Acquired: Chosen in Supplemental draft, 1989
Final 1990 Team: Phoenix Cardinals

PRODUCTIVITY

Nineteen-ninety was essentially Timm Rosenbach's rookie year (he appeared in less than three quarters during his inaugural 1989 season). Improving in all phases as the season progressed, Rosenbach went from a nervous kid (4 picks in the opener against Washington) to a confident triggerman who struck for 682 yards and 6 TDs in the final two games against the Giants and Eagles.

Rosenbach posseses a lively arm and excellent mobility, finishing as the second-leading rushing quarterback in the NFL with 470 yards, 3 touchdowns and a 5.5 yards per carry average. In his first season as an NFL starter, he completed 54.2 percent of his passes for 3,098 yards, 16 touchdowns and a 72.8 quarterback rating.

TOUGHNESS

The 6-2, 210-pound quarterback toughed out a forty-four-sack season, surviving five blind-side hits against Miami and six sacks at Philadelphia. Unafraid to run, Rosenbach attacked defenses with his tough scrambling ability, and recklessly dove for additional yards. Though his toughness impressed fans, Rosenbach must cool his act. A quick conversation with the departed Neil Lomax—once a scrambler himself—could teach him the wiles of NFL linebackers. "Timm is for real," says Phoenix head coach Joe Bugel. "He'll do what it takes."

CONSISTENCY

Rosenbach's numbers are the definite reflection of a young, maturing quarterback with a strong arm. He threw 4 interceptions against Washington, but finished the year with just 17. He also showed great poise during a three-game winning streak in the second half of the season. Rosenbach gave Cardinals fans something to cheer about for the first time since veteran Neil Lomax was forced out of action in 1988. But the charismatic offensive leader must reduce his interception ratio and increase his scoring production.

LEADERSHIP

With a supporting cast as youthful as its quarterback, Rosenbach's competitiveness was contagious—yet his inexperience cost Phoenix several close games. "Rosenbach is very confident in himself," says a veteran teammate. "As long as he keeps performing and moving the offense, nobody's complaining."

SUMMARY

Few quarterbacks throw for 3,000-plus yards in their first year as a starter. In fact, several veterans have never crossed that plateau. Scouts say the strong-armed Rosenbach has a bright NFL future, but must learn to be more patient in the pocket and to put some touch on his deep throws. Like most young, impatient firebrands, Rosenbach also looks deep too often, ignoring wide-open receivers running drag routes across the middle.

HANK'S RATING: A

Mark Rypien

Birthdate: October 2, 1962
College: Washington State
Height: 6-4
Weight: 234
How Acquired: Drafted in sixth round, 1986
Final 1990 Team: Washington Redskins

PRODUCTIVITY

In his fourth year, Washington's Mark Rypien may be earmarked for success. He has played very impressively at times while growing into the team leader that head coach Joe Gibbs believes he can be. He completed 54.6 percent of his passes for 2,070 yards in 1990, firing 16 touchdowns and 11 interceptions—including an impressive 3-touchdown performance against Phoenix on opening day.

TOUGHNESS

Rypien was placed on injured reserve in 1986 with a knee injury, then placed on injured reserve in 1987 with a back injury. Finally, in 1988, in his first full season, he threw for 1,730 yards—but missed two more games with a bad shoulder. In 1989, he played in the Pro Bowl after throwing for 3,768 yards—but was knocked out of the Atlanta game with a neck injury. "He's proven his toughness down the stretch," says Gibbs. "But he has to learn to make it through an entire season." To Rypien's credit, when he returned from his six-week layoff in 1990, he passed for 311 yards and 4 touchdowns in a 31-17 victory over New Orleans, and was named NFC Offensive Player of the Week. "From the first play, I kind of lost myself and got caught up in the game," says Rypien.

CONSISTENCY

Prior to the 1990 season, Rypien had a glowing 40-26 touchdown-interception ratio, sterling numbers that Rypien only added to with last year's performance. "Ryp is a young quarterback who has lost some confidence along the way, but has bounced back to show he has what it takes to be a factor in this league," says head coach Joe Gibbs. But he has yet to develop the full-time consistency that Gibbs seeks in his offensive leader, and when he falls apart, he does so in a big way—like his 5 interceptions against the Bears, or his late interception against the Colts that was returned for Indianapolis' winning score.

LEADERSHIP

His strongpoint going into Washington's 1991 training camp may be his ability to lead the offense. "Ryp usually makes the right decisions, he makes them quick, and he's gained everyone's respect," says Gibbs. And though injured often, he's used his health problems to his advantage, by not complaining and bouncing back to win big games. "He really came back strong from his knee injury," says wide receiver Gary Clark.

SUMMARY

The inconsistencies in Washington's offense leave doubts concerning Rypien's status for 1991. Gibbs won't rule out competition for the position. "We're not where we've had a quarterback who led us to the Super Bowl who we have no doubts about," the coach says. "We don't have a Joe Theismann situation. Our competition is closer than that." But Rypien has only started thirty games in his young career, and has a strong arm.

HANK'S RATING: A

Jeff Hostetler

Birthdate: April 22, 1961
College: West Virginia
Height: 6-3
Weight: 212
How Acquired: Drafted in third round, 1984
Final 1990 Team: New York Giants

PRODUCTIVITY

A career 50 percent passer, Jeff Hostetler became a cult hero when he led the New York Giants to their rousing 20-19 victory over Buffalo in Super Bowl XXV. And certainly, his efforts can in no way be discounted. But it must be noted that Hostetler's productivity—614 yards, 3 touchdowns, 1 interception—is still a result of the bruising New York running game. Hostetler's mobility adds another dimension to the Giants' offense. He has excellent escapability skills and run-by-design ability.

TOUGHNESS

Long before Hostetler became a New York hero for his passing heroics, he was an unknown special teams player for the Giants, barreling downfield on kickoff and punt teams. He's also appeared in several games as a wide receiver, and once blocked a punt. In the NFC title game against San Francisco, Hostetler missed three plays early in the fourth quarter after injuring his knee. But he came back to lead the Giants to field goals on their final two possessions—the last one the game winner.

CONSISTENCY

Like the other capable backups around the league—Carlson, Reich, Wilhelm—it's hard to gauge Hostetler's consistency over his few limited appearances. But Hostetler, obviously, has a Super Bowl ring to show for his outstanding efforts. "Hoss gives you a feeling of comfort," says former New York coach Bill Parcells. "Somehow, you know he's going to get it done."

LEADERSHIP

Hostetler's leadership has never been questioned. Every time he's been called on, he's performed. He ran for one touchdown and passed for another to bring the Giants back to a 24-21 victory over the Cardinals on December 23. In the NFC championship game, Hostetler completed critical passes of 19 yards and 13 yards on the final drive to set up the Giants' winning field goal. And, of course, the way he rallied his troops in the Super Bowl became New York legend.

SUMMARY

Hostetler, much like his tutor (Simms), is a very accurate and careful passer. He rarely forces the ball into coverage, and does an excellent job of "looking off" his primary receivers. He's an excellent quarterback in the Giants, run-oriented, ball-control scheme. And his ability to make big first downs running puts great pressure on the defense. Expect Hostetler to be in hot pursuit of Phil Simms for the starting spot.

HANK'S RATING: A

Vinny Testaverde

Birthdate: 11-13-63
College: Miami
Height: 6-5
Weight: 215
How Acquired: Drafted in first round, 1987
Final 1990 Team: Tampa Bay Buccaneers

PRODUCTIVITY

Vinny Testaverde has improved slowly since 1987, when Tampa Bay made him the first player selected in the draft. His 2,818 yards in 1990 were the third-best totals of his career, but managed to make him the second-highest passer in Tampa Bay history (behind Doug Williams).

TOUGHNESS

At 6-5, 215 pounds, Testaverde is one of the most physically capable quarterbacks in football. He seldom misses a game with injury.

CONSISTENCY

This is Testaverde's biggest problem. Scouts feel he makes too many poor reads, and has trouble picking out the open receivers. Though his completion percentage rose a few points in 1990 (from 53.8 percent in 1989 to 55.6), his horrendous interception ratio stayed the same. He threw 22 picks against 20 touchdowns in 1989; in 1990, 18 picks against 17 touchdowns. In his four-year career, Testaverde has now thrown 59 interceptions, and just 35 touchdowns, the worst among any starting quarterback, free agent or otherwise.

LEADERSHIP

In four years, Testaverde has failed to quarterback a winner in Tampa. He also has been quick to publicly complain and point blame in other directions in the media. His biggest problem, perhaps, has been maturity, something that typically comes slower to players on losing franchises. Tampa Bay needs a leader, and so far Testaverde has not stepped up to fill the role.

SUMMARY

Scouts still fault Testaverde's basic mechanics: He lacks the discipline to dump the ball off, instead of forcing it into downfield coverage or taking a sack. He often stares down the intended receiver. He telegraphs screens. And he's color-blind. All facts. Another fact—he is a player blessed with incredible God-given skills. If Tampa Bay's constant coaching changes cease, a more consistent Vinny Testaverde should be the result. And that could mean his best year so far.

HANK'S RATING: A

Chris Miller

Birthdate: August 9, 1965
College: Oregon
Height: 6-2
Weight: 200
How Acquired: Drafted in first round, 1987
Final 1990 Team: Atlanta Falcons

PRODUCTIVITY

Chris Miller's 6,194 passing yards and 33 touchdowns in the 1989 and 1990 seasons are the best two years since Steve Bartkowski's back-to-back efforts in 1980 and 1981. At the age of twenty-four, only Joe Namath, Fran Tarkenton, Dan Marino, and Bernie Kosar had passed for more yards. His 2.6 percent two-year interception rate is impressive. Miller completed more passes for more yards in 1990 than the quarterbacks of eight different playoff teams.

TOUGHNESS

Miller is mentally tough, physically tough, but generally brittle, which has been his biggest weakness to date. Injuries have kept Miller from performing at a peak level. Dating back to an injured leg during his sophomore year in high school, Miller has routinely suffered minor injuries that have forced him to miss all or parts of games. His collarbone injury against Tampa Bay in week 13 brought his 1990 season to a close, and effectively slammed the door on the Falcons' hopes.

CONSISTENCY

The 1990 season was probably the most consistent year for the fourth-year pro. He threw for 366 yards in a victory over the Saints, completed 28 passes against the Bears, fired 3 touchdowns against the 49ers, and completed 72 percent of his passes against the Bengals. He also had a streak of six games without an interception, including streaks of 110 and 77 throws without a pick.

LEADERSHIP

If Miller rebounds well from his collarbone injury, the NFL may get a chance to see what he truly is capable of under new offensive coordinator June Jones. A quiet leader, Miller leads by example.

SUMMARY

For Miller to rocket into the NFL's elite, it will take a combination of his improved efforts, a healthy season, and the response of the talent around him. A lot of ifs . . . but Miller has the potential.

HANK'S RATING: A

Bubby Brister

Birthdate: August 15, 1962
College: Northeast LA
Height: 6-3
Weight: 205
How Acquired: Drafted in third round, 1986
Final 1990 Team: Pittsburgh Steelers

PRODUCTIVITY

It might surprise some people to know that Brister's 1990 rating (81.6) was ahead of such notables as Jim Everett, John Elway, Boomer Esiason, and Chris Miller, and that his 20 touchdowns were a career high. All that in spite of Joe Walton's double-clutch, slam-bam-thank-you-ma'am offense, which seems to specialize in poor field position and punting. After the team went a month without scoring, Brister, a long-ball specialist trapped in a dink'em and dunk'em offense, responded to the boos in the stand. "If I was them," the blue-collar Brister said matter-of-factly, "I'd boo, too."

TOUGHNESS

Cajun cannon Bubby Brister has personified guts for so long, it's hard to pick a single example. There was the time he exchanged punches with 6-5, 290-pound defensive end Keith Gary. "I'd never seen a quarterback punch out a defensive end," says an amazed teammate. Or the time he cursed a Houston defensive lineman—at the line of scrimmage. But never was Brister tougher than last year, when trapped inside a predictable, methodical offense, he had one of his finest years—despite incredible physical punishment. He suffered five sacks against the Dolphins, and six against the Raiders. "When you talk about Bubby," says Houston defensive end Sean Jones, "you're usually talking about toughness. He never thinks he can't win."

CONSISTENCY

Brister tied with Marino in 1990 in completion percentage (57.6), the highest of his career. Prior to that, he'd been a career 49 percent passer, which scouts say is more indicative to the lack of talent around him. His 2,725 yards in 1990 and 2,634 yards in 1988 were the best for Pittsburgh since Terry Bradshaw in 1981. But in the past eighteen months, Brister has struggled under new offensive coordinator Joe Walton. The Steelers went a *month* without a touchdown. And when the team finally scored their first touchdown in 1990 against San Diego on an 8-yard Brister pass, the offensive scheme had nothing to do with it. "It was a broken play, the wrong formation, the whole damn thing," says Brister. "It's never easy."

LEADERSHIP

So intense is Brister, says Atlanta coach Jerry Glanville, "that I think he occasionally throws an interception just to knock the hell out of the guy who catches it." Two years ago, Brister boldly predicted that he would lead the Steelers to the playoffs. He did. "That wasn't enough," Brister says. "From now on, I'm gonna walk softly and carry a bigger stick." "With his attitude," says Glanville, "we should all thank God he's not a strong safety."

"I've just had it with excuses," Brister says. "I've been here six years. It used to be somebody always was blaming somebody else. This guy didn't block. This guy didn't run. This guy didn't tackle. Well, those days are over. A few years ago I stood up and told everybody, 'Hey, shut the hell up and let's play football.' If you get in my huddle, you better be there to win the damn ballgame."

SUMMARY

Brister may be the fastest-rising star of all the quarterbacks in the league. He taunts defensive linemen. He oozes emotion. He struts standing still. And he wins. Critics point to his erratic completion average, but the Steelers receiving corps has yet to live up to Brister's ability. And no quarterback in the league spits in the face of an oncoming blitz like Brister. "The last time I saw a guy with his confidence," says ESPN analyst Joe Theismann, "it was Joe Namath. You may not always get the right decision out of Bubby, but he is *always* decisive. Whatever he does, he does with confidence. Don't underestimate him."

HANK'S RATING: A

Ken O'Brien

Birthdate: November 27, 1960
College: California-Davis
Height: 6-4
Weight: 206
How Acquired: Drafted in first round, 1983
Final 1990 Team: New York Jets

PRODUCTIVITY

Ken O'Brien has found himself under the pile so many times that, at this point, it's hard to determine just how good he is. Despite an erratic season with a young offensive line and new faces everywhere, O'Brien still managed to complete 55.0 percent of his passes for 2,855 yards and 13 touchdowns. In 1989, when he suffered the worst physical beating of his career (68 sacks) his 3,346 yards were the *third best* totals of his career. O'Brien throws the slant route as well as anybody in football, and has excellent touch on the ball.

TOUGHNESS

No NFL quarterback has taken a worse physical beating over the past three years than O'Brien—108 sacks in the past two years alone. "Physically, Ken is the toughest guy on this football team," says center Jim Sweeney. "I honestly don't know how he takes the punishment he does." But the beatings might be taking their toll; he often throws in fear of being hit.

CONSISTENCY

O'Brien's career has been plagued by inconsistency, but it's often been a reflection of the inconsistency around him. He's been plagued by dropped balls, frequent sacks, and a sporadic running game. Until the Jets can put together more pieces of the puzzle, we may never know how good O'Brien can be. Ironically, when the team plays modestly well, O'Brien is brilliant.

LEADERSHIP

There's no question that Jets players respond to O'Brien. He's been a gutty performer who has played with injuries and held up under brutal media and fan scrutiny.

SUMMARY

Second-year coach Bruce Coslet, who built Cincinnati's attack offense, may be able to breathe new life into O'Brien's career, but first the Jets have to protect him. But there are doubts whether O'Brien can consistently make the big throws even if the "fear of sacks" is removed. The jury is still out as to whether GM Dick Steinberg believes O'Brien can get the job done.

HANK'S RATING: B

Jim Harbaugh

Birthdate: December 23, 1963
College: Michigan
Height: 6-3
Weight: 204
How Acquired: Drafted in first round, 1987
Final 1990 Team: Chicago Bears

PRODUCTIVITY

Jim Harbaugh won the starting job with an impressive 1990 training camp performance, beating out former Chicago handyman Mike Tomczak. Harbaugh guided the team to a 10–3 record before separating his right shoulder against the Lions in week 14. His 57.7 completion average and 1.9 interception percentage were Bears records, while his 173 passes without an interception is the longest streak in Chicago's seventy-one-year history. Harbaugh's 81.9 rating was fourth in the NFC.

TOUGHNESS

As recently as 1988, Harbaugh was still volunteering for kickoff coverage on special teams, a fact you seldom see on the resumé of an NFL quarterback taken in the first round. A very mobile quarterback, Harbaugh finished third on the team in rushing with 322 yards and 4 touchdowns—averaging 6.3 yards a carry. In 1990, after bruising his ribs against Green Bay, he came back the next week to have the best game of his young career—248 yards at Los Angeles, where he marched the offense to scores on its first four possessions.

CONSISTENCY

When Harbaugh started five games in 1989, then became the full-time starter last year, he set a pace that so far has been the earmark of his young career: In 1989, he completed 62.4 percent of his passes, a Bears' single-season record, and in 1990, he completed 57.7 percent. His career completion percentage of 57.85 percent is also a team record.

Harbaugh is a steady, consistent player, and dating back to his college days at Michigan, he avoids making the big errors that can kill a team. The first passer in Michigan history to throw for more than 2,000 yards, Harbaugh also owns the school's single-season efficiency record (63.3 percent) and touchdown mark (18).

LEADERSHIP

A gutsy player, Harbaugh is a get-it-done player who is still developing his on-the-field leadership skills. Many thought that Harbaugh would be culture-shock to a team that had responded under the likes of characters like Jim McMahon, but his teammates spoke differently. "We had this maniac running around, slobbering tacos and wearing headbands, and we couldn't count on the guy," said defensive end Dan Hampton, who retired at the end of the 1990 season. "Now we have a guy we can count on."

SUMMARY

Harbaugh is young, consistent, and talented. He makes few mistakes. He runs well, throws *well enough,* and performs within the limits of his offensive scheme and the players around him. He's vanilla in a world of chocolate swirl, but on a team like Chicago, that's all that's necessary. Harbaugh is a proven winner. His toughest job will be staving off the attack of colorful—and talented—backup Peter Tom Willis.

HANK'S RATING: B

David Krieg

Birthdate: October 20, 1958
College: Milton College
Height: 6-1
Weight: 192
How Acquired: Free Agent, 1980
Final 1990 Team: Seattle Seahawks

PRODUCTIVITY

Dave Krieg signed an $8.07-million contract prior to the 1990 season, then proceeded to have arguably the worst fall of his eleven-year career. Krieg's productivity dropped so far that he suffered his lowest quarterback rating since he became the starter in 1983—73.6, and had more interceptions (20) and fumbles (16) than he did touchdown passes (15). It was the first time in Krieg's career that his turnovers outnumbered his touchdown throws, and his inconsistency was largely the reason behind Seattle's twenty-first-place finish in total offense.

TOUGHNESS

Dave Krieg has battled his way back from multiple injuries throughout his career, including broken bones, concussions, and countless abrasions. He is a gutsy, team player who has used toughness as yet another avenue to earn respect from his teammates. He does possess small hands, however, which makes him one of the NFL's most fumbling quarterbacks. But he seldom allows punishment alone to remove him from a game.

CONSISTENCY

If history is any indication, 1990 was simply an off-year: going into last season, Krieg was the NFL's fourth ranked quarterback of all-time (based on a minimum number of 1,500 career attempts), and his 87.3 rating ranked behind only Joe Montana, Dan Marino, and Boomer Esiason. Though last year's debacle spoiled such heighty numbers, Seahawks coaches expect Krieg to return to his old form in 1991: Krieg has finished second in the AFC in quarterback ratings three times, and holds team records for completions (1,644), yards (20,858) and touchdowns (169).

Only two other quarterbacks in the history of football (Marino, Johnny Unitas) have thrown 100 touchdowns quicker than Krieg, who reached that plateau in his sixty-fifth professional game. Furthermore, Krieg has thrown more touchdown passes in his last seven seasons than any other NFL quarterback except Marino and Joe Montana.

LEADERSHIP

After being ignored in the 1980 draft, Krieg signed with Seattle as a free agent and, after several years of tutelage under Jim Zorn, became Seattle's starter. His uncanny leadership ability has made him a favorite among Seahawks coaches, as Krieg manages to win games that many other quarterbacks would lose. Last-minute heroics are his forte, a trait he displayed last year against Kansas City.

Despite being sacked seven times by linebacker Derrick Thomas, Krieg managed to throw for 30 yards and 2 touchdowns, including the game-winner to Paul Skansi on the game's last play. "I'm glad the officials didn't call 'in the grasp,'" says Krieg. "Thomas had his hands around my waist on my last throw."

SUMMARY

Krieg's career has been marred by only two things: turnovers and inconsistency. One scout describes Krieg this way: "When he's hot, there may be none better. But when he's not, there may be none worse. Krieg is a streaky quarterback who makes things happen, gets the big play, but tries to force too much when things aren't going his way." And Krieg has succeeded despite a predictable offensive scheme that limits his freelancing abilities.

HANK'S RATING: B

Billy Joe Tolliver

Birthdate: July 28, 1965
College: Texas Tech
Height: 6-1
Weight: 218
How Acquired: Drafted in second round, 1989
Final 1990 Team: San Diego Chargers

PRODUCTIVITY

In an up-and-down year, Billy Joe Tolliver had his best season as a professional, completing 52.7 percent of his passes in 1990 for 2,574 yards—but matched his 16 touchdowns with 16 interceptions. A talented, rocket-armed quarterback, Tolliver has the size and strength of a prototype NFL pocket passer, but his swaggering self confidence has been hard for head coach Dan Henning to deal with. He's a young (third year), raw player with a ton of ability.

TOUGHNESS

A broken collarbone benched him after the final preseason game of his rookie year in 1988, and Tolliver missed six games. But that has been the only injury to sideline him. "Tolliver has displayed the toughness this league requires," says a scout. "You have to play hurt every week. You have to live through the weekly bumps and bruises, and Tolliver has shown that kind of toughness."

CONSISTENCY

Bottom line: Tolliver throws far too many interceptions. But he has a cannon arm that many scouts compared to the 1983 version of Jim Kelly. His problem is he lacks passing touch. He throws the out route as well as any quarterback in the game, but must learn to put touch on his deep passes. Too often Tolliver relies on the strength of his arm to force a pass he shouldn't throw.

LEADERSHIP

In 1989, Tolliver finished the year with huge division wins over Kansas City and Denver. His 350 yards in week 14 was the most productive performance by a Charger rookie in history. "Some days his completion percentage might not be as good, but he'll hit for several touchdowns," says an AFC Central scout. "In time, he has a chance to be great."

SUMMARY

A great physical specimen with all the skills to succeed in the NFL except for one—patience. When Tolliver gets confused, frustrated or angry, he simply hurls it deep, trying to make something happen. His burning desire to win should be applauded. But he must learn to let things happen naturally within the confines of his offensive system. Has to learn to tone down his throws and develop some touch and accuracy if he wants to step up to the next level.

HANK'S RATING: B

Anthony Dilweg

Birthdate: March 28, 1965
College: Duke
Height: 6-3
Weight: 215
How Acquired: Drafted in third round, 1989
Final 1990 Team: Green Bay Packers

PRODUCTIVITY

After a quiet rookie year, Anthony Dilweg was thrust into the spotlight when Green Bay starter Don Majkowski was a contract holdout in 1990, leaving Dilweg as the starter against the Rams on opening day. In his first start, Dilweg cooly completed 20 of 32 passes for 248 yards and three scores. On the season, Dilweg completed 52.6 percent of his passes for 1,267 yards and 8 touchdowns, against just 7 interceptions.

TOUGHNESS

You won't rattle Dilweg. If this former Duke Blue Devil has one outstanding quality, it's his ability to focus on his job and remain virtually oblivious to the terror around him. He was sacked six times by Chicago and five times by Minnesota, yet never faltered.

CONSISTENCY

Dilweg's future clouded when the usually steady backup suddenly suffered through a stream of fumbles, interceptions, and indecision, though such spasms are not uncommon for players seeing their first real NFL playing time. Dilweg is a highly intelligent athlete (tied for the highest IQ score in the nation in the 1989 draft). At Duke, Dilweg was terribly consistent, throwing for more than 300 yards in nine of his last eleven games.

LEADERSHIP

The way Dilweg earned the No. 2 spot as a rookie—beating out two veterans—impressed Packer brass. In 1990, he led the team to back-to-back midseason victories over Phoenix and Tampa Bay. The win over Phoenix came after Dilweg rallied the team to two fourth-quarter scores. Dilweg is a very intellectual, highly motivated, quiet leader, who oozes self confidence. "Anthony retains things well and makes good decisions most of the time," says head coach Lindy Infante. "He has good poise and a good attitude for a quarterback. He has a lot of the intangibles."

SUMMARY

Like most backup players, Dilweg needs more playing time to prove his worth. With the injury to Majkowski, he may get it, and certainly more consistency will be high on his list of improvements. But so far he seems to be on his way.

HANK'S RATING: B

Frank Reich

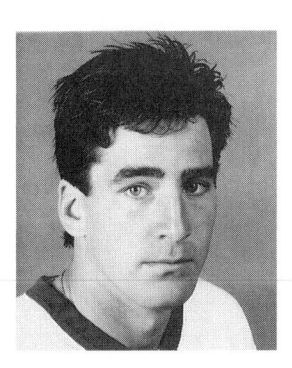

Birthdate: December 4, 1961
College: Maryland
Height: 6-4
Weight: 210
How Acquired: Drafted in third round, 1985
Final 1990 Team: Buffalo Bills

PRODUCTIVITY

When you lose your starter, it pays to have a good backup quarterback. Which is why the Bills rewarded Frank Reich with a five-year, $4.35 million contract at the end of the 1989 season, so the sixth-year quarterback wouldn't mind being patient.

Reich led Buffalo to a 24–14 victory over the arch-rival Miami Dolphins after Jim Kelly went down in the fifteenth week of the 1990 season. The win not only clinched the team's third successive AFC title, but also guaranteed Buffalo home advantage through the playoffs. In his first start of the year, Reich threw for a career-high 234 yards and 2 touchdowns.

TOUGHNESS

Reich was sacked six times in his brief appearances last season, but it didn't slow him at all. A proven, stand-in quarterback, Reich has survived physical beatings at the hands of the New York Giants and Los Angeles Rams. We have yet to see him play through a sixteen-game schedule, but in his limited action thus far, he's been more than capable.

CONSISTENCY

Based on his brief appearances, Reich has never failed to rally his team, carry his team, or lead his team. He produces in clutch situations, shows remarkable poise, "and basically just gets it done consistently," says head coach Marv Levy. "We're thrilled with him. Frank has come of age as an NFL quarterback, and he's proven that he is a fine one."

LEADERSHIP

There's no question that when called upon, Reich leads the Bills. He made his first career start in 1989, on a Monday night game against the Rams. Three games later, Reich was 3–0, having completed 40 of 66 passes for 482 yards with 6 touchdowns and only 1 interception.

SUMMARY

Reich completed 36 of 63 passes for 469 yards and 2 touchdowns in 1990 for a 91.3 rating. He throws a soft, catchable ball with the same pinpoint accuracy that carried him to an outstanding career at Maryland, where he once roomed with Boomer Esiason. If Kelly suffers a season-ending injury, Reich will have to prove he can step in and perform over the long haul.

HANK'S RATING: B

Cody Carlson

Birthdate: November 5, 1963
College: Baylor
Height: 6-3
Weight: 199
How Acquired: Drafted in third round, 1987
Final 1990 Team: Houston Oilers

PRODUCTIVITY

Cody Carlson has the misfortune of playing behind one of the NFL's premier quarterbacks in Warren Moon, which means he sees little playing time. But when he does play, he makes it count. He completed 67.3 percent of his passes in 1990 for 383 yards and 4 touchdowns. "Cody is a solid player," says Houston offensive coordinator Kevin Gillbride. "When we need him, he's as good as having another starter. Very few teams can say that."

TOUGHNESS

Like Buffalo's Frank Reich, Carlson hasn't been tested over a sixteen-game season. He has, however, shown incredible poise in the limited role he's played. There's no question he's mentally tough.

CONSISTENCY

Over his career, Carlson has completed 51.9 percent of his passes for 2,243, 8 touchdowns, and 9 interceptions. But most of his interceptions came very early in his career. He's started seven games and played in fourteen with Houston, and in recent years, has been a reliable performer with flashes of potential. Though there are two incoming quarterbacks we'd pick over Carlson, at least one scout feels differently. "Carlson is as good or better than any college quarterback that's currently available," says the scout. "And he's a proven NFL veteran."

LEADERSHIP

For those who have seen Cody Carlson practice in Houston in recent years, there's been little doubt that "The Commander," as he's been nicknamed by his teammates, could do the job in a live firefight. Which is why nobody on the Houston bench seemed surprised when Carlson, subbing for an injured Warren Moon, calmly picked apart the Pittsburgh defense in the final week of the 1990 season. Pittsburgh hadn't allowed a touchdown in its last three games, but Carlson was a technician, completing 22 of 29 passes for 247 yards and 3 touchdowns. "It was a blur at first," Carlson says. "But after the first three completions, I settled down." The win put the Oilers in the playoffs.

SUMMARY

Carlson, now in his fifth year, is a solid player who displays potential to start. He is young, has a powerful arm, and is healthy, but he has trouble making his reads quickly. The Oilers renegotiated his contract last year to keep him happy, aware that Warren Moon can't play forever. Problem is, Moon still looks young—and Carlson keeps looking better. He's asked to be traded in the past; don't be surprised if he starts asking again.

HANK'S RATING: B

Tommy Hodson

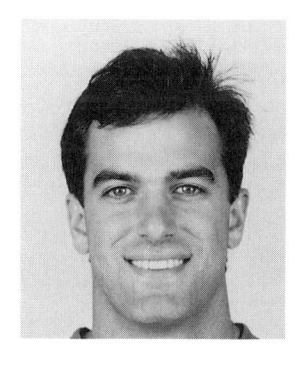

Birthdate: January 28, 1967
College: LSU
Height: 6-3
Weight: 195
How Acquired: Drafted in third round, 1990
Final 1990 Team: New England Patriots

PRODUCTIVITY

No quarterback had worse circumstances than rookie quarterback Tommy Hodson in 1990. Hodson, who flirted with Heisman Trophy candidacy during a stellar career at LSU, broke into the Pats' starting lineup in the eleventh week of the season against Phoenix. He finished the season with 85 completions on 156 attempts for 968 yards, 4 touchdowns and 5 interceptions—not bad numbers for a rookie thrown to the wolves.

TOUGHNESS

The fact that Hodson survived is testimony to his toughness. In just six games, he was sacked twenty times, for losses of 147 yards. Hodson took enough helmets in the back to last him a career.

CONSISTENCY

In spite of the controversy swirling around every Patriots game in 1990, Hodson played with valiant courage, and each week somehow mustered some offense for his club. He completed a career-long 56-yard pass to Irving Fryar, then found Fryar two weeks later with a 40-yard touchdown. His college career showed similar consistency: Hodson was the most prolific passer in the history of the Southeastern Conference.

LEADERSHIP

Hodson tried gamely to lead his team in his rookie year, but there were just too many outside distractions that kept the players' minds far from the field. Hodson will return in 1991 with a clear goal: Stave off the challenge of newcomer Hugh Millen, listen to everything veteran Steve Grogan has to say, and start putting the pieces together.

SUMMARY

Hodson has a strong arm and a good understanding of the game. He has been erratic dating back to college, but overcomes his shortcomings with big plays and an uncanny ability to win games. He could blossom into a decent professional quarterback—but it remains to be seen if new coach Dick McPherson can erase the horrible 1990 nightmares from Hodson's mind.

HANK'S RATING: B

Who's Missing

Rodney Peete

Birthdate: March 16, 1966
College: USC
Height: 6-0
Weight: 195
How Acquired: Drafted in sixth round, 1989
Final 1990 Team: Detroit Lions

Rodney Peete, in his second year, had his finest season in 1990, completing 52.4 percent of his passes for 1,974 yards, 13 touchdowns and 8 interceptions. But Peete has been plagued by small hands, a tendency to run too quickly, and poor reads. In 1991, the Lions, while staying in the run 'n' shoot, will occasionally utilize a more conventional two-back scheme, which may further hinder the six-foot Peete. The former Heisman runner-up is a fine athlete with 4.65 speed, but the jury is still out. "Rodney has the ability to scramble and is a young leader with a great deal of potential," says head coach Wayne Fontes. "He does need to improve on his reads, as well as other parts of his game."

HANK'S RATING: A

Jack Trudeau

Birthdate: September 9, 1962
College: Illinois
Height: 6-3
Weight: 213
How Acquired: Drafted in second round, 1986
Final 1990 Team: Indianapolis Colts

The Colts should trade Jack Trudeau and give him a chance to play. Pound for pound, Trudeau is one of the league's most physical players, and, if you believe Chiefs coach Marty Schottenheimer, he's one of its finest quarterbacks. "The Colts are a great team with Trudeau at quarterback," Schottenheimer says. "People don't give him enough credit. He's a very, very tough player."

In 1990, Trudeau was excellent in relief of Jeff George (1,078 yards, 6 touchdowns) before suffering injury in the season's eighth week. A vicious hit by Miami linebacker Cliff Odom tore ligaments in the quarterback's left knee.

But Trudeau is no stranger to injury. In 1989, through twelve starts, Trudeau played with a broken fifth finger on his left hand, which required surgery and three pins to hold together; he played with severely cut third and fourth fingers on his right hand; he played the week after being hospitalized for a concussion against Cleveland. Trudeau actually played two games with protective gloves on *both* hands. Yet he still finished the year with 2,317 yards and 15 touchdowns. And think about this—in his last three starts, he's been named AFC Player of the Week twice. Another Steve DeBerg in the making?

HANK'S RATING: B

Steve Walsh

Birthdate: February 1, 1966
College: Miami
Height: 6-2
Weight: 200
How Acquired: Trade, 1990
Final 1990 Team: New Orleans Saints

First, the Saints refused to talk contract with Bobby Hebert, as GM Jim Finks called him "a backup quarterback." Then they started John Fourcade, who quickly proved he wasn't the answer. So the Saints gave up first-, second-, and third-round draft picks to Dallas to get Steve Walsh. By season's end, Mora was welcoming Hebert back to camp.

Walsh, whose arm was suspect when he came out of Miami in 1988, had a frustrating year after being thrown into the fire five games into the regular season. Walsh threw for 2,010 yards, 12 touchdowns and 13 interceptions, and generally struggled in the Saints ball-control offense. Head coach Jim Mora predicts Walsh will be "vastly improved," in 1991, but also adds that "Walsh needs to be part of our offseason program—lifting, running, and getting ready to play. He needs to become more comfortable with our offensive scheme."

HANK'S RATING: B

Rich Gannon

Birthdate: February 20, 1965
College: Delaware
Height: 6-3
Weight: 197
How Acquired: Trade, 1987
Final 1990 Team: Minnesota Vikings

Rich Gannon got his first real look at pro action in 1990, his fourth year. After Wade Wilson went down with injury, Gannon somehow marched the injury-depleted Vikings to a .500 record, completing 52.1 percent of his passes for 2,278 yards and 16 touchdowns. But he also threw 16 interceptions, and floundered occasionally. Gannon shows great promise, displaying the fire and spunk that made him attractive to Minnesota coaches four years ago. But he must learn to be more consistent, study more, and recognize defenses quicker. Mentally, he's still another year away. Physically, he has all the tools—and his quick feet add problems against any defense.

HANK'S RATING: B

Gary Kubiak

Birthdate: August 15, 1961
College: Texas A&M
Height: 6-0
Weight: 192
How Acquired: Drafted in eighth round, 1983
Final 1990 Team: Denver Broncos

The 1983 draft produced more than John Albert Elway for the Denver Broncos. It also produced backup quarterback Gary Kubiak, an eighth-round pick, who has complemented Elway throughout their eight years together in Denver. Kubiak is one of the NFL's most reliable backups, and has proven his worth in every situation. Whether it's replacing an injured Elway in a must-win playoff game, or relieving him due to illness or poor performance, Kubiak —with few exceptions—has delivered. When given the opportunity to prove it, Kubiak's been a tough, valuable performer; his career completion percentage of 58 is the highest in team history.

HANK'S RATING: B

Peter Tom Willis

Birthdate: January 4, 1967
College: Florida State
Height: 6-2
Weight: 188
How Acquired: Drafted in third round, 1990
Final 1990 Team: Chicago Bears

After becoming the Bears third-round draft pick in 1990, Peter Tom Willis only played in one game—but he was impressive. After starter Jim Harbaugh went down to injury against the Lions with 2:42 to play, P.T.—in his first action as a pro—impressively completed 7 of 8 passes as he marched the Bears 76 yards. He capped the drive with an 8-yard touchdown to Wendell Davis. "This kid is a player," says Denver head coach Dan Reeves, who coveted Willis. "He's the kind of guy you want running your team in three or four years."

Many scouts think Willis is the best young backup in the league. He passed for over 300 yards six times as a senior at Florida State, and finished his college career with 4,291 yards and 33 touchdowns. Has a good arm and an uncanny ability to find the open receiver. Is very durable under pressure—a future star.

HANK'S RATING: B

Erik Wilhelm

Birthdate: November 19, 1965
College: Oregon State
Height: 6-3
Weight: 210
How Acquired: Drafted in third round, 1989
Final 1990 Team: Cincinnati Bengals

A third-round pick in 1989, Erik Wilhelm was virtually an unknown until Boomer Esiason suffered a bruised lung against the Raiders in 1989. Wilhelm entered the game and cooly threw for 200 yards and a touchdown. "Erik did things he never practiced," says head coach Sam Wyche. "The players have a lot of confidence in him. He's going to be a great one." An incredibly accurate quarterback, Wilhelm holds virtually every passing record at Oregon State. In his brief appearances, Wilhelm has shown uncanny ability to stand in against the rush, throws deep well, and displays mental toughness. Is the Esiason heir apparent in coming years.

HANK'S RATING: B

Gilbert Renfroe

Birthdate: February 18, 1963
College: Tennessee State
Height: 6-1
Weight: 195
How Acquired: Free Agent, 1990
Final 1990 Team: Atlanta Falcons

Gilbert Renfroe's inclusion in our quarterback section might seem surprising, but listen up. According to scouts, he is a *raw* Warren Moon. "He's exactly where Moon was ten years ago," says one. "He can throw it 100 mph, he's mobile, and he's intelligent." Renfroe, who runs a 4.65 in the 40, was a Canadian Football League all-star, including a 14–4 season in 1988 in which he threw for 4,113 yards. He also led his team to back-to-back playoff appearances, including a 1987 loss in the Grey Cup championship game. If Chris Miller falters in Atlanta, we may see Renfroe, who excelled in the run-and-shoot offense in Canada and has been a pet project for new offensive coordinator June Jones.

HANK'S RATING: C

Andre Ware

Birthdate: July 31, 1968
College: Houston
Height: 6-2
Weight: 205
How Acquired: Drafted in first round, 1990
Final 1990 Team: Detroit Lions

Andre Ware, after being the seventh player drafted in 1990, has depreciated considerably in the eyes of pro GMs. Word of Ware's bad attitude and horrible inconsistency has crept around the NFL, and many teams consider him a risk. The Lions have quietly offered the former Heisman Trophy winner as trade bait since February 1991, but few teams will bite. Ware repeatedly overthrows receivers underneath, and lacks the arm to throw deep accurately. Still, he's a name player making a lot of money—somebody is bound to give him a chance. But Andre Ware is a multi-year project. Believe it.

HANK'S RATING: C

Best of Plan B

Bob Gagliano

Birthdate: September 5, 1958
College: Utah State
Height: 6-3
Weight: 196
How Acquired: Free Agent, 1989
Final 1990 Team: Detroit Lions

After three straight 6–10 seasons, the Chargers were among the most active teams signing Plan B free agents this year, including former Lions quarterback Bob Gagliano. Gagliano will battle second-year player John Friesz to become Billy Joe Tolliver's backup. Gagliano was out of football when he signed as a free agent with the Detroit Lions in 1988, where he was reunited with former coach Darrel "Mouse" Davis, who revived his career. Gagliano completed 52 percent of his passes while throwing for 2,861 yards, 16 touchdowns, and 22 interceptions in two years with the Lions. But Gagliano will have to earn his keep. "You have to be realistic," says GM Bobby Beathard. "With Plan B, you're signing people that someone else either didn't want or at least didn't think enough of to protect."

HANK'S RATING: B

Mark Vlasic

Birthdate: October 25, 1963
College: Iowa
Height: 6-3
Weight: 206
Final 1990 Team: San Diego Chargers

Former San Diego Chargers quarterback Mark Vlasic was signed by the Chiefs off the Plan B list to add depth behind starter Steve DeBerg and backup Steve Pelluer. In his four years in San Diego, Vlasic was a 48 percent passer and threw for 438 yards, 2 touchdowns and 5 interceptions. A talented passer, Vlasic was a fourth-round draft pick in 1984 out of Iowa, where he finished fifth in the nation in pass efficiency as a senior. Prone to injury, Vlasic missed all of 1989 with a knee injury and one-third of his senior year with a shoulder injury.

HANK'S RATING: B

Hugh Millen

Birthdate: November 22, 1963
College: Washington
Height: 6-5
Weight: 216
Final 1990 Team: Atlanta Falcons

Former Atlanta quarterback Hugh Millen won both games he started in 1990, and when the Falcons didn't protect him, New England signed him. New England coach Dick McPherson says Millen will be expected to challenge second-year pro Tommy Hodson for the starting signal-caller job. The twenty-seven year-old Millen has played four seasons in the NFL since being drafted by the Los Angeles Rams in the third round of the 1986 draft. In 1988, Atlanta claimed Millen on waivers. The former University of Washington star has played in eleven NFL games, completing 83 of 145 passes for 1,074 yards, with 2 touchdowns and 4 interceptions.

HANK'S RATING: B

Mike Tomczak

Birthdate: October 23, 1962
College: Ohio State
Height: 6-1
Weight: 198
Final 1990 Team: Chicago Bears

When quarterback Mike Tomczak was left unprotected by the Chicago Bears, he immediately said he'd like to play for the Green Bay Packers, his division rival the past six years. "Coach [Lindy] Infante called my a couple days after I was put on Plan B," Tomczak says. "It was nice to get a phone call from a head coach."

The veteran quarterback will battle Anthony Dilweg for the number-two quarterback slot behind Don Majkowski. Tomczak, left unprotected by the Bears after a difficult 1990 season, was booed by fans and had troubles with Coach Mike Ditka. The rap on Tomczak is that he seemed to lose his confidence, and he lacks the ability to make the *tough* throws. Tomczak has thrown for 6,247 yards in his career, with 33 touchdowns and 47 interceptions. His career completion percentage is 49.6 percent.

HANK'S RATING: B

Todd Philcox

Birthdate: September 25, 1966
College: Syracuse
Height: 6-4
Weight: 209
Final 1990 Team: Cincinnati Bengals

The Cleveland Browns, uneasy over the health status of starter Bernie Kosar, signed former Cincinnati third-string quarterback Todd Philcox off the Bengals' Plan B list. Cincinnati was high on Philcox, but couldn't find room to protect him. "He's got a lot of poise and a good, fluid movement," says Bengals coach Sam Wyche. "He's very productive—he just needs to be in a place where he can play." Philcox threw for 2,076 yards and 16 touchdowns as a senior at Syracuse in 1988. After signing with the Bengals as a free agent in 1989, he has only thrown three passes in regular season games—two incompletes and an interception.

HANK'S RATING: B

Tailbacks

Barry Sanders

Birthdate: July 16, 1968
College: Oklahoma State
Height: 5-8
Weight: 203
How Acquired: Drafted in first round, 1989
Final 1990 Team: Detroit Lions

PRODUCTIVITY

Barry Sanders won his first NFL rushing title in 1990 with 1,305 yards in 255 attempts. In 1989, he conceded the NFL rushing title to Kansas City's Christian Okoye, but Okoye rushed for just 10 more yards on *90* more attempts, evidence of Sanders long-run potential. In 1990, he averaged 5.1 yards a carry, tops of any running back in the NFC with more than 100 carries. His 13 touchdowns were second in the NFC, and he also hauled in 35 passes for 462 yards and three more scores—a 13 yards per catch average.

SUMMARY

"Against Sanders, you're afraid to take out your heavy people," says a scout. "Most people ignored their passing game and played their heavy people all the time, because you're afraid he may bust a draw on third and long."

The Lions have gone to great lengths to bring their passing game up to par, which means Sanders should remain—for now—the NFL's most dominant back. His excellent quickness at the line of scrimmage allows him to get into the defensive backfield, which is why he is the top touchdown run threat in the NFL. And nobody personifies poetry in motion like Sanders. In a losing effort against the Raiders, Sanders left scores of defenders grabbing air as he danced his way to 176 yards and 2 touchdowns. "Barry Sanders is my new idol," said Raider running back Bo Jackson afterward. "When I grow up, I want to be just like him."

HANK'S RATING: AAA

Thurman Thomas

Birthdate: May 16, 1966
College: Oklahoma State
Height: 5-10
Weight: 198
How Acquired: Drafted in second round, 1988
Final 1990 Team: Buffalo Bills

PRODUCTIVITY

When Thurman Thomas became Buffalo's second-round draft pick in 1988, most scouts completely missed on his ability to catch the football. Thomas had 60 receptions in 1989, including 13 catches against Cleveland in the playoffs. And his 3,000-plus yards rushing over the past three seasons surpasses all other backs from the 1988 class.

His past two seasons have been sterling: in 1989 and 1990, he has led the league in total yards from scrimmage. Last year he led the AFC in rushing with 1,297 yards on 271 attempts, an average of 4.8 yards a carry, including 11 touchdowns and a long run of 80 yards. In 1989, Thomas totaled 1,913 yards rushing and receiving, carrying the ball 298 times for 1,244 yards.

SUMMARY

Thomas struggles as a blocker, which is largely due to his petite 5-10, 198-pound frame, but he is unafraid to go head up with any linebacker in the league. And when he's on, he can single-handedly control a game: Against the New York Jets on September 23, 1990, Thomas broke loose for non-scoring runs of 60, 39, 24, 15, and 15 yards, while rushing for 214 yards on just 18 carries. He has the ability to make tacklers miss at the line of scrimmage. And there aren't many who hit the line any harder.

HANK'S RATING: AA

James Brooks

Birthdate: December 28, 1958
College: Auburn
Height: 5-10
Weight: 180
How Acquired: Trade, 1984
Final 1990 Team: Cincinnati Bengals

PRODUCTIVITY

At the age of thirty-two, James Brooks seems like he's been around forever, but he keeps running like he's getting younger. Last year, in his tenth NFL season, Brooks hit the 1,000-yard plateau for the third time in his career: 195 attempts for 1,004 yards, an average of 5.1 yards per carry, and 5 touchdowns. He also caught four more passes for touchdowns. That came on the heels of his finest year in 1989, when he rushed for 1,239 yards and his 5.6 yards per carry led the AFC.

Brooks has played hurt so many times that his toughness is never questioned. But never was his toughness greater than during the seventh week of the 1990 season, when he rushed for 63 yards on just 6 carries against the Browns—despite a strained *neck*, which sizzled with pain every time he was tackled. He also set a club record with a 201-yard effort against Houston, scoring on a 56-yard run and setting up two more scores with runs of 45 and 40 yards.

SUMMARY

Opposing coaches praise Brooks for his physical toughness. "He doesn't dodge anybody," says head coach Sam Wyche. It's hard to critique Brooks; he seldom fumbles, gets the tough yards inside, and still has the deceptive speed to break it long. A super team player, Brooks may be the best all-around running back in the NFL. Some things still get better with age.

HANK'S RATING: AA

Neal Anderson

Birthdate: August 14, 1964
College: Florida
Height: 5-11
Weight: 210
How Acquired: Drafted in first round, 1986
Final 1990 Team: Chicago Bears

PRODUCTIVITY

Neal Anderson earned his third Pro Bowl appearance with his third-consecutive 1,000-yard season, finishing third in the NFC with 1,078 yards on 260 carries for a 4.1-yards-per-carry average. He scored 10 touchdowns, one below his 1989 mark.

In the past two years, Anderson has been the only consistent medicine for Mike Ditka's heartburn. He scored 2 touchdowns in three different games. Suffering from a sore hamstring against Denver, he rushed a career-high 28 times for 111 yards. In a 16–6 playoff win over New Orleans, he accounted for 166 yards in offense, including 102 yards rushing, 4 catches for 42 yards, and threw a 22-yard pass to Ron Morris.

In 1989, Anderson truly displayed the potential that made the Bears take him in the first round in 1986, when he rushed for 1,275 yards (11 touchdowns) and led the Bears in receptions with 50 catches.

SUMMARY

Anderson is a complete player. He runs hard, is great at the line of scrimmage, and is a very good receiver. And let's not forget that he is a team player.

Late in the 1990 season, stacked defensive lines made it difficult for Anderson to maintain his early-season form, perhaps revealing the deficiencies in Chicago's one-dimensional run offense. But Anderson touched the ball a total of 302 times, and he made it count every time: he finished second on the team in receiving yards with 484. In overtime against the Lions, he even called his own number in the huddle, then hauled in a 50-yard pass from Jim Harbaugh to win the game. "Neal keeps my heart ticking," says head coach Mike Ditka.

HANK'S RATING: AA

Many question Allen's desire to play for the Raiders in 1991. Even though it looks like Bo won't be ready to go this season, there is the matter of Roger Craig, signed during the offseason. And Marcus needs to be the No. 1 back to be productive. Will he see enough action to stay sharp? If he does he can still put up top numbers.

HANK'S RATING: AA

Marcus Allen

Birthdate: March 26, 1960
College: USC
Height: 6-2
Weight: 205
How Acquired: Drafted in first round, 1982
Final 1990 Team: Los Angeles Raiders

PRODUCTIVITY

When the 1990 season opened, rumors swirled that Marcus Allen wouldn't be part of the Raiders' plans. Allen, weary of riding sidesaddle to celebrity Bo Jackson, openly expressed his frustration. And sources close to Al Davis made it clear the maverick owner, who has never been fond of Allen, wouldn't mind a trade.

Allen responded to the maelstrom by rushing for 682 yards and a team-leading 12 touchdowns; against San Diego, Allen rushed for 45 yards, caught 3 passes for 50 yards, and set up a field goal with a 30-yard catch and a touchdown with a 27-yard run. "Marcus is a true professional," says head coach Art Shell. "You know what you're going to get when he steps on the field."

SUMMARY

No, Allen's quickness, or his toughness, is not what it once was. No, Allen is not a favorite of Davis and his yes-men in the front office. But, yes, Allen is the heart and soul of the Raiders' offense. Allen does the dirty work for injury-prone Bo Jackson, seldom fumbles, sacrifices his body on lead blocks, and still catches the ball well (15 catches for a 12.6-yard average in 1990). He does it all. "It's hard to appreciate everything Marcus does for their offense," says NBC analyst O.J. Simpson. "But there's no question he makes a difference."

Eric Dickerson

Birthdate: September 2, 1960
College: SMU
Height: 6-3
Weight: 217
How Acquired: Trade, 1987
Final 1990 Team: Indianapolis Colts

PRODUCTIVITY

The 1990 season was a tumultuous one for malcontent Eric Dickerson. The NFL's seventh-leading career rusher missed the team's first four games after the Colts suspended him when he refused to undergo team physicals. Dickerson then lost an appeal to NFL Commissioner Paul Tagliabue, and the suspension cost him $635,000 in pay.

Finally, Dickerson was reinstated October 17, and appeared in the October 21 game against Denver. Weeks later, after rushing for just 183 yards across a five-game stretch, he finally broke loose against Cincinnati, bursting for 143 yards and a touchdown. His year-end totals included 166 carries for 677 yards and 4 touchdowns.

SUMMARY

Team continuity was disrupted by the return of Dickerson, who a year ago criticized teammates, demanded a trade and threatened retirement. "I saw no lasting negative impact to the majority of our team by his return," says head coach Ron Meyer. "A couple of players expressed their opinions, but they were professionals. But his not being here early in the season was, no doubt, disruptive."

Dickerson has worn his welcome thin in the NFL. He is a once-great back who still possesses decent speed (4.6) and slashing ability, but he tends to over read at the line of scrimmage instead of attacking the holes. Most scouts feel he still has the skills to make an impact, but question his attitude and desire. If he puts maximum effort forward, the Colts will have a strong running game. If not, Ron Meyer could be in a tough spot.

HANK'S RATING: AA

Marion Butts

Birthdate: August 1, 1966
College: Florida State
Height: 6-1
Weight: 248
How Acquired: Drafted in seventh round, 1989
Final 1990 Team: San Diego Chargers

PRODUCTIVITY

In his third NFL season, Marion Butts emerged to finish second in the AFC in rushing in 1990; at 4.6 yards per clip, he barreled for 1,225 yards, a single-season Charger record. "After he hits you," says Raider nose tackle Bob Golic, "you refer to him as 'big' Butts." He eclipsed 100 yards in several critical games, and also showed a determination to play hurt: Nursing a deep thigh bruise against Denver, Butts came off the bench against the team doctor's wishes to rush for 114 yards.

Butts was the primary reason the Chargers offense improved over its 1989 output both in total yards gained and rushing yards. San Diego averaged 117 yards rushing in 1989, while it led the AFC with 141 yards a game in 1990. The result, according to Chargers officials, was a new team record of 2,257 yards, topping the 27-year-old record of 2,201 yards set in 1963. And get this: In four seasons at Florida State, Marion Butts carried the ball just 64 times.

SUMMARY

Butts missed the last two games with a foot injury, but aside from that setback, was highly durable throughout the course of the season, as his workload of 265 carries attests. He also caught 16 passes for 117 yards. "Butts shows surprising speed, balance, and agility for a man his size," says head coach Dan Henning. "He's an impressive player."

More impressively, however, is Butts' remarkable penchant for holding onto the ball: He didn't fumble once in 1990, has not fumbled in his last 284 attempts dating back to 1989, and has fumbled just twice in 435 *career* carries. Butts is a "natural" runner with good strength and agility. And he hasn't peaked yet—he will get better.

HANK'S RATING: AA

Dalton Hilliard

Birthdate: January 21, 1964
College: LSU
Height: 5-8
Weight: 204
How Acquired: Drafted in second round, 1986
Final 1990 Team: New Orleans Saints

PRODUCTIVITY

After a stellar year in 1989 (1,262 yards and 13 touchdowns) in which he earned his first Pro Bowl appearance, Hilliard suffered through a miserable year in 1990. Thanks to a knee injury that kept him out most of the season, Hilliard rushed just 90 times for 284 yards, for an average of 3.2 yards a carry. Can a player Hilliard's size (5-8, 204) survive the brutalities of a sixteen-week NFL season? Scouts think so. "What impresses me about Hilliard," says John Butler, Buffalo Bills director of pro personnel, "is that he's tough. For his size, he takes tremendous punishment."

SUMMARY

Defensive coordinators around the NFC seem to agree on one thing; Dalton Hilliard hits the hole faster than any back in the league. "He just explodes through there," says Tampa Bay's Floyd Peters. "He's a darting, slashing type back, who really makes you miss. He's a very difficult target." Along with Hilliard's ability to make tacklers miss at the line of scrimmage, he has the strength to keep moving even when hit. And he is an excellent receiver, too. But in 1991, all eyes will be on Hilliard's rehabilitated knee. Word is that it will never be 100% again, but look for him to bounce back with a great year anyway.

HANK'S RATING: AA

Emmitt Smith

Birthdate: May 15, 1969
College: Florida
Height: 5-9
Weight: 199
How Acquired: Drafted in first round, 1990
Final 1990 Team: Dallas Cowboys

PRODUCTIVITY

The easiest way to sum up Emmitt Smith's "Rookie of the Year" season in 1990 is one word: Production. When the Cowboys gave him the ball, he rewarded them with yards, touchdowns, and sensational plays. After a holdout that lasted through training camp, Smith was finally signed when the Cowboys agreed to pay him a $1 million signing bonus. After a 3–7 start in which Smith saw little action, the Cowboys pumped him the ball twenty times or more in the next four games: The Cowboys won all four.

Smith finished fifth in the NFC in rushing with 937 yards on 241 carries, an average of 3.9, and scored a whopping 11 touchdowns—outstanding considering his late start.

SUMMARY

On draft day, discussion of the talented Smith consisted mostly of questions over his breakaway speed and toughness in a sixteen-game schedule. Smith quickly laid those doubts to rest; he played physical and wasn't prone to fumbles or injury. And he repeatedly proved his big-play ability, including a 4-touchdown performance against Phoenix and a 132-yard, 2-touchdown display against Washington. "When you have a back like Emmitt Smith," says Cardinals head coach Joe Bugel, "you're a threat to score every time he touches the ball."

Smith will become an All-Pro running back. He is very tough running inside, and has the great vision at the line of scrimmage that sets apart the great backs. He is very simply the key to the future success of Dallas.

HANK'S RATING: A

Herschel Walker

Birthdate: March 3, 1962
College: Georgia
Height: 6-1
Weight: 223
How Acquired: Trade, 1990
Final 1990 Team: Minnesota Vikings

PRODUCTIVITY

Despite heated criticism from fans, teammates, and opponents, Walker—statistically—had a reasonable year. Walker rushed for 770 yards on 184 carries—a solid average of 4.2 yards per carry—and scored 5 touchdowns. But those aren't the kind of numbers that Minnesota management was thinking of when it sacrificed its first- and second-round draft picks until 1993. And, despite the numbers, it's hard to erase memories of Walker falling down without being touched on a kickoff, or fumbling in critical situations.

SUMMARY

The Herschel Walker mystique took a beating in 1990, but perhaps it should be noted that it was departed GM Mike Lynn, not Walker, who surrendered the franchise to get him in 1989. Nevertheless, Walker bears that burden like an anvil on his broad shoulders, and until he rushes for 1,500 yards and 20 touchdowns, his tag of "expensive failure" will never be overcome.

"Herschel simply doesn't run like he did in the USFL," says an AFC scout. "We call him 'lay-down.' In the USFL, when he hit the pile, he exploded through people. Now he just lays down." Walker did not perform at the level needed to make a positive contribution to the Vikings. The effort seemed to be lacking.

For strange reasons, the once surehanded Walker has developed fumbling habits and has disappeared from the passing game, as well. Further clouding the issue was Walker's expired contract. But the puzzling tailback has signed a new contract with Minnesota and says he's looking forward to a big season.

Walker has always been an I formation runner and has done it with great success. He is a much better runner from 7½ yards deep than 4. The Vikings must run him from the I formation in 1991.

HANK'S RATING: A

Gary Anderson

Birthdate: April 18, 1961
College: Arkansas
Height: 6-0
Weight: 181
How Acquired: Trade, 1990
Final 1990 Team: Tampa Bay Buccaneers

PRODUCTIVITY

The nomadic career of Gary Anderson has been marred by inconsistency, poor timing, and bad coaching decisions. In San Diego, the Chargers tried—and failed—to convert Anderson to wide receiver, despite his multi-dimensional abilities as a running back. After a year out of football during a contract dispute with the Chargers, he was traded back home to Tampa, site of his legendary rushing performances in the defunct USFL (2,731 yards).

Back in his familiar position at tailback, it took Anderson little time to make his case that, despite his small size, he is a tailback, and nothing else. He finished seventh among NFC running backs with 1,110 total yards from scrimmage in 1990, including 646 yards rushing on 166 attempts, and 464 receiving yards. He had long receptions of 74 and 58 yards, the latter against Dallas, which marked a team-record fifth consecutive game in which he scored a touchdown.

SUMMARY

Anderson was an electrifying, play-making speedster (4.35) in his college days at Arkansas. "Catching Gary Anderson in the open field," says Notre Dame's Lou Holtz, who coached Anderson at Arkansas, "is like chasing a rabbit through a cornfield." But Anderson has lost some of those skills. Yet, against Detroit, he rushed for 71 yards and caught passes for 37 more, including a spectacular, leaping, 11-yard touchdown run. "He did an Air Jordan," says quarterback Vinny Testaverde.

Anderson is still a threat to score from anywhere on the field. But, since he absorbs a lot of punishment—calf and rib injuries severely hampered him in at least four games—Tampa Bay should look for other running help and use Anderson as a third-down back.

HANK'S RATING: A

Johnny Johnson

Birthdate: June 11, 1968
College: San Jose State
Height: 6-2
Weight: 212
How Acquired: Drafted in seventh round, 1990
Final 1990 Team: Phoenix Cardinals

PRODUCTIVITY

Phoenix brass were openly gleeful the day they plucked Johnson in the seventh round of the 1990 draft, and the all-purpose back proved to be the steal of the year. Had an ankle injury not bumped him from three games, Johnson—at his 4.0 yards per carry pace—would've eclipsed 1,000 yards. But Johnson did finish with 926 yards and 5 touchdowns. Johnson, who proved his versatility in college by playing both football and basketball, caught an additional 25 balls for 241 yards—an outstanding 9.6 yards per catch. His efforts made him a Pro Bowl selection in his first NFL season.

SUMMARY

Johnson was a late-round selection due mostly to a reputation for a bad attitude in college, which he claims stems from a personal rift with his college coach. But Johnson put all criticism to rest in Phoenix by working hard in the weight room, spending additional time with his position coaches, and displaying a general team attitude. "Johnny worked hard to prove himself," says head coach Joe Bugel. "We're looking for him to be even better next season."

Johnson has a great future in the NFL. He's an All-Pro runner who can come out of the backfield to make the big catch. Look for 1990 first-round pick and Heisman-runner-up Anthony Thompson to join Johnson in an explosive backfield.

HANK'S RATING: A

Bobby Humphrey

Birthdate: October 11, 1966
College: Alabama
Height: 6-1
Weight: 201

How Acquired: Chosen in Supplemental Draft, 1989
Final 1990 Team: Denver Broncos

PRODUCTIVITY

Despite his relative inexperience, Bobby Humphrey has given the Broncos a sorely needed ground attack over the past two seasons—and seems to be improving with time. In 1990, he carried the ball 288 times 1,202 yards, for a 4.2 yards per carry average and 7 touchdowns. In 1989, his rookie year, he rushed for 1,151 yards. "We believe that Bobby will continue to take pressure off our passing game," says head coach Dan Reeves.

Many teams down-rated Humphrey before the Broncos drafted him because his left foot was twice broken during his senior year at Alabama. And though his foot seems fine, there are still doubts about his durability.

SUMMARY

Reeves has changed his offensive philosophy to feature more of Bobby Humphrey and less of quarterback John Elway. In Humphrey, the Broncos have a versatile back capable of running and catching.

Humphrey made a run at the league rushing title, but fell short of his goal when he suffered a sprained ankle against Cleveland during the season's fifth week. "The rushing title would've been nice," Humphrey says. "But I'm just trying to get this ballclub back on track so we can win some ball games."

At the time of his injury, Humphrey was leading the league in rushing and averaging 5.2 yards per carry—and had just finished his fourth-straight 100-yard game. Humphrey failed to break 100 yards the rest of the season.

When healthy, Humphrey can get it done, but the questions still remain about whether he can stay healthy for an entire season, and a long career.

HANK'S RATING: A

Earnest Byner

Birthdate: September 15, 1962
College: East Carolina
Height: 5-10
Weight: 215

How Acquired: Trade, 1989
Final 1990 Team: Washington Redskins

PRODUCTIVITY

Earnest Byner had the misfortune, while with the Browns, to fumble in a championship game. Now everytime he mishandles a ball, as he did against the arch-rival Giants when a potential go-ahead touchdown pass from quarterback Stan Humphries bounced off his hands and was intercepted by safety Greg Jackson, effectively ending Washington's comeback effort, the subject of Byner being a fumbler comes up. But Earnest Byner is *not* a fumbler.

Against New England in a driving rainstorm, Byner offered proof that he could carry the team, and hold on to the ball, rushing a career-high 39 times for 149 yards and a touchdown. Byner topped that two weeks later, darting for 154 yards in a losing effort against Indianapolis. When Gerald Riggs suffered an arch injury on November 12, Byner assumed a workhorse share of the offense: He won the heart of Joe Gibbs by rushing for 770 yards in the final eight weeks of the season.

SUMMARY

One of the NFL's most versatile performers, Byner rushed for 1,219 yards and 6 touchdowns, while catching 31 passes for another 279 yards in 1990. Byner is a tough back who knows how to get yardage. He has lost some of his quickness at the line of scrimmage, but you won't hear Joe Gibbs complain.

HANK'S RATING: A

Eric Metcalf

Birthdate: January 23, 1968
College: Texas
Height: 5-9
Weight: 180
How Acquired: Drafted in first round, 1989
Final 1990 Team: Cleveland Browns

PRODUCTIVITY

Since Eric Metcalf became the Browns first-round pick in 1989, he has been a loose piece in the Cleveland puzzle. He led the Browns in rushing in 1989 with 633 yards and 6 touchdowns, but those numbers fell way off to 80 carries for 248 yards and 1 touchdown in 1990. The list of problems is long and credible: Metcalf is small, light-footed, and injury-prone. He insists he's a running back, but he must run tougher at the line of scrimmage and prove he has the desire to be an every-down running back. Last year's coaching committee utilized him mostly as a receiver: Metcalf caught 57 passes for 452 yards and a touchdown.

His attributes are strong: 4.3 speed in the 40, dazzling footwork in the open field, and solid work habits. But don't ask Metcalf to block, run between the tackles, or catch a ball over the middle. Against Houston, he fumbled when hit after a 15-yard catch; against Pittsburgh, he fumbled three times. "He fumbled it to us even when we didn't want it," says Steelers cornerback Rod Woodson. One Cleveland newspaper described Metcalf last year as "a guy who runs with fear in his heart." And two regimes of coaches have yet to find a workable position for the talented, but limited, role player.

SUMMARY

Metcalf has yet to prove that he's durable, and fumbled eight times on the season. But he proved he's still capable of making sensational plays, breaking a bob-and-weave 101-yard kickoff return against Houston, and returning another kickoff 98 yards against the New York Jets. His kickoff return average of 41.25 is third-best in team history, but the Browns didn't draft him to simply return kickoffs. And if Metcalf wants more, he has to prove he has the desire to excel.

HANK'S RATING: B

Derrick Fenner

Birthdate: April 6, 1967
College: North Carolina
Height: 6-3
Weight: 229
How Acquired: Drafted in tenth round, 1989
Final 1990 Team: Seattle Seahawks

PRODUCTIVITY

In a classic rags-to-riches tale, second-year running back Derrick Fenner silenced critics and coaches by leading the AFC in touchdowns with 15, while rushing for 859 yards.

Fenner's story is remarkable. His college career had been marred by a first-degree murder charge, of which he was later acquitted. But Fenner, who didn't even play football in 1988, wound up a tenth-round pick in the 1989 draft.

After little action in 1989, Fenner rebounded—while earning just $75,000—to finish sixth in the AFC in rushing. And he proved his big-play worthiness at critical times, such as his 3-touchdown performance against Cincinnati.

SUMMARY

Though Fenner brought additional running punch to the Seahawks and took pressure off weary superback John L. Williams, the Seahawk running game remained inconsistent. But Fenner's injury-free—and relatively fumble-free season suggest that he'll see more of the football in 1991. He makes the tough yards and knows how to find the end zone. "Derrick did an outstanding job last year," says head coach Chuck Knox. "Now we'll look to him to establish some consistency and prove that he can maintain a high level of performance."

HANK'S RATING: B

Blair Thomas

Birthdate: October 7, 1967
College: Penn State
Height: 5-10
Weight: 195
How Acquired: Drafted in first round, 1990
Final 1990 Team: New York Jets

PRODUCTIVITY

After a great career at Penn State, Blair Thomas showed promise during his rookie year in 1990. Though some scouts question whether Blair's skill levels are those of a top NFL back, he did lead the Jets in rushing with 620 yards on 123 carries, scoring 1 touchdown.

SUMMARY

Though Thomas injected youth and energy into the Jets running game, he frustrated head coach Bruce Coslet by refusing to play through minor injuries. Coslet's biggest source of irritation was Thomas's contract holdout that caused him to miss training camp. Coslet believes the lack of conditioning made Thomas more susceptible to injury.

But the Jets head coach was pleased with Thomas's progress, and vows that he'll get more carries in 1991. "We accomplished a lot this year, but we didn't even scratch the surface," Coslet says. "There's a lot of work to be done."

HANK'S RATING: B

Mike Rozier

Birthdate: March, 1, 1961
College: Nebraska

Height: 5-10
Weight: 213
How Acquired: Free Agent, 1990
Final 1990 Team: Atlanta Falcons

PRODUCTIVITY

When Rozier rushed for 155 yards in the season finale against Dallas, it marked his third 100-yard game in five weeks. "He's the best hundred-dollar investment I've made since I bought a cheap suit in Texas," quipped Atlanta head coach Jerry Glanville, who plucked his old workhorse from the waiver wire after Houston waived Rozier in the season's first week.

Rozier finished the season with 163 carries for 717 yards for a very respectable 4.4 yards per carry average and 3 touchdowns. But what pleased Glanville most was the work ethic and toughness Rozier brought to the young Falcon backfield. "Rosey is dirt tough, and regardless of the circumstances, he plays," Glanville says. "He plays hurt, he plays in the mud, he plays in the snow. And he never, ever runs out of bounds. From a physical standpoint, he may be the toughest back to ever play this game."

SUMMARY

Glanville, for once, may be telling the plain truth. Rozier's ex-teammates in Houston still swap war stories of the former Heisman Trophy winner playing with every possible injury. "He came in at halftime once just beat to hell," says a former teammate. "He took his pads off, had the trainers shoot him [with painkillers] in about a half-dozen places, put his pads back on, and played the second half. He's a tough sonuvabitch."

Although Rozier broke a 67-yard touchdown run against Dallas, he lacks the speed to get outside and seldom breaks a run for more than ten yards. But he runs hard inside the tackles, comes up with the big play, and is a tenacious blocker. The run 'n' shoot offense improved Rozier's line of scrimmage run potential, but even without he still has plenty of skills remaining and he loves to play.

HANK'S RATING: B

Sammie Smith

Birthdate: May 16, 1967
College: Florida State
Height: 6-2
Weight: 225
How Acquired: Drafted in first round, 1989
Final 1990 Team: Miami Dolphins

PRODUCTIVITY

For the first time since the days of Larry Csonka and Jim Kiick, Sammie Smith—in his second year—made Miami a running threat in 1990, rushing for 831 yards, his career high. It was the most yards rushing by a Dolphin since Csonka's 837 yards in 1979. Smith scored 9 touchdowns, 8 rushing and 1 receiving, and carried the ball 226 times—the second-highest total in Miami history.

Smith, after an injury-plagued rookie year, showed remarkable improvement last season. His yards-per-carry average improved almost a half-yard to 3.7, and he showed dangerous speed on a 53-yard touchdown reception. Against New England, Smith rushed for a career-high 159 yards and a touchdown in a 27–24 victory.

SUMMARY

Though Smith showed marked improvement in 1990, he still must learn to protect the football. While Smith has posted the best two-year rushing totals for any Dolphin runner in his first two pro seasons, Smith still put the ball on the ground *eight times,* one shy of the club record. His biggest improvement was playing hurt, but some scouts still question his toughness and desire when it comes to moving a pile and getting the extra yard. Smith needs to continue to show improvement and prove he can make the step up to the next level.

HANK'S RATING: B

Cleveland Gary

Birthdate: May 4, 1966
College: Miami
Height: 6-0
Weight: 226
How Acquired: Drafted in first round, 1989
Final 1990 Team: Los Angeles Rams

PRODUCTIVITY

Cleveland Gary may be the Rams' answer to Herschel Walker, only without as much fanfare. When Gary plays well, he deserves billing as one of the NFL's Top 10 backs. But when he doesn't play well . . . look out. In what would have been an otherwise sound season, Gary was plagued by fumbles, dropped passes, and blown assignments. "It's a mystery," says a Rams official, who requested anonymity. "Some games, he just doesn't show up mentally. I don't know if it's a maturity thing or what. But we need him to make a move."

Indeed. Despite his Jekyll-and-Hyde level of play, Gary still led the listless Rams in 1990 with 808 yards, averaging

4.0 yards a carry. His 14 rushing touchdowns tied Seattle's Derrick Fenner for the league lead, as Gary tried to assume the leading role in the Rams slug-mouth attack. His 30 catches netted 150 yards and another touchdown.

SUMMARY

Gary has to be more careful. He fumbled away would-be victories against both Dallas and New Orleans, and, despite a 3-touchdown effort, nearly fumbled away the Rams upset win over San Francisco in week 12. With 2:31 remaining and Los Angeles inside the 49ers five-yard line, Gary took an Everett pitchout—and fumbled. Miraculously, the ball bounced right back in his hands, and he managed to score.

To win the heart of head coach John Robinson—and boost the Rams back into the playoffs—Gary will have to improve his mental toughness. Like several other former Hurricaines, scouts question Gary's efforts in tough situations. But as the Rams system becomes more instinct and less thinking for Gary, Robinson believes his young back could lead the league in rushing. Gary must learn quickly: In the NFL, consistency equals longevity. Blatant inconsistency . . . you get the picture.

HANK'S RATING: B

Barry Word

Birthdate: July 17, 1964
College: Virginia
Height: 6-2
Weight: 220
How Acquired: Free Agent, 1990
Final 1990 Team: Kansas City Chiefs

PRODUCTIVITY

In Kansas City, it was a year for comebacks. First, quarterback Steve DeBerg posted a sensational season. Not to be outdone, tailback Barry Word, who in 1986 was serving time in prison on federal drug charges, shocked critics by busting loose for the best numbers of his career. Word rushed for a team-leading 1,015 yards, good for seventh in the league, including a club-record, 200-yard effort against Detroit. He averaged five yards a carry and scored four times.

More surprising, perhaps, Word proved more durable than the punishing—but injury-prone—Christian Okoye, and Word may find himself in a starting role by September.

SUMMARY

When Word signed with Kansas City in May 1990, he had been working for a phone company and hadn't played since 1988. But the long-shot gamble by head coach Marty Schottenheimer paid big dividends. "Barry knew that the road ahead of him would be a tough one," the coach says. "And he has come through. He's lived up to everything we've asked him to do, both on and off the field." Word gives the Chiefs a unique, double-barrel, big-back punch. He seldom fumbles and is dependable, two of Schottenheimer's biggest prerequisites. But can Word sustain his level of performance in 1990 and put up the same type of numbers? The Chiefs hope so, but others believe he's not as good as his 1990 stats.

HANK'S RATING: B

Ottis Anderson

Birthdate: November 19, 1957
College: Miami
Height: 6-2
Weight: 225
How Acquired: Trade, 1986
Final 1990 Team: New York Giants

PRODUCTIVITY

The old man did it again. At the ripe age of thirty-four, Anderson put many backs ten years his junior to shame. Like a stubborn mule, Anderson ground out 784 yards in his twelfth NFL season, good for eighth in the NFC. And he did it with impressive style: 72 yards and 2 touchdowns against Miami; 92 yards in a 21–10 win over division-rival Washington; 91 yards against Detroit.

At Indianapolis, Anderson spanked the Colts, scoring touchdowns on two of the Giants first three possessions to give New York an insurmountable 17–0 halftime lead. And, though seldom used as a receiver, he managed to catch 18 passes for 139 yards. Anderson's fountain-of-youth performance continued right through the Super Bowl, where he was named the game's Most Valuable Player.

SUMMARY

Anderson won't outrun anybody, and he gets back to the huddle a little slower than he used to. But on third and short, you can bet number 24 will lumber for the first down. Anderson still runs with power, and shows good durability. He scored 11 touchdowns in 1990, evidence that old age hasn't affected his memory of what to do with the ball inside the five. After gaining just 932 yards rushing between 1985 and 1988, Anderson has been a vital cog in the Giants ground game the past two years.

Last season, he surpassed the 10,000-yard mark for his career. "The Cardinals thought I was burned out," Anderson says of his former team, who gave him away in 1986. "But my flame still burns."

The problem is that the Giants have Rodney Hampton looking for playing time. And Anderson, who has lost some quickness, only averaged 3.5 yards a carry to Hampton's 4.2. Don't be surprised if the capable veteran finds himself forced to watch a little more this season.

HANK'S RATING: B

and four more scores, and White was responsible for one-fifth of his team's record-breaking attack.

SUMMARY

White's sometimes hot-and-cold inconsistency should be shared by the Oilers' adjustment to the run 'n' shoot as an every-down offense. White's all-around improvement in 1991 will mirror that of the offense, as players become more acclimated to its nuances. "Lorenzo is a fantastic back," says quarterback Warren Moon. "When we call on him, he responds. He's young, and getting better."

At times, White showed dazzling ability; in a 27–24 upset victory over Buffalo, he rushed for 125 yards and caught 5 passes for 89 yards. Against Cleveland, White spent half his afternoon in the end zone, scoring on runs of 10, 1, 7, and 5 yards, while running for 116 yards in a 58–14 route. Historically, the run 'n' shoot has produced big yards with *average* backs. And though some scouts question whether White has top speed or quickness, he is not average.

HANK'S RATING: B

Lorenzo White

Birthdate: April 12, 1966
College: Michigan State
Height: 5-11
Weight: 209
How Acquired: Drafted in first round, 1988
Final 1990 Team: Houston Oilers

PRODUCTIVITY

The biggest break in Lorenzo White's pro career came in 1990, when Houston's new coaching staff elected to go with White as the single-back in the explosive run 'n' shoot. Prior to 1990, during White's first two pro seasons, he watched with frustration from the bench as coaching favorites Alonzo Highsmith, Mike Rozier, and Allen Pinkett rotated in the Red Gun offense.

But that ended under new coach Jack Pardee, who traded Highsmith, waived Rozier, and relegated Pinkett to a backup role. White, in his first full season as a starter, thanked his peers by rushing 168 times for 702 yards, and scoring 8 touchdowns. Tack on 39 receptions for 368 yards

John Stephens

Birthdate: February 23, 1966
College: NW Louisiana
Height: 6-1
Weight: 220
How Acquired: Drafted in first round, 1988
Final 1990 Team: New England Patriots

PRODUCTIVITY

The Patriots finished twenty-sixth in the NFL in total offense in 1990—twenty-fifth in rushing, twentieth in passing. And without bruising John Stephens, it would've been worse. Stephens finished with 212 carries for 808 yards and a pair of touchdowns. His 3.8 yards per carry average was just below his career-high 3.9 yards per carry average during Stephens' Pro Bowl year of 1988, when he rushed for more than 1,000 yards.

Stephens' dedication and hard work were the only bright spots on a team mired in frustration and mediocrity. He should be praised for his work ethic and positive attitude in the face of such adversity.

SUMMARY

Stephens has yet to regain his Pro Bowl form of 1988, but in his defense, he's had no help from his teammates. The Patriots coaching staff and front office has been completely overhauled, but it remains to be seen how new head coach Dick McPherson plans to utilize his talented tailback. Stephens is a strong, powerful, inside runner, with modest speed (4.7). But there are those who question whether his skills are good enough to become an impact player again.

HANK'S RATING: B

Heath Sherman

Birthdate: March 27, 1967
College: Texas A&I
Height: 6-0
Weight: 190
How Acquired: Drafted in sixth round, 1989
Final 1990 Team: Philadelphia Eagles

PRODUCTIVITY

For nearly a year and a half, Heath Sherman floundered as an obscure member of the Eagles backfield, starting only one regular-season game. But all that changed on November 11, 1990, when Sherman became the first Eagle in nine years to rush for 100 yards in successive games as Philadelphia rolled through the Patriots and Redskins.

"It's good that we have a back like Heath," says Philadelphia quarterback Randall Cunningham. "He's capable of gaining 200 yards someday." Sherman finished the season with 685 yards on 164 carries and a touchdown, averaging 4.2 yards a clip. He finished second on the team in rushing, behind quarterback Randall Cunningham.

SUMMARY

Sherman displayed amazing toughness with his 35 carries against Washington, which set a club record. "I've been high on him since the day we drafted him," says Eagles running backs coach Dave Atkins. "I knew he could come in here and do it." Sherman is a disciplined runner. He won't outrun many secondaries, but he makes few mistakes, is versatile, blocks well, and protects the football. A reliable performer.

HANK'S RATING: B

Tim Worley

Birthdate: September 24, 1966
College: Georgia
Height: 6-2
Weight: 216
How Acquired: Drafted in first round, 1989
Final 1990 Team: Pittsburgh Steelers

PRODUCTIVITY

After leading the Steelers in rushing during his 1989 rookie season, Tim Worley's sophomore effort in Pittsburgh was a great disappointment to fans and coaches alike. Worley finished the 1990 campaign with just 418 yards on 109 carries, for a sub-par 3.8 yards per carry average and no touchdowns. In Worley's defense, he struggled with the change to Joe Walton as offensive coordinator, as Walton got away from Pittsburgh's power attack of 1989 and utilized more of a finesse, multiple-set approach.

The new offense seemed to create indecision with Worley, who quit reacting and started thinking—and hesitating. Worley, a talented tailback with 4.65 speed and driving power and strength, fell victim to specialization and injuries, and failed to become the all-around back that Walton's complicated offense usually features. And this failure effected his attitude.

"When you look at game film from 1989, when they just gave Worley the rock and let him bang away, you wonder why they ever tried to change him," says an AFC scout. "He's not a multi-formation, thinking-man's running back. Worley is a power rusher, a give-it-and-go guy, as in give him the ball and go to hell."

SUMMARY

Worley has struggled with injuries and fumbles since the Steelers made him their first-round pick in 1989. At one time, Noll praised Worley, calling him Pittsburgh's "best running back since Franco Harris"; but thus far, Worley has failed to live up to such high expectations. After the 1990 setback, Noll has openly stated that Worley will not get the ball on a consistent basis until he applies himself to learning the offense. This season will go a long way in determining whether Worley will be a bigtime NFL running back, or a plugger who runs hard and will get you the tough yards here and there.

HANK'S RATING: B

Dexter Carter

Birthdate: September 15, 1967
College: Florida State
Height: 5-9
Weight: 170
How Acquired: Drafted in first round, 1990
Final 1990 Team: San Francisco 49ers

PRODUCTIVITY

It will surprise the masses if San Francisco enters the 1991 season with lightweight second-year man Dexter Carter as its primary go-to guy in its multi-formation offense. Carter, the team's first-round pick in 1990, has speed to burn (4.3) and is a multi-dimensional player, but there are powerful doubts among NFL scouts that his spry 170 pounds will stand up under the punishment. Many say Carter can not be the 49ers No. 1 runner if they expect to go all the way.

But Carter proved that, in spot duty, he has sensational ability. Against Pittsburgh, he gained 147 yards from scrimmage in a 27–7 win, rushing for 90 yards and catching passes for an additional 57 yards. "That game did a great deal for Dexter's confidence and for everyone else's on the team," says head coach George Seifert. Carter finished the season with 460 yards on 114 carries, for a 4.0 average, including a 74-yard touchdown.

SUMMARY

Expect Carter to become a critical weapon in San Francisco's third-down arsenal, much as Roger Craig once was when he rushed and caught passes for over 1,000 yards in 1986. Though there are questions as to whether Carter can develop his running skills enough, he did catch 25 balls for 217 yards in his brief rookie appearances.

Carter's resumé is highlighted by blazing speed and the ability to post out as a legitimate deep-pass threat. But he also bears the reputation as a fumbler. Against New Orleans, with San Francisco trailing 13–10 with 47 seconds remaining, the 49ers were driving at the Saints' 23-yard line when Carter muffed a handoff exchange with quarterback Steve Young. New Orleans linebacker Rickey Jackson fell on the ball to end the game. "Dexter has to develop his own rythym, his own consistency," says Seifert.

HANK'S RATING: B

Fullbacks

Albert Bentley

Birthdate: August 15, 1960
College: Miami
Height: 5-11
Weight: 214
How Acquired: Chosen in supplemental draft, 1984
Final 1990 Team: Indianapolis Colts

PRODUCTIVITY

From the time the Colts signed Eric Dickerson in 1987, Albert Bentley has been the forgotten man. But Bentley, in near anonymity, has been quietly spectacular, and out performed his backfield mate in 1990. His 1,220 yards from scrimmage were a personal best.

As a back, Bentley tied Dickerson in yards per carry (4.1), rushing for 556 yards and 4 touchdowns. And Dickerson couldn't match Bentley's production as a receiver, who had 664 yards in receptions and 2 touchdowns.

SUMMARY

Bentley's last two seasons have been superb. His 71 catches in 1991 were the second-highest of any AFC back. In 1989, he caught a pass in every game, recovered a blocked punt for a touchdown against San Francisco and had five tackles on punt coverage. Bentley's career average of 4.7 yards per carry is the second-highest mark in team history. Bentley is a versatile, multi-talented athlete, with All-Pro ability. A strong runner, Bentley runs great routes. Though he has previously played in the shadow of Eric Dickerson, that is all changing.

HANK'S RATING: A

John L. Williams

Birthdate: November 23, 1964
College: Florida
Height: 5-11
Weight: 226
How Acquired: Drafted in first round, 1986
Final 1990 Team: Seattle Seahawks

PRODUCTIVITY

The fact that John L. Williams failed to earn a berth in the Pro Bowl makes one wonder what criteria is necessary for such honors. Williams was fifth in Pro Bowl balloting, despite finishing second in the AFC in receptions (73) and total yards (1,413). He was spectacular as a receiver, piling up 699 yards, and averaged 3.8 yards a carry while running for 714 yards.

"There's no question that Williams is one of the NFL's best backs," says head coach Chuck Knox. "At times, he's carried our football team."

SUMMARY

Entering his sixth season, Williams has been a mainstay of the Seahawks. No other player has caught more passes over the past four seasons (245), and he was the first running back in team history to lead the team in receiving touchdowns, as he did with six scores in 1989. Williams has fumbled just five times in his career, gets the tough yards, and will pay the price as a blocker. He has the potential to be the best fullback in the NFL—but he has to prove he has the desire and the fire in his belly to take his productivity up a notch or two.

HANK'S RATING: A

Craig Heyward

Birthdate: September 23, 1966
College: Pittsburgh
Height: 5-11
Weight: 251
How Acquired: Drafted in first round, 1988
Final 1990 Team: New Orleans Saints

PRODUCTIVITY

In what was an injury-marred year for New Orleans Saints running backs, Craig "Ironhead" Heyward managed to lead the team in rushing with 599 yards, and occasionally flashed the brilliance that led the Saints to make him a number-one pick in 1988. He bulled for 122 yards and a touchdown against Cincinnati, then came back for an encore with a 155-yard game against Tampa Bay, scoring on runs of 47 and 2 yards. He tallied 4 touchdowns and a 4.6-yard average on the year, but still remained in head coach Jim Mora's doghouse.

SUMMARY

Historically, Heyward's problem always has been, and apparently, always will be, his attitude. "Craig always has had potential," says Mora. "It's his willingness to work for it that has been questioned." Heyward annually shows up for camp weighing upwards of 260 pounds, ignoring Mora's pleas of control. He was arrested for drunkenness after the 1990 season, and basically exudes an attitude of general disdain for the New Orleans front office.

But Heyward is still a great athlete who remains the best runner on the team. His skills are such that he could play as a tailback for an I-formation offense in the NFL. Several scouts reported that if the Saints heirarchy would leave him alone, Heyward could become an All-Pro fullback on a good, solid, experienced Saints team.

There is not a better blocking fullback in the league, but Heyward must run twenty to twenty-five times from the deep position to be effective.

HANK'S RATING: A

Kevin Mack

Birthdate: August 9, 1962
College: Clemson
Height: 6-0
Weight: 235
How Acquired: Chosen in supplemental draft, 1984
Final 1990 Team: Cleveland Browns

PRODUCTIVITY

Kevin Mack was the only bright spot on a dismal Browns football team in 1990. He carried the ball 158 times for 702 yards, an average of 4.4 yards per carry, and scored 5 touchdowns. He ran hard and played hurt, including a four-week stretch when he was forced to wear a cast on a broken left hand. And through it all, he somehow seemed oblivious to the controversy swirling around venerable Cleveland Stadium.

After serving time on a drug-related charge in 1989, Mack bounced back with conviction. He was visible in the community and carried his chin high through the Browns embarassing 3–13 season. His career-high 42 catches for 360 yards pushed him over the 1,000-yard mark in total yards from scrimmage for the season.

SUMMARY

In a season marred by controversy, inner-office feuds, and midseason firings, Mack kept quiet about the Browns internal problems and just played. Some question whether he wasn't quiet because he didn't care about the team or the other players. But no one can find fault in the toughness and strength he shows at the line of scrimmage. A great power runner. He was the Browns player of the game a record six times, including a consecutive four-week stretch.

HANK'S RATING: A

Merril Hoge

Birthdate: January 26, 1965
College: Idaho State
Height: 6-2
Weight: 226
How Acquired: Drafted in tenth round, 1987
Final 1990 Team: Pittsburgh Steelers

PRODUCTIVITY

Hoge's versatility makes him a favorite of blue-collar quarterback Bubby Brister. Oblivious to the high-salary, high-draft-pick choices around him, Hoge continues to shoulder the Steelers' running game. In 1990, his third season as a starter, Hoge had career highs in rushing yards (772) and touchdowns (7 rushing, 3 receiving), while catching 40 passes for 342 yards. "Merril is a tough player," says Brister. "He's just as valuable to us as a receiver as he is in the inside trapping game."

Before a national Monday night television audience last year, Hoge stung the Rams for 2 touchdown receptions, then later scored on a 1-yard run. He averaged 6 yards a carry in a 117-yard performance against the Patriots, and added 64 tough inside yards against a physical San Francisco defense.

SUMMARY

Hoge has been so consistent that rumors persist he might be moved to halfback in 1991, for two reasons. Obviously, to get him the football more often, and second, to accomodate hard-driving Barry Foster, a second-year fullback from Arkansas. Hoge doesn't fumble, and is a hard-working, conscientious football player. He has limited natural skills, but makes up for any deficiences with hustle and second effort. Hoge would be an invaluable addition to any run-oriented club.

HANK'S RATING: B

Gerald Riggs

Birthdate: November 6, 1960
College: Arizona State
Height: 6-1
Weight: 232
How Acquired: Trade, 1989
Final 1990 Team: Washington Redskins

PRODUCTIVITY

Inconsistency and injuries have tripped up Gerald Riggs in his past two seasons at Washington, forcing the Redskins to look elsewhere for a young, versatile player that could challenge him for his position. In 1990, it was an arch injury that ended his season, and he missed eight weeks. While healthy, he scored 6 touchdowns, rushing 123 times for 475 yards and a 3.9 average.

SUMMARY

Riggs is now in his tenth season, and the sun may be setting on what has been a tremendous career. He is still a force in short-yardage and goal-line situations, but the speed that once carried him outside as an Atlanta Falcon is no longer there. He has to show that he won't run too cautious and that he still has the desire to fight for the tough yards. Washington head coach Joe Gibbs had hoped to get several injury-free seasons from Riggs, whose size and attributes fit perfectly in the Redskins big-back scheme. Now Gibbs will be content to get one.

HANK'S RATING: B

Tom Rathman

Birthdate: October 7, 1962
College: Nebraska
Height: 6-1
Weight: 232
How Acquired: Drafted in third round, 1986
Final 1990 Team: San Francisco 49ers

PRODUCTIVITY

Tom Rathman rushed 101 times for 318 yards in 1990, for an average of 3.1 yards per carry and 7 touchdowns. He also added 48 catches for 327 yards. Modest numbers, but to the 49ers, Rathman is the quintessential utility player who does his best work in critical situations. His 73 receptions in 1989 were the most among NFL running backs. And despite the disappearance of the 49ers' rushing game last year (eighteenth in the NFL), Rathman remained a durable, punishing blocker.

SUMMARY

Tom Rathman is a perfect example of a player who can't be measured by statistics. A long-shot, third-round pick in 1986, Rathman has blossomed into a top NFL fullback; he blocks, he catches, he runs. "He's an awesome talent," says Buffalo director of pro personnel John Butler. "Rathman is everything you want in a fullback."

Some chinks are beginning to show in Rathman's armor. Never possessing more than limited run skills, some scouts report that his pass route skills are slipping. The ultimate team player, Rathman knows that for San Francisco to be successful they need a fullback like himself. Look for him to work hard at keeping the 49ers near the top.

HANK'S RATING: B

Alonzo Highsmith

Birthdate: February 26, 1965
College: Miami
Height: 6-1
Weight: 234
How Acquired: Drafted in first round, 1987
Final 1990 Team: Dallas Cowboys

PRODUCTIVITY

For two-plus years, Highsmith was among the NFL's best blocking fullbacks in Houston's two-back, slug-mouth scheme. Those days are gone, as Highsmith was traded to the Cowboys in 1990, then suffered through an injury-plagued year. Highsmith's dismal numbers reflect his frustrating 1990 season—19 carries for 48 yards. But he remains a big, strong talent who, when healthy, is among the Top 10 fullbacks in football.

SUMMARY

Highsmith is big (6-1, 234), he's fast (4.5), and he's a devastating blocker. But he must prove that he can stay healthy long enough to fulfill the potential that led the Oilers to make him their first-round pick in 1987. And there have also been questions about his willingness to play hard. "I know I have the ability," he says. "I just want the chance to prove it." The Cowboys are praying that Highsmith's troubled knees hold up long enough for him to complement tailback Emmitt Smith in what could be an explosive backfield.

HANK'S RATING: B

Anthony Toney

Birthdate: September 23, 1962
College: Texas A&M
Height: 6-0
Weight: 227
How Acquired: Drafted in second round, 1986
Final 1990 Team: Philadelphia Eagles

PRODUCTIVITY

Slowed by injuries in recent seasons, Anthony Toney rebounded for a reasonable 1990 season. His 132 carries for 452 yards was second among Eagles running backs. Though much more limited as a receiver, Toney caught 17 passes for 133 yards.

SUMMARY

Toney is a tough, durable, inside runner who is a spot-duty player. His ferocious blocks made him a favorite of departed coach Buddy Ryan, but there are questions as to what Toney's role will be under new head coach—and former offensive coordinator—Rich Kotite. Injuries to both ankles make Toney a question mark.

HANK'S RATING: B

Christian Okoye

Birthdate: August 16, 1961
College: Azusa Pacific
Height: 6-1
Weight: 253
How Acquired: Drafted in second round, 1987
Final 1990 Team: Kansas City Chiefs

PRODUCTIVITY

With the emergence of free agent Barry Word, Christian Okoye's production dropped considerably in 1990; after being the NFL's leading rusher in 1989, he finished last season with 805 yards on 245 carries—an average of 3.3 yards, nearly a yard off his career average of 4.1. He scored 7 touchdowns, which was also below his career best.

In 1989, Okoye finished with 1,480 yards, and carried the ball a whopping 370 times en route to eight 100-yard games. But the 253-pound "Nigerian Nightmare" suffered the punishment that goes with such a workload, and some scouts believe that could be to blame for his lose of quickness and toughness at the line of scrimmage. The same scouts wonder if Okoye isn't done as a *top* runner.

SUMMARY

Okoye still sorely needs to work on his receiving skills, he has the poorest hands in the NFL. And despite his size, Okoye remains an average blocker who is prone to nagging injuries. Scouts are quick to point out, however, that Okoye, now entering his fifth NFL season, is still relatively new to sport. Others question whether he isn't older than he claims to be. Look for Okoye to produce this year, but he will again fail to match his 1989 numbers.

HANK'S RATING: B

Brad Muster

Birthdate: April 11, 1965
College: Stanford
Height: 6-3
Weight: 231
How Acquired: Drafted in first round, 1988
Final 1990 Team: Chicago Bears

PRODUCTIVITY

Brad Muster finally came into his own in 1990, averaging 4.7 yards per carry and leading the Bears with 47 receptions. He had the best year of his three-year career with 664 rushing yards and 452 receiving yards. A two-dimensional weapon, Muster rushed for 50 yards and caught passes for 93 yards against Tampa Bay, and had a season-high 99 yards rushing against Phoenix. He also caught at least one pass in seventeen of eighteen games.

SUMMARY

Going into the 1990 season, there was concern whether Muster, the twenty-third player taken in the 1988 draft, would live up to his potential. In his first two seasons, Muster was terribly inconsistent, fumbled too often, and suffered from a nagging back injury and various illnesses. But in the face of criticism, Muster responded with his best season to date. He stayed healthy, threw precision blocks for Neal Anderson, and did a good job running and catching the football. "Brad's improvement was a high point of the season," says Mike Ditka.

If Muster can build on his performance in 1990, look for him to leap into the Top 10 for fullbacks. If not, the rap that he is overrated and lacks the speed, running skills, and toughness at the line of scrimmage will resurface. As will the talk that he is better suited for tight end.

HANK'S RATING: B

Tony Paige

Birthdate: October 14, 1962
College: Virginia Tech
Height: 5-10
Weight: 235
How Acquired: Plan B free agent, 1990
Final 1990 Team: Miami Dolphins

PRODUCTIVITY

A versatile, veteran player, Paige played a number of roles for the Dolphins in 1990. His thunderous blocks opened huge holes for tailback Sammy Smith, who enjoyed the finest year of his young pro career. His tender hands and well-executed routes out of the backfield resulted in 35 catches for 247 yards and 4 touchdowns, good for third among other Dolphins. And he rushed for 95 yards on 32 carries, an average of 3.0 yards a carry.

SUMMARY

Paige added a veteran's instincts and work habits to the Dolphin running game, teaching Miami's young backs the demands of the NFL. He played the whole season with a bad knee, and shook off an assortment of sprained ankles and muscle bruises.

Paige, who the Dolphins took from Detroit's Plan B list in 1990, isn't particularly fast (4.78), or talented. He is a top blocker, but doesn't have good running skills. He does make some big plays in critical games: Against the Colts, he had a career-high 8 catches; his 7-yard, diving touchdown catch against New England with 1:46 remaining beat the Patriots. "I tell my teammates that I'm going to make something happen," Paige says. "And I do." It might be time for Miami to start looking for more talent at the fullback position.

HANK'S RATING: B

Ickey Woods

Birthdate: February 28, 1966
College: UNLV
Height: 6-2
Weight: 232
How Acquired: Drafted in second round, 1988
Final 1990 Team: Cincinnati Bengals

PRODUCTIVITY

Ickey Woods, who hadn't played since the second game of the 1989 season when he suffered a career-threatening injury, came back with a bang in the seventh week last year with a slashing 1-yard score against Cleveland. Woods is no where near his rookie form of 1988, but he proved that he can still produce, battering the Raiders 11 times in the playoffs for 73 yards. But Woods is battling time, and numbers, as hard-charging, third-year player Craig Taylor continues to press for playing time.

Woods carried 64 times for 268 yards, a 4.2 average, and 6 touchdowns, but he was clearly slower and more tentative than the flamboyant runner who captured the nation's heart with his power touchdowns and high-brow dance moves three seasons ago. The injury will make big production days few and far between.

SUMMARY

Though Ickey's comeback, by any standards, must be considered a success (some doctors felt he'd never play again), there is reason to believe that the days of the Ickey Shuffle are numbered in Cincinnati. A Cincinnati favorite, Woods is loved by Bengals fans, but his maverick attitude, sloppy work habits, and poor morale may hinder the development of youngsters like Taylor and Harold Green. He's still a good bet to score inside the five, but he can't bear the brunt of the load over the course of sixteen games. And many question whether he isn't too heavy and if he has the "fire" to be a top runner.

HANK'S RATING: B

Rod Bernstine

Birthdate: February 8, 1965
College: Texas A&M
Height: 6-3
Weight: 235
How Acquired: Drafted in first round, 1987
Final 1990 Team: San Diego Chargers

PRODUCTIVITY

Bernstine teamed with Marion Butts to boost the Chargers to the number-one rushing attack in the AFC in 1990. The former tight end flashed good skills and versatility. A vicious blocker with solid form and technique, Bernstine was San Diego's second-leading rusher with 589 yards on 124 carries—an impressive average of 4.8 yards per. When Marion Butts missed the final two games of the 1990 season to injury, Bernstine busted loose for 190 yards in the final two games, including a career-high, 27-carry, 114-yard effort against the Raiders in the season finale.

SUMMARY

Bernstine's high per-carry average helped the Chargers tie for first in the NFL (with Philadelphia) for average yards per carry, at 4.7. But Bernstine's recurring injuries irritated management, who questioned his attitude and reliability. They need him to spend more time on the field and less time in the tub. His contract expired February 1. "We'd like to sign him," says GM Bobby Beathard. "But it won't be easy."

HANK'S RATING: B

Michael Haddix

Birthdate: December 27, 1961
College: Mississippi State
Height: 6-2
Weight: 227
How Acquired: Plan B free agent, 1989
Final 1990 Team: Green Bay Packers

PRODUCTIVITY

It's not often that a fullback leads a team in rushing, but Michael Haddix paced the Packers in 1990 with less-than-impressive numbers. He ran for 311 yards, good for exactly fifty-eighth overall in the NFL, averaged just 3.2 yards a carry, and failed to crack the end zone once. Though Haddix, whom the Packers plucked from Plan B in 1989, has been a valuable addition as a blocker, head coach Lindy Infante never had any intention of him carrying the team's ground attack. His 13 catches for 94 yards were way off his career average of 22 a season.

"We've got to have a running game," says GM Tom Braatz, acknowledging the Packers declining ground attack. "When you run well, the passing game gets in tune with it." Not lost on Braatz is a simple fact: The Packers are 10–0 under Infante in games in which they've rushed for 125 yards or more. But when talking those heady numbers, don't look at Haddix, who was Philadelphia's first-round pick in 1983.

SUMMARY

Haddix is an extremely talented blocking back, cut from the mold of a Maurice Carthon or Jamie Mueller. But he lacks the run skills to be the catalyst of a team's running attack. With a career average of just three yards a carry, Haddix has rushed for just a little more than 1,600 yards in his nine-year career, most of it between the tackles. Within his limitations, he's a solid, tough runner who won't commit costly turnovers.

HANK'S RATING: B

Reggie Cobb

Birthdate: July 7, 1968
College: Tennessee
Height: 6-0
Weight: 225

How Acquired: Drafted in second round, 1990
Final 1990 Team: Tampa Bay Buccaneers

PRODUCTIVITY

Reggie Cobb, who finished third among NFC rookies in 1990 with 480 yards on 151 carries (2 touchdowns), should be praised for his rebound from a college career shortened by injuries and allegations of drug use. And, like Atlanta's Steve Broussard, Cobb had seldom been asked to block or catch passes in college, but he adapted well to his new duties.

Cobb caught 39 passes for 299 yards, and dropped just 3 passes. "Reggie worked hard last year and showed a lot of improvement," says Tampa Bay head coach Richard Williamson. "We expect his development to continue this year."

SUMMARY

Cobb had his best game against Green Bay, when he rushed for 54 yards and caught 5 passes for 48 yards, giving the Tampa Bay coaching staff reason to be optimistic. But, like most other second-year players, Cobb must develop consistency. When paired with scatback Gary Anderson, Cobb lines up at fullback, but was used as the primary back in Tampa Bay's one-back set. Cobb may be fending off the challenge of Bruce Perkins, who was impressive last year in a limited role, but we feel Cobb has fine NFL potential and will get *much* better.

HANK'S RATING: B

Anthony Thompson

Birthdate: April 8, 1967
College: Indiana
Height: 5-11
Weight: 207
How Acquired: Drafted in second round, 1990
Final 1990 Team: Phoenix Cardinals

PRODUCTIVITY

A superbly conditioned athlete, Anthony Thompson fell victim to the oldest NFL rule: He who shows up for camp usually plays. And seventh-round pick Johnny Johnson beat him there, as Thompson held out. Nevertheless, Thompson worked hard, didn't complain about his lack of playing time, and when given the chance, "he played his ass off," says head coach Joe Bugel. When Johnson went down with injury, it gave Thompson his chance: Over three games, he rushed for 306 yards, and finished with 390 yards and 4 touchdowns on 106 attempts.

SUMMARY

Thompson, who Bugel says may start at fullback, but will also challenge Johnson for the starting tailback job, has all the running skills you want in an NFL back. He is an outstanding open-field runner with great acceleration (4.69) and strong, powerful legs, virtues that helped him set an NCAA record of 68 career touchdowns at Indiana. And Thompson's natural running style is to attack the line of scrimmage—perfect for the NFL. Thompson also has soft hands—he caught 25 balls for 241 yards in 1990. "We feel good about our backfield," says Bugel. "And Thompson has a lot to do with that attitude." He certainly does. Look for Thompson to become a fine NFL back this season.

HANK'S RATING: B

Brad Baxter

Birthdate: May 5, 1967
College: Alabama State
Height: 6-1
Weight: 231
How Acquired: Free Agent, 1989
Final 1990 Team: New York Jets

PRODUCTIVITY

Brad Baxter developed a reputation in 1990 as a sledgehammer fullback, throwing ear-ringing blocks and battering his way to 539 yards on 124 attempts (4.3). Baxter, though nonexistent in the passing game (8 catches for 73 yards), earned a starting job the old-fashioned way: Hard work and physical play. "You know how leaves will be piled up on the lawns, and you run and jump into them and they disperse?" says tailback Freeman McNeil. "That's the way it seems when Brad hits the pile."

SUMMARY

Baxter was a little-known free agent signee in 1989 out of Alabama State, and appeared in just one game before last season. He is loaded with raw potential, and has attributes that could make him a top NFL fullback: modest speed (4.7), powerful legs, and good technique. We especially like his ability in short yardage and goal-line situations. He must learn to catch the football, however, if he intends to remain a vital part of Bruce Coslet's attack offense.

HANK'S RATING: B

Rick Fenney

Birthdate: December 7, 1964
College: Washington
Height: 6-1
Weight: 240
How Acquired: Drafted in eighth round, 1987
Final 1990 Team: Minnesota Vikings

PRODUCTIVITY

Unlike several of his backfield mates—D.J. Dozier, Herschel Walker—unsung Rick Fenney created little controversy in 1990, choosing instead to bear the burden of the Vikings running game on his shoulder. Fenney carried 87 times last year for 376 yards—an impressive 4.3 yards per carry, and a shade better than Walker. Fenney's yards were tough yards, typically short-yardage situations, but the spunky fullback seems more suited to the Vikings trapping and sweeping schemes than his more visible backfield mates.

SUMMARY

Fenney has never been an every-down back, but is a consistent role player. "Rick is a tough, tough guy," says guard Todd Kalis. "He's a terribly hard-working back who gives it 110 percent every week." He is a hard driving, tackle-to-tackle runner, with excellent blocking skills. Though he caught 17 passes for 112 yards, Fenney is primarily a one-dimensional, blocking fullback, with exceptional work habits and strength. He seems to be slipping as a runner, and it will be a challenge for him to perform at the same level as he has in the past.

HANK'S RATING: C

Maurice Carthon

Birthdate: April 24, 1961
College: Arkansas State
Height: 6-1
Weight: 225
How Acquired: Free Agent, 1985
Final 1990 Team: New York Giants

PRODUCTIVITY

Maurice Carthon built his reputation in New York while punching open holes for Herschel Walker and the New Jersey Generals in the USFL. Now, six years later, the blue-collar Carthon still earns his keep doing what he does best: pounding linebackers, running for tough inside yards, and maintaining the consistency in the New York offense.

In 1990, Carthon rushed 36 times for 143 yards, a 4.0 yards per carry average. But his numbers, though not spectacular, hardly reflect what Carthon meant to the Giants offense. His explosive blocking opened holes for Super Bowl MVP Ottis Anderson and was a big reason star tailback Rodney Hampton was able to gain 455 yards in his rookie campaign.

SUMMARY

Carthon will never rush for 1,000 yards. But he is the consummate team player and never fumbles. When necessary, Carthon has stepped forward and made the big play on his own: In a touch-and-go battle last year with Washington, he flashed his seldom-seen breakaway speed when he hauled in a 63-yard, game-winning, down-the-seam strike from quarterback Phil Simms.

"Power wins," says Giants former head coach Bill Parcells. "We're not trying to fool you with our running game." But some argue that Carthon's running skills have slipped enough that he may have trouble making the final roster.

HANK'S RATING: C

Jamie Mueller

Birthdate: October 4, 1964
College: Benedictine
Height: 6-1
Weight: 225
How Acquired: Drafted in third round, 1987
Final 1990 Team: Buffalo Bills

PRODUCTIVITY

Jamie Mueller has earned his bruising reputation for his sledgehammer blocks and no-nonsense style of play. Like the Giants' Maurice Carthon, Mueller seldom carries the ball—he rushed for 207 yards on 59 attempts in 1990, scoring just 2 touchdowns—but was brutally effective in short-yardage situations. He is a career 3.5 yards-per-carry fullback; another of the NFL's unsung heroes.

SUMMARY

Mueller is a throwback to the fullbacks of earlier eras, who seemed oblivious to everything except stimulating pain among opposing linebackers and defensive backs. On rare occasion does Mueller share the spotlight with the Bills' talent-laden offense, but when he does, he makes the best of it.

Just nineteen seconds remained last year against the Jets when quarterback Jim Kelly ducked under center at the New York 14-yard line on the game's final play. Mueller, who was designated as a blocker on the play, pancaked his man, then noticed that Kelly was in trouble. He took off, drifting over the middle until he found himself completely alone in the end zone. A disbelieving Kelly fired the ball into Mueller's chest, giving the fullback his first touchdown reception of his four-year career. When reporters kiddingly asked Mueller to describe his secret on how he got so wide open, he responded with a grin, "Actually, I pretended I was going for water . . ."

Most agree Buffalo needs a better fullback athlete, saving Mueller for the late down, short yardage plays.

HANK'S RATING: C

Steve Smith

Birthdate: August 30, 1964
College: Penn State
Height: 6-1
Weight: 235
How Acquired: Drafted in third round, 1987
Final 1990 Team: Los Angeles Raiders

PRODUCTIVITY

Steve Smith performed his yeoman's duty once again in 1990, rushing 81 times for 327 yards and 2 touchdowns. He caught just four passes, but three of them went for touchdowns. With the sudden demise of the Cowboys' Alonzo Highsmith, Smith may now be the most devastating blocking fullback in the NFL. In his fifth pro season, Smith has solid cutback ability as well as enough quickness to bounce it outside.

SUMMARY

Smith is a selfless, consistent player who doesn't make waves, performs when called on, and can be counted on in critical situations; it was his 17-yard touchdown catch that gave the Raiders a 12–10 win over San Diego in the season finale, giving Los Angeles its first division title since 1985.

"Smith is a lot better player than he gets credit for," says one scout. "There's a lot of teams who have looked at him and wondered how he'd do as an every-down back. He has sneaky speed and lots of potential." But there are others who question his skills and feel Oakland may need to look elsewhere for higher production.

HANK'S RATING: C

Who's Missing

Bo Jackson

Birthdate: November 30, 1962
College: Auburn
Height: 6-1
Weight: 225
How Acquired: Drafted in seventh round, 1987
Final 1990 Team: Los Angeles Raiders

With his career jeopardized by his injured left hip, Jackson faces the 1991 season with terrible uncertainty. Certainly his annual ten-week impact on the Raiders cannot be denied, but many Los Angeles players have grown tired of living in the shadow of Jackson, who never goes to training camp, doesn't play hurt, yet gets most of the praise.

"It's a problem," says one veteran. "Bo cruises in after baseball, makes a few spectacular plays, makes a million dollars, and goes home. I hope his injury isn't career-ending, but I do believe he's become a distraction to our team. He's not out for the team. He's out for Bo."

But when Bo was motivated, he was spectacular, like his 8-carry, 117-yard performance in a 24–7 win over Cincinnati. It was his third straight 100-yard game, and offered one of the most amazing runs in Jackson's well-storied career: Bo started left, encountered heavy traffic, reversed his field, and ran 88 yards to the Cincinnati 1-yard line, where a diving tackle by former 400-meter sprinter Rod Jones finally brought him down. "I thought [Jones] was going to chase him into the parking lot," said amazed Raider defensive tackle Bob Golic.

Bo, if healthy, is the No. 1 skill player in the NFL. He is simply the best runner we've ever seen. A Hall of Fame player. But his hip injury is so bad that he may not play again. But if he is able, Bo will return to the Raiders.

HANK'S RATING: AAA

Keith Byars

Birthdate: October 14, 1963
College: Ohio State
Height: 6-1
Weight: 238
How Acquired: Drafted in first round, 1986
Final 1990 Team: Philadelphia Eagles

If you're scrolling the year-end rushing statistics in search of Keith Byars, you might be looking awhile. The sixth-year running back only carried the ball 37 times for 141 yards, but never has Byars' all-around worth meant more to the Eagles. Byars lined up all the over field in 1990—tailback, fullback, tight end, even wide receiver—and led the team with 81 catches for 819 yards and 3 touchdowns.

In one game, Byars *threw* an 8-yard scoring pass to Anthony Toney, then minutes later caught a 12-yard touchdown from Randall Cunningham. In the season's final game, Byars threw his fourth touchdown strike of the year to rookie receiver Calvin Williams. Though Byars has never rushed for more than 577 yards in a single season, he has caught 221 passes over the last three years.

Byars may have the best hands in the NFL. A unique talent, he has become an amazingly productive player. A definite All Pro, and a great asset to the Eagles.

During the off-season, the players looked to Byars to hear out the gripes of numerous Eagles upset over the dismissal of Buddy Ryan. A team leader, Byars has worked hard to restore order to a floundering, but talented, Philadelphia team. "We have to get back the team unity we had in the strike year of 1987," Byars says.

HANK'S RATING: AA

Rodney Hampton

Birthdate: April 3, 1969
College: Georgia
Height: 5-11
Weight: 215
How Acquired: Drafted in first round, 1990
Final 1990 Team: New York Giants

The Giants were rotating Rodney Hampton and Ottis Anderson on a regular basis until Hampton broke his fibula in the NFC divisional playoff game against the Bears and was lost for the season. But his 455 yards on just 109 carries sheds some light on what the rookie was capable of in 1990, as he broke one run for 41 yards and scored 2 touchdowns. He added 32 receptions for 274 yards, including a 27-yard touchdown, to his sterling freshman numbers. Hampton wowed Giants veterans and coaches in 1990—has All-Pro potential. A possible future star, 1991 could be a big year for Hampton if he stays healthy.

HANK'S RATING: A

Dave Meggett

Birthdate: April 30, 1966
College: Towson State
Height: 5-7
Weight: 180
How Acquired: Drafted in fifth round, 1990
Final 1990 Team: New York Giants

David Meggett, as one of the league's most dangerous players, doesn't fit a certain niche. But his contribution to the World Champion Giants is quite impressive. He led the team in receptions last year with 39, and his 410 yards was second among all New York receivers.

As a running back, Meggett is used as a scatback, attacking defenses outside the tackles. He carried the ball 22 times in 1990 for 164 yards, a whopping 7.5-yard average, including a 51-yard scamper. He also rolled up over 900 yards in kickoff and punt returns to lead the Giants in both categories. "Meggett is an outstanding player who can hurt you in a number of ways," says former head coach Bill Parcells. "He's a special kind of player."

Meggett is most effective running the Giants' "scat" option on passing downs, in which he finds any hole he can and releases as a safety-valve receiver. The Bears successfully stopped that strategy in the playoffs, however, by constantly blitzing to Meggett's side of the formation, which forced him to block backside.

A productive player, Meggett has a bright future in the NFL.

HANK'S RATING: A

Harold Green

Birthdate: January 29, 1968
College: South Carolina
Height: 6-2
Weight: 218
How Acquired: Drafted in second round, 1990
Final 1990 Team: Cincinnati Bengals

The Bengals have been waiting for someone to step forward as the successor to the ageless James Brooks. Harold Green just might be their man, as he proved in 1990 that, with playing time, he can carry the rock. His 353 yards on 83 carries was good for a solid 4.3 yard average in his rookie year, and head coach Sam Wyche was impressed by the youngster's powerful inside running and durability over the course of a sixteen-game season. He has NFL running and receiving ability. A top talent. "He might have been the steal of the [1990] draft," says Bengals running back coach Jim Anderson. "He's got size, quickness, speed. He's got it all."

HANK'S RATING: A

Rueben Mayes

Birthdate: June 16, 1963
College: Washington State
Height: 5-11
Weight: 200
How Acquired: Drafted in third round, 1986
Final 1990 Team: New Orleans Saints

Reuben Mayes was the NFL rookie of the year in 1986, rushing for 1,353 yards and 8 touchdowns, including six 100-yard games. But a nagging Achilles' heel problem resulted in three operations over the next four years, and, after another Pro Bowl season in 1987, Mayes suffered torn knee ligaments, requiring more surgery. The result was a slower, more tentative Mayes, who saw more time on the bench in 1990 than he did on the field.

In a 28–7 win over Phoenix, Mayes ran for 99 yards on 16 carries, scoring 3 touchdowns on runs of 10, 4, and 14 yards. On the game's final drive, he carried 9 times for 58 yards. "I felt like I found another gear, the gear I had been looking for," he said then. "This time I just ran and reacted. After today, I feel like I'm over the hump."

But it was not to be a Cinderella story. Mayes finished the 1990 season 510 yards on 138 carries and 7 touchdowns, for an average of 3.7 yards a carry. Mayes, never fully recovered from his leg injuries, has lost his great quickness at the line of scrimmage. The Saints, whose backfield has been plagued with injury, are hoping Mayes can add some consistency to his game. "Reuben was not productive," says head coach Jim Mora. "Maybe it was the year off. Maybe he lacked confidence." Some insiders feel Mayes may not make the 1991 roster.

HANK'S RATING: B

Steve Broussard

Birthdate: February 22, 1967
College: Washington State
Height: 5-7
Weight: 201
How Acquired: Drafted in first round, 1990
Final 1990 Team: Atlanta Falcons

After Steve Broussard got off to a quick start as a rookie in 1990, he found himself in Jerry Glanville's doghouse, for reasons common among first-year running backs: He fumbled too often, failed to understand the importance of playing through minor bumps and bruises, and resisted learning to catch the football out of the backfield.

Broussard displayed some speed and moves in the open field, and developed blocking skills that he had seldom been asked to use at Washington State. When the Falcons added reliable Mike Rozier from Houston, Glanville limited Broussard's NFL baptism, choosing to slowly develop his talented rookie. "Bruiser," as he is called by his teammates, finished the year with 126 carries for 454 yards, a 3.6 yards per carry average, while catching 24 passes for 160 yards.

Most feel Broussard's problems can be traced to his attitude. He had the reputation of having a bad attitude coming out of college, and last year did nothing to improve it. There is talent here, but his NFL future is still up in the air.

HANK'S RATING: B

Marcus Dupree

Birthdate: May 22, 1964
College: Oklahoma
Height: 6-3
Weight: 225
How Acquired: Free Agent, 1990
Final 1990 Team: Los Angeles Rams

One of the finest players to ever line up at Oklahoma, Marcus Dupree opted for the USFL as a junior in 1984. His pro career was cut short, however, when he suffered what was believed to be a career-ending knee injury while playing for the defunct Portland Breakers in 1985. After collecting a Lloyd's of London insurance policy and remaining out of football for five years, Dupree, in a comeback bid, joined the Rams in mid-1990 as a free agent.

"He really looks impressive," says Dick Coury, who coached Dupree in the USFL and was the Rams quarterback coach last season. "He came in in excellent shape, and in practice, he looked like the old Marcus Dupree. It could be an amazing story." Dupree saw spot duty, rushing for just 72 yards on 19 carries. But he averaged 3.8 yards an attempt, and nearly broke one 13-yard run for a touchdown. "I'm eager to play a whole game, get in a rhythm, and see what I can do," he says.

We have to question whether Dupree can return to the skill level needed to produce in the NFL. Last year, his reactions at the line of scrimmage were poor, but his long layoff could be to blame. By preseason, we'll all know.

HANK'S RATING: D

Best of Plan B

Roger Craig

Birthdate: July 10, 1960
College: Nebraska
Height: 6-0
Weight: 224
Final 1990 Team: San Francisco 49ers

Much like Cincinnati's James Brooks, thirty-one-year-old Roger Craig keeps surprising opponents, like he did in a brilliant 97-yard effort against the Bengals in 1990. But Craig enters the 1991 season facing the biggest hurdle in his career: Coming back from a miserable 1990 season and a torn posterior cruciate ligament in his right knee.

Craig carried the ball 141 times last year for 439 yards, a 3.1 yards per carry average. The 49ers' charmed 1990 season ended abruptly when Craig fumbled while the 49ers were protecting a one-point lead in final minutes of the NFC title game; the Giants drove to the winning field goal for a 15–13 triumph as time expired.

Craig's injury and drop in production last year led the 49ers to put Craig on Plan B, but the Raiders would rather remember his 1989 numbers: 1,054 yards and 6 touchdowns. They are hoping Craig can ease the possible loss of Bo Jackson.

Craig's best season was 1985 when he gained 2,066 total yards, 1,050 rushing and 1,016 receiving. But the knee injury has cost Craig much of the cutting ability and quickness that made him such an effective runner. Scouts question whether Craig can regain his confidence enough to help the Raiders. We think he will. And he still catches low balls better than anyone we have ever seen.

HANK'S RATING: B

John Settle

Birthdate: June 2, 1965
College: Appalachian State
Height: 5-9
Weight: 210
Final 1990 Team: Atlanta Falcons

John Settle carried just 9 times for 16 yards in Atlanta in 1990 for a dismal 1.8 yard average, which was a radical departure from his Pro Bowl season of 1988, or even his 689-yard season of 1989. But Settle didn't adjust well to new head coach Jerry Glanville or his Red Gun offense, and the frustrated back voiced his opinion often and loudly.

The Redskins hope Settle can find his old skills. He has the size to fit into the Redskins scheme. Questions as to whether his top performance days are over, and if his bad attitude was a one-year problem, do exist among scouts.

HANK'S RATING: B

Don Smith

— 55 —

Birthdate: October 30, 1963
College: Mississippi State
Height: 5-11
Weight: 200
Final 1990 Team: Buffalo Bills

The Miami Dolphins signed former Buffalo utility back Don Smith just before the Plan B deadline, moments after they lost Troy Stradford, who signed with the Kansas City Chiefs.

Smith was the fifth Plan B player signed by Miami, and Stradford was the tenth player the Dolphins lost. Smith, a quarterback at Mississippi State, has played running back and wide receiver in three seasons with Tampa Bay and one with the Buffalo Bills. He sat out his first season at Tampa Bay with a back injury.

Last year with the Bills, he played in all sixteen regular season games and all three postseason games with two starts. He gained 82 yards in 20 carries and caught 21 passes for 225 yards. He also returned 32 kickoffs for 643 yards, a 20 yard average. Smith has excellent balance and ballhandling skills, as well as fine speed and moves in the open field.

Miami hopes Smith will be productive as a third-down receiver. As long as they don't expect too much, they shouldn't be disappointed.

HANK'S RATING: B

Joe Morris

Birthdate: September 15, 1960
College: Syracuse
Height: 5-7
Weight: 195
Final 1990 Team: Did Not Play

Joe Morris was not actually a Plan B acquisition, but he was an unconditional free agent after being waived by the Giants in 1990, just one year removed from the third 1,000-yard season of his career. That was before former New York Giants defensive coach Bill Belichick became head coach of the Browns, when he signed Morris as an unconditional free agent.

Morris gained 1,083 yards in 1988, then spent 1989 on injured reserve after breaking his foot in the final exhibition game. He was the No. 1 back in the 1989 training camp, but in 1990, the New York Giants had Ottis Anderson and Rodney Hampton, which meant they no longer needed Morris, who was released on the final cut. Belichick, then with the Giants, encouraged Morris to stay in shape.

"He said 'Keep working out, keep yourself in shape, and keep working for the season,'" Morris says. "'If something doesn't work out this year, you'll get a shot next year.' He said 'You can play, Joe. I know that and you know that.'"

"The reason why we signed Joe Morris is we think he can play," Belichick said as the Browns went through the second day of the three-day minicamp at Baldwin-Wallace College. "Even though he's a veteran player, I still think he has some good football left in him." Morris holds Giants' career records with 1,318 carries for 5,296 yards and 48 rushing touchdowns, and he also holds single-season records for the 1,516 yards he gained in 1986 and the 21 rushing touchdowns he scored in 1985. Morris gained 1,336 yards in 1985 and had four games that year in which he scored 3 touchdowns.

There is no doubt that the old Joe Morris would help the Browns. But after his layoff, can the veteran regain his quickness at the line of scrimmage and his running confidence?

HANK'S RATING: B

Wide Receivers

Only wideouts who finished with *more* than 500 yards receiving in 1990 were evaluated by the cast of NFL assistant coaches, personnel directors, and scouts who assisted with this book. Some of the receivers who were mentioned by the evaluators, but who did not receive enough votes are listed in the "Who's Missing" section.

Jerry Rice

Birthdate: October 13, 1962
College: Mississippi Valley State
Height: 6-2
Weight: 200
How Acquired: Drafted in first round, 1985
Final 1990 Team: San Francisco 49ers

TECHNIQUE

What makes Jerry Rice special is one simple quality: his stride. "He doesn't look that fast," says a scout. "But when the ball's in the air, he has the ability to stride away from you." Add to that his ability to run great 45-degree routes, and you can see why Rice is No. 1. Bottom line: Don't cover him man-to-man. Atlanta tried, and failed, on two miserable occasions.

In Rice's first confrontation with the Falcon's bump-and-run coverage, he pulled in 8 passes for 171 yards and a touchdown. Three weeks later, Rice answered with 5 touchdowns, including a 49ers-record 13 catches for 225 yards. His five scores equaled the NFL record co-held by Bob Shaw of the 1950 Chicago Cardinals and former Charger star Kellen Winslow. "It's impossible," says San Francisco quarterback Joe Montana, "to cover Jerry Rice one-on-one."

PRODUCTIVITY

Rice finished the Atlanta game with 6,938 career receiving yards, which was another club record—and he was just six weeks into the 1990 season. And he wasn't through. Tack on 12 catches against Dallas for 147 yards, and 8 more for 101 yards against Cincinnati—including 3 on the game-winning drive in overtime. "There's great chemistry between us," says 49ers quarterback Joe Montana, in classic understatement.

SUMMARY

The 49ers found Rice the perfect complement when they added John Taylor to the arsenal three years ago. How can you argue with a tandem that routinely turns 6-yard hitches into long touchdowns? Rice is bigger (6-2, 200), but together Rice and Taylor have routinely piled up the yards: 2,250 yards and 20 touchdowns in 1990. Mike Sherrard, whose thrice-broken leg limited his production in 1990, still showed—with frightening results—what could happen if the 49ers added a *third* wideout with 4.4 speed.

HANK'S RATING: AAA

Al Toon

Birthdate: April 30, 1963
College: Wisconsin
Height: 6-4
Weight: 205
How Acquired: Drafted in first round, 1985
Final 1990 Team: New York Jets

TECHNIQUE

Watch Al Toon run and you won't believe he's *that* fast. At 6-4, 205, he always appears to be loping. But line up next to him, and his quickness will startle you; he has great vertical seam speed. "If he's even, he's leavin'," says a scout.

His 4.4 speed, combined with textbook routes, remarkable strength, and unbelievable hands make Toon the prototype, pro-set wide receiver. Such attributes were evident in the Jets' 17–12 surprise of Houston in 1990. Toon caught 7 passes for 119 yards, including a 42-yard touchdown and a 28-yard catch that set up the winning field goal.

— 57 —

PRODUCTIVITY

The Jets unveiled their new attack offense in 1990 under new head coach Bruce Coslet, and three things were certain: the wide receivers did more downfield blocking, the quarterback seldom threw down the middle of the field when there was a free safety, and Al Toon caught 57 passes for 757 yards and 6 touchdowns. But while opposing defenses were unsuccessful in stopping Toon, injuries did.

SUMMARY

Toon's toughness is worthy of the purple heart. In 1989, he played six full games and parts of five despite a sprained shoulder, contused thigh, two sprained ankles (which occurred in the same game), and a concussion. In 1990, he played despite painful back and groin problems. Best one-on-one receiver in the NFL.

HANK'S RATING: AA

Andre Rison

Birthdate: March 8, 1967
College: Michigan State
Height: 6-0
Weight: 191
How Acquired: Trade, 1990
Final 1990 Team: Atlanta Falcons

TECHNIQUE

Andre Rison isn't the fastest receiver in the NFL; in fact, on draft day in 1989, when the Colts took him in the first round, scouts had him as a low 4.6, but combined with his tremendous strength, "it makes him a thoroughbred," according to one scout. He earned a reputation as a route technician as a rookie in Indianapolis in 1989, where he carved up defenses for 52 catches for 820 yards and 4 touchdowns. But he has also proved he is a deep vertical threat. The Colts stunned the league when they included Rison for trade bait to draft quarterback Jeff George. "This year," says an AFC scout, "Rison will prove that he's the best wideout in the league. He runs precision routes. He's physical. He stays healthy. He's a secondary's nightmare."

PRODUCTIVITY

Rison caught 11 passes in his first meeting with San Francisco, and answered with 9 more (and 172 yards and 2 touchdowns) when he played the then-world champs again three weeks later. Those two nationally televised games gave the nation a taste of Rison's ability; he finished with a team record 82 catches, 1,208 yards, and 10 touchdowns —despite the fact that Atlanta seldom threw to him in the second half of the season due to the myriad of coverages teams used to stop him.

Few receivers have had such an impact so early in their careers: Rison reached the 100-career-catch plateau in 24 games, third behind Gary Clark (21) and Al Toon (23). Over a three week stretch last year, he caught 30 passes. Against New Orleans, he caught 4 passes for 77 yards, including a touchdown—all in the final two minutes of the game. Against Cleveland, he pulled in 6 catches for 100 yards—*in the fourth quarter alone.*

SUMMARY

Part of Rison's problems last year stemmed from confusion among the young receivers—and young coaches—in the Red Gun offense. By midseason, opponents were correctly guessing Atlanta's tendencies, and the receivers struggled with the offense's complex route conversions. Under new offensive coordinator June Jones, that will change: Jones is a run 'n' shoot wizard, and his mastery of the offense will result in Rison having an even bigger year as a pro. "When I looked at film of Rison," Jones says, "I realized we had a very special player on our hands."

HANK'S RATING: AA

Anthony Carter

Birthdate: September 17, 1960
College: Michigan
Height: 5-11
Weight: 166
How Acquired: Trade, 1985
Final 1990 Team: Minnesota Vikings

TECHNIQUE

Anthony Carter, dating back to his days in the defunct United States Football League, has relied on darting speed to survive the wiles of opposing defenses. "Carter has great speed, and runs decent routes," says a scout. "What he does best is break back toward the football and run with the football after the catch."

PRODUCTIVITY

Carter had 70 catches for 1,008 yards and 8 touchdowns in 1990, including an incredible 56-yard touchdown against the Packers in which he outleaped three defenders at the goal line. Carter is still capable of the dazzling, game-winning play, as he proved—again—against Denver; Carter paced a Minnesota rally by catching 5 passes for 146 yards, helped set up a touchdown and two field goals, and outjumped cornerback Alton Montgomery for a 56-yard, fourth-quarter score that iced the game for Minnesota.

SUMMARY

Carter, of late, has been the victim of an inconsistent offense and poor quarterback play. He runs great routes that he is able to adjust to the coverage. And he is the best in the NFL at running with the ball after a catch. In the Top 5 among NFL receivers.

HANK'S RATING: AA

John Taylor

Birthdate: March 31, 1962
College: Delaware State
Height: 6-1
Weight: 185
How Acquired: Drafted in third round, 1986
Final 1990 Team: San Francisco 49ers

TECHNIQUE

John Taylor uses his size and strength to his advantage. Few corners are physically capable of tying him up in bump-and-run, and Taylor is a master of rubbing off defenders in the 49ers "picking" schemes. It worked against Houston last year, when Taylor rubbed off Oiler cornerback Cris Dishman on a 10-yard slant, then sprinted in for a 46-yard touchdown. He did the same thing on a 23-yard, first-half touchdown against the Giants.

PRODUCTIVITY

Short or long, Taylor can be brutally effective and normally holds up well under extreme workloads; against the Redskins, he caught 8 passes for 160 yards. But for the first time in his career, he was bothered by slight injuries throughout the season, yet still caught 49 passes for 748 yards. He averaged 15.3 yards per catch, and his 7 touchdowns tied him for fifth in the NFC, proof that even a banged-up John Taylor is better than no John Taylor at all.

SUMMARY

Taylor is not only quick, but physical. In the 1989 opener against the Colts, Taylor threw a crushing block that allowed Rice to turn a quick slant into a 70-yard touchdown. That same year, lightning struck twice against the Rams—Rice returned the favor by throwing downfield blocks that allowed Taylor to convert two hitch routes into 92- and 95-yard scores. "More amazing," says a scout, "is that on all of those plays, the play started on one side of the field, weaved through the defense, and came down to the other guy's block being the difference."

HANK'S RATING: AA

Willie Gault

Birthdate: September 5, 1960
College: Tennessee
Height: 6-1
Weight: 180
How Acquired: Trade, 1988
Final 1990 Team: Los Angeles Raiders

TECHNIQUE

Willie Gault's technique equals one word: Speed. Gault is great in the open-field, often runs away from corners, and is perenially one of the NFL's fastest men. But he has few moves, little side-to-side lateral movement, and doesn't comeback well to the football. Gault is a pure deep threat.

PRODUCTIVITY

No one has ever questioned Gault's pure speed, and in obvious mismatches, Gault shines. His 68-yard touchdown against Detroit on "Monday Night Football" was such a mismatch, when Gault simply outran the Lions secondary. Likewise, he set up two more scores with 56- and 61-yard bombs against Minnesota. He finished the season with 50 catches for 985 yards and 3 touchdowns.

SUMMARY

Scouts, and cornerbacks, question Gault's current dedication to play at the peak of his ability. In a recent issue of *SPORT* magazine, cornerbacks around the league voted Gault as the NFL's "most fearful" wide receiver. He shuns physical contact, dislikes going over the middle, and is prone to fumbling. In 1990, with the Raiders trailing the Bills, Gault allowed Buffalo cornerback Nate Odomes to wrest the ball from him after a sideline catch; Odomes rumbled 49 yards for the deciding touchdown. But Raider coaches love Gault because his speed can loosen up a secondary. He is the Raiders' Cliff Branch of the 1990s.

HANK'S RATING: AA

Andre Reed

Birthdate: January 19, 1964
College: Kutztown State
Height: 6-1
Weight: 190
How Acquired: Drafted in fourth round, 1985
Final 1990 Team: Buffalo Bills

TECHNIQUE

Andre Reed flourished in Buffalo's wide-open, anticonservative, no-huddle approach. For a team that once threw only out of necessity, the Bills are now pass-happy, and their talented quarterback and receiver corps rank among the NFL's most productive crews. "They proved in the playoffs that [Jim] Kelly and Reed can be unstoppable," says an NFC assistant coach. "Reed is an awesome talent."

Reed's secret is in his release: He quickly gets off the line of scrimmage, runs crisp, precise routes, and, unlike many other talented receivers, comes back to the football. "Reed gets great position on the football," says one scout. "He knows how to keep his body between the ball and a defender." But others question Reed's ability to adjust his routes.

PRODUCTIVITY

Reed had a remarkable year in 1989, making 88 catches. He followed that with a 71 catch season in 1990.

Over the past two seasons, Reed has repeatedly flashed big-play ability at the most critical times: His 56-yard touchdown crushed Philadelphia in 1990; in 1989, he racked up 115 yards against San Francisco. In the Bills' 44–34 playoff win over Miami, Reed caught 40- and 26-yard touchdowns.

SUMMARY

A rumor is circulating in the AFC: Andre Reed is fragile. He went to the bench against Phoenix with a sprained ankle. And he allowed himself to be intimidated by the Giants in Super Bowl XXV, dropping two critical second-half passes.

"That's the only time I've seen Reed completely neutralized," says a scout. "People are realizing they can physically take him out of the game. But if you let him become a factor, he'll kill you."

Reed could be in for some big hits now that some DBs question whether he can handle them.

HANK'S RATING: AA

Flipper Anderson

Birthdate: March 7, 1965
College: UCLA
Height: 6-0
Weight: 172
How Acquired: Drafted in second round, 1988
Final 1990 Team: Los Angeles Rams

TECHNIQUE

Great vertical speed gives Flipper Anderson opportunities that slower receivers don't have. He can stretch a defense in the seams, run past tight bump-and-run coverage, or wreak havoc underneath soft zones. And though he's still learning, Anderson knows what to do with the ball; in 1989, he piled up 336 yards on 15 catches *in one game* against the Saints.

PRODUCTIVITY

Flipper's 21.5 yards per catch led the NFL in 1990, as Anderson had another banner year with 1,097 yards on 51 catches. Anderson's 8 catches for 149 yards against San Francisco helped Los Angeles upset the 49ers. "Flipper has the ability to be the difference," says Rams head coach John Robinson.

SUMMARY

In 1989, Anderson beat the Giants in the playoffs with 2 touchdowns and caught 2 passes for 77 yards to help beat the Eagles in the wildcard game. "Anderson has excellent speed on top," says a scout. "It's amazing that he got a shot only because Aaron Cox and Henry Ellard were hurt. But this kid is a championship player."

HANK'S RATING: A

Henry Ellard

Birthdate: July 21, 1961
College: Fresno State
Height: 5-11
Weight: 182
How Acquired: Drafted in second round, 1983
Final 1990 Team: Los Angeles Rams

TECHNIQUE

Henry Ellard, now in his eighth pro season, is a textbook receiver. Ellard has great body control, makes excellent adjustments in his routes, protects the football, and is very fluid in the open field, with no wasted movement. Ellard is a technician who isn't flashy, wastes little time in needless conversation, and gives a solid performance every week. A consummate professional with a great attitude.

PRODUCTIVITY

Ellard had another phenomenal season and was the picture of consistency in 1990, catching 5 or more passes in ten games. He finished with 76 receptions, and his 1,294 receiving yards were second in the NFL only to Jerry Rice.

SUMMARY

The emergence of Willie "Flipper" Anderson has revitalized Ellard, who, until Anderson's rise to stardom, had grown used to double coverage. But now that teams can no longer isolate against either receiver, Ellard has responded with a vengeance, displaying the brilliant ability that led the Rams to be so high on him as a budding collegiate receiver in 1983.

HANK'S RATING: A

Art Monk

Birthdate: December 5, 1957
College: Syracuse
Height: 6-3
Weight: 209
How Acquired: Drafted in first round, 1980
Final 1990 Team: Washington Redskins

TECHNIQUE

Art Monk will be remembered as one of the toughest, most productive receivers in NFL history. And for all his record-breaking afternoons, Monk performs quietly and professionally. After an outstanding 1989 season, Monk was ignored in Pro Bowl voting, a fact that infuriated head coach Joe Gibbs. "Art is a gifted athlete who takes care of himself," Gibbs says. "He is a guy who works hard at his craft, but he does it so quietly that his accomplishments often get overlooked."

PRODUCTIVITY

In 1990, Monk's brilliance continued. Against the Lions, Monk caught 13 passes for 168 yards, including a 40-yard catch in overtime that set up Chip Lohmiller's winning 34-yard field goal. His 4 catches and a touchdown against New Orleans made him the third player in NFL history to surpass 700 receptions. Only Steve Largent, who had ten 50-plus catch seasons, is ahead of Monk on the all-time list. Monk finished the 1990 season with 68 catches for 770 yards.

SUMMARY

Monk, who now has 730 career receptions, joined Steve Largent and Charlie Joiner as the only players in league history to reach the 700-catch plateau. He needs just 33 receptions in 1991 to surpass Joiner for second on the all-time list. Monk also stretched his regular season consecutive receiving streak to 116 games, which is fourth on the all-time list. One of the toughest receivers in the NFL, Monk seems to catch everything, no matter how hard he is hit. There is no receiver more consistent.

HANK'S RATING: A

Mervyn Fernandez

Birthdate: December 29, 1959
College: San Jose State
Height: 6-3

Weight: 200
How Acquired: Drafted in tenth round, 1983
Final 1990 Team: Los Angeles Raiders

TECHNIQUE

Swervyn Mervyn Fernandez has decent speed (4.5), catches everything thrown to him (52 catches for 839 yards in 1990), and works hard. But his secret to success is his precise route running. Fernandez is tall, blessed with good quickness and lateral movement, and is very agile. The result is a very big, mobile target. Has to "think" more and take full advantage of coverage holes.

PRODUCTIVITY

Throughout the 1990 season, Fernandez had a penchant for the big play. His 66-yard, fourth-quarter touchdown against Pittsburgh clinched the game. In 1989, he led the Raiders in receiving (57 catches), receiving yardage (1,069 yards), and touchdowns (9). He stays healthy too: He hasn't missed a game due to injury since 1987.

SUMMARY

Fernandez played his first five years of professional football for the British Columbia Lions in the Canadian Football League, and CFL corners were thrilled when he excused himself in 1987 to play for the Raiders. He was the top receiver in Canada in the 1980s, catching 374 passes for 6,408 yards and 55 touchdowns. "Mervyn works hard, and that work is evident in his play," says head coach Art Shell.

HANK'S RATING: A

TECHNIQUE

Much of Green Bay's offense centers around Sterling Sharpe, with good reason. Sharpe is one of the NFL's most physical, attacking receivers, though he's not the most gifted. He will catch over the middle and has no fear. Good receiver in the clutch. "Sterling will go up and get the ball," Infante says. "He protects it and he finds a way to get the extra 5 or 10 yards. He's a tough player." How tough? The last five weeks of the 1990 season, Sharpe played with broken ribs.

PRODUCTIVITY

Head coach Lindy Infante deserves kudos for Sharpe's development; in many other offensive schemes, Sharpe wouldn't be as productive. Sharpe led the NFL in 1989 with 90 catches, and was second only to Jerry Rice in total yards (1,423). He was also a large reason why the Pack's number of dropped passes fell from 53 in 1988 to 33 in 1989, and his 12 touchdowns were the most by a Packer since Billy Howton in 1956. In 1990, it was more of the same: 67 catches for 1,105 yards in an injury-plagued season. "But give him credit," says a scout. "He may get hurt, but he plays. That's more than most the receivers in this league can say." Which is why he gets our vote for one of the toughest receivers in the NFL.

SUMMARY

Teammate Perry Kemp has done little to take the pressure of Sharpe, and Infante has been openly critical of the receiver position. Infante is fond of second-year speedster Charles Wilson, who could develop this year into a full-time threat. Jeff Query has shown big-play potential, but for now, the burden of the Packers' passing game rests on Sharpe's shoulders.

HANK'S RATING: A

Sterling Sharpe

Birthdate: April 6, 1965
College: South Carolina
Height: 5-11
Weight: 202
How Acquired: Drafted in first round, 1988
Final 1990 Team: Green Bay Packers

Webster Slaughter

Birthdate: October 19, 1964
College: San Diego State
Height: 6-0
Weight: 170
How Acquired: Drafted in second round, 1986
Final 1990 Team: Cleveland Browns

TECHNIQUE

Nothing brings a smile to the face of Webster Slaughter quicker than man-to-man coverage. "When I think of Slaughter," says Atlanta head coach Jerry Glanville, "I think of toughness. When I was with Houston, we pounded him, and he laughed at us. It's hard to believe he's just 170 pounds."

PRODUCTIVITY

Despite Cleveland's poor overall showing in 1990, Slaughter stepped forward with a banner year. His 59-catch, 847-yard, 4-touchdown performance was second only to his Pro Bowl year of 1989.

Slaughter came of age as a deep threat in 1989 against Houston, when he caught 4 passes for 184 yards. Twice he split the Oilers vaunted hard-hitting secondary for easy touchdowns, one covering 80 yards and another 77. He followed that performance with an 8-catch performance against Chicago, including a 97-yard touchdown.

SUMMARY

Slaughter may be the league's finest down-field blocker (Art Monk comes to mind, too). Despite his relative lack of size, Slaughter is physical, emotional, and quick to anger. Lacks discipline, but there's not a corner in football that can handle him one-to-one. The most underrated wide receiver in the NFL.

HANK'S RATING: A

Drew Hill

Birthdate: October 5, 1956
College: Georgia Tech
Height: 5-9
Weight: 174
How Acquired: Trade, 1985
Final 1990 Team: Houston Oilers

TECHNIQUE

Don't ask him how, but Drew Hill gets open. Up the seam against a zone, or on the corners against man to man, Hill gets free. He reads and adjusts to coverages quickly. Hill runs the run 'n' shoot's "bubble" and "broom" routes to perfection, and is ideal for an offense that depends on receivers to create space and run to the open area.

PRODUCTIVITY

When Haywood Jeffires led the Oilers—and the AFC—in receiving in 1990, it was the first time in the past six years that Drew Hill wasn't on top of the Oilers gushing receiving corps. But in most years, with most teams, Hill's 1,019 yards and 5 touchdowns would have led the conference.

Hill averaged 13.8 yards a catch and caught a 57-yard touchdown, proving that his speed is still more than adequate in the seams of most secondaries. Houston's commitment to the run 'n' shoot under new head coach Jack Pardee increased Hill's catches from 66 in 1989 to 74 in 1990—at the age of thirty-four. Expect more of the same in 1991.

SUMMARY

When the Oilers are in a critical situation, you can bet that Warren Moon still looks for Drew Hill. In spite of his age, Hill always reports to camp in excellent shape and comes up with the big play, year after year. Hill still drops too many throws to be considered in the NFL's Top 10, but his lack of notoriety is a crime.

HANK'S RATING: A

Mark Duper

Birthdate: January 25, 1959
College: Northwestern Louisiana
Height: 5-9
Weight: 190
How Acquired: Drafted in second round, 1982
Final 1990 Team: Miami Dolphins

TECHNIQUE

Mark Duper was once a speed-reliant wide receiver whose deceptive quickness and great routes made him one of the AFC's toughest receivers to cover. But that has changed. Duper often struggles to break from the line of scrimmage, appears to have lost a step, and lacks the quickness to beat a good cornerback back to the football. He still has great hands, but his other skills are quickly fading.

PRODUCTIVITY

Duper's productivity has tailed off dramatically since 1987, but he still displayed that, on occasion, he could still make the big play. Going into the Jets game in the fifth week of the 1990 season, Duper had caught just 2 touchdowns in three years. But he caught 2 against New York, including the game winner with 1:03 remaining. And his 6-yard scoring catch against Philadelphia boosted Miami to a 10-point, fourth-quarter surge that beat the Eagles.

SUMMARY

After the Jets game, Dolphins head coach Don Shula said that, "Duper's back, for you people who are wondering." Duper finished the season with 52 passes for 810 yards and 5 touchdowns, but is no longer the deep threat he once was. Duper is still an asset to the Miami offense, but not the constant threat he once was. Some insiders blame this more on the lack of adjustments in the Miami offense over the last few years and a not-quite-as-sharp Marino than Duper.

HANK'S RATING: A

Eric Martin

Birthdate: November 8, 1961
College: LSU
Height: 6-1
Weight: 207
How Acquired: Drafted in seventh round, 1985
Final 1990 Team: New Orleans Saints

TECHNIQUE

A gifted receiver with sneaky speed, Martin lacks the sizzling speed of many other NFC receivers, yet his consistent production is proof of his ability to get open. Martin is physical, displays excellent footwork, and doesn't drop the football. He is New Orleans' all-time leading receiver with 332 catches.

PRODUCTIVITY

Martin is a proven, big-play, third-down receiver for the Saints. "On that touchdown to Eric Martin, I sat back there, had a couple of Cokes and a hot dog, and just waited on him to get open," says quarterback Steve Walsh.

Martin finished 1989 with 1,090 yards on 68 catches, but his production dropped off slightly in 1990 to 63 catches for 912 yards, perhaps evidence of the Saints beleaguered quarterback position. Martin had a respectable 14.5 yards per catch average with 5 touchdowns.

SUMMARY

New Orleans' seeming constant upheaval at the quarterback position, as well as head coach Jim Mora's ultra-conservative approach, makes Martin's numbers that much more impressive. If the Saints start Bobby Hebert at quarterback, look for Martin's numbers to increase: He was Hebert's favorite target in 1989. If Martin will work harder and improve his short routes, he could make the jump into the Top 10.

HANK'S RATING: A

Haywood Jeffires

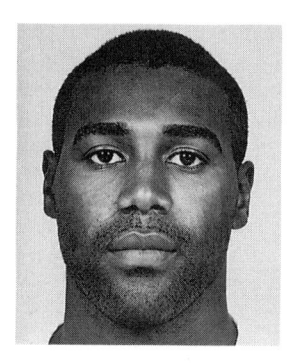

Birthdate: December 12, 1964
College: North Carolina
Height: 6-2
Weight: 201
How Acquired: Drafted in first round, 1987
Final 1990 Team: Houston Oilers

TECHNIQUE

The Houston Oilers drafted Haywood Jeffires in 1987 for two reasons: He possessed speed and size. After two disappointing seasons, Jeffires flourished in the run 'n' shoot in 1990, and had those two attributes to thank for it. The offense often relied on its receivers to "freelance" their way into open passing lanes, and Jeffires developed a unique mental rapport with quarterback Warren Moon. This "connection" with Warren Moon helped hide Jeffries lack of route discipline.

PRODUCTIVITY

Jeffires was more than remarkable in Houston's new run 'n' shoot offense—he was spectacular. His 1,048 yards led the AFC, as Jeffires finished with a 14.2 yards per catch average and 8 touchdowns. During Warren Moon's record-setting 527-yard afternoon against Kansas City, Jeffires reeled in an 87-yard touchdown, and had another 30-yard-plus catch taken away by a controversial replay.

SUMMARY

A big, rangy receiver, Jeffires can hurt a secondary in multiple ways. "He can run by you," says Houston offensive coordinator Kevin Gilbride, "or he can sit down in the zone." Though Jeffires has held up well under punishment, he can be intimidated, though his ability to "play physical" has improved with maturity. But some still question his ability to make the "contact" catch. An improving receiver that soon may challenge for a spot among the NFL's Top 10.

HANK'S RATING: A

Gary Clark

Birthdate: May 1, 1962
College: James Madison
Height: 5-9
Weight: 173
How Acquired: Free Agent, 1985
Final 1990 Team: Washington Redskins

TECHNIQUE

Clark's 75 catches in 1990 marked the sixth straight year he's had at least 50 catches, indicating he's doing something right. Clark runs smooth routes and breaks well to the ball, but his biggest assets are toughness and intensity. He is always making clutch catches over the middle. Says head coach Joe Gibbs "He's one of the greatest competitors I've ever been around. He's at his best when the stakes are highest."

PRODUCTIVITY

In years past, Clark has described himself as "a go-to guy." As usual, he backed it up again in 1990, finishing fourth in the league in receiving and leading Washington in scoring. Against Phoenix, he caught back-to-back 42-yard touchdowns from Mark Rypien. Against Detroit, he pulled down 8 huge catches for 132 yards and a touchdown. In a 31-17 victory over New Orleans, he snagged 8 balls for 131 yards and 2 touchdowns.

When the dust settled on the season, Clark had 1,112 yards and 8 touchdowns. Clark now has 415 career receptions in Washington, which trails Jerry Smith.

SUMMARY

Clark is not your classic outside, one-on-one receiver, but only he and Jerry Rice have put together four 1,000-yard receiving seasons since 1986. Clark has also moved closer to former Washington great Bobby Mitchell for third place on the Skins' all-time yards receiving list. Clark now has 6,490 yards receiving, and needs just 2 yards to surpass Mitchell, who finished his Hall of Fame career with 6,491 yards.

HANK'S RATING: A

Anthony Miller

Birthdate: April 15, 1965
College: Tennessee
Height: 5-11
Weight: 185
How Acquired: Drafted in first round, 1988
Final 1990 Team: San Diego Chargers

TECHNIQUE

In the past two seasons, Anthony Miller has evolved into one of the NFL's biggest threats, whether it be on the opening kickoff, a punt return, or at wide receiver. In three pro seasons, Miller has played in two Pro Bowls.

Miller's breakaway speed and good hands have been the difference for the flashy wideout. "Miller doesn't run the greatest routes in the world [that is an understatement]," says a scout. "But he's incredibly fast, and he catches in traffic." San Diego receiver coach Charlie Joiner agrees. "Anthony has worked hard to become one of the best," says Joiner, a receiving legend in his own right.

PRODUCTIVITY

Surrounded by mediocrity, Miller got little attention his rookie season. But nobody overlooked his 1989 numbers: 75 catches, 10 touchdowns, five 100-yard games, a 162-yard effort against Houston, and a 91-yard touchdown on the opening kickoff against the Raiders. For those who thought Miller's performance was a fluke, he answered the call in 1990 with more outstanding results, despite increased coverage: 63 catches for 933 yards and 7 touchdowns. Miller was third on the team in scoring with 42 points.

SUMMARY

When Joiner talks about Miller, he can't stop smiling. The reason is simple: If quarterback Billy Joe Tolliver can show more consistency, Miller could jump into the Top 10. San Diego coaches also believe that Miller will benefit from the emergence of Walter Wilson, a third-round pick in GM Bobby Beathard's first draft who averaged 20 yards a catch in 1990.

HANK'S RATING: A

Curtis Duncan

Birthdate: January 28, 1965
College: Northwestern
Height: 5-11
Weight: 184
How Acquired: Drafted in tenth round, 1987
Final 1990 Team: Houston Oilers

TECHNIQUE

Curtis Duncan is a long striding outside receiver who began coming into his own in late 1990. He is blessed with speed, strength and height, and excels on the corners in the Oilers' run 'n' shoot.

PRODUCTIVITY

Duncan, in his best year as a pro, pulled in 66 passes for 785 yards and a touchdown in 1990. He was used largely as a possession receiver, indicated by his 11.9 yards per catch average. In years previous, Duncan was marred by inconsistency and injuries, but played well enough in 1990 to make his bid as a full-time starter in 1991.

SUMMARY

Duncan is a rapidly improving wideout with the skills and work habits to become a force in the AFC. The Oilers have the finest complement of young receivers in the NFL, and Duncan, if his progress continues, could be a Top 10 wideout in the future.

HANK'S RATING: A

Tim McGee

Birthdate: August 7, 1964
College: Tennessee
Height: 5-10
Weight: 179
How Acquired: Drafted in first round, 1986
Final 1990 Team: Cincinnati Bengals

TECHNIQUE

Tim McGee, like former Tennessee teammate Willie Gault, is a big-play performer who has speed to burn. But McGee's years in the league have been marred by inconsistency and his inability to make the big catch over the middle. Just not a "tough-hit" receiver. But to his credit, he recognizes his problem. "I know speed is my advantage," McGee says. "I've tried not to concentrate on being just a speed receiver. Going across the middle is one thing I've tried to do, and I think it's turned me into a complete receiver."

PRODUCTIVITY

Proof of McGee's superstar ability came in 1990 against the Rams, when he caught 8 passes for 142 yards. In just his second full season as a starter, he finished the season with 43 catches for 737 yards and a touchdown. "This season was one of consistent performances for myself," he says.

SUMMARY

McGee's speed is deceptive, evidenced by how long he waited for a slow-arriving 52-yard Esiason touchdown pass against New England. "It was like being on an island with nobody around," McGee says. McGee is still learning to be a complete receiver; he catches fifty extra balls each Thursday afternoon from head coach Sam Wyche. "Tim is an excellent pattern runner," says Wyche. "That's good, because it takes the heat off of Eddie Brown."

HANK'S RATING: A

Ernest Givins

Birthdate: September 3, 1964
College: Louisville
Height: 5-9
Weight: 172
How Acquired: Drafted in second round, 1986
Final 1990 Team: Houston Oilers

TECHNIQUE

Chasing Ernest Givins, according to Chicago linebacker Mike Singletary, "is like chasing a waterbug," the Bears' linebacker says. "He's everywhere." Givins has deceptive speed, and is capable of changing gears several times in a single route. Though he isn't a great strider, Givins lulls defenders to sleep when he's not the intended receiver, then bursts past them for big plays. In other words, the perfect run 'n' shoot receiver.

PRODUCTIVITY

Givins caught 72 passes for 979 yards, a 13.6 yards per catch average, and 9 touchdowns. It was another banner year for the young wideout, who has posted huge numbers during his short career. But most impressive to Oilers quarterback Warren Moon is Givins ability to make the big catch. "Ernie's not afraid to go up and get the ball," Moon says. "He's a tough player who's not easily intimidated."

SUMMARY

Again, like Jeffires and Hill, Givins is just one more piece of artillery in the Houston Oilers' lethal arsenal. In a normal situation, Givins would lead his team in receiving. But not in Houston, where Givins is just one of several talented receivers.

HANK'S RATING: A

Ricky Proehl

Birthdate: March 7, 1968
College: Wake Forest
Height: 5-10
Weight: 181
How Acquired: Drafted in third round, 1990
Final 1990 Team: Phoenix Cardinals

TECHNIQUE

Two things impressed Phoenix scouts with Ricky Proehl during his senior year at Wake Forest: His leaping ability and speed, two attributes that had made him a double-threat as both a deep threat and possession receiver. Proehl more than lived up to the scouts estimations in 1990. He runs a 4.5, but his 34-inch vertical jump gives him a sizable leaping advantage over many smaller defensive backs. And he *wants* to make every catch.

PRODUCTIVITY

On draft day, critics scoffed the Cardinals third-round pick. But by season's end, the jeers had turned to cheers for Proehl, who caught more passes (56) for more yards (802) than any rookie in the Cardinals' history—and any rookie during the 1990 season.

SUMMARY

Proehl is an excellent downfield blocker who thrived under new head coach Joe Bugel's system. "Our whole system is based on time of possession," says Bugel. "But big plays are built into the offense. Ricky proved he was a valuable part of our football team."

HANK'S RATING: A

Rob Moore

Birthdate: September 27, 1968
College: Syracuse
Height: 6-2
Weight: 201
How Acquired: Chosen in supplemental draft, 1990
Final 1990 Team: New York Jets

TECHNIQUE

Rob Moore looked brilliant at times in 1990, but the Syracuse product also struggled due to his relative college inexperience. Several veteran NFL cornerbacks stifled Moore, and he enters 1991 with several goals: He needs to get off the ball quicker, recognize defenses faster, and run sharper routes. But he possesses tremendous physical assets and soft hands that should give him a bright NFL future.

PRODUCTIVITY

Second-year Jet GM Dick Steinberg elected to give up the team's 1991 first-round pick to take Moore in the July supplemental draft, and the move was well worth it: Moore led AFC rookies in receptions (44 catches for 692 yards), and set a new Jet rookie record with 6 touchdown catches. His yards per catch average was 15.7, including one long score of 66 yards.

SUMMARY

Steinberg is hoping a healthy Al Toon and Moore can put some punch back in the Jets lifeless passing game, which ranked twenty-first in the league in 1990. Moore needs to let his natural abilities take over as he did in college. With the addition of new quarterback Browning Nagle, the Jets are back on the runway.

HANK'S RATING: A

Stephone Paige

Birthdate: October 15, 1961
College: Fresno State
Height: 6-2
Weight: 185
How Acquired: Free Agent, 1983
Final 1990 Team: Kansas City Chiefs

TECHNIQUE

Stephone Paige is noted for colorful, acrobatic catches—but he relies on his 4.4 speed and quick feet to get him into position to make such catches. Paige is a swift, physical receiver, oblivious to punishment, and seldom fails to make the critical catch.

PRODUCTIVITY

Paige, in his ninth year, finished with 1,021 yards, including an 86-yard touchdown catch against Denver—just one of his 5 touchdowns. But Kansas City fans have expected great things from Paige since he made the club in 1983 as a free agent. Until Steve DeBerg's shocking comeback, Paige—for years—was often all the offense the Chiefs could muster, such as his 309-yard game against San Diego in 1985 attests.

SUMMARY

Paige is a talented, reliable receiver with great hands who has managed to survive long enough to see the Chiefs rally around him. Kansas City, under head coach Marty Scottenheimer, is a legitimate AFC championship contender, and Paige will again be a major cog in the offense.

HANK'S RATING: A

James Lofton

Birthdate: July 5, 1956
College: Stanford
Height: 6-3
Weight: 190
How Acquired: Free Agent, 1989
Final 1990 Team: Buffalo Bills

TECHNIQUE

James Lofton was revived by the Bills' no-huddle attack, as it prevented opponents from substituting key personnel and allowed Lofton to take advantage of severe mismatches. His biggest asset is speed, but make no mistake: Lofton is a big, rangy receiver, whose crafty experience and excellent hands present a formidable challenge for any cornerback.

PRODUCTIVITY

On occasion, Lofton was reminiscent of his youth during the 1990 season. Trailing the Los Angeles Raiders 24–14 in the fourth quarter, Lofton started a 3-touchdown barrage with a 42-yard bomb from quarterback Jim Kelly. Against the Eagles, he caught 5 balls for 174 yards, including a 63-yard touchdown. In the playoffs against Miami, Lofton caught 7 passes for 149 yards, including a game-clinching 13-yard touchdown.

SUMMARY

Lofton's lofty 1990 numbers—35 catches, 712 yards—pushed him to third on the NFL's list for all-time receiving yardage and catches. His 20.3 yards per catch led all AFC receivers. "My God, Lofton was unbelievable," says former Eagles coach Buddy Ryan, whose defense was pillaged by the veteran wideout. "He just ran right through our secondary."

Perfect receiver for Buffalo—four and five wide receiver offense gives Lofton a high percentage of single coverage opportunities.

HANK'S RATING: A

Louis Lipps

Birthdate: August 9, 1962
College: Southern Mississippi
Height: 5-10
Weight: 190
How Acquired: Drafted in first round, 1984
Final 1990 Team: Pittsburgh Steelers

TECHNIQUE

Eight-year veteran Louis Lipps is the closest the Steelers come to having a speed receiver, but the former speedster is now reliant on deceptive quickness and solid routes to get open. Once one of the AFC's most dominant receivers, Lipps now struggles to out run even average cornerbacks, but still possesses great hands and the willingness to fight for the ball. His skills, however, are quickly fading.

PRODUCTIVITY

Lipps' productivity has tailed off dramatically since early in his career, but he still can, on occasion, make the big play. He's had 50 receptions in each of the last three seasons, without the benefit of a dangerous receiver opposite him to relieve double coverage. Although Lipps averaged 13.6 yards per catch (682 total yards), he scored just 3 touchdowns and didn't catch a pass over 40 yards. He represents the only real receiving threat in the offense, which greatly simplifies coverages for opponents.

SUMMARY

Offensive coordinator Joe Walton, whose double-barreled tight-end set took the focus away from Lipps, perhaps failed to notice that in 1989 Lipps was the team's third-best runner, with 180 yards on 13 reverses. Lipps is a hard worker, but is now little more than a dependable possession receiver.

HANK'S RATING: A

Wendell Davis

Birthdate: January 3, 1966
College: LSU
Height: 5-11
Weight: 188
How Acquired: Drafted in first round, 1988
Final 1990 Team: Chicago Bears

TECHNIQUE

The Bears liked Wendell Davis in the 1988 draft because he fit the Chicago mold: a strong, heady receiver, who was not afraid to block and worked well from a possession offense. Since turning pro, Davis has added more skills to his repertoire: He reads defenses well and reacts well to the ball. Davis deceives defensive backs with short, choppy steps. He's not a strong one-on-one performer, but his quickness makes him a good, short-yardage, high percentage receiver.

PRODUCTIVITY

Mike Ditka's decision to sacrifice veteran Dennis McKinnon to Plan B prior to the 1990 season was a testimony to Davis's development. Instead of alternating with backups or substituting receivers based on down and distance, Morris became an every-down player, and with solid results. Davis took over a starting role in the tenth week of the 1990 season, and has quickly become a receiving force for Chicago. His 1990 numbers were modest—39 catches for 572 yards and 3 touchdowns—but acceptable, considering Chicago's ball-control offense. He also posted his first 100-yard day against Atlanta, with 5 catches for 105 yards and 1 touchdown.

SUMMARY

Davis has become a big third-down receiver who runs good routes, is a savvy downfield blocker, and, if quarterback Jim Harbaugh can improve, could turn into a big-play receiver. Davis catches the ball well in traffic, but is prone to injury—he missed four games in 1990.

HANK'S RATING: A

Mark Jackson

Birthdate: July 23, 1963
College: Purdue
Height: 5-9
Weight: 180
How Acquired: Drafted in sixth round, 1986
Final 1990 Team: Denver Broncos

TECHNIQUE

Mark Jackson is a speed merchant with a strong upper body. Opposing defensive backs say Jackson is very difficult to jam at the line of scrimmage, and is a modest downfield blocker. His biggest asset, perhaps, is his straightaway speed. Against zone defenses, Jackson freelances often, depending on mobile quarterback John Elway to find him. And when Elway is forced to scramble, Jackson has a great feel for coming back to him.

PRODUCTIVITY

From the time Jackson slid under John Elway's 5-yard touchdown pass for "The Catch" against Cleveland in the AFC championship in 1987, he has carried the label of a big-play receiver with pride. And he lived up to his billing in 1990, giving Denver fans one of their few reasons to celebrate. Jackson caught 57 passes for 926 yards and 4 touchdowns.

SUMMARY

Jackson has heard the criticism that he's lost a step, that he can't stay healthy, and that he's lost the desire to make the "tough" catch. All Jackson continues to do is catch the ball, especially in clutch situations. Against division-rival Seattle, Jackson caught 2 touchdowns in a 34–31 victory, while his 66-yard catch against Indianapolis set up a critical fourth-quarter field goal that cinched the game for Denver.

HANK'S RATING: A

Mark Carrier

Birthdate: October 28, 1965
College: Nicholls State
Height: 6-0
Weight: 185
How Acquired: Drafted in third round, 1987
Final 1990 Team: Tampa Bay Buccaneers

TECHNIQUE

Consistency may be Mark Carrier's greatest asset. Not blessed with jet speed, Carrier relies on his other skills to weave his way through opposing defenses. Carrier credits tae kwon do for his considerable eye-hand skills and flexibility, which enable him to make circus-style catches.

PRODUCTIVITY

Carrier finished 1990 with 49 receptions for 813 yards, a 16.6 average, and just missed his third consecutive 50-catch season. He stayed healthy, starting all sixteen games, and was consistent, catching at least one pass in all sixteen games. His club-record streak of consecutive games with a catch now stands at forty-eight. Carrier is third in Buccaneer annals in career yards.

SUMMARY

His 86 catches for 1,422 yards and a league-high nine 100-yard games in 1989 pushed Carrier into the upper echelon of NFL receivers. And despite erratic performances by Tampa Bay quarterbacks, Carrier managed to continue his excellence in 1990: His 35-yard over-the-shoulder touchdown pass with 39 seconds left beat Atlanta, and he scored touchdowns in the season's last four games.

HANK'S RATING: A

Fred Barnett

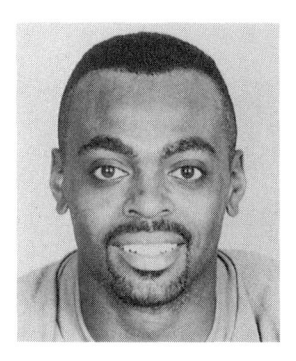

Birthdate: June 17, 1966
College: Arkansas State
Height: 6-0
Weight: 203
How Acquired: Drafted in third round, 1990
Final 1990 Team: Philadelphia Eagles

TECHNIQUE

In 1990, Fred Barnett did all the things most NFL rookies do: He made mistakes, he ran some bad routes, he dropped a few passes. But what Philadelphia fans remember most is what he did best: Run fast and make sensational plays. His threatening speed (4.3) forced corners to play off in respect, which opened up the underneath passing game.

PRODUCTIVITY

Barnett caught 36 passes for 721 yards and 8 touchdowns in 1990. Against Buffalo, Barnett hauled in a 95-yard rainbow from quarterback Randall Cunningham, who had somehow scrambled his way through a myriad of defenders. In the-season finale against Phoenix, he pulled in two more scores. "Fred showed he had the ability to make the big play," says head coach Rich Kotite. "With hard work, we expect him to play a major role in the offense this season."

SUMMARY

Barnett is a strong, quick receiver with lots of raw ability. But, he must improve his route-running technique. As his knowledge of the game—and recognition of defenses—improves, so will his numbers. Jury is still out on whether he'll become a complete receiver or just a deep threat.

HANK'S RATING: A

Bill Brooks

Birthdate: April 6, 1964
College: Boston University
Height: 6-0
Weight: 185
How Acquired: Drafted in fourth round, 1986
Final 1990 Team: Indianapolis Colts

TECHNIQUE

One scout described Bill Brooks in a unique way: "His body looks bad, his form looks bad, his technique looks bad, and he's not very fast. But he catches the ball, gets open in traffic, and in all the film I've seen, he's never dropped a single pass." Brooks has had a spectacular pro career in the face of many critics when he was drafted from tiny Boston University in 1986.

PRODUCTIVITY

Brooks has quietly produced for years, evidenced not just by his numbers, but by his performance in critical games. Against Philadelphia, he gave the Colts their first victory of the 1990 season with a gutty, 6-catch performance on Indy's final 82-yard drive; Brooks caught 6 of quarterback Jeff Trudeau's last 7 passes on the drive, including the winning 6-yard catch with Eagle cornerback Izell Jenkins draped across his back. Against New England, his 26-yard touchdown reception with 2:05 remaining won the game.

SUMMARY

Brooks finished 1990 with another solid year: 823 yards on 62 catches, with 5 touchdowns. His 13.3 yards per catch average indicates that he's becoming more and more of a possession receiver, but seldom fails to make the big catch. "Bill is a gutty player," says head coach Ron Meyer. "He's a consistent player who is an asset to our offense."

HANK'S RATING: A

Vance Johnson

Birthdate: March 13, 1963
College: Arizona
Height: 5-11
Weight: 185
How Acquired: Drafted in second round, 1985
Final 1990 Team: Denver Broncos

TECHNIQUE

Vance Johnson's 4.36 in the 40 during his rookie camp in 1985 set a Denver record, prompting the Broncos to convert him from tailback to wide receiver. The transition was not an easy one, as Johnson struggled early to learn the nuances common to NFL receivers. He still has trouble occasionally against tight man coverage, and shows timidness over the middle.

PRODUCTIVITY

Johnson produced in spurts, but he made them count. Denver trailed the Chiefs 23–21, and faced fourth down and 10 on its own 17 with barely a minute to play, when Johnson made an acrobatic 49-yard catch that led to the game-winning field goal. But Johnson's year—54 catches for 747 yards and 3 touchdowns—was still among the best of his career. Newcomer Shannon Sharpe, a seventh-round pick in 1990, was used both at both wide receiver and H-back, and should help take some pressure off Johnson and Mark Jackson in 1991.

SUMMARY

For all his ability, Jackson is injury prone and can be intimidated, a fact that might make quarterback John Elway look to Mark Jackson in tough situations. Against the Raiders, with Denver winning 9–7, Elway threaded a perfect pass over the middle to Johnson, who was hit first by cornerback Garry Lewis, and then by safety Eddie Anderson, who jarred the ball loose. Cornerback Terry McDaniel returned Johnson's fumble 42 yards for the winning touchdown.

HANK'S RATING: A

Stephen Baker

Birthdate: August 30, 1964
College: Fresno State
Height: 5-8
Weight: 160
How Acquired: Drafted in third round, 1987
Final 1990 Team: New York Giants

TECHNIQUE

Dependent on speed and intelligence, Stephen Baker has matured into one of the NFL's most solid receivers. Although he remains overshadowed by the Giants' marquee running game, Baker runs skilled, precision routes, has great deep speed, and releases off the line of scrimmage quickly. "Baker is a perfect complement to the Giants running game," says a scout. "He could put up big numbers in a more pass-oriented offense." The only question on Baker is his ability to react and change his route to coverages.

PRODUCTIVITY

Granted, Baker is seldom asked to do yeoman's duty in the Giants' slug-mouth running scheme. In 1990, he caught just 26 passes for 541 yards, but his 20.8 yards per catch average was second in the NFC. Baker is a tried and proven performer, and when the Giants do go to the air, he's there. Baker hauled in an 80-yard touchdown in the season's sixth week against arch-rival Washington. Weeks later, with quarterback Phil Simms nursing a sprained ankle against Phoenix, Baker salvaged a poor performance by his teammates with a diving, 38-yard touchdown with 3:21 to play, and the Giants won the game with a field goal on their next series.

SUMMARY

As long as Baker stays with the Giants, he'll probably never break 1,000 yards or score 12 touchdowns. But he is a reliable performer who is capable of much more, but still responds well within the limitations of the Giants offense.

HANK'S RATING: B

Ernie Jones

Birthdate: December 15, 1964
College: Indiana
Height: 5-11
Weight: 191
How Acquired: Drafted in seventh round, 1988
Final 1990 Team: Phoenix Cardinals

TECHNIQUE

Ernie Jones was a pleasant surprise for the Cardinals in the 1988 draft. Going into the 1990 season, his per-catch average was 19.6, and though it fell off to 16.8 in 1990, Jones still displayed flashy ability to gain considerable yards *after* the catch. Jones still struggles against the league's finer cornerbacks, but is a fine athlete who is still learning. A definite long ball threat, Jones loves the "Go" route.

PRODUCTIVITY

Jones caught 43 passes for 724 yards and 4 touchdowns in 1990. Though rookie Ricky Proehl led the team, Jones made it clear that he will test aging veteran Roy Green for the starting job in 1991. Jones is a big-play performer who will complement the faster Proehl in years to come; his 93-yard touchdown catch against Philadelphia in 1988 still stands as the Cardinals' longest scoring pass since 1958.

SUMMARY

Jones' biggest hurdle is still dropped passes—but it's an area in which he's immensely improved. And Jones remains a tough, physical player, and is a brutal downfield blocker. He is not easily intimidated; against the Raiders in 1989, he came back from a vicious hit to catch a 35-yard touchdown.

HANK'S RATING: B

Mark Ingram

Birthdate: August 23, 1965
College: Michigan State
Height: 5-10
Weight: 188
How Acquired: Drafted in first round, 1987
Final 1990 Team: New York Giants

TECHNIQUE

Mark Ingram is a surehanded, quick-footed receiver who runs precise routes but lacks quickness in and out of his cuts. He lacks the strength to power his way off the line of scrimmage, but is a brilliant open-field runner.

PRODUCTIVITY

Ingram had his best game in the Super Bowl, where his critical third-down catch and subsequent run of a Jeff Hostetler pass late in the second half may have saved the game for the Giants. Ingram, like teammate Stephen Baker, sees little action due to New York's bruising ground game. But he averaged 19.2 yards per catch en route to 499 yards in 1990. He also scored 5 touchdowns.

SUMMARY

With more work, Ingram could easily be more of a factor. But due to the Giants scheme, he'll never post numbers good enough to put him among the NFL's Top 25.

HANK'S RATING: B

Shawn Collins

Birthdate: 2/20/67
College: Northern Arizona
Height: 6-2
Weight: 207
How Acquired: Drafted in first round, 1989
Final 1990 Team: Atlanta Falcons

TECHNIQUE

Shawn Collins took the league by storm as a rookie in 1989, using his height, strength, and speed to overwhelm smaller defensive backs. A tight end in college, Collins understands the fine art of separation—creating space between himself and defenders. He runs smooth routes and has adapted well in recent minicamps to a purer version of the run 'n' shoot, which Atlanta will use this year under new offensive coordinator June Jones.

PRODUCTIVITY

Collins had one of the finest rookie seasons (1989) in history; the only receiver whose rookie year compares to Collins is Art Monk. He caught 58 balls for 862 yards (Monk had 58 catches for 797 yards in 1980). General manager Ken Herock traded second-, fourth- and tenth-round picks to move up in the first round to draft Collins. But Collins found himself in new coach Jerry Glanville's doghouse in 1990, and, in the shadow of new acquisition Andre Rison, he caught just 34 passes for 503 yards and 2 touchdowns.

SUMMARY

Collins is an extremely capable player who has the size, speed, and skill to play in Atlanta's Red Gun offense. His biggest deficiency, which irritated Glanville, was his attitude. "He had a hard time dealing with the presence of Rison," says an Atlanta source. "But he seems to be dealing with it much better this season." If Collins works hard and cooperates, his size could pose a serious threat—much like Houston's Haywood Jeffires—in Atlanta's wide-open offense. Must become a more alert receiver, or he may be destined to be a number two type weapon.

HANK'S RATING: B

Hassan Jones

Birthdate: July 2, 1964
College: Florida State
Height: 6-0
Weight: 195
How Acquired: Drafted in fifth round, 1986
Final 1990 Team: Minnesota Vikings

TECHNIQUE

Now in his fifth season with the Minnesota Vikings. Hassan Jones has proven himself as an excellent leaper with soft hands. Jones is generally unafraid to catch the ball in traffic, has adequate speed, and does his best work when opposite the speedier Anthony Carter.

PRODUCTIVITY

Jones' final 1990 numbers reflect his consistency: 51 catches, 810 yards, and a sterling 15.9 yards per catch average. Jones also scored 7 touchdowns, including a 75-yard bomb. Such statistics put him in fine company, but in the NFL, one season doesn't make a career: Jones must maintain such production over a period of several years to elevate himself into the league's Top 25 receivers.

SUMMARY

Jones is a reliable receiver who will make the big catch. One completely healthy season might attract the national spotlight he's looking for. Certainly, playing in the pass-dependent offense of coordinator Tom Moore won't hurt his chances. It's time for Jones to prove he deserves consistent praise.

HANK'S RATING: B

Jessie Hester

Birthdate: January 21, 1963
College: Florida State
Height: 5-11
Weight: 172
How Acquired: Free Agent, 1990
Final 1990 Team: Indianapolis Colts

TECHNIQUE

Jessie "The Jet" Hester got his nickname for obvious reasons: He can run. Nothing fancy. But Hester is a much different player than he was at Florida State; perhaps more important than his speed is Hester's savvy and veteran intelligence. He knows how to get open, runs well-timed routes, and reacts quickly to a thrown ball.

PRODUCTIVITY

Hester came out of forced retirement and had his best NFL season. Hester was also involved in one of 1990's more bizarre plays: Against the Jets, quarterback Jeff George completed a 43-yard pass to Hester, which bounced off his shoulder pads, then bounced off cornerback James Hasty, then tumbled back into the hands of Hester for a touchdown. That circus catch illustrated his entire season—the ball bounced his way.

SUMMARY

Hester, who caught 1 pass in 1987 before being released by the Raiders and 12 in 1988 with the Atlanta Falcons, had career highs in receptions (54) and yards (924) and scored 6 touchdowns. He has always been a capable player, and Colts officials say Hester will again play a big role in the offense in 1991.

HANK'S RATING: B

Calvin Williams

Birthdate: March 3, 1967
College: Purdue
Height: 5-11
Weight: 181
How Acquired: Drafted in fifth round, 1990
Final 1990 Team: Philadelphia Eagles

TECHNIQUE

After Purdue made the switch from a wishbone offense midway through his senior season, Calvin Williams prospered behind a run 'n' shoot scheme designed to get him the football. "Calvin reads defenses extremely well," says Dan Lounsbury, a former Purdue assistant who is currently with the WLAF's New York Knights. "He has a knack for getting back to the football."

PRODUCTIVITY

Williams displayed traits in 1990 that suggest he has a bright future in the NFL. He finished the year with 37 catches for 602 yards and 9 touchdowns. Against the Cowboys, Williams capped an 85-yard drive when he tucked in Randall Cunningham's 10-yard lob with 44 seconds to play to give the Eagles a 21–20 victory. In a 31–13 surprise of the Giants, Williams out-jumped two Giants for a fourth-quarter touchdown that put the game away. And his late touchdown against Phoenix cinched the game.

SUMMARY

Eagles assistants believe Williams will turn into Philadelphia's primary possession receiver. Scouts note his aggressiveness in going to the ball. It was the emergence of Williams that eased Philadelphia's loss of receiver Mike Quick, who, it appears, will not recover from his badly injured knees.

HANK'S RATING: B

Reggie Langhorne

Birthdate: April 7, 1963
College: Elizabeth City State
Height: 6-2
Weight: 200
How Acquired: Drafted in seventh round, 1985
Final 1990 Team: Cleveland Browns

TECHNIQUE

Outstanding speed is Langhorne's greatest asset, which makes him a legitimate deep threat. Like his counterpart, Webster Slaughter, Langhorne is an outstanding blocker who works the hashmarks extremely well and is unafraid to go over the middle.

PRODUCTIVITY

Going into the 1990 season, Langhorne had been the Browns' leading receiver over 1988–89 with 117 catches. Despite Cleveland's troubled season, he still pulled down 45 catches for 585 yards and 2 touchdowns in 1990. Langhorne has played in every game—excluding three strike contests—since joining the Browns.

SUMMARY

Langhorne is a tough player who is not swayed by injuries. He didn't miss a game in 1990 after arthroscopic knee surgery in the preseason; in 1989, he played with broken ribs, a broken toe, and played one week after an emergency appendectomy. "Reggie Langhorne is one of the toughest receivers in the league," says Green Bay head coach Lindy Infante. "He's all football player, and he leaves his heart on the field every week." The type of team player coaches love.

HANK'S RATING: B

Brian Blades

Birthdate: July 24, 1965
College: Miami
Height: 5-11
Weight: 184
How Acquired: Drafted in second round, 1988
Final 1990 Team: Seattle Seahawks

TECHNIQUE

Scouts assessing Brian Blades' 1990 performance noticed one thing: The speed that carried him to a stellar Pro Bowl season in 1990 simply wasn't there. Some attributed his dropoff in performance to quarterback Dave Krieg's up-and-down year, who had his lowest rating since becoming the starter in 1983. But Blades will have to work hard, nonetheless, to reestablish the respect he earned in years past.

PRODUCTIVITY

Blades finished 1990 with 49 catches for 525 yards and 3 touchdowns, far off his 1989 numbers of 77 catches for 1,063 yards. The biggest drop, though, was in Blades' yards per catch, which fell from a 14.9 career mark to 10.7 in 1990.

SUMMARY

Blades is a solid player with good coordination and modest speed. He will take the hit and hold on to the ball. But his 1990 season was marred by inconsistency. He has the potential to be a 1,000-yard receiver, and should benefit greatly from the emergence of Tommy Kane. Blades needs more help from the quarterback position.

HANK'S RATING: B

Ricky Sanders

Birthdate: August 30, 1962
College: Southwest Texas State
Height: 5-11
Weight: 180
How Acquired: Trade, 1986
Final 1990 Team: Washington Redskins

TECHNIQUE

You don't overthrow Ricky Sanders. "Ricky does a fine job of running to the ball," says head coach Joe Gibbs. Separating Sanders from Clark and Monk is his light, quick feet, soft hands, and his ability to flow to the long ball without breaking stride. Watching a Sanders workout is a baffling experience; try as you may, you can't hear him run *or* catch. But to complement his speed, Sanders needs to show more discipline with his routes.

PRODUCTIVITY

Sanders best game of the season came against the Lions, when he tucked in 8 catches for 132 yards and a touchdown. He finished the season with 56 catches for 727 yards and 3 touchdowns, with a per-catch average of 13.0—nearly 2 yards better than Art Monk. "Ricky has put together several great seasons," says Washington wide receiver coach Charley Taylor. "Ricky has great work ethic and never lets up. He not only puts up big numbers, he makes the big catches."

SUMMARY

Sanders has lived in the shadow of Art Monk and Gary Clark. Monk, is better than Sanders, but Sanders might live up to Clark's numbers with the same amount of work. It remains a mystery why the Redskins fail to use Sanders to his potential. But quarterbacks throw to receivers they can rely on and that they know will make the play in the tough situation. But Joe Gibbs vows to work Sanders into the offense more.

HANK'S RATING: B

Kelvin Martin

Birthdate: May 14, 1965
College: Boston College
Height: 5-9
Weight: 162
How Acquired: Drafted in fourth round, 1987
Final 1990 Team: Dallas Cowboys

TECHNIQUE

When the Cowboys drafted Michael Irvin in the first round in 1988, Dallas fans automatically assumed that Irvin would take over the workhorse share of the receiving load. But Kelvin Martin, without Irvin's fanfare, dancing, and taunting, continues to quietly produce. Martin is a long-striding, elusive receiver, with great cutback ability. And to date, anyway, he's Troy Aikman's clutch target.

PRODUCTIVITY

Martin piled up 732 yards on 64 catches in 1990 as he continued his work as the Cowboys most consistent receiver. Though Martin lacks the deep speed to stretch a defense, he averaged 11-plus-yards a catch, but failed to get in the end zone.

SUMMARY

Dallas is hurt by its lack of a speed receiver that can neutralize an all-out blitz. Alexander Wright, the Cowboys' second-round pick in 1990 out of Auburn, has legitimate 4.3 speed. But he had a pitiful 11-catch rookie season after a lengthy training camp holdout. While the Cowboys wait patiently for one of their young stars to step to the head of the class, Martin will continue to play a critical role in moving the chains for Aikman and the Cowboys. So the Cowboys went out and drafted Alvin Harper in the first round this year. Though Martin has been productive, Cowboys will be hard pressed to win with him as their number one receiver.

HANK'S RATING: B

Irving Fryar

Birthdate: September 28, 1962
College: Nebraska
Height: 6-0
Weight: 200
How Acquired: Drafted in first round, 1984
Final 1990 Team: New England Patriots

TECHNIQUE

Technique is perhaps Irving Fryar's greatest flaw. Just as he did during his collegiate years at Nebraska, Fryar runs stiff, predictable routes, and fails to use his blazing speed to his advantage. "When you watch Fryar, the word 'clunky' comes to mind," says a scout. "He has yet to develop a fluid, graceful style."

PRODUCTIVITY

For just the second time in his seven years with the team did Fryar catch more than 40 passes. He finished the year with 54 catches for 856 yards, a 15.9 yards per completion average and 4 touchdowns. Fryar, for all his off-the-field problems, still rates as one of the NFL's best downfield blockers and, when called on, can still stretch a defense. But he does not always show dependable hands. He did double-duty as a punt returner, but was hardly spectacular. He averaged 4.8 yards a return on 28 attempts. His most impressive number was a streak of consecutive catches in twenty-one games.

SUMMARY

Fryar's career has been marked by the utterance of a single word every year: Consistency, or for the record, Fryar's lack of it. He occasionally plays brilliant football, but for all the trouble and money the Patriots have spent on him, he repeatedly falls short of his potential. You have to question his desire to play well. Scouts point to Fryar's poor work habits and off-field distractions as key reasons behind his mediocre career. Fryar should be helped by 1989's second-round pick Greg McMurtry, who will take away some of the pressure.

HANK'S RATING: B

the right time. And he's played in the offense so long, he probably knows more about it than anybody but Lindy." But his lack of top receiver skills will always limit him. Kemp will battle Charles Wilson, 1990's fifth-round pick, for playing time in 1991.

HANK'S RATING: B

Perry Kemp

Birthdate: December 31, 1961
College: California State
Height: 5-11
Weight: 170
How Acquired: Free Agent, 1988
Final 1990 Team: Green Bay Packers

TECHNIQUE

When Perry Kemp came to the Packers two years ago, he had a headstart on the other Packer receivers: He played for head coach Lindy Infante for two years in the USFL (Jacksonville) and one year in Cleveland. Infante wanted him for the same reasons: consistent routes and fine adjustments to what he sees after a play begins. Kemp doesn't have great physical skills, but, for the most part, he makes up for it with his smarts.

PRODUCTIVITY

Kemp caught 48 passes in his first two seasons in Green Bay, then dropped off to 44 receptions in 1990. His 12.0 yards per catch were in line with his previous two seasons. Thus Infante truly has an idea of the annual contribution he will get from the consistent Kemp. "Perry has been very productive," Infante says. "But wide receiver is going to be a very competitive position for us."

SUMMARY

"There's one word for Perry Kemp," says Packers receiver coach Buddy Geis. "That's consistency. You can always count on Perry Kemp. You know he'll be in the right place at

Tommy Kane

Birthdate: January 14, 1967
College: Syracuse
Height: 5-11
Weight: 176
How Acquired: Drafted in third round, 1988
Final 1990 Team: Seattle Seahawks

TECHNIQUE

A former high school basketball and hockey player, Tommy Kane shows good feet and physical form in his pass routes. Kane's excellent lateral movement helps against pressing corners, and his deceiving stride enables him to occasionally run past opponents. But some question whether he has NFL receiver skills and if he can make the mental adjustments needed to be a Top 25 wide receiver.

PRODUCTIVITY

Kane performed admirably in 1990, considering he was recovering from major surgery to an injured knee suffered in 1989. The Canadian-born receiver caught 52 passes for 776 yards and 4 touchdowns for a 14.9 yards per catch average. It was by far his best season: Prior to 1990, Kane had 13 career receptions for 126 yards.

SUMMARY

Kane has to learn to somehow avoid injury. He missed seven games due to injury during his rookie season, then missed more than half of the 1989 season with a knee injury. But give Kane credit: Few players come back so strong from the type of injuries he's suffered.

HANK'S RATING: B

Bruce Hill

Birthdate: February 29, 1964
College: Arizona State
Height: 6-0
Weight: 180
How Acquired: Drafted in fourth round, 1987
Final 1990 Team: Tampa Bay Buccaneers

TECHNIQUE

Now in his fifth season, Bruce Hill has proven himself as a crafty receiver who is unafraid to catch the ball in traffic and has adequate speed to stretch a defense. But once again, he failed to stay healthy, suffering throughout 1990 from a myriad of injuries: bad shoulder, broken finger, broken ribs.

PRODUCTIVITY

Though his final numbers really didn't do him justice, Hill improved in 1990 in virtually every respect. Despite his injuries, he managed to play in thirteen games, though his poor health limited him in several contests. Hill finished the season with 42 receptions for 641 yards, and scored touchdowns in each of the last two games to tie for the team lead with five.

SUMMARY

Hill has the skills to be a big-play receiver. He caught 5 passes for 104 yards, including an 11-yard touchdown pass to tie Minnesota with 24 seconds remaining. His 26-yard reception late in the fourth quarter helped the Bucs score the winning touchdown over Detroit. A completely healthy season is the only thing Hill needs to have a major-impact season.

HANK'S RATING: B

Who's Missing

Eddie Brown

Birthdate: December 17, 1962
College: Miami
Height: 6-0
Weight: 185
How Acquired: Drafted in first round, 1985
Final 1990 Team: Cincinnati Bengals

Eddie Brown suffered an off-year in 1990, but still posted 706 receiving yards on just 44 catches—a per-catch average of 16.0 yards. His 9 touchdowns tied Houston's Ernest Givens for the best in the AFC. He started the 1990 season with a bang against San Diego in the second week, catching 10 balls for 178 yards, including 30- and 23-yard touchdown passes. But the last six weeks of the Bengals' 10–8 season, Brown, and teammate Tim McGee, virtually vanished from the offense; Brown caught just 10 passes for 88 yards during that span.

Brown has all the skills, and should be one of the top NFL wide receivers. But something is holding him back. Some question his attitude and whether he gives his all. If Brown would work at his game, he could become the big-catch receiver the Bengals are looking for.

HANK'S RATING: A

Hart Lee Dykes

Birthdate: September 2, 1966
College: Oklahoma State
Height: 6-4
Weight: 218
How Acquired: Drafted in first round, 1989
Final 1990 Team: New England Patriots

Hart Lee Dykes has been considered a bust by many scouts, primarily because of his lofty selection in the 1989 draft (the first receiver taken) and his very limited role in the New England offense. But in Dyke's defense, the quarterbacks throwing the ball have been horribly inconsistent, too. Nevertheless, the numbers simply don't support Dykes' salary: In 1989, he had 49 catches and 5 touchdowns; in 1990, he had 34 catches and just 2 touchdowns. Dykes must run better routes and learn to be more consistent. His one-on-one skills aren't great, but don't close the book on Dykes. With a more consistent offense, Dykes could be a good producer.

HANK'S RATING: A

Emile Harry

Birthdate: April 5, 1963
College: Stanford
Height: 5-11
Weight: 178
How Acquired: Free Agent, 1986
Final 1990 Team: Kansas City Chiefs

Emile Harry has suffered from injuries throughout his career, but when he can play, he gives the Chiefs a multi-purpose offensive weapon. He finished 1990 with 41 catches for 519 yards and 2 touchdowns. Harry has decent speed, moves, and hands. He is a reliable receiver who doesn't fail to produce. Harry may see less playing time if youngster Robb Thomas continues to improve.

HANK'S RATING: A

Mark Clayton

Birthdate: April 8, 1961
College: Louisville
Height: 5-9
Weight: 184
How Acquired: Drafted in eighth round, 1983
Final 1990 Team: Miami Dolphins

Clayton's severe drop-off in numbers in 1990—33 catches for just 425 yards—reflected the Dolphins change in focus: No longer a long-ball offense, Miami was content to batter defenses with a revived running game as its passing shootouts of years past became more and more infrequent. "I never dreamed I'd be part of a dink offense," Clayton says ruefully.

But on occasion, Clayton still flashed ability. His fourth-quarter, 12-yard touchdown against Kansas City with 3:28 remaining was the difference in Miami's 17–16 playoff victory. Clayton, in perfect communication with quarterback Dan Marino, baited cornerback Albert Lewis on the play. "I knew Lewis would go for the interception," says Marino. "But Mark ran a perfect route, made him think the interception was there, and I threw it low and outside. Mark made the catch."

Mark has to come into camp in shape and show he's ready for a new season. With his old desire intact, he can still get in done.

HANK'S RATING: A

Brian Brennan

Birthdate: February 15, 1962
College: Boston College
Height: 5-10
Weight: 185
How Acquired: Drafted in fourth round, 1984
Final 1990 Team: Cleveland Browns

Brian Brennan produced startling numbers in the Browns' madcap 1990 season. He tied for third on the team in receptions, with 45 catches for 568 yards and 2 touchdowns. His reception and yardage totals, surprisingly, were the third-best in his seven-year career. And Brennan came through with several clutch catches, including a 24-yard touchdown against Denver with 3:21 remaining, which led to the Browns 30–29 upset of the Broncos.

Brennan does not have a lot of speed, but he is an outstanding short-yardage receiver—12-yard hooks and hitches. He runs good routes, and has as good of hands as any receiver in the NFL. A complete team player.

HANK'S RATING: A

Michael Irvin

Birthdate: March 5, 1966
College: Miami
Height: 6-2
Weight: 202
How Acquired: Drafted in first round, 1988
Final 1990 Team: Dallas Cowboys

Michael Irvin danced his way into the hearts of Cowboys fans as a number-one pick in 1988, but has failed to live up to his potential—or self-promotion—since. Irvin caught 20 passes for 413 yards and 5 touchdowns in 1990, but developed a reputation as a player who didn't like to catch over the middle and could be pushed around by physical corners. Many quesiton whether Irvin can fully recover from knee surgery—he seems to worry about the knee when he makes his cuts.

HANK'S RATING: A

Clarence Verdin

Birthdate: June 14, 1963
College: Southwest Louisiana
Height: 5-8
Weight: 170
How Acquired: Trade, 1988
Final 1990 Team: Indianapolis Colts

Clarence Verdin's productivity dropped off severely in 1990, as he caught just 14 balls for 178 yards and a touchdown. But he still led the AFC in punt returns with a 12.8 average on 31 attempts, and set up the winning field goal against the Jets with a 33-yard punt return. Verdin has been plagued by dropped balls, an indication that he's not getting enough reps in practice. Verdin proved in the USFL that he could wow opponents with tough catches and blazing speed, but Colts coaches have yet to focus his role. A reliable, veteran backup receiver who won't disappoint in the occasional start.

HANK'S RATING: B

Brett Perriman

Birthdate: October 10, 1965
College: Miami
Height: 5-9
Weight: 180
How Acquired: Drafted in second round, 1988
Final 1990 Team: New Orleans Saints

Brett Perriman came to the Saints in 1988 with the mindset of taking over as the team's dominant receiver. But thus far, that hasn't been the case. Despite good speed, Perriman has struggled as a professional, suffering from injuries, bad reads, and drops. He caught just 36 passes for 386 yards in 1990, and cracked the end zone just twice. Many scouts feel Perriman has the skills to be a quality receiver, but question his desire to improve and his work habits. And his attitude was also questioned after he said, "We've got more mistakes [in the passing game] than Van Camp's has pork and beans." "We're killing ourselves."

HANK'S RATING: B

Ronnie Harmon

Birthdate: May 7, 1964
College: Iowa
Height: 5-11
Weight: 200
How Acquired: Plan B free agent, 1990
Final 1990 Team: San Diego Chargers

Ronnie Harmon is a running back by nature, but the Chargers threw to him so much that, for our purposes, he ended up in the receiving files. Harmon, who came to San Diego as a Plan B acquisition from Buffalo, caught 46 passes for 511 yards and 2 touchdowns—an average of 11.1 yards per catch. In the Chargers offense, Harmon was a dependable H-back and scatback capable of moving the chains.

"Ronnie was used mainly as a third-down specialist," says head coach Dan Henning. "He was a steal." Harmon also added 363 yards rushing, and made numerous big plays—including a thrilling 41-yard run against the Raiders in the season finale.

HANK'S RATING: B

Robb Thomas

Birthdate: March 29, 1966
College: Oregon State
Height: 5-11
Weight: 171
How Acquired: Drafted in sixth round, 1989
Final 1990 Team: Kansas City Chiefs

Second-year man Robb Thomas became a critical part of the Kansas City offensive attack in 1990, as he combined with another second-year player—third-down running back Todd McNair—to make 81 catches for 1,052 yards. Thomas showed flashy running ability after the catch, and survived major-league blows from several teams. Thomas is a young, talented player. If he can stay healthy, he could become a versatile weapon in the Kansas City offense.

HANK'S RATING: B

Robert Clark

Birthdate: August 8, 1965
College: North Carolina Central
Height: 5-11
Weight: 173
How Acquired: Plan B free agent, 1989
Final 1990 Team: Detroit Lions

Robert Clark enjoys playing in the Detroit Lions run 'n' shoot offense. And he is a perfect receiver for the offense. Small and quick, Clark is good at finding the open area. He finished the 1990 season with 53 receptions for 932 yards —an impressive 17.6 yards per catch. And Clark proved he could find the end zone, notching a team-leading 8 touchdown receptions. With Richard Johnson departed, Clark is the top returning wide receiver. Like other receivers who have found success in a run 'n' shoot offense, scouts argue Clark would not be nearly as successful in a "regular" offensive scheme.

HANK'S RATING: B

Best of Plan B

Richard Johnson

Birthdate: October 19, 1961
College: Colorado
Height: 5-6
Weight: 184
Final 1990 Team: Detroit Lions

"Nobody reads coverage better or makes better decisions than Richard," says WLAF head coach and run 'n' shoot guru Mouse Davis, who coached Johnson in both the USFL and NFL. "He has that little extra boost of speed when you need it, but the bottom line is he gets open."

And if anybody ever deserved to thumb their nose at management, it's Johnson. Nobody wanted the 5-6, 184-pound speedster after he graduated from Colorado, where he was a running back. Davis converted him to receiver in 1984 as a USFL free agent, and Johnson proceeded to catch 218 passes for 2,400 yards in two seasons. But again, the NFL turned its head.

Finally, after two years as a computer programmer for IBM, Johnson was summoned by Davis to the Lions. As before, Detroit scouts openly expressed their doubts. Johnson responded with the most receptions by a receiver inf Lions' history (70), and his 1,091 yards in 1989 were second in Detroit history. He caught 727 yards worth of passes for 6 touchdowns in 1990. Scouts argue that Johnson will only be productive in a run 'n' shoot offense. Though signed by the Houston Oilers, Johnson was let go in late June. Should end up on a team before the 1991 season begins.

HANK'S RATING: A

James Milling

Birthdate: February 14, 1965
College: Maryland
Height: 5-9
Weight: 156
Final 1990 Team: Atlanta Falcons

James Millings, who played in 1988 and 1990 for Atlanta, was a three-year letterman at Maryland who played well during his brief stints with the Falcons. He caught 18 passes for 161 yards and a touchdown in 1990, and in a limited role in 1988, caught 5 passes for 66 yards. Milling has quick feet and blazing speed, but is very small and needs work on his routes. He could be an asset, however, to a run-heavy team, due to his speed. The Giants signed him in hopes that he would add some vertical stretch to their offense.

HANK'S RATING: B

Jason Phillips

Birthdate: October 11, 1966
College: Houston
Height: 5-7
Weight: 168
Final 1990 Team: Detroit Lions

Jason Phillips caught 8 passes for 112 yards for the Detroit Lions in 1990, an average of 14 yards per catch. The former University of Houston product—who led the nation in receiving in back-to-back seasons—could flourish under Atlanta's evolution to a purer form of the run 'n' shoot. Atlanta offensive coordinator June Jones had Phillips in Detroit, and is impressed with his hands and work ethic. Some scouts question his route-running ability, though.

HANK'S RATING: C

Tight Ends

Keith Jackson

Birthdate: April 19, 1965
College: Oklahoma
Height: 6-2
Weight: 250
How Acquired: Drafted in first round, 1988
Final 1990 Team: Philadelphia Eagles

BLOCKING

Surprisingly, Keith Jackson has yet to realize his potential as a blocker, despite the fact that he learned his trade at Oklahoma, a school noted for its running game. But don't expect Philadelphia coaches to hold that against the playmaking tight end. "He has so much talent," says head coach Rich Kotite, "it's unbelievable."

RECEIVING

Keith Jackson may be the best pass-catching tight end in the league. He has 144 receptions and two Pro Bowl starts in his first two seasons. Despite being injured through half of 1989, Jackson still finished tops among tight ends in receptions (63) and yards (648). He had comparable numbers in 1990, finishing with 50 catches for 670 yards and 6 touchdowns.

SUMMARY

The premier tight end in 1989, Keith Jackson possesses all the tools to be one of the greatest ever. His 1990 holdout severely cramped his production, but in a full season, Jackson is among the league's most dominant players.
HANK'S RATING: AAA

Rodney Holman

Birthdate: April 20, 1960
College: Tulane
Height: 6-3
Weight: 238
How Acquired: Drafted in third round, 1982
Final 1990 Team: Cincinnati Bengals

BLOCKING

One of the best blocking tight ends in the league, Rodney Holman has raised his game to new heights. A bit undersized (6-3, 238), Holman still takes pride in his blocking ability. "If I get a good block and the back runs for 15 or 20 yards, I'm just as happy as if I make a catch," says Holman.

RECEIVING

According to Cincinnati tight end coach Bill Johnson, who is entering his forty-third season in professional football, Holman "is as good a tight end as I've been around." The ten-year pro helped restore the roar into the vaunted Bengal offense in 1990, catching 40 passes for 596 yards and 5 touchdowns.

SUMMARY

Holman has emerged as one of the best in the NFL at his position. His best year was in 1989, when he posted career highs with 50 catches for 736 yards and 9 touchdowns.

HANK'S RATING: AA

Eric Green

Birthdate: June 22, 1967
College: Liberty College
Height: 6-5
Weight: 274
How Acquired: Drafted in first round, 1990
Final 1990 Team: Pittsburgh Steelers

BLOCKING

Eric Green emerged as a strong run blocker in 1990, which helped the Steelers running game immensely. However, Pittsburgh's deficient passing game relied too heavily on Green, both as a blocker and receiver. "Green could easily be another offensive lineman," says a scout. "But in blocking situations, he's got great upper body strength and quick feet. He's an earth-mover."

RECEIVING

Green showed surprising route-running skills for a big man, catching 34 passes for 387 yards for a respectable, chain-moving 11.4 yards per catch average for 7 touchdowns. Against San Diego, Green caught touchdown passes of 8 yards and 1 yard, then two weeks later shredded Denver for three scores. "He's hard to miss," says quarterback Bubby Brister. "He's as big as a house."

SUMMARY

The Steelers' 1990 first-round pick out of Liberty College, Eric Green offered something Pittsburgh sorely missed for years: A big (6-5, 274), underneath target that can block and catch. In Joe Walton's offensive scheme, Green will became an instant starter, giving him ample opportunity to display the skills that made him a first-round choice. "He's a strong blocker and has excellent hands," says head coach Chuck Noll. "We feel like he's a prototype tight end."

HANK'S RATING: AA

Steve Jordan

Birthdate: January 10, 1961
College: Brown
Height: 6-3
Weight: 236
How Acquired: Drafted in seventh round, 1982
Final 1990 Team: Minnesota Vikings

BLOCKING

The most cunning tight end in our Top 10, Steve Jordan often opts for brains over brawn. "He's a tough player who blocks well, but one who is smart enough to get open in the seams," says a scout.

RECEIVING

Jordan caught 45 passes in 1990 for 636 yards, a 14.1 yards per catch average, and scored 3 touchdowns. Although Jordan is in the twilight of his career, expect him to excel under second-year offensive coordinator Tom Moore.

SUMMARY

A consensus All Pro since entering the league as a little-known prospect from Brown University, Jordan expects his ninth season to be his best.

HANK'S RATING: AA

Ferrell Edmunds

Birthdate: April 16, 1965

College: Maryland
Height: 6-6
Weight: 252
How Acquired: Drafted in third round, 1988
Final 1990 Team: Miami Dolphins

BLOCKING

Blocking is Ferrell Edmunds' biggest weakness. He is extremely quick for his size, has powerful lateral movement, but often displayed short sustain balance in blocking situations. With effort, however, Edmunds has the physique to become a dominating blocker.

RECEIVING

The 6-6, 252-pound Edmunds is an ideal target and an added dimension for the pass-happy Dolphins. "He is such a good receiver that on second-and-long, it's an advantage to keep him in the game, instead of bringing in a third wide receiver, because the defense won't be sure if we're going to run or pass," says head coach Don Shula. In 1990, Edmunds —en route to another Pro Bowl—caught 31 balls for 446 yards and a touchdown. He averaged 14.4 yards per catch.

SUMMARY

Edmunds benefits from Miami's talented group of receivers —especially the venerable Jim Jensen—on third down plays. Jensen—who caught 44 passes for 365 yards himself—draws so much defensive attention, it creates passing lanes for Edmunds.

But despite Edmunds' back-to-back Pro Bowl seasons, his penchant for dropping passes still occasionally draws icy stares from quarterback Dan Marino.

HANK'S RATING: AA

Mark Bavaro

Birthdate: April 28, 1963
College: Notre Dame
Height: 6-4
Weight: 245
How Acquired: Drafted in fourth round, 1985
Final 1990 Team: New York Giants

BLOCKING

Mark Bavaro has been hurt much of the past two years, a fact that infuriates the most acclaimed tight end of the 1980s. New York coaches expect him to be 100 percent in 1991, but Bavaro's oft-injured bad knees have stifled his quickness. At half his ability, however, Bavaro is still better than many of the league's starting tight ends.

RECEIVING

Former head coach Bill Parcells marvels at Bavaro's ability to catch the ball in traffic. "He's a great competitor in two areas where you ask the most of a tight end—blocking and catching the ball inside," Parcells says. In 1990, Bavaro had 33 catches for 393 yards and 5 touchdowns, which tied him for the team lead. Bavaro caught a 61-yard down-the-middle pass against Washington which helped New York outlast the Redskins, 24–20.

SUMMARY

Bavaro allows the Giants to stretch defenses from the inside-out with the three-tight-end "load" formation pioneered by New York prior to Bavaro's succession of knee injuries. The Giants favor possession-type short passes and screens to the tight ends. Word is that Bavaro might not be able to overcome his injury problems. If he is still injured, we have to give him a C rating. But if he's not he is one of the best.

HANK'S RATING: A

Keith McKeller

Birthdate: July 9, 1964
College: Jacksonville State
Height: 6-4
Weight: 245
How Acquired: Drafted in ninth round, 1987
Final 1990 Team: Buffalo Bills

BLOCKING

En route to the Super Bowl, the Bills relied often on Keith McKeller for his powerful blocking in certain run situations. Ironically, however, McKeller is on the sidelines in

Buffalo's no-huddle offense, which running back Thurman Thomas seems to thrive from. But in must short-yardage situations, McKeller is a force.

RECEIVING

The Bills use McKeller almost exclusively—and extensively—on possession-type passes. He caught 34 passes for 464 yards in 1990, for a 13.7 yards per catch average and 5 touchdowns.

SUMMARY

McKeller is one more example of the outstanding work done by Buffalo's scouting department; one-third of the Bills played at Division I-AA or smaller schools, and half of the drafted starters were selected *after* the first round. An excellent young prospect, McKeller has improved markably over his three pro seasons. Expect his improvement to continue—McKeller has Pro Bowl potential.

HANK'S RATING: A

Jay Novacek

Birthdate: October 24, 1962
College: Wyoming
Height: 6-4
Weight: 235
How Acquired: Plan B Free Agent, 1990
Final 1990 Team: Dallas Cowboys

BLOCKING

Jay Novacek impressed a lot of people during his tenure in Phoenix—Dallas officials were baffled, but happy, when they were able to snag Novacek on Plan B in 1990. Novacek's sustaining run block efforts were a big reason for the rapid success of rookie running back Emmit Smith.

RECEIVING

Novacek has only modest speed, but is an effective receiver. His 59 catches for 657 yards and 4 touchdowns were among the league leaders. Quarterback Timm Rosenbach of Phoenix, in particular, fell in love with Novacek's good hands.

SUMMARY

Novacek is a hard-working, blue-collar player. "I just want to play," he says. He lacks speed, but boasts decent strength and near perfect technique.

HANK'S RATING: A

Brent Jones

Birthdate: February 12, 1963
College: Santa Clara
Height: 6-4
Weight: 230
How Acquired: Free Agent, 1987
Final 1990 Team: San Francisco 49ers

BLOCKING

On the 49ers' star-laden offense, blue-collar Brent Jones has found his niche primarily as a successful blocker. He has size, good feet, and benefits from sound technique. "Brent understands leverage," says a coach.

RECEIVING

Jones possesses amazingly soft hands for a big man. Add the constant outside threats of Jerry Rice and John Taylor, and Jones is frequently open underneath and across the middle. He really became involved in the passing game in 1989, catching 40 passes for 500 yards. In 1990, he caught 56 balls for 747 yards and 5 touchdowns.

SUMMARY

This fifth-year pro out of Santa Clara has emerged into a pleasant surprise for the 49ers. Jones is a naturally gifted player who needs only to refine his skills to become an every-down player.

HANK'S RATING: A

Ed West

Birthdate: August 2, 1961
College: Auburn
Height: 6-1
Weight: 243
How Acquired: Free Agent, 1984
Final 1990 Team: Green Bay Packers

BLOCKING

Ed West built his reputation in the NFL as primarily a blocker for a simple reason: He is strong at the point of attack. West excels in short-yardage, man-to-man blocking situations.

RECEIVING

Though West doesn't make his living as a receiver, he still managed 27 catches in 1990 for 356 yards, a 13.2 yards per catch average. He also scored 5 touchdowns, including a 1-yard score with 16 seconds left to beat Phoenix, 24–21.

SUMMARY

West has been a mainstay in the Packer offense, and many talented players have failed to beat him out. However, impressive 1990 fourth-round draft pick Jackie Harris (out of Northeast Louisiana) will give West another run for his money in 1991.

HANK'S RATING: A

Arthur Cox

Birthdate: February 5, 1961
College: Texas Southern
Height: 6-2
Weight: 277
How Acquired: Free Agent, 1988
Final 1990 Team: San Diego Chargers

BLOCKING

San Diego head coach Dan Henning grew partial to Arthur Cox for his devastating blocking ability. At 277 pounds, Cox is literally like adding another lineman, which means everything to a ground-attack team like the Chargers.

RECEIVING

Cos is a limited receiver, evidenced by his modest 14 catches for 93 yards and a lone touchdown. When Cox is in the game, it's in almost exclusively running situations.

SUMMARY

Cox is a gigantic, talented blocker with excellent speed and strength for his size. He has all the tools to become a great NFL player. However, Cox's fumbles cost San Diego at least one game, a fact that could result in Derrick Walker—sixth-round pick in 1990—getting a chance to play more.

HANK'S RATING: A

Marv Cook

Birthdate: February 24, 1966
College: Iowa
Height: 6-4
Weight: 234
How Acquired: Drafted in third round, 1989
Final 1990 Team: New England Patriots

BLOCKING

Marv Cook's toughness on special teams impressed opponents during his rookie year of 1989, and his continued improvement last year hints of a bright NFL future. A gritty, hard-nosed blocker, Cook "is still learning how to use his body," says a scout. "He's learning the fine points of blocking, but he's got the attitude for it."

RECEIVING

Cook had his best year as a pro, catching 51 passes for 455 yards and 5 touchdowns. A former record-setting high school quarterback, Cook understands the passing game and displays excellent pass-catching form in the open field.

SUMMARY

As the Patriots begin the rebuilding process, they'd be wise to make Cook an integral part of their plans. He is a solid, consistent player who is a natural leader, with the size, speed, and talent to become a Mark Bavaro-type player.

HANK'S RATING: A

Ron Hall

Birthdate: March 15, 1964
College: Hawaii
Height: 6-4
Weight: 245
How Acquired: Drafted in fourth round, 1987
Final 1990 Team: Tampa Bay Buccaneers

BLOCKING

Teammates nicknamed Ron Hall "Ironman" for his mental and physical toughness. Despite a rash of injuries in 1989, he didn't miss a game. Hall honed his toughness while playing at Hawaii, when he literally walked on hot coals not once, but three times. "To improve my concentration," he says.

RECEIVING

Hall is established as one of the most surehanded tight ends in the NFL. He caught 31 passes for 464 yards, good for a 15.0 yards per catch average, and scored two touchdowns. It was his third straight season with 30 or more receptions.

SUMMARY

Hall was named to an assortment of postseason media All-Pro teams. He received the 1990 Ed Block Courage Award at the end of the season, as teammates rewarded his ability to play despite painful injuries.

HANK'S RATING: A

Walter Reeves

Birthdate: April 9, 1964
College: Auburn
Height: 6-5
Weight: 244
How Acquired: Drafted in third round, 1987
Final 1990 Team: Phoenix Cardinals

BLOCKING

A tough, physical player who learned his craft at Auburn, where he honed his skills against numerous future NFL linebackers in the Southeastern Conference.

RECEIVING

Reeves caught his first NFL pass against the Cowboys in 1989, when he pulled in the ball in a fourth-and-three situation to preserve a late fourth-quarter Phoenix drive. Head coach Joe Bugel was impressed with Reeves, who caught 18 passes for 126 yards in 1990.

SUMMARY

Reeves made considerable progress under Bugel's new offensive scheme. Scouts believe he could mature into Top 10 material in 1991, and will certainly be used more in goal-line situations.

HANK'S RATING: B

Clarence Kay

Birthdate: July 30, 1961
College: Georgia
Height: 6-2
Weight: 237
How Acquired: Drafted in seventh round, 1984
Final 1990 Team: Denver Broncos

BLOCKING

Each season, Clarence Kay's physique gets a little worse and his blocking skills decline a little more. In his prime, during the mid-1980s, Kay was a capable blocker. In recent years, however, Kay has been used almost exclusively in passing situations. "When Kay is asked to block," says a scout, "he does more pushing and shoving than blocking. His technique is terrible."

RECEIVING

Kay's receiving production in 1990 was hardly star quality: 29 catches, 282 yards, no touchdowns. "We have to get more production out of the tight end position," says head coach Dan Reeves. Kay is a naturally gifted receiver, but doesn't work at his trade.

SUMMARY

Kay has been troubled by numerous off-the-field problems that have scouts doubting his dedication and work habits. If he can't put these problems behind him, his future is limited. Reeves is merely waiting for a capable replacement for Kay, which is too bad—Kay was once considered among the league's brightest prospects.

HANK'S RATING: B

Who's Missing

James Thornton

Birthdate: February 8, 1965
College: Cal State-Fullerton
Height: 6-2
Weight: 242
How Acquired: Drafted in fourth round, 1988
Final 1990 Team: Chicago Bears

James Thornton is an accomplished body-mover. His blocking and impressive physique (he gets our vote for having the best "guns" of any tight end in the NFL) made him a Mike Ditka favorite since he entered the league in 1988. An improving player, Thornton caught 19 passes for 254 yards, a 13.4 yards per catch average. In the playoffs against New Orleans, quarterback Mike Tomczak connected with Thornton on an 18-yard touchdown that iced the game. In the past, Thornton hasn't fulfilled his potential as a receiver or learned to match his brawn with brains. An excellent tight end athlete, this could be the year Thornton finally fulfills his potential.

HANK'S RATING: A

Don Warren

Birthdate: May 5, 1956
College: San Diego State
Height: 6-4
Weight: 242
How Acquired: Drafted in fourth round, 1979
Final 1990 Team: Washington Redskins

Don Warren is a veteran tight end with crafty skills and football knowledge that make him one of the NFL's savviest players. But age has taken its toll, and his 1990 stats reflect it: 15 catches, 123 yards. But despite his age, Warren is still one of the Redskins' more dependable blockers. Some scouts question whether his blocking will be enough to keep him on the team this year.

HANK'S RATING: B

Bob Mrosko

Birthdate: November 13, 1965
College: Penn State
Height: 6-5
Weight: 270
How Acquired: Trade, 1990
Final 1990 Team: New York Giants

Bob Mrosko is a young, talented tight end whose best football is still ahead of him. He was an understudy in 1990 to Bavaro and Howard Cross, but has a chance to stand out in the Giants big-back attack. Mrosko is a hard-working football player who is a leader on and off the field. In a very limited role, he managed to catch 3 passes for 27 yards and 1 touchdown. And he has proven to be a strong run blocker!

HANK'S RATING: B

Gary Wilkins

Birthdate: November 23, 1963
College: Georgia Tech
Height: 6-2
Weight: 235
How Acquired: Free Agent, 1989
Final 1990 Team: Atlanta Falcons

Gary Wilkins was one of the Falcons' most pleasant surprises in 1990. Despite Atlanta's reliance on the four-receiver Red Gun offense, Wilkins shined in running situations, and managed to catch 12 balls for 175 yards and 2 touchdowns. He averaged 14.6 yards per catch. Atlanta will use even fewer tight end formations in 1991, but when they do, Wilkins has proven himself as more than capable.

HANK'S RATING: C

Mark Boyer

Birthdate: September 16, 1962
College: USC
Height: 6-4
Weight: 252
How Acquired: Trade, 1990
Final 1990 Team: New York Jets

Mark Boyer came to the Jets in a trade with Indianapolis prior to the 1990 season, but performed capably under new Jets head coach Bruce Coslet, racking up 40 catches for 334 yards, a humble 8.4 yards per catch average. He scored just one touchdown. Boyer is not a reliable run blocker, limiting him to passing situations. Though he has been inconsistent, Boyer has the tools to become a third-down specialist.

HANK'S RATING: C

Ethan Horton

Birthdate: December 19, 1962
College: North Carolina
Height: 6-4
Weight: 240
How Acquired: Free Agent, 1989
Final 1990 Team: Los Angeles Raiders

After being out of football two of the previous four years, Ethan Horton responded to his last-chance offer from Al Davis with what many considered to be a Pro Bowl season in 1990. The former running back took well to his new position, catching 33 passes for 404 yards, a 12.2 yards per catch average. He scored 3 touchdowns. "Ethan played good, hard-nosed football," says head coach Art Shell. "When we called on him, he responded." The problem with Horton is he has not shown the ability needed to run block in the NFL.

HANK'S RATING: C

The Best of Plan B

Pete Holohan

Birthdate: July 25, 1959
College: Notre Dame
Height: 6-4
Weight: 232
Final 1990 Team: Los Angeles Rams

Pete Holohan has long been one of the league's finest pass-catching tight ends, and 1990 was no exception. He caught 49 balls for 475 yards and 2 touchdowns. While his yards per catch dropped off to 9.7, he still has a lot of football left in him. A smart receiver, Holohan knows how to get open. Kansas City, which has been deficient at the tight end position, will improve from his acquisition.

HANK'S RATING: A

Eric Sievers

Birthdate: November 9, 1957
College: Maryland
Height: 6-4
Weight: 238
Final 1990 Team: New England Patriots

Eric Sievers caught 8 passes in 1990 for 77 yards and failed to score a touchdown. Just three years ago, Sievers was considered an awesome talent by scouts, but has been bothered by injuries—he was limited to 3 receptions from 1986 through 1988. In 1989, his first year with the Patriots, he caught 54 passes, flashing the skills that had made him a star in San Diego. The Miami Dolphins are gambling that Sievers can stay healthy. If so, he could become a strong third-down contributor.

HANK'S RATING: B

Offensive Linemen

More than 140 linemen appear in the following section. For the sake of simplicity and identification, linemen are grouped together as a team unit, but critiqued individually. All players are subject to last-minute trades, cuts, or position changes. The names and positions are as of April 30, 1991.

Due to the enormous number of linemen and our limited amout of space, it is impossible to critique every one. However, this list represents each team's best at each position. If a position is left uncovered, it means either a) the player who held that spot was waived, b) the player was lost to Plan B, or c) the position is open for competition among current free agents, veterans, and draft picks.

Buffalo Bills

Will Wolford

Birthdate: May 18, 1964
College: Vanderbilt
Height: 6-5
Weight: 280
How Acquired: Drafted in first round, 1986
Position: Left Tackle

Will Wolford, one of Buffalo's two first-round picks in 1986, is capable of playing either tackle or guard, and has done so very capably in the past few seasons. A Pro Bowl alternate in 1990, he made the move from right guard to left tackle in 1987, and started three games at left tackle that season. He started all sixteen games as a rookie in 1986. Wolford has suffered few serious injuries, but has shown a willingness to play through them. Pro Bowl potential.

HANK'S RATING: AA

Jim Ritcher

Birthdate: May 21, 1958
College: North Carolina State
Height: 6-3
Weight: 265
How Acquired: Drafted in first round, 1980
Position: Left Guard

Jim Ritcher played in fourteen of sixteen games as a rookie in 1980, and since 1983, has started every game he's played in, missing just three games. Only Fred Smerlas (who was recently waived by San Francisco) have played more games for the club among active players. He began his career at left guard, after being one of the nation's most celebrated collegiate linemen at North Carolina State. A powerful, punishing drive blocker, Ritcher is also adequate in pass protection.

HANK'S RATING: A

Kent Hull

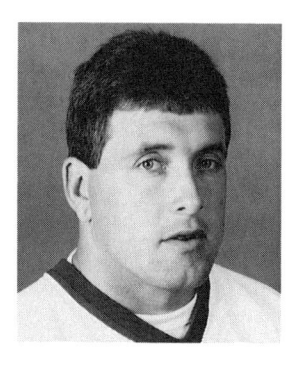

Birthdate: January 13, 1961
College: Mississippi State
Height: 6-4
Weight: 275
How Acquired: Free Agent, 1986
Position: Center

Kent Hull had a banner year in 1990, and was rewarded with his third starting berth in the Pro Bowl. And he made a statement for toughness: In his last eight pro seasons, he has yet to miss a start. Hull began his career in 1983 as a seventh-round draft pick with the New Jersey Generals of the defunct USFL, and never missed a snap in three years, despite nagging injuries. He has gained more than twenty pounds since coming to the Bills, and, in an emergency, could play virtually anywhere on the line. An outstanding all-around athlete, Hull grades out each year as the Bills best lineman.

HANK'S RATING: AA

John Davis

Birthdate: August 22, 1965
College: Georgia Tech
Height: 6-4
Weight: 310
How Acquired: Free Agent, 1989
Position: Right Guard

John Davis' Buffalo career began on a tough note: In a move that surprised some Buffalo assistants, Davis beat out several other drafted players to win the honor of replacing thirteen-year veteran standout Joe Devlin. Buffalo coaches like his work ethic, strength, and discipline. "For a man his size, he moves incredibly well," says director of personnel John Butler. "He's a big, rangy, physical player."

HANK'S RATING: A

Howard Ballard

Birthdate: November 3, 1963
College: Alabama A&M
Height: 6-6
Weight: 315
How Acquired: Drafted in eleventh round, 1987
Position: Right Tackle

Howard Ballard moved into the starting lineup full-time in 1989, and hasn't budged since. A long shot in the 1987 draft, this wide-body earned the respect of coaches through sheer power blocking. Ballard boasts good arm and upper body strength, and has truly blossomed as a pass protector in the last eighteen months. Ballard overcame sharp, undeserved criticism from quarterback Jim Kelly in 1989 when he missed a pass block that resulted in a sack. Kelly later apologized, and rightfully so: Some NFL observers consider the maturing tackle tandem of Ballard and Wolford as potentially the AFC's best.

HANK'S RATING: A

Cincinnati Bengals

Anthony Munoz

Birthdate: August 19, 1958
College: USC
Height: 6-6
Weight: 284
How Acquired: Drafted in first round, 1980
Position: Left Tackle

Anthony Munoz has been the standard of the consummate NFL offensive lineman from the time he became the Bengals number-one draft choice in 1980. Last year he played with the enthusiasm of a rookie, en route to being selected as a consensus All-Pro left tackle for the tenth consecutive time.

"Anthony doesn't blow guys off the line like he did when he first came here," says Bengals line coach Jim McNally, "but that is only because the game has changed. He doesn't dominate every play of every game like he did then, but he's still the best athlete I've ever been around. He could be a linebacker or a tight end." Munoz has three career touchdown receptions on the tackle eligible, including one that beat Cleveland in overtime. Still a powerful run blocker, Munoz is clearly the best.

HANK'S RATING: AAA

Bruce Reimers

Birthdate: September 18, 1960
College: Iowa State
Height: 6-7
Weight: 294
How Acquired: Drafted in eighth round, 1984
Position: Left Guard

Injuries hampered Bruce Reimers in 1990, forcing him to miss two regular season games before a sprained ankle knocked him out of the playoffs against the Raiders. Reimers is a quiet, hard-working, and usually durable player. He is versatile, can play both guard and tackle, and has helped the Bengals to lead the NFL in rushing in 1988 and 1989. "He's tough physically and tough mentally," says line coach McNally. "He's a good run blocker and a more than adequate pass blocker. He's got size and has a mean streak, and that I like."

HANK'S RATING: A

Bruce Kozerski

Birthdate: April 2, 1962
College: Holy Cross
Height: 6-4
Weight: 287
How Acquired: Drafted in ninth round, 1984
Position: Center

Bruce Kozerski is capable of playing any position on the offensive line, but won the center job in 1988 and has settled in with authority. McNally calls him "one of our keys . . . he makes dominating blocks, and his man spends a lot of time on the ground." Kozerski is a smart player with great technique, agility, and instincts. "He can play all positions," says McNally. "He's a quick, tough guy, he uses his head, and keeps us in the right line calls."

HANK'S RATING: A

Brian Blados

Birthdate: January 11, 1962
College: North Carolina
Height: 6-5
Weight: 296
How Acquired: Drafted in first round, 1984
Position: Right Guard

The Bengals were hoping that Brian Blados could fill in for the departed Max Montoya, who left for the Raiders. But the normally dependable Blados suffered a neck injury in 1990 and played in just four games. Like many of his talented offensive linemates, Blados has played all five positions on the line. Prior to the 1990 season, Blados cut his weight down to prepare for his new starting role. A competent player, Blados is made even better by his linemates.

HANK'S RATING: B

Joe Walter

Birthdate: June 18, 1963
College: Texas Tech
Height: 6-6
Weight: 290
How Acquired: Drafted in seventh round, 1985
Position: Right Tackle

Joe Walter returned to the starting lineup in 1990 after recovering from an operation on a torn anterior cruciate ligament and miniscus cartilage in his left knee suffered against the Washington Redskins in the 1988 season finale. He played in 1989 sooner than anticipated, but failed to return to form until last year. "I've worked hard," he says. "It's something I'm going to play with the rest of my life." Wyche likes Walter, saying that "he is an outstanding tackle." He has excellent strength, good balance, and his 48-inch arms give him great leverage over pass rushers like Reggie White. A very good pass blocker. "He can pass block forever," says McNally.

HANK'S RATING: AA

Cleveland Browns

Paul Farren

Birthdate: December 24, 1960
College: Boston University
Height: 6-6
Weight: 270
How Acquired: Drafted in twelfth round, 1983
Position: Left Tackle

Paul Farren started all sixteen games in 1990 after being a training camp holdout. The holdout might explain the inconsistency in his normally reliable play. But at times Farren was the lone bright spot of a unit that was the Browns Achilles' heel last season. In his career, Farren has started 91 games, while playing in 119. A durable lineman, he missed only part of a fourth quarter in 1990 with a knee injury against New Orleans. He beat the odds after being the 316th player selected in the 1983 draft.

HANK'S RATING: C

Ralph Tamm

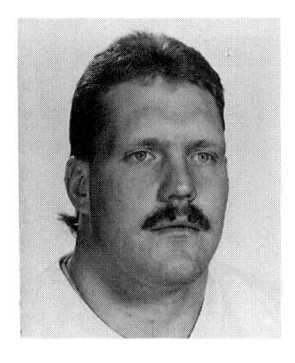

Birthdate: March 11, 1966
College: Westchester
Height: 6-4
Weight: 280
How Acquired: Plan B free agent, 1990
Position: Left Guard

Ralph Tamm was signed by the Browns as an unprotected free agent from the Washington Redskins, who, in 1989, also signed him unprotected from the New York Jets. A ninth-round draft pick in 1988, Tamm has been plagued by inconsistency and was repeatedly beaten for sacks in 1990. He can play both center and guard and is a deep snapper. In his defense, he is a hard worker, but possesses limited ability.

HANK'S RATING: D

Mike Baab

Birthdate: December 6, 1959
College: Texas
Height: 6-4
Weight: 275
How Acquired: Plan B free agent, 1990
Position: Center

Mike Baab did what he could to help the Browns suffering offensive line in 1990. As a unit, their play was so bad that one former Cleveland assistant said simply that "it's embarrassing lining up with these guys." But in a mediocrity-ridden situation, Baab's blue-collar work ethic was a motivating factor. He spent hours in the weight room and maintained his poise throughout the season.

In 1990, he wore an armband in every game in honor of his father Glenn, who was in the Texas National Guard airlifting provisions in Saudi Arabia during Operation Desert Storm. "I asked my dad what it was like to be in the war," Baab says. "He said it was just like football: Keep your head up, your butt down, and go like hell." A fifth-round draft pick in 1982, Baab played with Cleveland from 1982 to 1987 before being traded to New England. The Browns got him back when New England left him unprotected in 1990.

HANK'S RATING: B

Gregg Rakoczy

Birthdate: May 18, 1965
College: Miami
Height: 6-6
Weight: 290
How Acquired: Drafted in second round, 1987
Position: Right Guard

The highest draft pick among the Browns offensive linemen, Rakoczy started thirty-two straight games at center in 1988 and 1989, and was moved to right guard in 1990. He started the last twelve games at right guard. A toughnosed, aggressive player, he was ejected against Houston for fighting with the Oilers Glenn Montgomery. He has started forty-four games and played in sixty. At his best he is an average pass blocker and a sufficient run blocker. The problem is he often performs below that level, which makes it tough for the offense to establish consistency.

HANK'S RATING: D

Tony Jones

Birthdate: May 24, 1966
College: Western Carolina
Height: 6-5
Weight: 290
How Acquired: Free Agent, 1988
Position: Right Tackle

Nicknamed T-Bone, Tony Jones started all sixteen games at right tackle. The new coaching regime believes Jones may be the Browns best offensive lineman. Jones started the final three games and both playoff games in 1989 before moving in as a full-time starter last season. He has nineteen career starts and twenty-eight games played, and took over the right tackle spot after Cody Risien shocked the Browns with his sudden retirement. A talented young player, Jones could mature into a promising lineman *if* he works hard enough. So far he hasn't consistently done that.

HANK'S RATING: C

Denver Broncos

Doug Widell

Birthdate: September 23, 1966
College: Boston College
Height: 6-4
Weight: 287
How Acquired: Drafted in second round, 1989
Position: Left Guard

Doug Widell moved into the Denver starting lineup full-time in 1990, and quickly established himself as a budding star. Widell has excellent size and strength, and is a powerful drive blocker who continues to make great strides as a pass protector. A consistent and aggressive player who is very difficult to knock off his feet, Widell displays fine balance, but only average foot speed, for a player his size.

HANK'S RATING: B

Keith Kartz

Birthdate: May 5, 1963
College: California
Height: 6-4
Weight: 270
How Acquired: Free Agent, 1987
Position: Center

After joining the team as a free agent in 1987, Keith Kartz quickly built a reputation as a powerful drive blocker, with quick feet and long arms. He settled into a starting position in 1988, and since has proven himself as a reliable, hard-working player. Kartz possesses great strength at the point of attack.

HANK'S RATING: A

Jim Juriga

Birthdate: September 12, 1964
College: Illinois
Height: 6-6
Weight: 275
How Acquired: Drafted in fourth round, 1986
Position: Left Guard

Jim Juriga saw his first regular season action as a professional in 1988, starting the first twelve games at left tackle and the next three at right guard. He moved into a full-time starting position in 1989 after impressing Denver coaches with his outstanding pass blocking abilities. Though he lacks the physical standards to dominate opponents outright, Juriga is a skilled, versatile player.

HANK'S RATING: B

Ken Lanier

Birthdate: July 8, 1959
College: Florida State
Height: 6-3
Weight: 290
How Acquired: Drafted in fifth round, 1981
Position: Right Tackle

Ken Lanier is the ironman of the Denver Broncos, seldom missing action due to injury. Lanier owns the longest active streak for consecutive starts. He is an extremely intelligent player with extraordinary quickness. He was named a full-time starter at right tackle in 1982 and has held the position ever since, and despite being slightly undersized, remains a pass-blocking force.

HANK'S RATING: A

Houston Oilers

David Williams

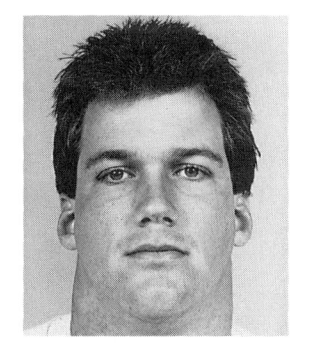

Birthdate: June 21, 1966
College: Florida
Height: 6-5
Weight: 292
How Acquired: Drafted in first round, 1989
Position: Left Tackle

Former Gator David Williams has taken a slower track to stardom than other linemen in his draft class, but he certainly has excellent mentors to learn from. Williams was considered by many scouts to be a bust during his 1989 rookie season in Houston, but came on in 1990 and had a consistent, if modest, sophomore season.

Williams is a powerful run blocker with tremendous size, but is still learning the footwork and lateral movement that he must have to play well in the run and shoot offense. "Pass pro has been his toughest problem," says a Houston assistant. "But David works hard, and he's getting there. He'll be a great player within another twelve to eighteen months." He's solid already, but with the likes of Matthews and Munchak next door, just being good still isn't enough.

HANK'S RATING: B

Don Maggs

Birthdate: November 1, 1961
College: Tulane
Height: 6-5
Weight: 285
How Acquired: Chosen in supplemental draft, 1984
Position: Left Guard

Don Maggs had one of the softest bodies ever seen among professional linemen, but credit Houston strength coach Steve Watterson for his unbelievable development in strength. Sources claim that Maggs, when he came to the Oilers from the USFL, "was so terrible in the weight room that nobody believed he'd been playing the last couple years." But Watterson, perhaps the league's best strength coach, put the baby-faced Maggs on a relentless strength and conditioning program, and presto, three years later, he's one of the NFL's strongest players.

Maggs still struggles when matched up alone with powerful straight-ahead pass rushers, but his lateral quickness has improved over the past three seasons. Despite his NFL tenure, Maggs is still relatively inexperienced, having become an every-down player just last season. He should continue to improve in 1991.

HANK'S RATING: A

Bruce Matthews

Birthdate: August 8, 1961
College: USC
Height: 6-5
Weight: 288
How Acquired: Drafted in first round, 1983
Position: Center

Bruce Matthews, along with teammate Mike Munchak, has long set a standard among AFC linemen for his play at guard. And when Houston was forced to play him often at center last year, nothing changed in the excellence department. In Houston's wide-open offense, he was a brilliant pass protector, and also tacked up numerous pancakes during run-blocking duties. Matthews is a leader on a team that didn't give up a sack in a six-game stretch in 1989. He's dirt strong, spends his offseason in the weight room, and works at his craft. Excellent blocking strength.

HANK'S RATING: AAA

Mike Munchak

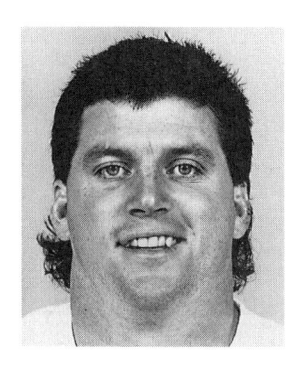

Birthdate: March 5, 1960
College: Penn State
Height: 6-3
Weight: 284
How Acquired: Drafted in first round, 1982
Position: Right Guard

Like partner Matthews, Mike Munchak has also spent years honing his trade—and it shows by his number of Pro Bowl appearances. "From a strength standpoint, Mike does everything right," says Houston strength coach Steve Watterson. "He understands his body, he knows how to deliver thrust and power, and he studies his opponents. In the weight room, he and Bruce [Matthews] set an example that few can follow."

HANK'S RATING: AAA

Dean Steinkuhler

Birthdate: January 27, 1961
College: Nebraska
Height: 6-3
Weight: 287
How Acquired: Drafted in first round, 1984
Position: Right Tackle

Dean Steinkuhler's greatest asset is consistency. Little is heard from the right side of the Houston line, and although Steinkuhler lacks the standout skills of linemates Matthews and Munchak, he is nonetheless a quiet, physical, talented performer. Weight is an occasional problem for Steinkuhler, but performance isn't: He works in the weight room, he works on the practice field, he works in games. He isn't error-free, but certainly solidifies the line of scrimmage for the Oilers.

HANK'S RATING: A

Indianapolis Colts

Zefross Moss

Birthdate: August 17, 1966
College: Alabama State
Height: 6-6
Weight: 361
How Acquired: Trade, 1989
Position: Left Tackle

Now in his third season with the Colts, Zefross Moss earned a starting job in 1990 after being largely just a special teams performer in 1989. He took an indirect route to the Colts, who obtained him from Dallas in 1989 for a tenth-round draft pick. A huge player, Moss interested the Colts coaches immediately, who believed that, with some technique and some weight loss, he could become a dominant NFL lineman. His 1990 performance couldn't be described as dominating. Though he is capable of controlling two players by himself, Moss doesn't do it very often. Scouts say that his feet must get quicker and that his upper body strength must improve. Until Moss makes these adjustments, he'll be the weak link on this line.

HANK'S RATING: D

Randy Dixon

Birthdate: March 12, 1965
College: Pittsburgh
Height: 6-3
Weight: 302
How Acquired: Drafted in fourth round, 1987
Position: Left Guard

Randy Dixon had another solid season in 1990—starting fourteen games—after playing in every offensive snap for the Colts in 1989. But he held out of camp until September 12, three days after the opening loss at Buffalo. He went on to struggle often during the rest of the reason, greatly disappointing the coaching staff.

Dixon's run blocking ability makes him an asset on the run-oriented Colts, as he and left guard Zefross Moss give the left side of the line a combined weight of more than 600 pounds. A durable player with good strength.

HANK'S RATING: B

Ray Donaldson

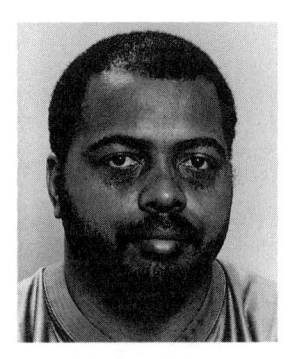

Birthdate: May 18, 1958
College: Georgia
Height: 6-3
Weight: 300
How Acquired: Drafted in second round, 1980
Position: Center

For the past three years, Ray Donaldson has started every Colts' game, and, as a perennial Pro Bowl performer, he enjoys a reputation as one of the finest centers in the NFL. Donaldson hasn't missed a game due to injury in his ten-year career and is an established team leader who truly drives the other offensive linemen. Colts coaches considered Donaldson as one of the primary reasons the team allowed the NFL's fourth-fewest sack total in 1989.

HANK'S RATING: A

Brian Baldinger

Birthdate: January 7, 1959
College: Duke
Height: 6-4
Weight: 278
How Acquired: Free Agent, 1988
Position: Right Guard

Considered the Colts' most versatile lineman, Brian Baldinger has played all five positions on the offensive line. In 1988, he proved his worth as a valuable backup player, then in 1989, he started three games while seeing significant action in all sixteen. More proof of his versatility occurred in 1988, when Baldinger lined up as a tackle eligible, and in a critical short-yardage situation, caught a 37-yard pass out of the wishbone formation. He is also a proven special-teams performer. Though Baldinger is the lightest of the Colts' linemen, he sees the most action.

HANK'S RATING: C

Kevin Call

Birthdate: November 13, 1961
College: Colorado State
Height: 6-7
Weight: 308
How Acquired: Drafted in fifth round, 1984
Position: Right Tackle

After Dixon's holdout, the Indianapolis offensive line was dealt another blow when veteran Kevin Call went down with a shoulder injury in the season's ninth week. Prior to 1990, Call was noted for being injury-prone, but had usually managed to ignore pain and play through serious injuries. His greatest asset is his pass blocking, and is instrumental in the Colts' passing game. Nicknamed "The Creature" due to his size, Call is a hard-working, tenacious player.

HANK'S RATING: B

Kansas City Chiefs

John Alt

Birthdate: May 30, 1962
College: Iowa
Height: 6-7
Weight: 300
How Acquired: Drafted in first round, 1984
Position: Left Tackle

Despite being hampered by injuries early in his career, John Alt has proven himself as a full-time player who can perform with consistency. A tight end as a college sophomore, Alt's excellent run blocking ability nudged Iowa coaches to move him to tackle, where he eventually grew into his new role. Alt is agile, quick, and intelligent; a consistent performer who gets the most out of his ability.

HANK'S RATING: AAA

Rich Baldinger

Birthdate: December 31, 1959
College: Wake Forest
Height: 6-4
Weight: 292
How Acquired: Free Agent, 1983
Position: Left Guard

Once considered among the Chiefs most versatile linemen, Rich Baldinger has seen action all over the Kansas City line during his Chiefs' tenure. As a critical cog in the team's grind-it-out approach, Baldinger reacted well to pressure from youngster Michael Harris, who played well but failed to take away Baldinger's job in 1990. He might have trouble holding off Harris for a second year.

HANK'S RATING: C

Tim Grunhard

Birthdate: May 27, 1968
College: Notre Dame
Height: 6-2
Weight: 292
How Acquired: Drafted in second round, 1990
Position: Center

It took a special player to move old veteran Mike Webster out of the Chiefs lineup, and that task fell to rookie Tim Grunhard in 1990. Grunhard obviously benefitted from working next to such a mentor, as his level of play radically improved over the course of the season. Like most young linemen, however, Grunhard needs more work on pass protection, but proved he can begin to control opponents in straight-ahead run blocking. A good player with the potential to improve.

HANK'S RATING: A

David Lutz

Birthdate: December 30, 1959
College: Georgia Tech
Height: 6-6
Weight: 303
How Acquired: Drafted in second round, 1983
Position: Right Guard

David Lutz made a smooth transition from tackle to guard in 1989, and his typical error-free, heady style of play matched well with head coach Marty Schottenheimer's philosophy. A prototype player for a run offense, Lutz plays all out every season, and has started more games than anybody on the Chiefs roster.

HANK'S RATING: B

Irv Eatman

Birthdate: January 1, 1961
College: UCLA
Height: 6-7
Weight: 298
How Acquired: Drafted in eighth round, 1983
Position: Right Tackle

Irv Eatman built a reputation in the defunct USFL destroying opposing linemen and crushing safeties, and he hasn't disappointed anybody since joining the Chiefs in 1985. Like Lutz, Eatman is a good run blocking lineman with quick feet and sound pass protection technique. A former collegiate defensive tackle, Eatman ranks among the tallest, fastest, quickest offensive linemen.

HANK'S RATING: B

Los Angeles Raiders

Rory Graves

Birthdate: July 21, 1963
College: Ohio State
Height: 6-6
Weight: 290
How Acquired: Free Agent, 1988
Position: Left Tackle

Another free-agent acquisition for the Raiders, Rory Graves, though not particularly agile, represents what the Raiders love in their offensive linemen: size, strength, and decent quickness. Surprisingly, Graves wasn't drafted out of college, before he signed as a free agent with the Seattle Seahawks in 1986. After a modest career in Seattle, Graves has flourished under the Raiders system.

HANK'S RATING: B

Max Montoya

Birthdate: May 12, 1956
College: UCLA
Height: 6-5
Weight: 280
How Acquired: Plan B free agent, 1990
Position: Left Guard

Two words best describe Max Montoya: mean and nasty. Behind Houston's Munchak and Matthews, Montoya is the third-best pass blocking guard in the NFL. While playing for Cincinnati in 1989, Montoya's opponents had only *hit* (not sacked) Esiason once in 237 attempts (scouts consider a ratio of one to twenty-five as excellent). Montoya is a good run blocker, although he is better at pass protecting, trapping, and making adjustments. A very smart player who has all the physical tools, too.

HANK'S RATING: AA

Don Mosebar

Birthdate: September 11, 1961
College: USC
Height: 6-6
Weight: 280
How Acquired: Drafted in first round, 1983
Position: Center

Don Mosebar, like Jim Otto before him, has played classic football in relative anonymity, despite being named to the 1990 Pro Bowl. Throughout his career, he's been consistent and versatile—playing every position along the line. Mosebar is a superb, mobile athlete who also does double-duty on special teams, despite his nine-year NFL tenure. Only the third starting center in Raider history, Mosebar has carried the torch with pride. His professional work ethic and personal discipline have been critical qualities on the Raiders improving offensive line.

HANK'S RATING: AA

Steve Wisniewski

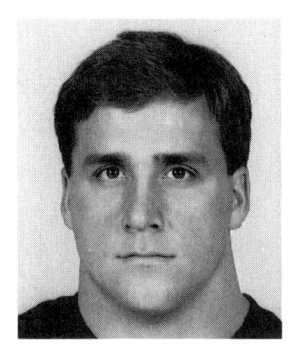

Birthdate: April 7, 1967
College: Penn State
Height: 6-4
Weight: 280
How Acquired: Drafted in second round, 1989
Position: Right Guard

The Raiders were high on Steve Wisniewski when they picked him in the 1989 draft, and thus far, he's lived up to expectations. Despite his basic run orientation at Penn State, Wisniewski has nonetheless excelled in pass protection. In 1989, despite being the youngest player on the Raiders roster at twenty-two, he had a brilliant rookie year, starting fifteen games. Solid skills with outstanding potential.

HANK'S RATING: AA

Steve Wright

Birthdate: April 8, 1959
College: Northern Iowa
Height: 6-6
Weight: 280
How Acquired: Free Agent, 1987
Position: Right Tackle

Steve Wright had a career season in 1990 as he experienced a rebirth under head coach Art Shell. Wright is a perfect fit in the Raiders' ball-control offense, able to wear down weaker defensive linemen on runing plays or stalemate them on passing plays. "Wright played the best football of his career last year," says a scout. "His pass pro can still use some work, but he's become a very impressive player in what they do."

HANK'S RATING: B

Miami Dolphins

Richmond Webb

Birthdate: January 11, 1967
College: Texas A&M
Height: 6-6
Weight: 291
How Acquired: Drafted in first round, 1990
Position: Left Tackle

Richmond Webb, in a performance that was hardly typical of a rookie offensive linemen, quickly became a key member of a Dolphin unit in 1990 that allowed an NFL low 16 sacks. He also wrote his name into the history books: Webb started next to another rookie, Keith Sims, making the tandem the first rookie draft choices ever to start in the season opener on the offensive line, and just the third and fourth rookie draft choices to start on opening day in the history of the Dolphins. In just his first season, Webb was selected as a backup lineman for the Pro Bowl, as he dominated many of his opponents. He picked up the passing game quickly, where his quick feet and agility made him an instant star. Barring injury, Webb should be a dominating player for many years.

HANK'S RATING: AA

Keith Sims

Birthdate: June 17, 1967
College: Iowa State
Height: 6-2
Weight: 310
How Acquired: Drafted in second round, 1990
Position: Left Guard

Like Webb, Keith Sims enjoyed a fine rookie year, despite an injury to his left knee that interrupted his stellar season. Although the injury required surgery, Sims missed just two weeks of action after undergoing arthroscopic surgery, and returned to play dominating football. And, unlike Webb, Sims displays versatility and is capable of playing guard, tackle, or center.

HANK'S RATING: AA

Jeff Uhlenhake

Birthdate: January 28, 1966
College: Ohio State
Height: 6-3
Weight: 282
How Acquired: Drafted in fifth round, 1989
Position: Center

Like his two new rookie partners in 1990, Jeff Uhlenhake was a rookie star himself for the Dolphins when he entered the league in 1989. He was the first rookie center to ever start for Miami, and played in all sixteen games. A durable, reliable player, Uhlenhake makes few mistakes and possesses great upper body strength. Primarily a run blocker in college, Uhlenhake has developed into a fine pass protector, but still has work to do in that area.

HANK'S RATING: A

Harry Galbreath

Birthdate: January 1, 1965
College: Tennessee
Height: 6-1
Weight: 275
How Acquired: Drafted in eighth round, 1988
Position: Right Guard

Harry Galbreath has been a steady performer since he entered the league in 1988, and once again started all sixteen regular season games in 1990. A versatile player, Galbreath's first nineteen career starts were at right guard, which also happened to coincide with quarterback Dan Marino's sackless streak. In the four previous games prior to Galbreath's starting assignment, the Dolphins gave up seven sacks, several of them through the right tackle spot. Johnny Majors, Galbreath's college coach, once called him "the best run blocker I've ever coached," which is another skill that Galbreath has brought with him to the Dolphins.

HANK'S RATING: A

Mark Dennis

Birthdate: April 15, 1965
College: Illinois
Height: 6-6
Weight: 290
How Acquired: Drafted in eighth round, 1987
Position: Right Tackle

There is no question the Dolphins will seek improvement at this position in 1991. Whether it will come from improving veteran Mark Dennis is the question. Dennis, while starting in all sixteen games in 1990, displayed good strength and speed, but lacked the dominating run-blocking skills that head coach Don Shula seeks. "We have to look at continuing to improve our running game and keep working to find that balance between pass and run," Shula says. A quick look at Miami's solid unit indicates that Dennis will have to work hard to maintain his position in 1991.

HANK'S RATING: C

New England Patriots

Bruce Armstrong

Birthdate: September 7, 1965
College: Louisville
Height: 6-4
Weight: 284
How Acquired: Drafted in first round, 1987
Position: Left Tackle

Bruce Armstrong has started in every game he's played as a Patriot since New England drafted him in 1987, when he was the first rookie to start on the club's offensive line since John Hannah in 1973. And in recent years, his play has been somewhat reminiscent of Hannah: After New England suffered what might have been the worst season ever experienced by an NFL franchise, Armstrong still made the Pro Bowl and drew rave reviews from his peers. A power drive blocker and agile pass protector, Armstrong is a bright, heady player. Coaches rave about his positive attitude, good work habits, and willingness to play with pain.

HANK'S RATING: AA

Sean Farrell

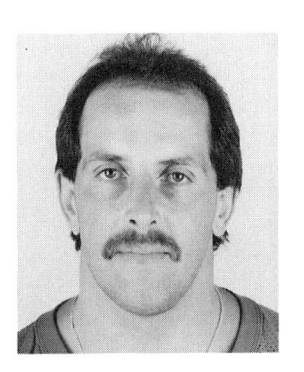

Birthdate: May 25, 1960
College: Penn State
Height: 6-3
Weight: 260
How Acquired: Trade, 1987
Position: Left Guard

Sean Farrell is an underrated player who exhibits tremendous ability when he stays healthy. He missed games in 1989 with a sprained ankle, in 1988 with a hamstring injury, and in 1987 with a shoulder injury. But it's not as if he isn't tough: In 1984, while playing with Tampa Bay, he played an entire game against Green Bay with an injured knee. After being the country's most decorated offensive lineman as a senior in 1981, Farrell has evolved into a workman-like pro lineman. He makes few errors and is a very reliable, effective player.

HANK'S RATING: AA

Danny Villa

Birthdate: September 21, 1964
College: Arizona State
Height: 6-5
Weight: 305
How Acquired: Drafted in fifth round, 1987
Position: Center

Danny Villa has started thirty out of the Patriots' past thirty-two games, missing but one outing in each of the past two years due to injury. A consistent player, Villa is a reliable, veteran performer, who is capable of playing guard, tackle or center, and is also adept as a long-snapper on special teams.

HANK'S RATING: A

Paul Fairchild

Birthdate: September 14, 1961
College: Kansas
Height: 6-4
Weight: 270
How Acquired: Drafted in fifth round, 1984
Position: Right Guard

A workman-like player, Paul Fairchild has given the Patriots a consistent performance since he moved into the starting lineup in 1986. Though not blessed with outstanding skills, Fairchild is a capable veteran, but should be challenged in camp.

HANK'S RATING: B

David Viaene

Birthdate: July 14, 1965
College: Minnesota-Duluth
Height: 6-5
Weight: 300
How Acquired: Plan B free agent, 1989
Position: Right Tackle

David Viaene came to the Patriots in 1990 as a Plan B signee from the Houston Oilers, and wound up as a starter on the right side of the Patriots' line. Viaene proved his versatility in college, where he played both center and defensive tackle. He spent his entire rookie season (1988) with the Oilers on injured reserve due to a back injury suffered in the preseason against Dallas. During the 1990 season with New England, Viaene showed signs of ability, but must work harder at pass protection if he expects to keep his position under the Pats' new regime.

HANK'S RATING: B

New York Jets

Dave Zawatson

Birthdate: April 13, 1966
College: California
Height: 6-5
Weight: 275
How Acquired: Plan B free agent, 1990
Position: Left Guard

Dave Zawatson, free agent signee, played adequately in 1990. Zawatson made few mistakes, but scouts question his speed and agility. Jets management will certainly hope to challenge him in training camp in 1991, however, as they seek a larger, more dominant player at this position.

HANK'S RATING: B

Jim Sweeney

Birthdate: August 8, 1962
College: Pittsburgh
Height: 6-4
Weight: 270
How Acquired: Drafted in second round, 1984
Position: Center

Jim Sweeney provided the veteran leadership along New York's makeshift, band-aid line during 1990, and was a primary reason the Jets finished fourth in the NFL in rushing with a 132.9 yards per game average. Sweeney delivered a consistent performance typical of his seven-year career, helping the Jets decrease their sacks allowed from an NFL-worst 62 in 1989 to just 40 in 1990. Sweeney still has several good years left in him, but management must provide additional help. "One problem we have right now," says GM Dick Steinberg, "is there aren't enough guys in the prime of their careers to build some solidity around. We're looking to the draft, the free agent market, and other avenues to help us. And we're not against trading, either."

HANK'S RATING: A

Dave Cadigan

Birthdate: April 6, 1965
College: USC
Height: 6-4
Weight: 280
How Acquired: Drafted in first round, 1988
Position: Right Guard

Dave Cadigan was lost during the fifth week in 1990 to a season-ending knee injury. Rookie Dwayne White, a seventh-round pick last year out of Alcorn State, started the last five games and played surprisingly well. At least one Jets' source believes White's development will push Cadigan from guard to tackle, especially since that position remains a severe team weakness. So far Cadigan hasn't played as well as you want a first rounder to play. Young and determined, but recovering from injury, Cardigan has to show he's not an overrated player, but the type of player that new head coach Bruce Coslet can build around.

HANK'S RATING: C

Ron Mattes

Birthdate: August 8, 1963
College: Virginia
Height: 6-6
Weight: 302
How Acquired: Trade, 1991
Position: Right Tackle

Ron Mattes, who lost his starting left tackle job in Seattle last year to rookie Andy Heck, moved to right tackle in 1990 to replace retiring starter Mike Wilson, and played capably if not spectacularly. Mattes was a starter for the Seahawks since his first season on the roster in 1986, and is a durable, but not dominating, player. He should provide instant help, however, to a patchwork Jets line.

HANK'S RATING: B

Pittsburgh Steelers

John Jackson

Birthdate: January 4, 1965
College: Eastern Kentucky
Height: 6-6
Weight: 288
How Acquired: Drafted in tenth round, 1988
Position: Left Tackle

The youngster of Pittsburgh's front five, John Jackson established himself in 1990 with tremendous improvement. Jackson started twelve games in 1989, then earned a full-time starting job last year. Coaches praised him for "growing into the position," and believe he has Pro Bowl potential. He was a large reason that sack numbers dramatically decreased to the left side of Pittsburgh's line.

HANK'S RATING: B

Dermontti Dawson

Birthdate: June 17, 1965
College: Kentucky
Height: 6-2
Weight: 275
How Acquired: Drafted in second round, 1988
Position: Center

After an inconsistent year in his first season as a starter in 1989, Dermontti Dawson followed with more of the same in 1990. But scouts feel Dawson has the tools to develop into a very good lineman. A good all-around athlete, Dawson offers Pittsburgh a solid combination of agility, mobility, and strength. He has played both guard and center, and, thanks to his quickness, excels in Pittsburgh's trapping system. If called on, Dawson is also a capable long-snapper on punts and placekicks.

HANK'S RATING: B

Terry Long

Birthdate: July 21, 1959
College: East Carolina
Height: 5-11
Weight: 275
How Acquired: Drafted in fourth round, 1984
Position: Right Guard

Terry Long is a crafty veteran who has overcome a lack of size to perform well in Pittsburgh's pulling and trapping schemes. Long possesses incredible hand, arm and upper body strength, and maintains an intense year-round training program. He has been the Steelers' regular starter at guard for more than six seasons, despite being the shortest lineman in the NFL.

HANK'S RATING: B

Tunch Ilkin

Birthdate: September 23, 1957
College: Indiana State
Height: 6-3
Weight: 266
How Acquired: Drafted in sixth round, 1980
Position: Right Tackle

A two-time Pro Bowl player, Tunch Ilkin is Pittsburgh's most solid lineman. The team's offensive captain, Ilkin is noted for his leadership, savvy experience, and reliability: He gives up an average of just one sack every eight games, and has the second-longest starting streak among active Steelers. A versatile player, Ilkin is also capable of lining up at tight end on short-yardage downs.

HANK'S RATING: A

San Diego Chargers

Frank Cornish

Birthdate: September 24, 1967
College: UCLA
Height: 6-4
Weight: 281
How Acquired: Drafted in sixth round, 1990
Position: Left Guard

A college center, Frank Cornish surprised San Diego with his rapid development last season by earning a starting job at left guard. Cornish is a physical, tough drive blocker with good strength and modest mobility. He ranks fourth in UCLA's notable weightlifting record book with a three-lift (bench, squat, and clean) total of 1,253 pounds. A dependable, productive player, Cornish started all sixteen games in 1990.

HANK'S RATING: A

Courtney Hall

Birthdate: August 26, 1968
College: Rice
Height: 6-1
Weight: 269
How Acquired: Drafted in second round, 1989
Position: Center

It took Dan Marino to debunk the myth that it takes five years for a quarterback to excel in the NFL. Then offensive lineman Courtney Hall proved again that experience isn't everything—there is something to be said for pure ability. Hall, the youngest player in the league at twenty-one, started every game two years ago as a rookie, and impressed some of the league's best critics. "Great quickness, quick hands, exceptional strength . . . he has the whole package," says the Raiders' Howie Long. Scouts compare Hall to former Miami center Dwight Stephenson, who, when healthy, was considered the league's best.

HANK'S RATING: AA

David Richards

Birthdate: April 11, 1966
College: UCLA
Height: 6-4
Weight: 310
How Acquired: Drafted in fourth round, 1988
Position: Right Guard

David Richards made the difficult switch from right tackle to right guard during the 1989 training camp, yet still started in all sixteen games. A huge, overpowering player, he has started and played in every NFL game since he was drafted in 1988. Like many of his teammates along the Chargers line, Richards has outstanding potential but is yet unproven against championship caliber opponents.

HANK'S RATING: B

Leo Goeas

Birthdate: August 15, 1966
College: Hawaii
Height: 6-4
Weight: 285
How Acquired: Drafted in third round, 1990
Position: Right Tackle

Leo Goeas started ten games in his rookie season and played with brilliant versatility, displaying explosive run blocking technique and impressive pass protection ability. San Diego scouts like his upper body strength against quicker pass rushers, and his ability to consistently run 5.0 in the 40. A promising young player.

HANK'S RATING: B

Seattle Seahawks

Andy Heck

Birthdate: January 1, 1967
College: Notre Dame
Height: 6-6
Weight: 291
How Acquired: Drafted in first round, 1989
Position: Left Tackle

After earning unanimous all-rookie honors from several news publications in 1989, Andy Heck turned in a solid sophomore year. Evidence of Heck's quick feet and athletic ability came in 1989 when he started the Cincinnati game at tight end. A proven run blocker in college, Heck matured last year as a pass protector.

HANK'S RATING: B

Edwin Bailey

Birthdate: May 15, 1959
College: South Carolina State
Height: 6-4
Weight: 273
How Acquired: Drafted in fifth round, 1981
Position: Left Guard

Edwin Bailey is certainly one thing: durable. He has been a starter at guard since his rookie year in 1981. He has played and started more games than any other offensive lineman in team history, and ranks sixth in starts and seventh in games played among all players. He has played both guard and tackle for the Seahawks, but is best at guard. An intelligent veteran, Bailey often relies on experience to dominate more skilled opponents.

HANK'S RATING: A

Grant Feasel

Birthdate: June 28, 1960
College: Abilene Christian
Height: 6-7
Weight: 279
How Acquired: Free Agent, 1987
Position: Center

Grant Feasel moved into the starting lineup two seasons ago and hasn't missed a play. A consistent, quiet player, Feasel is a strong, experienced lineman whose strength is run blocking. A former free agent, Feasel has missed few games due to injury, and along with teammate Edwin Bailey, provides the developing Seahawks with solid leadership.

HANK'S RATING: A

Bryan Millard

Birthdate: December 2, 1960
College: Texas
Height: 6-5
Weight: 281
How Acquired: Free Agent, 1984
Position: Right Guard

Bryan Millard joined the Seahawks after two solid seasons in the defunct USFL, and took over as a starter in 1986. Versatile, Millard has played every position on the line. A capable run blocker and pass protector, Millard gives a good account of himself.

HANK'S RATING: B

Atlanta Falcons

Mike Kenn

Birthdate: February 9, 1956
College: Michigan
Height: 6-7
Weight: 277
How Acquired: Drafted in first round, 1978
Position: Left Tackle

Perhaps one of the league's toughest tackles, Mike Kenn has missed just eight full games to injury during his thirteen years as a pro. A five-time Pro Bowl choice, Kenn has long set the standard for other Falcon linemen, even through the numerous mediocre seasons Atlanta has suffered. Kenn is a consummate professional linemen, equally capable of dominating at both run and pass blocking. Though age has slowed him, he still remains a vital link in the Falcon front.

HANK'S RATING: A

Houston Hoover

Birthdate: June 2, 1965
College: Jackson State
Height: 6-2
Weight: 290
How Acquired: Drafted in sixth round, 1988
Position: Left Guard

Houston Hoover was Atlanta's biggest surprise of the 1989 season, as the sixth-round draft pick moved into the starting lineup and earned praise from coaches and trainers alike. His rookie year, Hoover played with a bad knee, a bad ankle and a bad shoulder, yet refused to succumb to those injuries. His 1990 year was equally impressive, as he started eleven of sixteen games. Hoover is easily one of the league's strongest players: he routinely does twenty repetitions of squats with two-and-a-half times his body weight, and bench-presses more than 400 pounds.

HANK'S RATING: A

Jamie Dukes

Birthdate: June 14, 1964
College: Florida State
Height: 6-1
Weight: 285
How Acquired: Free Agent, 1986
Position: Center

Jamie Dukes, like Hoover, earned his starting job in 1989, as he overcame the "utility" role he played during his first three seasons with the team. "Jamie can be one heck of a center," says former Falcon legend Jeff Van Note. "A center needs leverage, and his big, long arms are an asset. He's light on his feet. He's a natural pass blocker." Dukes fit perfectly in the Falcons new pass-oriented Red Gun offense, and his skills should continue to thrive in the Glanville system.

HANK'S RATING: A

Bill Fralic

Birthdate: October 31, 1962
College: Pittsburgh
Height: 6-5
Weight: 280
How Acquired: Drafted in first round, 1985
Position: Right Guard

Bill Fralic comes out of the same mold as Anthony Munoz: big, strong, and an exceptional athlete. Touted in college as one of the best ever, Fralic hasn't disappointed anyone since joining the league seven years ago. This past season, Fralic was the anchor in the Falcons new Red Gun offense, serving as a perfect tutor to the team's youth infusion along the offensive line.

HANK'S RATING: AAA

Chris Hinton

Birthdate: July 31, 1961
College: Northwestern
Height: 6-4
Weight: 300
How Acquired: Trade, 1990
Position: Right Tackle

Chris Hinton earned his fifth consecutive Pro Bowl starting assignment in 1989 while a member of the Indianapolis Colts, but his production lagged in 1990 due to a nasty holdout after his trade to Atlanta. Hinton found himself in Glanville's doghouse early in the season, after his lackadaisical conditioning habits irked the coaching staff. But by midseason, Hinton was back to form: When he chooses, Hinton can control virtually any opponent he faces. Look for Hinton to prove he is one of the Top 5 tackles in the league.

HANK'S RATING: AA

Chicago Bears

Jimbo Covert

Birthdate: March 22, 1960
College: Pittsburgh
Height: 6-4
Weight: 278
How Acquired: Drafted in first round, 1983
Position: Left Tackle

Jimbo Covert earned an All-NFC second-team berth from UPI for his play in 1990, evidence that he had overcome injuries that hampered him in 1989. Covert fought off lower back problems most of the 1989 season, but still started the season's final six games, as well as two additional playoff games. A team leader, Covert has been the offensive captain since 1984, but injuries have marred an otherwise brilliant pro career. In the past five years, Covert has been troubled by back, shoulder, ankle, elbow, and knee injuries. But to his credit, he's played hurt. A durable, powerful lineman who can neutralize even the best pass rushers.

HANK'S RATING: AA

Mark Bortz

Birthdate: February 12, 1961
College: Iowa
Height: 6-6
Weight: 272
How Acquired: Drafted in eighth round, 1983
Position: Left Guard

Mark Bortz earned his second-consecutive selection as a Pro Bowl starter, as the talented left guard continued to improve in his seventh pro season. A defensive tackle in college, the Bears pegged him as an offensive lineman, and the athletic Bortz made the switch with relative ease. Bortz is a year-round weightlifter, and his game relies heavily on his power, quickness, and strength.

HANK'S RATING: A

Jay Hilgenberg

Birthdate: March 21, 1960
College: Iowa
Height: 6-3
Weight: 260
How Acquired: Free Agent, 1981
Position: Center

Add Jay Hilgenberg to taxes and death among the sure things you can count on in Chicago. Hilgenberg has played in more consecutive games than any player in Bears' history. And he's done more than play; "he's dominated," says head coach Mike Ditka. Hilgenberg, like San Francisco's Guy McIntyre, is not as big or as strong as many of his peers, but his opponents know to button their chinstraps. "He doesn't really have the size you look for and he's not the best athlete, but he's productive," says Ditka. "He gets it done on hard work, intelligence, technique, and competitiveness."

Hilgenberg plays every snap like it's his last, and that dedication has put him in the last six Pro Bowls.

HANK'S RATING: AA

Tom Thayer

Birthdate: August 16, 1961
College: Notre Dame
Height: 6-4
Weight: 270
How Acquired: Drafted in fourth round, 1982
Position: Right Guard

Tom Thayer has played in every game with the Bears in his last six seasons with the club. He posted a sterling season in 1989; Thayer didn't miss a play due to injury, and wasn't called for a holding penalty all season. A tremendously strong, physical player, Thayer is a vicious run blocker and a capable pass blocker.

HANK'S RATING: A

Keith Van Horne

Birthdate: November 6, 1957
College: USC
Height: 6-6
Weight: 283
How Acquired: Drafted in first round, 1981
Position: Right Tackle

Keith Van Horne has been a mainstay at right tackle for the Bears since 1981, missing just seven games since he joined the team. He has more career starts than any other Chicago player, and his pro tenure is earmarked by one accomplishment after another. In 1989, Van Horne turned heads when he played several weeks with a severely injured neck. In 1988, he earned a game ball by shutting out perennial All-Pro pass rusher Reggie White. Van Horne rises to the level of his competition, and when healthy, has few peers.

HANK'S RATING: A

Dallas Cowboys

Mark Tuinei

Birthdate: March 21, 1960
College: Hawaii
Height: 6-5
Weight: 286
How Acquired: Free Agent, 1983
Position: Left Tackle

Mark Tuinei is a talented tackle whose two greatest assets are size and strength. On occasion, Tuinei has lacked mental concentration, jumping offsides in critical situations and committing holding penalties at the worst times. But head coach Jimmy Johnson has shown much faith in Tuinei, and Tuinei has produced. Though short of the Top 10, Tuinei is a consistent, reliable player. Scouts credit much of his staying power to run blocking and balance, the finer points of Tuinei's game.

HANK'S RATING: AA

Mark Stepnoski

Birthdate: January 20, 1967
College: Pittsburgh
Height: 6-2
Weight: 269
How Acquired: Drafted in third round, 1989
Position: Left Guard

A giant man with a baby face, Mark Stepnoski is one of the Cowboys most productive young linemen. A powerful player, Stepnoski bench-presses 500 pounds and squats 600 pounds. But despite his strength, "Mark takes a very cerebral approach to the game," says Bill Meyers, Stepnoski's collegiate position coach. "He's a thinking player." Stepnoski has shown marked improvement during his short tenure in the NFL. "We're very pleased with his progress," says Dallas head coach Jimmy Johnson. Has a chance to make a real mark in the NFL.

HANK'S RATING: AA

Nate Newton

Birthdate: December 20, 1961
College: Florida A&M
Height: 6-3
Weight: 318
How Acquired: Free Agent, 1986
Position: Right Tackle

The largest and certainly strongest of the Dallas linemen, Nate Newton, if he controls his weight, has the chance to become a superstar NFL player. A dominating run blocker, Newton possesses quick feet, quick hands, and superior upper body strength, and his explosion off the snap is rivaled by few. Newton also brings a tremendous will to win to the game.

"Newton is among the most competitive linemen we see all year," says an opposing scout. "He really works hard, and if he gets his hands on you, you can kiss your butt goodbye. If Newton would work harder, we're convinced he could be one of the league's top two or three tackles." There is talk Newton may be moved to guard for the 1991 season.

HANK'S RATING: AA

Detroit Lions

Lomas Brown

Birthdate: March 30, 1963
College: Florida
Height: 6-4
Weight: 287
How Acquired: Drafted in first round, 1985
Position: Left Tackle

Lomas Brown, long considered a Pro Bowl-caliber player, finally got the votes in 1990 to go with his reputation. "Lomas always had the ability to be an All-Pro," says head coach Wayne Fontes. "And he finally started playing like an All-Pro. Lomas knows he has to work harder in the offseason, and he's doing that." Brown has long, powerful arms, quick feet, and excellent upper body strength.

HANK'S RATING: A

Eric Andolsek

Birthdate: August 22, 1966
College: LSU
Height: 6-2
Weight: 286
How Acquired: Drafted in fifth round, 1988
Position: Left Guard

Eric Andolsek wrote himself into NFL history in 1990 when he pancaked Chicago defensive tackle William Perry, a feat once considered impossible. In just his third year, Andolsek blossomed into one of the league's best young linemen with a brilliant 1990 season. "Eric is a young, tough, enthusiastic player who is continuing to learn and improve," says Fontes.

HANK'S RATING: A

Kevin Glover

Birthdate: June 17, 1963
College: Maryland
Height: 6-2
Weight: 282
How Acquired: Drafted in second round, 1985
Position: Center

Kevin Glover turned in another dependable, if not flashy, season in 1990. "Kevin must continue to improve for us to be a better football team," Fontes says. Glover is capable of playing both guard and center and possesses above-average skills, but scouts still criticize his base technique and pass blocking.

HANK'S RATING: A

Mike Utley

Birthdate: December 20, 1965
College: Washington State
Height: 6-6

Weight: 279
How Acquired: Drafted in third round, 1989
Position: Right Guard

Mike Utley joined the Lions with lots of promise in 1989, but missed most of the season due to a knee injury. He returned in 1990, however, and displayed flashes of talent that excited Detroit brass. "Mike is a giant who needs to work hard," says Fontes. "He can play both guard and tackle, which gives us some flexibility." Some scouts question whether he has the strength to excel at his position.

HANK'S RATING: D

Harvey Salem

Birthdate: January 15, 1961
College: California
Height: 6-6
Weight: 289
How Acquired: Trade, 1986
Position: Right Tackle

Lions coaches credit Harvey Salem with being the team's most consistent linemen. "He's strong, an excellent pass blocker, and a smart player who makes excellent adjustments," says Fontes. "I think Harvey is on the verge of something. He's happy with our program and he is confident we can become winners." But scouts from other teams still consider Salem a just-above-average pass protector and an average run blocker. They also point to his attitude, which hasn't always been good—sometimes giving less than a consistent effort. But in the Lions run-and-shoot offense, Salem's experience and technique make him a valuable player.

HANK'S RATING: A

Green Bay Packers

Ken Ruettgers

Birthdate: August 20, 1962
College: USC
Height: 6-5
Weight: 280
How Acquired: Drafted in first round, 1985
Position: Left Tackle

Ken Ruettgers is noted among Packer linemen for spending hours on end in the film room and weight room in "the relentless pursuit of perfection," according to Packer officials. "Ken had an outstanding year as a pass protector," says offensive line coach Charlie Davis. "He is getting to a point where he's ready to move into the upper echelon of the NFL's offensive linemen." Ruettgers is a very intelligent player who excels through hard work. His hard work could move him into the Top 20.

HANK'S RATING: A

Rich Moran

Birthdate: March 19, 1962
College: San Diego State
Height: 6-2
Weight: 275
How Acquired: Drafted in third round, 1985
Position: Left Guard

Rich Moran has impressed Packer coaches with his consistency, both in practice and in games. Moran runs extremely well, and is an excellent trap- and pull-blocker. "When Rich gets into the game, he can let himself go," says line coach Charlie Davis. "He prepares so well that he doesn't have to involve himself in a lot of thinking during the game. He really studies hard, to the point that he's a pain in the butt because he asks so many questions."

HANK'S RATING: A

Blair Bush

Birthdate: November 25, 1956
College: Washington
Height: 6-3
Weight: 272
How Acquired: Plan B free agent, 1989
Position: Center

A conservative player who takes a very business-like approach to the game, Blair Bush gave the Packers everything they wanted when they plucked him off the Plan B list in 1989: stability, leadership, and execution, three things that helped settle down Green Bay's younger players. Now in his fourteenth year, Bush is no longer the physical run blocker he once was, but survives on skill and experience.

HANK'S RATING: A

Ron Hallstrom

Birthdate: June 11, 1959
College: Iowa
Height: 6-6
Weight: 290
How Acquired: Drafted in first round, 1982
Position: Right Guard

The Packers incumbent offensive captain, Ron Hallstrom has built a reputation of being a conscientious, steady performer, who takes the time to carefully learn every facet of his responsibilities. Hallstrom has played every position in the offensive line during his nine-year career, and hasn't missed a game since his rookie year in 1982. A solid Top 20 guard.

HANK'S RATING: A

Tony Mandarich

Birthdate: September 23, 1966
College: Michigan State
Height: 6-5
Weight: 300
How Acquired: Drafted in first round, 1989
Position: Right Tackle

Tony Mandarich is a mystery to NFL scouts, who were awed when the former Michigan State product ran the 40 in 4.65 and bench-pressed 545 pounds prior to the 1989 draft. Mandarich denies having ever used steroids, yet his weight has declined nearly thirty pounds since he left college and Green Bay sources report his strength has declined, too. "We've got to expect more out of Mandarich, and I'm sure he does of himself," says head coach Lindy Infante. To his credit, Mandarich is one of the hardest-working players on the team: He lives in Green Bay and spends his offseason in the weight room. "There are no more excuses now," Mandarich says. "It's time to play." We agree. It is now time to see if Mandarich has the toughness needed to move up in the NFL.

HANK'S RATING: C

Los Angeles Rams

Irv Pankey

Birthdate: February 15, 1958
College: Penn State
Height: 6-5
Weight: 295
How Acquired: Drafted in second round, 1980
Position: Left Tackle

Like several other Ram starters, Irv Pankey's greatest foe is age. Now entering his eleventh pro season, Pankey has made a living from being one of the game's most dominant run blockers for nearly a decade, but the passing of time is slowly eroding his most outstanding skills: quickness and power. "Pankey still gets off the ball like a young man," head coach John Robinson said at one point in 1990, but fact is that the lineman was stalemated on occasion and he's simply losing the dominant edge that had so long been his credo.

Scouts say Pankey is still a physical challenge whose strength and experience present problems. But Pankey can't play forever, so the Rams must start grooming his replacement immediately, for when he goes, a gaping hole will be left behind.

HANK'S RATING: A

Tom Newberry

Birthdate: December 20, 1962
College: Wisconsin-Lacrosse
Height: 6-2
Weight: 285
How Acquired: Drafted in second round, 1986
Position: Left Guard

Next to Jackie Slater, Tom Newberry is probably the Rams' best lineman, but newcomer Gerald Perry may push him in 1991 for that honor. Newberry is a touch short, but has all the other skills: size, speed, and, say scouts, "a streak of meanness that can cause a guy serious problems. The more physical a game gets, the more Newberry seems to enjoy it. He's one guy who you'll never physically intimidate."

Though Newberry struggles occasionally when faced with a speed pass rusher, Rams coaches say 1991 could be his finest season. "He's come along very well in his first five years," says a former Los Angeles assistant. "He's a steady guy. But I'm told that many of the coaches are convinced he still hasn't reached his potential. If he really busts his butt, he's got a chance to be a great, great player. Adding Gerald Perry will really help him, and Slater, too."

HANK'S RATING: AA

Doug Smith

Birthdate: November 25, 1956
College: Bowling Green
Height: 6-3
Weight: 272
How Acquired: Free Agent, 1978
Position: Center

Few free agents end up being the cornerstone of one of the premier run-blocking lines in professional football, but that's what happened to Doug Smith. Now in his fourteenth season, Smith has long been a quiet and damn-near-perfect technician in the middle of the Rams line. But Father Time is slowly chipping away at the Los Angeles offensive front, and despite consistency, Smith may find himself fighting for his job in the near future.

Good upper body strength, power, and intelligence have kept Smith's L.A. tenure intact. Few mistakes, few sacks allowed, and even fewer missed blocks in the running game make him a consummate pro. And attitude, too, is another Smith asset: Head coach John Robinson once said that "Smith brings his lunchbox ... he's just a determined guy who is very, very consistent in his level of play."

HANK'S RATING: A

Gerald Perry

Birthdate: November 12, 1964
College: Southern University
Height: 6-6
Weight: 305
How Acquired: Trade, 1991
Position: Right Guard

Gerald Perry, after a 1990 season in which he was clearly the Broncos best offensive lineman, sought a change of atmosphere and a new environment after several off-the-field incidents put him under intense media scrutiny. Unfortunate for the Broncos, yes, but an outstanding stroke of luck for the Los Angeles Rams.

One NFC Central scout calls Perry "one of the best pulling guards in the business," citing Perry's size, quick feet, and great burst as "uncoachable" attributes. "He's a very powerful man," the scout says. "He can pull, he can run, he moves side to side very well, and he's a big man. In the right package, he's a consistent All-Pro caliber player." Perry must, however, improve his work ethic and off-the-field behavior before he earns the league-wide respect—and peace of mind—that he so dearly covets.

HANK'S RATING: A

Jackie Slater

Birthdate: May 27, 1954
College: Jackson State
Height: 6-4
Weight: 285
How Acquired: Drafted in third round, 1976
Position: Right Tackle

At 6-4, 285 pounds, Jackie Slater looks like the ideal offensive tackle; fans forget that he has maintained this remarkable size and quickness after fifteen years of battling in the trenches. Slater may be among the last of the dinosaurs, but his desire rivals that of any rookie. "He leads by example," says head coach John Robinson. "Some guys talk about leadership. Jackie is a leader." Has shown the great veteran consistency that many only dream about.

HANK'S RATING: AAA

Minnesota Vikings

Gary Zimmerman

Birthdate: December 13, 1961
College: Oregon
Height: 6-6
Weight: 277
How Acquired: Trade, 1986
Position: Left Tackle

A former Pro Bowler, Gary Zimmerman remains a picture of consistency on the Minnesota offensive line. Size, strength and outstanding technique are Zimmerman's qualities. "If you were to draw up the perfect offensive lineman, it'd be Zimmerman," says a scout.

Zimmerman built his reputation in the defunct USFL, where he was one of the trump cards held by the Los Angeles Express that made former Brigham Young quarterback Steve Young sign with the then-fledgling league.

"Zimmerman was the best offensive lineman in the draft that year, in my opinion," says Don Klosterman, formerly a general manager with the Rams and the USFL. "He is one of the best linemen in the game. He can run, he can think, he can overpower you, he can run around you, he can pull. Hell, he can do it all. He's still in the Top 20 linemen in the NFL."

HANK'S RATING: AA

Randall McDaniel

Birthdate: December 19, 1964
College: Arizona State
Height: 6-3
Weight: 268

How Acquired: Drafted in first round, 1988
Position: Left Guard

Randall McDaniel earned another Pro Bowl spot in 1990, and justifiably so: Since his rookie year, he has made his mark as one of the league's best guards. But his popularity in the media, according to Minnesota team sources, has often caused McDaniel's linemates to overachieve in virtual anonymity.

But in McDaniel's defense, all he's guilty of is great football. "McDaniel was a very good rookie, and that is a big reason he keeps going to the Pro Bowl," says an AFC defensive lineman. "He made a name for himself his rookie year. Since then, he's been terribly consistent, but nothing super. He pass blocks as well as anybody, but he could improve in the running game. He's good, but he's not their best player."

Sorry, but we have to disagree. McDaniel is the best "athlete" in the NFL amongst offensive linemen, and he gets our vote for the best guard in the league.

HANK'S RATING: AAA

Kirk Lowdermilk

Birthdate: April 10, 1963
College: Ohio State
Height: 6-3
Weight: 263
How Acquired: Drafted in third round, 1985
Position: Center

Head coach Jerry Burns doesn't spare praise when talking about Kirk Lowdermilk. "He's one of the top three or four centers in football," Burns says. "We're very fortunate to have a guy with his consistency snapping the football." Consistency is a good word to describe Lowdermilk—his play is virtually error-free. Though small by today's NFL standards, Lowdermilk is still a tremendously gifted, physically talented lineman. "Like a lot of other undersized centers, Lowdermilk uses position and leverage to control his man," says a scout. "There are better centers, but not many. This guy really works hard."

HANK'S RATING: A

Todd Kalis

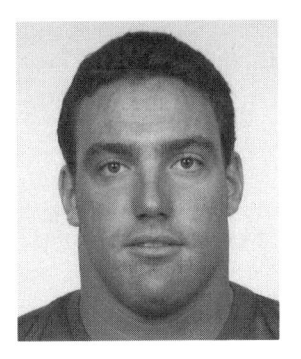

Birthdate: June 10, 1965
College: Arizona State
Height: 6-5
Weight: 269
How Acquired: Drafted in fourth round, 1988
Position: Right Guard

If you're checking the Minnesota newspapers, it's doubtful you'll read much about lineman Todd Kalis. But if you're reading the grading reports from the Minnesota coaching staff, you'll see his name pretty often: Since joining the Vikes as a fourth-round pick in 1988, Kalis has regularly graded out among the best Viking linemen, and for a two-year period, graded out as their best lineman. Yet Kalis, a unique physical specimen, continues to thrive despite his lack of attention.

But his efforts aren't lost on opponents: Against the Raiders last year, he pancaked Howie Long; against Chicago, he easily handled William Perry and the rest of Chicago's media darlings on the Bears defensive line. "I really don't care about publicity, or awards, or anything else like that," Kalis says. "I care about winning, about doing my job, about being the best player I can be. The cream always rises." With continued improvement, Kalis will move up in our rankings.

HANK'S RATING: B

Tim Irwin

Birthdate: December 13, 1958
College: Tennessee

Height: 6-6
Weight: 289
How Acquired: Drafted in third round, 1981
Position: Right Tackle

Right tackle Tim Irwin has been a solid, consistent performer for the Vikings for several years, but now in his eleventh year, he will be tested in 1991 to hold on to his starting job. Irwin is a tall, physically blessed athlete who has long been noted for his versatility and range: long arms, good instincts, and great judgement have helped him overcome a lack of dominating physical skills. But time has taken its toll, and Irwin faces an uphill battle in the coming seasons as he moves into the latter stages of his career.

"I'm concerned about this position," says head coach Jerry Burns. "We have nobody, really, behind Gary Zimmerman and Tim Irwin. But Irwin is a really durable, good football player. But he can't play forever, and I hate to think about what might happen if he goes down. Our priority is to find some more young, backup strength on the offensive line."

HANK'S RATING: B

New Orleans Saints

Kevin Haverdink

Birthdate: October 20, 1965
College: Western Michigan
Height: 6-5
Weight: 285
How Acquired: Drafted in fifth round, 1989
Position: Left Tackle

Originally recruited by colleges as a defensive lineman, Kevin Haverdink became an offensive lineman during his freshman year at Western Michigan, but kept his defensive mentality. The result is an offensive lineman with good straight-ahead quickness and speed; Haverdink is capable of running a sub-5.0 40. Haverdink also has to be one of the greatest physical stories of the league: Intense weight training in college evolved him from a 195-pound freshman to his current 285 pounds. A solid, strong drive blocker, Haverdink must improve his pass protection. He missed parts of three games with a nagging knee injury in 1990, but coaches say he'll be 100 percent by training camp.

HANK'S RATING: C

Jim Dombrowski

Birthdate: October 19, 1963
College: Virginia
Height: 6-5
Weight: 298
How Acquired: Drafted in first round, 1986
Position: Left Guard

Jim Dombrowski became serious about his craft in 1988, when a rigorous off-season conditioning program helped him drop ten pounds and increased his strength and stamina. Dombrowski didn't miss a down in 1990, and played exceptional run football. Possesses quick feet for his size, and has good upper body strength, as well as excellent explosion at the point of attack.

HANK'S RATING: A

Joel Hilgenberg

Birthdate: July 10, 1962
College: Iowa
Height: 6-2
Weight: 252
How Acquired: Drafted in fourth round, 1984
Position: Center

Like Dombrowski, Joel Hilgenberg also played every down in 1990, and played near error-free football. Though somewhat small for an NFL lineman, Hilgenberg draws praise from scouts for his near-perfect technique. A reliable player, Hilgenberg plays hurt, motivates the younger players, and can be counted on for critical blocks in key situations. Hilgenberg is also a veteran long-snapper, a craft he mastered during his four-year college career, where he never botched a long snap.

HANK'S RATING: A

Steve Trapilo

Birthdate: September 20, 1964
College: Boston College
Height: 6-5
Weight: 281
How Acquired: Drafted in fourth round, 1987
Position: Right Guard

Steve Trapilo was in on every offensive play in 1990 for his second consecutive year, evidence of his toughness and reliability. Trapilo set the tone for his career during his rookie year in 1987, when he started every game he was healthy for. A player with NFL size, speed and power, Trapilo has all the skills, but must stay healthy. His career has been plagued by nagging injuries, though few have kept him out of the lineup.

HANK'S RATING: A

Stan Brock

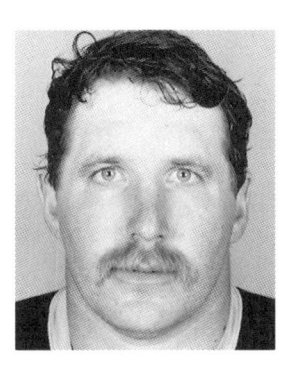

Birthdate: June 8, 1958
College: Colorado
Height: 6-6
Weight: 292
How Acquired: Drafted in first round, 1980
Position: Right Tackle

Considered one of the best pass blockers in the NFL, Stan Brock is a blue-collar veteran who is a master of his trade. Brock didn't miss a down in 1990, seldom makes mistakes, and is virtually error-free in pass situations. His run blocking could improve, but coaches say he consistently grades out among the highest of the Saints linemen. A solid Top 20 tackle.

HANK'S RATING: A

New York Giants

John Elliott

Birthdate: April 1, 1965
College: Michigan
Height: 6-7
Weight: 305
How Acquired: Drafted in second round, 1988
Position: Left Tackle

The humidity was so thick atop the damp Tampa Stadium grass during Super Bowl XXV in January that even reserve players standing calmly on the sidelines had broken into a steady sweat. Imagine, then, the exhaustion of Buffalo's vaunted pass rusher Bruce Smith, who was forced to line up across from the Giants' 305-pound tackle Jumbo Elliott all evening. By the fourth quarter, Smith was calling on all the reserve strength he could muster. Elliott pancaked Smith a half-dozen times, as well as several of his teammates. On a night when size, strength, and conditioning played the biggest role, Elliott outplayed everybody in the trenches. "Jumbo wore down every guy who lined up against him," says Giants head trainer Ronnie Barnes, "and he kept coming. That was what was so impressive. This guy's 300 pounds, and he never ran out of gas."

HANK'S RATING: AAA

William Roberts

Birthdate: August 5, 1962
College: Ohio State
Height: 6-5
Weight: 280
How Acquired: Drafted in first round, 1984
Position: Left Guard

William Roberts won his job during his rookie season, then missed his second season with what many believed was a career-ending knee injury. But Roberts proved himself as a dedicated and relentless worker when he battled his way back into the starting lineup his third year (1986), and has never looked back.

Roberts is a strong run and pass blocker, but excels most in man-to-man drive blocking situations. His weight fluctuates between 280 and 290, but as a freshman at Ohio State, he weighed just 240 pounds. After being plagued with injuries his first three seasons, Roberts has been relatively injury free in recent years and in the running game, plays with good consistency.

HANK'S RATING: B

Bart Oates

Birthdate: December 16, 1958
College: Brigham Young
Height: 6-3
Weight: 265
How Acquired: Free Agent, 1985
Position: Center

Bart Oates built his reputation with an outstanding career in the defunct USFL, where he was a two-time All-Pro player and helped the Philadelphia/Baltimore Stars win two league titles. His consistency has only improved since he joined the Giants in 1985, where he was a unanimous All-Rookie selection (1985) and ranks among the league's steadiest linemen.

Though slightly undersized, Oates makes up for it in hustle and discipline, and understands how to use his body to his advantage. Scouts say Oates has "tremendous strength for his size," according to one, "and is capable, just with intelligence, of kicking your ass all day long. You don't think he's blocking you effectively then you look at the film, and he's embarrassed you." A Top 10 center.

HANK'S RATING: A

Eric Moore

Birthdate: January 21, 1965
College: Indiana
Height: 6-5
Weight: 290
How Acquired: Drafted in first round, 1988
Position: Right Guard

Giants brass expected big things when they selected Eric Moore in 1988, and the former first-round pick hasn't disappointed. He earned a starting job in his second season, and went on to play strong football during last year's Super Bowl. If not for such outstanding linemates as Jumbo Elliott and Bart Oates, Moore might attract more recognition, but good line play in the land of Giants is virtually taken for granted.

Moore has nice quickness, and is a "very tough, very powerful player," says a scout. "With this guy, you're talking about scary size. When a man like Moore gets an angle on you, the best chance you have is to hope he doesn't kill you." Moore has good vision and awareness, and shows remarkable poise in the passing game. "He doesn't get frustrated," the scout says. "He works hard, does his job, doesn't get excited or mad. He's just a solid, even-keeled guy." Has a chance to make a mark in the NFL.

HANK'S RATING: B

Doug Reisenberg

Birthdate: July 22, 1965
College: California
Height: 6-5
Weight: 275
How Acquired: Drafted in sixth round, 1987
Position: Right Tackle

The Giants took Doug Reisenberg early in the sixth round in 1987 based on his potential. "When he was in college," says a scout, "you got the idea that nobody really knew how good he could be. He had some outstanding games, but he wasn't anything special. He wasn't a guy that you would risk in the first or second round. But since he's been with New York, he's really worked hard to become a contributing factor to their offense."

Indeed. Reisenberg is most effective as a power-thrusting run blocker, although he possesses average speed and quickness. In the passing game, he presents a huge and formidable obstacle. Though limited in pure ability, Reisenberg, like many of his linemates—thanks to New York strength coach Johnny Parker—has tremendous upper-body strength. Hard work and discipline round out his package of assets, as Reisenberg maintains a quiet, steady presence on the right side of the New York line.

HANK'S RATING: B

Philadelphia Eagles

Matt Darwin

Birthdate: March 11, 1963
College: Texas A&M
Height: 6-4
Weight: 275
How Acquired: Drafted in fourth round, 1986
Position: Left Tackle

Hampered by a knee injury in 1989, Matt Darwin returned from arthroscopic knee surgery in 1990 and despite physical limitations, played consistent football. At one time, Darwin was considered among the Eagles most reliable players, and was one of only two linemen to start every game in 1988. When Darwin is healthy, Philly running backs have averaged four yards a carry to his side of the line.

Darwin was once called "our most improved, consistent lineman" by departed head coach Buddy Ryan, but his development has tapered off due to injuries and general inconsistency by other positions on the rest of the offensive line. "In my opinion," says a scout, "Darwin is a better pass protector than run blocker. He doesn't have the speed and general movement he once had, but in pass pro, he still has the technique and strength to control you." Historically, pass protection has been Darwin's greatet strength: His entire senior year at Texas A&M, he didn't give up a single sack.

HANK'S RATING: B

Mike Schad

Birthdate: October 2, 1963
College: Queens College, Canada
Height: 6-5
Weight: 290
How Acquired: Plan B free agent, 1989
Position: Left Guard

Signed as a Plan B free agent from the Rams in 1989, Mike Schad was immediately penciled into the starting lineup and has lived up to expectations with a pair of fine seasons. A versatile player, Schad played defensive end, linebacker, and offensive tackle during his decorated collegiate career. The former first-round pick struggled during his tenure in Los Angeles, sitting behind All-Pro Tom Newberry and suffering several minor injuries. But scouts say his level of play has shown "sound development" since he became an Eagle, where he has stabilized the Philadelphia offensive line.

HANK'S RATING: B

David Alexander

Birthdate: July 28, 1964
College: Tulsa
Height: 6-3
Weight: 282
How Acquired: Drafted in fifth round, 1987
Position: Center

David Alexander's streak of forty-six straight regular-season starts is the longest among Eagle offensive linemen, and it doesn't appear things will change soon. Alexander is one of the very few linemen in the league to have started and played an entire pro game at each of the five line positions—and he also contributes as a long-snapper on both field goals and extra-point attempts. An outstanding all-around athlete, Alexander needs only to gain in overall strength to become a dominant player.

HANK'S RATING: A

Ron Solt

Birthdate: May 19, 1962
College: Maryland
Height: 6-3
Weight: 288
How Acquired: Trade, 1988
Position: Right Guard

Ron Solt came back from off-season knee surgery in 1989 and a month's suspension for testing positive for steroid use to become one of the Eagles' finest linemen. Some scouts believed the Solt trade was a bad decision when he developed tendonitis in both knees shortly after coming to Philadelphia. But the surgery was a success, giving Solt the chance to return to his Pro Bowl form of 1987. "One good thing to come out of it," says Solt, "is that in the past, I would rely on strength alone. But when my knees got bad, I learned to compensate, to become sharper mentally, and use more technique."

HANK'S RATING: A

Ron Heller

Birthdate: August 25, 1962
College: Penn State
Height: 6-6
Weight: 280
How Acquired: Trade, 1988
Position: Right Tackle

In 1989, Ron Heller's hustling, go-to-the-whistle style of play earned him team offensive MVP honors in a vote among Eagle players. And in 1990, Heller upped the tempo a little more. Heller is renowned around the NFL for his downfield blocking—he's always looking for someone to hit. While his run blocking could stand to be sharper, Heller pass protects with authority. He is an intelligent player who makes few mistakes.

HANK'S RATING: A

Phoenix Cardinals

Luis Sharpe

Birthdate: June 16, 1960
College: UCLA
Height: 6-4
Weight: 260
How Acquired: Drafted in first round, 1982
Position: Left Tackle

Long considered one of the NFL's finest pass blockers, Luis Sharpe is a thoroughbred tackle blessed with strength, quickness and intelligence. After being voted an alternate in 1983 and 1984, Sharpe earned a Pro Bowl invitation for three consecutive years (1987 to 89). But in 1990, he didn't use his "tools" enough to maintain his former status. Phoenix hopes this can be attributed to the preseason he missed due to a contract squabble. A durable player, Sharpe once played a string of forty-four games in sixteen months in 1984–85 after signing with the Memphis Showboats of the defunct USFL; he played sixteen games as a Cardinal in the fall of 1984, twelve games with Memphis in the spring of 1985, then re-signed with the Cardinals that fall and started sixteen more games.

HANK'S RATING: B

Derek Kennard

Birthdate: September 9, 1962
College: Nevada-Reno
Height: 6-3
Weight: 309
How Acquired: Chosen in supplemental draft, 1984
Position: Left Guard

Originally cast as an NFL guard, Derek Kennard wound up as the Cardinals center in 1987, then was shifted back to guard when Phoenix signed free agent center Bill Lewis in 1990. Kennard is a steady, reliable player who doesn't dominate opponents but does a capable job. He has battled weight problems throughout his career, and seems to perform best when tipping the scales around 300 pounds. Kennard played two seasons with the Los Angeles Express of the defunct USFL, where he played in twenty games.

HANK'S RATING: B

Bill Lewis

Birthdate: July 12, 1963
College: Nebraska
Height: 6-7
Weight: 265
How Acquired: Plan B free agent, 1990
Position: Center

Cardinals brass was thrilled in 1990 when the team was able to pluck former Raider starting center Bill Lewis off the Plan B list. Size and intelligence give Lewis an edge on the opposition, although his speed and strength are questionable. All in all a productive, consistent player. With Sharpe's problems, could be the Cardinal's best lineman.

HANK'S RATING: A

Lance Smith

Birthdate: November 1, 1963
College: LSU
Height: 6-2
Weight: 278
How Acquired: Drafted in third round, 1985
Position: Right Guard

The intensity of Lance Smith in the trenches has made him legend among his o-line teammates. A dependable player, Smith has started the last fifty-five games at right guard, after filling in at both guard and tackle early in his career. Smith overcomes his general lack of size with burning determination and fiery intensity, and has developed into a productive, though physically limited, NFL lineman.

HANK'S RATING: B

Tootie Robbins

Birthdate: June 2, 1958
College: East Carolina
Height: 6-5
Weight: 307
How Acquired: Drafted in fourth round, 1982
Position: Right Tackle

After a brilliant rookie season in 1982, Tootie Robbins has never realized his full potential, thanks to a host of minor injuries that have slowed his development. Though Robbins has yet to enjoy a full season without some type of injury. At one time, when healthy, he was capable of dominating the line of scrimmage.

HANK'S RATING: C

San Francisco 49ers

Bubba Paris

Birthdate: October 6, 1960
College: Michigan
Height: 6-6
Weight: 306
How Acquired: Drafted in second round, 1982
Position: Left Tackle

Bubba Paris is a huge, talented interior lineman who has had his best games against superior competition, but his weight—which has swollen to 350-pounds-plus in the offseason—could result in Paris being relegated to a backup role. Has had superb games at a modest weight (300), and has proven in the past that he can be a skilled, effective performer. But Paris' drop in production in recent years has disappointed coaches, and sources say 1991 training camp will be sink or swim for the rotund tackle.

HANK'S RATING: A

Bruce Collie

Birthdate: June 27, 1962
College: Texas Arlington
Height: 6-6
Weight: 275
How Acquired: Drafted in fifth round, 1985
Position: Left Guard

Bruce Collie has been a steady performer for the 49ers since he became a full-time starter in 1989. A large, powerfully strong man, Collie can play either guard or tackle. Collie is a quiet leader, often choosing to let his actions speak for him. He has also proven his worth as a valuable special teams performer. Could be ready to crack the Top 10.

HANK'S RATING: A

Jesse Sapolu

Birthdate: March 10, 1961
College: Hawaii
Height: 6-4
Weight: 260
How Acquired: Drafted in eleventh round, 1983
Position: Center

Though slightly undersized for his position, Jesse Sapolu brings strength, speed, and flexibility to the 49ers interior line. Sapolu has been effective at both guard and center since becoming a full-time player in 1987, and has evolved into a good position player despite a myriad of injury problems early in his career.

HANK'S RATING: A

Guy McIntyre

Birthdate: February 17, 1961
College: Georgia
Height: 6-3
Weight: 265
How Acquired: Drafted in fourth round, 1984
Position: Right Guard

Versatility alone should earn Guy McIntyre a spot among the NFL's top linemen. A legitimate right guard, McIntyre has been flip-flopped to left guard numerous times (reversing all his assignments) in his career due to injuries and assignments. "He is unbelievable," says George Siefert. "His ability to pull left or right is a rarity among linemen." McIntyre is not very large (6-3, 265 pounds) by o-line standards, but his heart may be the league's biggest.

HANK'S RATING: A

Harris Barton

Birthdate: April 19, 1964
College: North Carolina
Height: 6-4
Weight: 290
How Acquired: Drafted in first round, 1987
Position: Right Tackle

Though not the most gifted 49er lineman, Harris Barton may qualify as the team's most intense. A versatile, steady player, Barton openly exhibits a high level of emotion and effort on every snap, and ignores most injuries. He played twelve weeks in 1989 with a cast on his right hand, and played all of a game against Detroit in 1988 despite a severe ankle injury. "Harris is obsessed with bettering each previous performance," says head coach George Siefert. Continued improvement could mean a move into the Top 10.

HANK'S RATING: A

Tampa Bay Buccaneers

Paul Gruber

Birthdate: February 24, 1965
College: Wisconsin
Height: 6-5
Weight: 290
How Acquired: Drafted in first round, 1989
Position: Left Tackle

Referred to by Buccaneer officials as "Mr. Dependable," Paul Gruber has played every down during his three seasons with the Bucs. His consistent, often outstanding, 1990 season earned him numerous accolades from the print media, and he earned two game balls for his steady play—a rarity for an offensive lineman. At one point, Gruber went thirty-five games without a holding penalty, and in four games against rush specialists Richard Dent and Chris Doleman last year, he didn't give up a sack. Should be in the Top 5 for years to come.

HANK'S RATING: AAA

Randy Grimes

Birthdate: July 20, 1960
College: Baylor
Height: 6-4
Weight: 275
How Acquired: Drafted in second round, 1983
Position: Center

Randy Grimes had his streak of seventy-eight consecutive starts snapped against Detroit last year when a bicep injury kept him out of the game; it had been six years since reliable Grimes hadn't started for the Bucs. Grimes has started 117 games, which ties him for third in club history. A relatively light, quick player, Grimes is noted for his pass protection and modest run blocking abilities.

HANK'S RATING: A

Ian Beckles

Birthdate: July 20, 1967
College: Indiana
Height: 6-1
Weight: 295
How Acquired: Drafted in fifth round, 1990
Position: Right Guard

Ian Beckles surpassed even the highest hopes of the Tampa Bay coaching staff with his 1990 rookie season, starting sixteen games; fifteen at right guard one at tackle. A dominating run blocker during his college days at Indiana, Beckles quickly caught on to the pro passing game and played exceptional at times. He also demonstrated hustle after a Chris Chandler interception against San Diego, when he crushed Chargers safety Gill Byrd. An intelligent player (he is fluent in French and English), Beckles is expected to continue to improve.

HANK'S RATING: B

Washington Redskins

Jim Lachey

Birthdate: June 4, 1963
College: Ohio State
Height: 6-6
Weight: 290
How Acquired: Trade, 1988
Position: Left Tackle

Jim Lachey (6-6, 290 pounds) may be the league's most dominant lineman. This eight-year pro out of Ohio State simply dominates opponents, and has the physical tools to do it any way he likes. Lachey can lock up his man, matching pound for pound, or turn him, utilizing perfect technique, to completely take his man out of the play.

He also gets our vote for the most vicious hitter for a lineman. In 1989, Raider linebacker Jerry Robinson had just picked off a Mark Rypien pass and was headed for the opposite end zone when Lachey got off the ground (where he had pinned his man), ran forty yards crossfield, and simply crushed Robinson. Robinson, who was knocked completely unconscious, fumbled; Lachey recovered. "Maybe the best single play by an offensive lineman I've ever seen," says CBS analyst John Madden.

HANK'S RATING: AAA

Raleigh McKenzie

Birthdate: February 8, 1963
College: Tennessee
Height: 6-2
Weight: 270
How Acquired: Drafted in eleventh round, 1985
Position: Left Guard

Raleigh McKenzie is certainly one of the league's most versatile linemen. In 1989, he was asked to fill in for four former Pro Bowlers at four different spots along the line. Not only did he play admirably in relief, he battled his way to a starting job in 1990. "Rollo proved that he is a complete football player," says head coach Joe Gibbs. "He improved not only in his pass protection, but his run blocking was really upgraded." A hard-working player, McKenzie made the Redskins in 1985 as an unheralded eleventh-round draft choice.

HANK'S RATING: A

Jeff Bostic

Birthdate: September 18, 1958
College: Clemson
Height: 6-2
Weight: 260
How Acquired: Free Agent, 1980
Position: Center

For the past two seasons, Jeff Bostic hasn't missed a game at center. Gibbs has called Bostic "the glue that holds the offensive line together," and for good reason: Every week, Bostic rallies the Hogs with his leadership, toughness, and intelligence. "What Jeff gives us is continuity at the center of the line," says Gibbs. "He makes all the line calls, and he's a real leader out there." A superb, take-charge, skilled player that seldom gets outplayed.

HANK'S RATING: A

Mark Schlereth

Birthdate: January 25, 1966
College: Idaho
Height: 6-3
Weight: 285
How Acquired: Drafted in tenth round, 1989
Position: Right Guard

Mark Schlereth may hold the distinction of being the first native Alaskan to play in the NFL, but there's nothing cold about his level of play. He experienced trial by fire in 1989, when Gibbs threw him into an injury-marred starting lineup in the tenth week of the season: He played the entire game without giving up a quarterback hurry or sack, and has since proven himself time and again against the NFL's better linemen. "Mark has super strength, he's an excellent athlete, and he has all the pro standards," Gibbs says.

HANK'S RATING: A

Ed Simmons

Birthdate: December 31, 1963
College: Eastern Washington
Height: 6-5
Weight: 300
How Acquired: Drafted in sixth round, 1987
Position: Right Tackle

The 1989 season was Ed Simmons' proving ground, as he earned a position with the vaunted Hogs after filling in for other injured veterans. During a six-week stint, Simmons proved to be durable, solid, and most of all, consistent. "This year, Ed showed that he can go sixteen weeks and do a fantastic job," says Gibbs. Scouts praise his skills as a technician and pass blocker, as well as his prototype size.

HANK'S RATING: B

Best of Plan B

Roy Foster

Birthdate: May 24, 1960
College: USC
Height: 6-4
Weight: 275
Position: Guard
Final 1990 Team: Miami Dolphins

A strong and durable player, Roy Foster excelled for years as a starting member of the Miami Dolphins offensive line. He was a key member of the unit that set an NFL record by not allowing a sack through almost two consecutive seasons in 1988 and 1989, and has missed just one game due to injury in his career. Foster offers a mixture of speed and strength, and excels in short-yardage situations. Foster will challenge for playing time on an already talented 49ers offensive line.

HANK'S RATING: A

Mark May

Birthdate: November 2, 1959
College: Pittsburgh
Height: 6-6
Weight: 295
Position: Guard
Final 1990 Team: Washington Redskins

After years of moving up and down the line with the Redskins, Mark May finally found a home in 1989 at the right guard position before a knee injury finished his season. He came back strong in 1990 with an outstanding year, and San Diego GM Bobby Beathard—who drafted May in Washington—quickly snapped him up. A former Pro Bowler, May will add incredible depth and experience to the San Diego line. May has played through a myriad of serious injuries—broken wrist, injured knees, broken ribs, broken nose, hip pointer—and brings a powerful work ethic to the young Chargers. "Mark has a lot of football left in him," says Washington head coach Joe Gibbs. "He's a tremendous football player."

HANK'S RATING: B

Joel Patten

Birthdate: February 7, 1958
College: Duke
Height: 6-7
Weight: 307
Position: Tackle
Final 1990 Team: San Diego Chargers

Joel Patten's size and strength helped him develop as a powerful—and surprising—force at left tackle for San Diego. Chargers scouts were pleased with Patten in recent years, watching him hold his ground against such premier NFL pass rushers as Lawrence Taylor and Reggie White. Willing to play hurt, Patten has played during his six-year career despite knee and ankle injuries. He'll put pressure on both Rory Graves and Steve Wright for playing time on the Los Angeles Raiders.

HANK'S RATING: B

John Rienstra

Birthdate: March 22, 1963
College: Temple
Height: 6-5
Weight: 268
Position: Tackle
Final 1990 Team: Pittsburgh Steelers

Personal problems and injury woes made John Rienstra expendable to the Steelers, who once believed he had the potential to become the team's best lineman. Rienstra is well-suited in a pulling and trapping system, with explosive quickness, strength, and mobility. He is also a dedicated weightlifter. The Cleveland Browns hope Rienstra can clear his mind and focus purely on football, since he has the skills to be a dominating NFL lineman.

HANK'S RATING: C

Harry Swayne

Birthdate: February 2, 1965
College: Rutgers
Height: 6-5
Weight: 270
Position: Tackle
Final 1990 Team: Tampa Bay Buccaneers

Harry Swayne began his pro career with Tampa Bay as a defensive end, and played both ends of the defensive line before the Bucs switched him to offensive tackle in 1989. Swayne quickly proved his athleticism by making the move with relative ease. Swayne has tremendous potential but his career has been marred by injuries, dating all the way back to his freshman year in college. If he can stay healthy, he could add depth to the Chargers improving offensive line.

HANK'S RATING: C

Defensive Ends

Reggie White

Birthdate: December 19, 1961
College: Tennessee
Height: 6-5
Weight: 285
How Acquired: Chosen in supplemental draft, 1985
Final 1990 Team: Philadelphia Eagles

If defensive linemen were rated like quarterbacks, Reggie White would be the NFL's Montana—perhaps the best ever. "He is a devastating pass rusher," says former Eagles' skipper Buddy Ryan. "You've got to be ready to put two men on him." White, at 6-5, 285 pounds, improves the Eagles' defense "at least 25 percent," says Ryan, "because he doesn't give the quarterback and receivers time to let the patterns develop."

Despite constant double- and triple-teams, White still has managed 96 sacks in eighty-nine contests. And he plays the run and pass with equal greatness. A future Hall of Famer, White was selected last year to the NFL's "Team of the 1980s" by the Pro Football Hall of Fame Voters. But White, along with his Eagle linemates, will face a huge hurdle in 1990, when they are forced to adjust to a new defensive style: Buddy Ryan is gone, and defensive coordinator Jeff Fisher departed to join the Rams staff.

HANK'S RATING: AAA

Bruce Smith

Birthdate: June 18, 1963
College: Virginia Tech
Height: 6-4
Weight: 280
How Acquired: Drafted in first round, 1985
Final 1990 Team: Buffalo Bills

How great is Bruce Smith's contribution to the Buffalo Bills? The six-year veteran out of Virginia Tech is already Buffalo's career leader in sacks (76.5), and has quickly become the AFC's most dominant lineman. Smith is a master of the rip and spin; combining brute strength and explosive speed, he physically overwhelms opponents, then spins off the block into the quarterback.

Smith is the sole difference between Buffalo having an average defensive line and a great one. "His presence improves everybody around him," says head coach Marv Levy. Normally, Smith lines up at right end, but on passing downs, he moves to left end and linebacker Cornelius Bennett moves to right end. While Bennett was third on the team with 4 sacks, Smith's linemates, nose tackle Jeff Wright and left end Leon Seals, contributed just 5 and 4 sacks, respectively.

In a physical, 30–23 win over Philadelphia, Smith had 8 tackles, including 2 sacks and another tackle for a loss, and added 4 quarterback hurries. The very next week, against Indianapolis, Smith had 4 sacks, 9 total tackles, broke up a pass, and had 2 quarterback pressures. He was named Player of the Week for both weeks.

HANK'S RATING: AA

Chris Doleman

Birthdate: October 16, 1961
College: Pittsburgh
Height: 6-5
Weight: 250
How Acquired: Drafted in first round, 1985
Final 1990 Team: Minnesota Vikings

With help from defensive tackle Keith Millard, Chris Doleman has become a devastating pass rusher; last year he totaled a team-high 11 sacks, his second consecutive year he's led the team (21 in 1989). "He's really a dominating player and an excellent inside pass rusher," says an NFC Central coach. "But it's easier for him to dominate because he plays next to Keith Millard."

Millard is healthy again, which bodes well for one Chris Doleman; in the past, teams have double-, even triple-teamed Millard, allowing Doleman to come free. Doleman's selfless, steady performance in 1990 earned him a trip to the Pro Bowl. Doleman can alter the flow of a game by himself, and with the help of Millard, he can dominate. Excellent pass rush ability and incredible pass rush speed are what put Doleman in our Top 5 for defensive ends.

HANK'S RATING: AA

Leslie O'Neal

Birthdate: May 7, 1964
College: Oklahoma State
Height: 6-4
Weight: 259
How Acquired: Drafted in first round, 1986
Final 1990 Team: San Diego Chargers

Just how bad was the injury to Leslie O'Neal's left knee in 1986? So bad that he didn't play a full season until 1989; then, miraculously, he made the Pro Bowl with 12.5 sacks. However, there were teammates that thought he wouldn't play again in 1990. "When he walks to his locker after practice, he looks like he's 100 years old," said one player, who requested anonymity. "But when you put him on the field . . . I've never seen such determination in my life."

O'Neal continued his success in 1990, finishing third in the AFC with 13.5 sacks. A miracle, perhaps, when you consider the seriousness of his injury. Doctors cut a piece of his patella tendon, which goes across the kneecap, and used it to replace his anterior cruciate ligament. They locked it down with three screws, then sewed some of the medial collateral ligament. Part of his tibia had chipped off, so they drilled holes to get blood flowing through it to help it heal.

The Chargers often list O'Neal as a linebacker, but make no mistake: His greatest impact is at defensive end, where speed, quickness, upper body strength, and powerful explosion give him an edge over virtually any opponent he faces. "If my game is on, then nobody can beat me," he says. Believe it.

HANK'S RATING: AA

Charles Haley

Birthdate: January 6, 1964
College: James Madison
Height: 6-5
Weight: 230
How Acquired: Drafted in fourth round, 1986
Final 1990 Team: San Francisco 49ers

The only sure place to find Charles Haley in 1990 was in the Pro Bowl. During the regular season, there was no way to be sure where he might appear, as he not only played linebacker, but appeared at just about every position on the defensive line en route to harrassing opposing quarterbacks for 16 sacks, third in the NFL. For his outstanding versatility, Haley was named the NFC Defensive Player of the Year.

Haley, who some scouts considered a reach when San Francisco made him a fourth-round draft pick in 1986, truly came of age in 1990. At times, he dominated games; against Pittsburgh, he posted devastating, back-to-back sacks against quarterback Bubby Brister. Brister fumbled on the second sack, San Francisco recovered, and promptly scored. Against Houston, he made 11 tackles, including 2 sacks, forced a fumble, and broke up a pass in a 24–21 victory.

HANK'S RATING: AA

Lee Williams

Birthdate: October 15, 1962
College: Bethune-Cookman
Height: 6-5
Weight: 271
How Acquired: Chosen in Supplemental Draft, 1984
Final 1990 Team: San Diego Chargers

Defensive end Lee Williams' sack total fell to 7.5 in 1990, but it was largely due to the attention the two-time Pro Bowler received from his opposition. Williams, who possesses some of the most awesome physical skills in the NFL, started in back-to-back Pro Bowls in 1988 and 1989, as he demonstrated a combination of speed, quickness, durability, and strength like few had ever seen at his position.

He has accumulated more quarterback sacks at his position over the past six seasons (64.5) than any other AFC player, and with 3 sacks in 1991 will become San Diego's all-time career sack leader. Williams moved inside to tackle in 1990, which limited his sack total, but the position wasn't completely foreign to him: After playing left end in 1985, he has mostly played tackle, which makes his numbers even more astounding. Williams had 63 tackles on the season, good for sixth on the team. Questions have arisen over his sometimes inconsistent "game efforts."

HANK'S RATING: AA

Charles Mann

Birthdate: April 12, 1961
College: Nevada Reno
Height: 6-6
Weight: 270
How Acquired: Drafted in third round, 1983
Final 1990 Team: Washington Redskins

Charles Mann learned two years ago that becoming one of the league's better defensive linemen is a mixed blessing: not only do you reap lots of notoriety, you also earn lots of unwanted attention, in the form of numerous offensive linemen. Mann put together three consecutive All-Pro seasons from 1987 to 1989, but his productivity fell in 1990 as more and more teams geared their attacks toward blocking him.

The defensive end finished with 5.5 sacks, down from 9.5 in 1989, but led the team in quarterback hurries with 23. He also forced a fumble and added 59 tackles, while missing just one game due to injury. Against Philadelphia in the playoffs, Mann had one and a half sacks against Randall Cunningham, and was in on several turnovers. Though Mann is now the "old man" along the Skins defensive front, he is still its most reliable. Mann possesses great pass rush quickness and is great "getting off pass blocks." Still a Top 10 defensive end.

HANK'S RATING: AA

Richard Dent

Birthdate: December 13, 1960
College: Tennessee State
Height: 6-5

Weight: 268
How Acquired: Drafted in eighth round, 1983
Final 1990 Team: Chicago Bears

Richard Dent made his third Pro Bowl in 1990, and with good reason. The former Super Bowl MVP returned to mid-1980s form, finishing with 12 sacks and returned a fumble 45 yards for a touchdown. He had a 2-sack day against Green Bay, then followed that outing with an incredible effort against Minnesota: first, he ripped apart the Minnesota offensive line for 4 tackles and a sack, then broke up 2 passes and intercepted another to set up a field goal, which led the Bears to a 19–16 victory.

Dent's impact on the Chicago defensive line is unprecedented, and his numbers speak for themselves: He is Chicago's career sack leader with 94, and owns the team's single-season sack record with 17.5 in 1985. His 10.5 playoff sacks are the best in NFL history. Dent is a proven, tested, talented performer, who excels in high-pressure situations. Bears vice president of personnel Bill Tobin calls him "the best pure pass rusher" in football.

HANK'S RATING: AA

Pierce Holt

Birthdate: January 1, 1962
College: Angelo State
Height: 6-4
Weight: 280
How Acquired: Drafted in second round, 1988
Final 1990 Team: San Francisco 49ers

Some scouts thought San Francisco defensive end Pierce Holt deserved a Pro Bowl spot in 1990 for his outstanding play. He was third on the team in sacks (6), and his rapid improvement opened the eyes of many offensive coordinators around the league. "It's getting ridiculous," says one. "Between Haley, Fagan and Holt, there is little room to attack their front."

Holt is a thick, powerful interior lineman, who might have the quickest lateral movement in the league. It has taken him little time to become one of the team's steadiest players. "Pierce has a chance to be a major contributor on this team," says head coach George Seifert. "He's very impressive in his work habits and dedication."

HANK'S RATING: AA

Leonard Marshall

Birthdate: October 22, 1961
College: LSU
Height: 6-3
Weight: 285
How Acquired: Drafted in second round, 1983
Final 1990 Team: New York Giants

End Leonard Marshall had 4.5 sacks in 1990, and it was his crushing sack of 49ers' quarterback Joe Montana that forced a fumble, ended Montana's season, and helped put New York in the Super Bowl. So devastating was the hit that Montana suffered a concussion, broken ribs, and a broken little finger on his passing hand. "He had no idea the guy was coming," said backup quarterback Steve Young after the game.

Marshall has consistently played a big role for the Giants since his first Pro Bowl year in 1985, when he set a then-club record with 15.5 sacks. His size and quickness has always made him a force against the run, but his vertical speed and hand strength make him a terror when rushing the passer. "Marshall really uses his body well," says a scout. "He understands the game, and can not only outsmart an offensive tackle, he can physically overpower him if he chooses."

Although the well-liked Bill Parcells has moved on, Marshall still believes the Giants have an excellent chance to repeat. "If we can contain teams like we did last year," he says, "there's no telling how far we can go."

HANK'S RATING: AA

Jacob Green

140

Birthdate: January 21, 1957
College: Texas A&M
Height: 6-3
Weight: 254
How Acquired: Drafted in first round, 1980
Final 1990 Team: Seattle Seahawks

How long will it take before Jacob Green earns the respect he rightfully deserves? For years Green has excelled in virtual anonymity on the Seahawks' defensive front, semingly always outshined a year at a time by more publicized names like Easley, Young, or Bosworth. But those shooting stars are gone—hurt, waived or traded—while Green's excellence continues: He led the team, again, with 12.5 sacks, good for fifth in the AFC.

Green was a major factor in the resurgence of the Seahawks defense, a unit that allowed just 7 rushing touchdowns and only 26 overall, both club records. Against Detroit, Green had 3 sacks and 6 tackles to pace a 30–10 victory, and earned Defensive Player of the Week honors for his effort.

HANK'S RATING: AA

Greg Townsend

Birthdate: November 3, 1961
College: Texas Christian
Height: 6-3
Weight: 260
How Acquired: Drafted in fourth round, 1983
Final 1990 Team: Los Angeles Raiders

Defensive end Greg Townsend went to the Pro Bowl in 1990, and never was a defensive lineman more deserving. Townsend's progress as a defensive end was remarkable, as he matured into an every-down player, instead of just the pass-rush specialist he had been for so many years.

Townsend also produced the big-play in 1990, and even returned a fumble for a touchdown. "I know it was only a 1-yard run," he says, "but by the time I tell my grandchildren, I'll make it sound like it was a 50-yarder." Against Denver, it was his harrassment of quarterback John Elway that prompted Elway to throw the ball away in desperation —into the waiting arms of linebacker Jerry Robinson, who returned the interception for a touchdown.

Townsend led the team in sacks with 12.5, and, along with linemates Howie Long and Scott Davis, helped the Raiders defensive front return to its intimidating form of years past. And Townsend continued his assault on quarterbacks in the playoffs, sacking Boomer Esiason three times in the Raiders' 20–10 victory over the Bengals.

HANK'S RATING: AA

Burt Grossman

Birthdate: April 10, 1967
College: Pittsburgh
Height: 6-6
Weight: 270
How Acquired: Drafted in first round, 1989
Final 1990 Team: San Diego Chargers

Burt Grossman continued to talk a lot in 1990, but like his rookie year in 1989, he also continued to back it up. Grossman had his second-consecutive, 10-sack campaign last year, and was relentless in his pursuit of opposing quarterbacks. Scouts describe the thick, powerful lineman as a "rangy pass rusher... who still has overpowering strength against the run." Grossman was fifth on the team in tackles with 67, forced 2 fumbles and defensed 2 passes.

He also showed the speed to range sideline to sideline, and played with an impressive intensity. He was a large reason why the Chargers defensive line led the AFC in 1989 with 48 sacks. A controversial first-round pick, Grossman rewarded the Chargers with 10 sacks in 1989, the most by an NFL rookie linemen since fellow Charger Leslie O'Neil had 12.5 sacks in 1986.

Grossman also led the team with 45 quarterback hits and 38 quarterback pressures. Named to almost every all-rookie team, the 6-6, 270-pound Grossman leads a stable full of young thoroughbreds on the Chargers fast-improving defense.

HANK'S RATING: AA

Trace Armstrong

Birthdate: October 5, 1965
College: Florida
Height: 6-4
Weight: 259
How Acquired: Drafted in first round, 1989
Final 1990 Team: Chicago Bears

After a rollercoaster rookie season, Trace Armstrong emerged as a force at defensive end, and helped Richard Dent make a return trip to the Pro Bowl in 1990. Armstrong finished second only to Dent in sacks with 10, and in the opinion of coaches, was a much better player against the run than his linemates. Runs to the ball with outstanding speed.

Against Green Bay, he literally took control of the game, sacking Packer quarterbacks twice, forcing 2 fumbles and recovering another fumble that set up a touchdown. He was named NFC Defensive Player of the Month for September after he piled up 25 tackles, 5 sacks, 2 forced fumbles, 1 fumble recovery and 1 pass defensed—all in just four games.

His dependability is another plus: In 1989, he missed just one game, despite a severely sprained ankle. Armstrong is also versatile; the Bears often move him from end to tackle in nickel situations. In his rookie year, he earned the team's Brian Piccolo award for courage, loyalty, teamwork, dedication, and sense of humor.

HANK'S RATING: AA

Sean Jones

Birthdate: December 19, 1962
College: Northeastern
Height: 6-7
Weight: 273
How Acquired: Trade, 1988
Final 1990 Team: Houston Oilers

If a single player ever benefitted from a coaching change, it was defensive end Sean Jones. Acquired from the Raiders in 1988 to fuel Houston's low-octane pass rush, Jones wallowed in obscurity for three seasons in Glanville's linebacker-oriented 3–4 defense. But when new defensive coordinator Jim Eddy put him back at home in the 4–3, the tall, athletic Jones was given the opportunity to once again pin his ears back and attack the quarterback. And he did it with gusto, finishing fifth in the AFC in sacks with 12.5, ahead of his more-publicized teammate Ray Childress.

Jones is capable of being a dominating player, and should receive more credit from Houston coaches. "We had a hard time with Jones," says an NFC West assistant coach. "He gets upfield well, has excellent technique, and really stretches the tackle. He's not physically overpowering, but he's cat-quick, has patience, and might be the most intelligent player at his position in the league. He got robbed in the Pro Bowl."

Few players work as hard in the offseason as Jones. Due to a contract holdout, Jones didn't report last year until four days before the season's first game. He played the whole game. "He might have been in better shape than anybody who'd been in camp for the last month," confides a Houston assistant. The fact that he went on to have his best season as a pro is evidence of his non-drinking, non-smoking, restricted-diet, health regimen.

Though Jones didn't have 5- or 6-sack performances like Cornelius Bennett or Derrick Thomas, he did record sacks in nine consecutive games—the only NFL player to do so. Look for him in the highlight reels in 1991.

HANK'S RATING: AA

Kevin Greene

Birthdate: July 31, 1962
College: Auburn
Height: 6-3
Weight: 250
How Acquired: Drafted in fifth round, 1985
Final 1990 Team: Los Angeles Rams

In his fifth season out of Auburn, Kevin Greene made incredible strides in 1990, positioning himself at the brink of greatness. A devastating pass rusher, Greene tallied 13 sacks, good for third-best in the NFC and down just 3 from his career-high of 16.5 sacks in 1989. "Kevin Greene has all the tools you look for in a defensive end," says head coach John Robinson. "He's big, has great lateral movement, and is extremely physical."

Which is exactly why Greene appears among the top defensive ends, because he plays the position with the same ability as he does linebacker. Most of all, he thrives on pressure, a critical point for playoff-bound teams. Robinson says Greene has the ability to "turn it up a notch" in the big games, and cites the Rams' 1989 playoff victory over Philadelphia as proof: Green tallied 5 unassisted tackles, 2 sacks, and recovered a fumble late in the game. He played in his first Pro Bowl in 1989. "I liked it so much," he says, "that I want to go back."

But the Rams haven't sent a pure defensive lineman to the Pro Bowl since 1980, and the limited talent that does exist is floundering. Former first-round pick Bill Hawkins had 3 sacks last year, but was hurt often and played inconsistently. Nose tackle Alvin Wright, another solid tackler and run-stopper, registered but one sack. Had Greene not been versatile enough to play linebacker and down lineman, it could've been worse. "Defensive line is an area of need," says head coach John Robinson. And that's an understatement, coach.

HANK'S RATING: AA

Leon Seals

Birthdate: January 30, 1964
College: Jackson State
Height: 6-5
Weight: 267
How Acquired: Drafted in fourth round, 1987
Final 1990 Team: Buffalo Bills

Leon Seals, in his first season as a starter, played with modest success. He finished the season with 4 sacks, but improved rapidly as the year wore on. Scouts consider Seals a promising young lineman who must learn only consistency against the run to play at a higher level.

Seals has always been noted as a pass-rusher, but has worked hard to acquire all-around skills. His nickname at Jackson State was "Dr. Sack," but his indoctrination to the pro game has taken time. But his season showed major progress: Against Denver, Seals tipped a pass that was intercepted and returned for a touchdown by safety Leonard Smith that led Buffalo to a come-from-behind victory. Seals could be on the verge of putting it all together.

HANK'S RATING: AA

Neil Smith

Birthdate: April 10, 1966
College: Nebraska
Height: 6-4
Weight: 271
How Acquired: Drafted in first round, 1988
Final 1990 Team: Kansas City Chiefs

Defensive end Neil Smith, considered by some pundits to be a bust after his rookie year in 1988, came of age in 1990. After developing into one of the league's best run defenders in 1989, Smith continued his maturity in 1990, finishing with 9.5 sacks, second best on the team, and generally controlling the line of scrimmage.

Though the words "physical speciman" are frequently overused, they certainly apply to Smith. He went to Nebraska as a 208-pound freshman, and left weighing 260 pounds, capable of running the 40 in 4.59 with a vertical jump of 35 inches. He has huge arms (arm length of 45 inches, wingspan of 7 feet, 1 inch), and can bench-press 500 pounds. The only question seems to about his mental reaction.

"Smith had a tough rookie year because he struggled with the mental part of the pro game," says a scout. "Once he re-learned his position, it was just a matter of reacting to what he saw. He's a hellacious talent, and the scary part is that he's getting better." Awesome position motor skill potential.

HANK'S RATING: AA

Renaldo Turnbull

Birthdate: January 5, 1966
College: West Virginia
Height: 6-4
Weight: 248
How Acquired: Drafted in first round, 1990
Final 1990 Team: New Orleans Saints

Renaldo Turnbull turned in one of the finest rookie performances ever at defensive end. He finished the season with 9 sacks and showed the dominating form that the Saints were hoping for when they drafted him.

He also nearly provided the Saints with the best defensive play of the season: In the playoffs against Chicago, with New Orleans trailing 10–3, Turnbull blocked a Kevin Butler field goal attempt and returned it 61 yards for the apparent tying touchdown. But it was nullified when officials ruled that Robert Massey had lined up in the neutral zone. He also had 2 sacks in that game, neither of which were nullified.

Although Turnbull is one of the fastest defensive linemen ever to play his position (4.6 in the 40), he has to build more upper body strength. "Renaldo's a fine pass rusher, but he has to get bigger and stronger to do a better job against the run," says head coach Jim Mora. "He got hammered against the Bears." Insiders question his run strength, his reads, and his reaction "feel."

HANK'S RATING: A

Mike Gann

Birthdate: October 19, 1963
College: Notre Dame
Height: 6-5
Weight: 270
How Acquired: Drafted in second round, 1985
Final 1990 Team: Atlanta Falcons

Defensive end Mike Gann was revitalized by the attack defense new head coach Jerry Glanville implemented in Atlanta, and his season-ending numbers reflected it: He had his best professional season, finishing with 116 tackles and 3.5 sacks, while being a major reason why Atlanta finished third in the NFL against the run. He also had 19 quarterback pressures, third-best on the team. Not bad for a player who several scouts say is not a natural pass rusher.

Gann is also dependable; he hasn't missed a game in six years and has 560 tackles over that span. Gann is a strong, physical player who anchors Atlanta's defensive line. "Sometimes you wonder how he does it," says Glanville. "But when the bodies unpile, he's always under there somewhere."

HANK'S RATING: A

Tony Woods

Birthdate: September 11, 1965
College: Pittsburgh
Height: 6-4
Weight: 259
How Acquired: Drafted in first round, 1987
Final 1990 Team: Seattle Seahawks

Veteran linebacker Tony Woods put on twenty-five pounds in 1990 and moved to defensive end, where the Seahawks put his explosive quickness to work as a pass rusher. He played sixteen games, starting fifteen, and was credited with 43 tackles, including 6 for losses, and 3 sacks. He improved steadily as the season wore on, and his forced fumble against Houston led to Seattle's game-winning, overtime field goal.

Woods will have to bounce back from minor knee surgery in 1991, which became necessary after he suffered an injury against Detroit. But he raised his value among the coaching staff, demonstrating versatility, hustle, and desire.

HANK'S RATING: A

Jon Hand

Birthdate: November 13, 1963
College: Alabama
Height: 6-7
Weight: 301
How Acquired: Drafted in first round, 1986
Final 1990 Team: Indianapolis Colts

Defensive end Jon Hand didn't sign until September 12, three days after the Colts' opening loss at Buffalo, then failed to live up to expectations the rest of the season. In a mid-season loss to the Giants, Hand was steamrolled by the New York offensive line, and on the year had just 63 tackles.

Hand finished with 3 sacks and 7 quarterback pressures, and defensed two passes. Much like Atlanta's Aundrey Bruce, Hand has been an enigma since coming out of Alabama as a first-round pick in 1986. He has been plagued by injuries throughout his career, and has never developed the consistency of other players with similar talent. A Top 25 end, many felt he would develop into much more.

HANK'S RATING: A

David Grant

Birthdate: September 17, 1965
College: West Virginia
Height: 6-4
Weight: 288
How Acquired: Drafted in fourth round, 1988
Final 1990 Team: Cincinnati Bengals

Defensive end David Grant, now in his fourth season, proved in 1990 that he could help solve Cincinnati's d-line woes if he ever learns to play with consistency. Though he had one less sack than defensive linemate Skip McClendon, he outplayed McClendon against the run, and generally proved he has the talent to become a force in the trenches. Grant is a quiet, determined, hard-working player, but his development has been slowed by several nagging injuries.

"It's helped David that he can play nose and defensive end," says defensive line coach Chuck Studley. "But he needs to get stabilized in one position. He's a very good athlete and has some natural pass-rush ability." Scouts say Grant exhibits a perfect blend of size, quickness and strength, "but it's up to him to put the intangibles together."

HANK'S RATING: A

Wayne Martin

Birthdate: October 26, 1965
College: Arkansas
Height: 6-5
Weight: 275
How Acquired: Drafted in second round, 1989
Final 1990 Team: New Orleans Saints

Defensive end Wayne Martin improved considerably in 1990 over his rookie year of 1989, the year the Saints made him a first-round pick. He finished with 4 sacks before being put on injured reserve with a knee injury in December. He finished with 24 tackles, defensed 3 passes and forced 1 fumble.

Scouts say Martin is an outstanding athlete, with a reputation as an aggressive, punishing player. He has been favorably compared to Dan Hampton, another former Arkansas Razorback. He runs the 40 in 4.92 and is very agile. But, much like teammate Renaldo Turnbull, Martin needs to gain in size and strength. His maturity is critical to the development of the Saints line, due largely to the aging of eleven-year veteran Jim Wilks.

HANK'S RATING: A

Brent Williams

Birthdate: October 23, 1964
College: Toledo
Height: 6-4
Weight: 275

How Acquired: Drafted in seventh round, 1986
Final 1990 Team: New England Patriots

Defensive end Brent Williams played brilliantly in 1990, despite the controversy around the New England franchise. He finished the season with 71 tackles and a team-best 6 sacks, marking the sixth time that the twenty-six-year-old Williams has led the team in sacks. Williams moved ahead of defensive end Garin Veris into second place on the Patriots' all-time list with 34 career sacks.

Over his five-year career, Williams has steadily increased his production, and appears poised on the brink of becoming a steady, dependable NFL lineman. But the new Patriots regime has made it clear there will be much competition at the defensive line position in 1991, and Williams will have to work hard to maintain his starting job.

HANK'S RATING: A

Ray Agnew

Birthdate: December 9, 1967
College: North Carolina State
Height: 6-3
Weight: 272
How Acquired: Drafted in first round, 1990
Final 1990 Team: New England Patriots

Rookie Ray Agnew showed much promise during his freshman campaign with the Patriots in 1990. He played in twelve games with nine starts at defensive end, while missing two games with a calf injury and two games with a knee injury.

Agnew was ninth on the team with 52 total tackles, and had 2.5 sacks, 1 fumble recovery and 1 forced fumble. Against the Redskins, he had a season-high 7 total tackles. Agnew was named to several all-rookie teams by several publications, and is the odds-on favorite to nail down the starting defensive end job in 1991. He can bench more than 500 pounds, runs the 40 in 4.83, and has a vertical leap of 33 inches.

"Agnew is a strong, young player," says GM Sam Jankovich. "He'll get better if he continues to work at his game and make the effort it takes to play at this level."

HANK'S RATING: A

Reuben Davis

Birthdate: May 7, 1965
College: North Carolina
Height: 6-4
Weight: 285
How Acquired: Drafted in ninth round, 1988
Final 1990 Team: Tampa Bay Buccaneers

Why Reuben Davis doesn't fulfill his Pro Bowl potential is a mystery to Tampa coaches, but it wasn't from a lack of dedication in 1990. Davis was the Bucs' top defensive lineman, and started every game at left end, and played despite a series of nagging injuries.

Davis is very tough against the run, and led all Tampa Bay defensive linemen with 62 tackles. Against the Bears, he posted a season-high 9 stops, and was Tampa's Defensive Player of the Game against the Vikings with 2 tackles and 3 quarterback pressures.

Shoulder problems kept him out of several practices and part of one game, but his hard work and effort made him a favorite of the coaching staff. If Davis could ever survive a season injury-free, he has the potential to become one of the league's finer linemen.

HANK'S RATING: A

Jeff Cross

Birthdate: March 25, 1966
College: Missouri
Height: 6-4
Weight: 270

How Acquired: Drafted in ninth round, 1988
Final 1990 Team: Miami Dolphins

After Miami's defense finished the 1989 season ranked twenty-fourth in the NFL, head coach Don Shula called on his troops to step forward. At least one warrior heeded the call: defensive end Jeff Cross, who played his way right into the Pro Bowl in 1990 and had 8 sacks in the season's first seven weeks.

By season's end, Cross had finished with a career-high 11.5 sacks, up from his 1989 total of 10, and tallied 60 tackles. Cross became the lowest-drafted Dolphin ever to play in the Pro Bowl, but after October, nobody questioned his selection: over four games, he had 12 tackles, 3 sacks and a forced fumble.

Cross continued his assault through December: The Dolphins earned home-field advantage in the playoffs with two weeks to play when Cross pressured Colts quarterback Jeff George into grounding a pass in the end zone for a safety, then slapped the ball out of George's hands on the next series, which nose tackle Brian Sochia returned for a touchdown.

"Jeff Cross showed dramatic improvement," says head coach Don Shula. "He tapered off late in the season, but is regarded as one of the best young linemen in the NFL. My goal is to have Jeff play with more consistency all year long."

HANK'S RATING: A

William Fuller

Birthdate: March 8, 1962
College: North Carolina
Height: 6-3
Weight: 269
How Acquired: Trade, 1986
Final 1990 Team: Houston Oilers

Defensive end William Fuller had his best year as an Oiler, recording 8 sacks over the course of the 1990 season. Fuller, like Sean Jones and Ray Childress, greatly benefitted from Houston's switch to the 4-3 defense, and returned to the form that once made him a feared pass rusher in the USFL.

"The switch to the 4-3 really helped that team," says a scout. "Jones and Fuller were average players under Glanville in the 3-4. But in the 4-3, all of a sudden, they're turning the corner and harrassing the quarterback. But Fuller, in particular, really needs to do a better job against the run."

Fuller doesn't have overwhelming strength, but is a heady, aggressive player with quick recognition and solid lateral movement. He shares time with veteran Ezra Johnson, who had 2.5 sacks. Even rookie Jeff Alm got into the action, with a lone sack. "I think the 4-3 better suits the personality of this team," says defensive coordinator Jim Eddy. "And I think the success of guys like William Fuller and Sean Jones are proof of that."

HANK'S RATING: A

Natu Tuatagaloa

Birthdate: May 25, 1966
College: California
Height: 6-4
Weight: 270
How Acquired: Drafted in fifth round, 1989
Final 1990 Team: Cincinnati Bengals

Defensive end Natu Tuatagaloa played well enough in 1990 to be a part-time starter, and finished the season with 4.5 sacks. He played well enough in his rookie year (1989) to excite Cincinnati coaches, who believe the Dutch-Samoan has a bright NFL future. "He has real good quickness, and he's a big guy," says head coach Sam Wyche. "He's 270, and it's not a pumped up 270. I think he can get bigger as he matures."

He is a gifted athlete, who takes full advantage of his power and hands to shed blockers. Scouts like his aggressiveness at the point of attack, and credit his long arms and hand-eye coordination as his two greatest assets.

HANK'S RATING: A

Marvin Washington

Birthdate: October 22, 1965
College: Idaho
Height: 6-6
Weight: 260
How Acquired: Drafted in sixth round, 1984
Final 1990 Team: New York Jets

Jets scouts are high on Marvin Washington—tons of potential. A former basketball at the University of Idaho who has added forty pounds of bulk to his six-foot-six frame.

Scouts believe that Washington will become the full-time starter at left end in 1991. The only question is whether he will be able to handle the large weight gain. Forty extra pounds is a lot to carry for a whole season.

HANK'S RATING: A

Alphonso Carreker

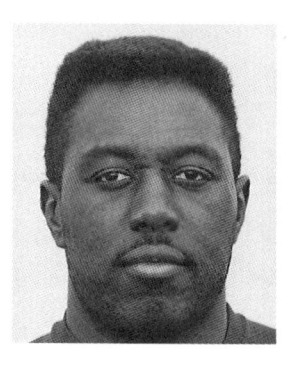

Birthdate: May 25, 1962
College: Florida State
Height: 6-6
Weight: 272
How Acquired: Plan B free agent, 1989
Final 1990 Team: Denver Broncos

Many scouts insisted that Alphonso Carreker didn't deserve to be rated so low, based on his history of adequate performances. But there were others who argued that, until he proves he can return from 1990's season-ending knee injury, there is no guarantee that he will play at the same level in 1991. Carreker was a Plan B signee from Green Bay, where he was once the Packers' first-round pick and the twelfth player taken overall in the 1984 draft.

But Carreker has never really lived up to his potential, providing consistent, though not outstanding, play. He has great size, good quickness, decent strength, and solid work habits. "Carreker is still a good situation player," says a scout. "You could surround him with more impact players and he might look like a different player. But if you ask him to be the guy, the stud on the defensive line, he just isn't capable."

HANK'S RATING: A

Daniel Stubbs

Birthdate: January 3, 1965
College: Miami
Height: 6-4
Weight: 260
How Acquired: Trade, 1990
Final 1990 Team: Dallas Cowboys

How talent-laden is the San Francisco defensive line? So deep that they could afford to ship the talent-rich Daniel Stubbs off to Dallas, where he will likely grow into the Cowboys next dominant pass rusher. Stubbs tied for the team lead in sacks with 7.5, and excelled in pass-rush situations. Much like New Orleans' Renaldo Turnbull, he lacks the upper body strength to play the run with consistency, not tough versus the run, but scouts believe he can acquire that strength—and those skills—over time.

Stubbs, says one scout, "reminds me of [former Charger and 49er] Fred Dean. He really has tremendous explosions, and uses his hands well to fend off traffic. He needs to really work on his technique and play recognition to become a consistent player. But he's blessed with all the physical tools." Still has to harness "tools" and play within defensive coordination.

HANK'S RATING: A

Keith Willis

Birthdate: July 29, 1959
College: Northeastern
Height: 6-1
Weight: 263
How Acquired: Free Agent, 1982
Final 1990 Team: Pittsburgh Steelers

Keith Willis, the Steelers' most experienced lineman, is a six-year starter and three-time sack leader. His 5 sacks in 1990 were good for second on the team, but Willis will likely give up his starting job to one of the team's challengers—Lorenzo Freeman, Aaron Jones, and Kenny Davidson, all promising young pros.

Willis is now thirty-two, and he has been inconsistent throughout his career. Pittsburgh needs at least one lineman to step forward as a dominating player, and coaches believe Davidson has a chance to be that player. Willis will have to battle the third-year player for playing time in 1991.

HANK'S RATING: A

Dan Owens

Birthdate: March 16, 1967
College: USC
Height: 6-3
Weight: 285
How Acquired: Drafted in second round, 1990
Final 1990 Team: Detroit Lions

Detroit defensive coordinator Woody Widenhofer called Dan Owens the Lions' "most consistent lineman" in 1990. "And he's a lot bigger and stronger now that he has a year under his belt," Widenhofer says. Owens finished with 46 tackles and 3 sacks, and was a mainstay on the defensive line. Owens has bulked up to 285, runs well, tackles well, and works hard. "We have a lot of young, talented players on the defensive line," says Widenhofer. "All they lack is experience."

HANK'S RATING: A

Bill Maas

Birthdate: December 19, 1960
College: Pittsburgh
Height: 6-5
Weight: 277
How Acquired: Drafted in first round, 1984
Final 1990 Team: Kansas City Chiefs

As the Kansas City Chiefs have improved under new head coach Marty Schottenheimer, the defensive recognition—and subsequent praise—gets spread around a little more these days. But two-time Pro Bowler Bill Maas still distinguishes himself on the suddenly talented Kansas City defensive line. Though Maas does not play with the same intensity he once did, causing up and down performance levels, he is helped by the fact that teams can no longer double-team him, for fear of giving up quick tackles to linemates Neil Smith and Dan Saleaumua.

Maas earned Player of the Week honors during the season's sixth week when he sacked Detroit quarterback Bob Gagliano on successive series, forcing a fumble to set up a field goal and scoring a safety, as Kansas City rallied to beat Detroit, 43–24. Maas finished the game with 5 tackles in all. "Bill is a steady player, and has really worked hard to maintain his level of play," says head coach Marty Schottenheimer. One only wonders how great Maas might have been had the Chiefs' enjoyed such outstanding defensive talent earlier in his career.

HANK'S RATING: B

Al Noga

Birthdate: September 16, 1966
College: Hawaii
Height: 6-1
Weight: 245
How Acquired: Drafted in third round, 1988
Final 1990 Team: Minnesota Vikings

Al Noga has bloomed into a dependable NFL defensive end. He finished the year with just 6 sacks, down from his 11.5 total in 1989, but that was perhaps more indicative of the loss of Keith Millard on the defensive line. But his explosion and quickness still gave opponents nightmares. In the Vikings' second meeting against Green Bay, Noga earned Player of the Week honors when he sacked quarterback Anthony Dilweg, forced a fumble, and recovered it in the end zone to lead Minnesota to victory.

"So much gets said about Doleman and Millard," says a scout, "that Noga's contributions get overlooked. He's a powerful player who is capable of controlling the line of scrimmage. He's lightning quick, getting off blocks quickly, has good moves and good technique, and is difficult to block." Noga's biggest weakness is his lack of upper body strength. "He's a little small," the scout says. "If you can lock him down, you have a chance of handling him." Not in the class of Doleman or Millard, but a consistent performer for the Vikings. A 100 percent effort player.

HANK'S RATING: B

Robert Brown

Birthdate: May 21, 1960
College: Virginia Tech
Height: 6-2
Weight: 267
How Acquired: Drafted in fourth round, 1982
Final 1990 Team: Green Bay Packers

Ten-year veteran Robert Brown epitomizes durability for the Green Bay Packers, having dressed for every game the Packers have played since he joined them as a fourth-round pick in 1982. He registered 3 sacks in 1990, but compiled just 32 tackles from his defensive end position. Primarily a run-stopper, Brown was once again capable and consistent holding down his end of the line.

"Robert isn't a spectacular player," says defensive line coach Greg Blache. "He's not flashy. He's just solid and sound. He's a blue-collar guy. He's what I call a fox-hole guy—a guy you can count on." Maybe so, but his production has dropped considerably in recent years. He had 51 tackles in 1989, and 39 solo tackles in 1988.

HANK'S RATING: B

Eric Dorsey

Birthdate: August 5, 1964
College: Notre Dame
Height: 6-5
Weight: 280
How Acquired: Drafted in first round, 1986
Final 1990 Team: New York Giants

Defensive end Eric Dorsey was another product of the Giants 1986 draft, which netted five defensive starters in the first three rounds (Dorsey, cornerback Mark Collins, nose tackle Erik Howard, linebacker Pepper Johnson, and defensive end John Washington). Dorsey gives the Giants an imposing physical dimension at defensive end, and is capable of playing both tackle and nose in New York's 3–4 scheme.

Despite his huge size, he runs a consistent 4.7 in the 40, and scouts praise his strength against the run. Dorsey, like many of the other unsung Giants, is a reliable cog in the suffocating New York defense. Some question whether he didn't get too bulky due to weight lifting—may have hurt his production.

HANK'S RATING: B

Tim Green

Birthdate: December 16, 1963
College: Syracuse
Height: 6-2
Weight: 245
How Acquired: Drafted in first round, 1986
Final 1990 Team: Atlanta Falcons

Nobody worked harder for head coach Jerry Glanville in Atlanta's new defensive scheme than defensive end Tim Green, and what he lacked in talent he made up for in intelligence, hustle, and hard work. "There's no comparison between 1990 and the year before," he says. "When 1989 ended, all we had were questions. We know, now, that we aren't far away from being a good football team."

Green flourished in the attack defense; at times his lack of speed limited him in obvious pass-rush situations, but he still finished with 6 sacks. Scouts question if he is strong enough to handle run blocks. An overachiever, he made some big plays: Against Pittsburgh, he forced 2 fumbles. Against the Rams, he had 6 quarterback pressures. Against Tampa Bay, he had 2 sacks. Green finished fifth on the team with 121 tackles, and had a team-high 37 quarterback pressures.

HANK'S RATING: B

Jeff Lageman

Birthdate: July 18, 1967
College: Virginia
Height: 6-5
Weight: 250
How Acquired: Drafted in first round, 1989
Final 1990 Team: New York Jets

Former first-round pick Jeff Lageman was an average success at linebacker in 1989, and new coach Bruce Coslet moved him to defensive end in 1990, in an effort to bolster the team's pass rush. Lageman tacked up 4 sacks and provided solid play against the run, but again, was relatively average.

Scouts say Lageman's selection in the first round has always been a mystery. "First of all, let's admit the kid does have some talent," says one. "But he's a stiff linebacker, and too small for a defensive lineman. In other words, he's a project, for maybe another two or three years. He would have still been there in the third round."

But don't fault Lageman. Coaches say he works hard, displays a great attitude, and attacks his job with zeal. "Jeff really plays with desire," says Coslet. But he adds that "...we have to improve our line play in 1991." Indeed. Buffalo alone ran through the Jets defensive line for more than 200 yards—in one game.

HANK'S RATING: B

Darrell Davis

Birthdate: March 10, 1966
College: Texas Christian
Height: 6-2
Weight: 255
How Acquired: Drafted in twelfth round, 1990
Final 1990 Team: New York Jets

Rookie Darrell Davis, like second-year man Jeff Lageman, was moved from linebacker to defensive end, and with similar success. Davis showed potential, with a good burst and impressive upfield speed. He finished the season with 5 sacks (good for third on the team), and made at least one outstanding play that resulted in a New York victory: Against Houston, he sacked Warren Moon, forced a fumble, and fell on it in the end zone for a touchdown. The Jets added a field goal and won, 17–12.

HANK'S RATING: B

Shawn Patterson

Birthdate: June 13, 1964
College: Arizona State
Height: 6-5
Weight: 261
How Acquired: Drafted in second round, 1988
Final 1990 Team: Green Bay Packers

Defensive end Shawn Patterson has shown more potential than production during his short career. Although he recovered relatively quick from knee surgery in 1989, he finished next-to-last among defensive linemen on the Packers in tackles in 1990 with just 17. This low total can be somewhat contributed to the fact that the Packers used him almost exclusively in pass-rush situations. And in this role he did notch 4 sacks.

Patterson is a strong, cat-quick player who is adequate against the run but shows great promise rushing the passer. Scouts believe he has the opportunity to become a star if he works hard enough. "His strength is back, his weight is back, and it appears that his quickness is back," says defensive line coach Greg Blache. "When he is fully recovered, which he is, he can take some of the pressure off Tim Harris because he gives us another guy who can make plays."

HANK'S RATING: B

Rod Saddler

Birthdate: September 26, 1965
College: Texas A&M

Height: 6-5
Weight: 280
How Acquired: Drafted in fourth round, 1987
Final 1990 Team: Phoenix Cardinals

Rod Saddler had a disappointing 4 sacks in 1990, and failed to live up to the expectations of the coaching staff. Phoenix scouts thought Saddler, now a fifth-year player, would step up and be an impact player last season, but such hopes never materialized. Saddler, it appears, will be little more than a consistent, aggressive end, who doesn't make many mistakes but may never reach stardom, either.

Saddler is versatile, capable of playing tackle or end, and is very active against the run. Phoenix hopes to get a big push from Dexter Manley and top-pick Eric Swann in 1991, with hopes that their presence will jump-start Saddler into a career-type season.

HANK'S RATING: B

Matt Brock

Birthdate: January 14, 1966
College: Oregon
Height: 6-4
Weight: 267
How Acquired: Drafted in third round, 1989
Final 1990 Team: Green Bay Packers

Left end Matt Brock, in a fairly one-dimensional role as a run lineman, finished the season with an unspectacular 59 tackles and 4 sacks in 1990. He did earn a starting assignment after impressing coaches in training camp, but reached a plateau and failed to continue the progress he'd shown since his rookie season in 1989. But defensive line coach Greg Blache is convinced Brock's development will continue.

"Do not underestimate Matt Brock," says Blache. "Assignment-wise, he's a sharp kid. The one thing he gives you is flexibility." He also works hard: Since becoming a Packer, he has tripled his production in the bench press. He also has excellent genes: He is the son of Clyde Brock, a defensive tackle who played for both Dallas and San Francisco in the early 1960s.

HANK'S RATING: B

Sam Clancy

Birthdate: May 29, 1958
College: Pittsburgh
Height: 6-7
Weight: 254
How Acquired: Plan B free agent, 1989
Final 1990 Team: Indianapolis Colts

Pass-rush specialist Sam Clancy had 48 tackles and a team-high 7.5 sacks in 1990, and tied for the team lead with 7 quarterback pressures. Though Clancy was below average against the run, he was used primarily in pass-rush situations.

The success of Clancy, a journeyman pass rusher who didn't play college football and has now played with four professional teams, is perhaps more proof of the deficiencies of the Indianapolis defense. In defense of Clancy, however, he is a selfless, rugged, dependable team player, who works hard and sets an example for younger players.

HANK'S RATING: B

Dexter Manley

Birthdate: February 2, 1959
College: Oklahoma State
Height: 6-3
Weight: 257
How Acquired: Free Agent, 1990
Final 1990 Team: Phoenix Cardinals

When Dexter Manley was banned from the NFL for drug use in the middle of the 1990 season, it was, perhaps, the greatest waste of defensive line talent the league had ever seen. Manley forfeited a year of his career for cocaine, but when the league reinstated him, Joe Bugel, a former Redskins assistant, gave Manley a second chance.

Now thirty-two, Manley faces an uphill road to regain the form that made him the most dominant pass-rusher in Washington Redskins history.

Though Manley has participated in but one training camp in the past six years, he remains the Redskins career sack leader (96). Though he signed too late in 1990 to have much impact with the Cardinals, there are those who still believe Manley has the ability to fight his way back to the top of the NFC sack standings. "The missed time . . . has hurt him," says Washington defensive line coach Torgy Torgeson. "But he has shown us that when he is in top form he can rush the passer as well as anybody."

Joe Bugel agrees. "I know what Dexter is capable of," he says. "If he works hard, he can make an impact on the right side of our defensive line." To be honest, the Cardinals might be in serious trouble if he doesn't: Defensive end Freddie Joe Nunn, a converted linebacker who led the team with 9 sacks last year, has been moved back to linebacker for 1991. First-round pick Eric Swain, a defensive end with no college experience, suffered a knee injury in the team's minicamp and might miss part of training camp. The burden might fall on Manley's shoulders. We have our doubts whether Manley can regain his old form, but if he can Phoenix will be an improved team.

"People in recovery have to have hopes to cling to," says Manley. "I have high hopes. I made a bad decision to do cocaine. But I have to believe in my second chance. Football is very important right now, because I know I have some great years left in me. But I know now that there are things more important than football. Like my life. From 1986 until 1989, I was living for football, because I was so caught up in material things. Today, I just live for me. And, for the critics who say whatever they say, hey, that's great, because the longer I stay sober, the more dignity I get back. And that's what I live for now."

HANK'S RATING: C

Defensive Tackles

Ray Childress

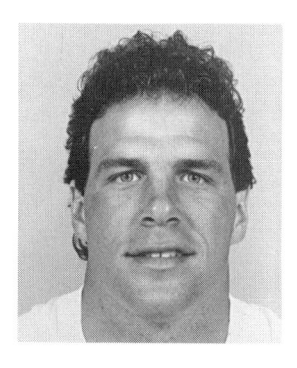

Birthdate: October 20, 1962
College: Texas A&M
Height: 6-6
Weight: 278
How Acquired: Drafted in first round, 1985
Final 1990 Team: Houston Oilers

Former Houston head coach Jerry Glanvlle used to say that "Ray Childress knows one speed, and that's wide open." He proved it again in 1990 with another Pro Bowl season, finishing with 85 tackles and 8 sacks. And he did that from his new position of defensive tackle, after having played end the past five years. Childress also benefitted from the inspired play of defensive end Sean Jones, who, like Childress, thrived in Houston's new 4-3 scheme.

To measure Childress's worth to the Oilers, one needs only to look back at the 1989 season, when he fractured his leg in week 15 and was unable to finish the season: the Oilers pass rush went to hell, as did their ability to stop the run. In the playoffs against Pittsburgh, the defensive line became so thin that coaches prepared tight end Bob Mrosko to enter the game at end, in an effort to muster a pass rush.

The Oilers depend on Sean Jones, Childress, and Doug Smith to anchor the line, while William Fuller, Ezra Johnson, and Jeff Alm are rotated through the lineup depending on down and distance.

Prior to his injury, Childress played the Oilers defensive line like a piano, as injuries forced him to play a different position virtually every week. The Oilers drafted much-needed defensive help, however, and when Childress was able to concentrate on a single position—defensive tackle—he quickly developed into one of the league's best. "Ray Childress," says Chicago head coach Mike Ditka, "may be the best out there at his position." Childress joined the NFL's elite in the Pro Bowl in 1990, and it was a well-earned trip: Nobody works harder at his craft than Childress.

HANK'S RATING: AAA

Keith Millard

Birthdate: March 18, 1962
College: Washington State
Height: 6-5
Weight: 263
How Acquired: Drafted in first round, 1984
Final 1990 Team: Minnesota Vikings

Ask any scout about Keith Millard and he'll likely use words like "nasty" or "physical" or "animal." Millard may be the most physical lineman in the league; he's only 6-5, 263 pounds, but the six-year veteran plays like he weighs 300. His coaches praise him for being extremely physical at the point of attack, without giving up outside speed and quickness.

The Vikings sorely missed Millard when he fell to injury during the season's first month. Because of his versatility, Millard flip-flops around nose tackle Henry Thomas, as the down and distance dictates. And if you watch film of Millard, it's easy to spot what the Vikings lose when he's not in the game: backside pursuit down the line of scrimmage.

"He has incredible acceleration," says former Minnesota defensive coordinator Floyd Peters. "He explodes when he's chasing somebody from behind. He simply runs them down." He's unselfish, too, usually occupying two or three offensive linemen while other Vikings make the big sacks. But don't kid yourself: When healthy, Millard is the most valuable tackle in the NFC.

HANK'S RATING: AAA

Jerome Brown

Birthdate: February 4, 1965
College: Miami
Height: 6-2
Weight: 295
How Acquired: Drafted in first round, 1987
Final 1990 Team: Philadelphia Eagles

Jerome Brown is one reason why Reggie White will continue to be the league's most dominant lineman for years to come: Because of Brown, you can't double-team White. Brown is an inside force, collapsing the pass pocket and actively stuffing the run. "Jerome is what I call the tempo guy," says defensive line coach Dale Haupt. "He takes a lot of the pressure off Reggie [White]."

At one time scouts questioned the former Miami Hurricane's pain tolerance, but Brown hushed critics by playing most of 1989 with a bruised shoulder and bum knee. "The big turnaround for Jerome was his willingness to work," says a coach. "He finally realized to play at this level it takes more than just ability."

Though he registered just 1 sack in 1990, Brown so dominated play from his position that his peers voted him into his first Pro Bowl. But his attitude towards authority and lack of discipline created some problems in the Philadelphia locker room; new head coach Rich Kotite vows he won't tolerate the open strife and backbiting that plagued the 1990 club. Brown has been known to have trouble with his weight and conditioning. If those are taken care of, look for Brown to have another stellar year in 1991.

HANK'S RATING: AA

Dennis Byrd

Birthdate: October 5, 1966
College: Tulsa
Height: 6-5
Weight: 270
How Acquired: Drafted in second round, 1989
Final 1990 Team: New York Jets

If the Jets showed great progress at any position in 1990, it was on the defensive line, where tackle Dennis Byrd emerged as New York's first pass-rushing force since the team had Joe Klecko and Mark Gastineau in their prime. Byrd finished the season with 13 sacks, fourth in the AFC. "We've got a lot of good young players," says GM Dick Steinberg. "And certainly Dennis Byrd is one of them."

Byrd's physical strength makes him an overpowering, bull-rush type lineman, and scouts compare him to a raw Keith Millard. But two areas Byrd has to improve on—common among young players—are learning to recognize opposing formations quicker and filling the right holes. He must also learn better technique on the line of scrimmage. The Jets hope to find another young pass rusher among their free agents and draft picks that can offer Byrd immediate help in 1991.

HANK'S RATING: AA

Kevin Fagan

Birthdate: April 25, 1963
College: Miami
Height: 6-4
Weight: 265
How Acquired: Drafted in fourth round, 1986
Final 1990 Team: San Francisco 49ers

The entire nation watched as defensive tackle Kevin Fagan made perhaps the most critical sack of the 49ers' regular season, when he dropped Giants' quarterback Phil Simms with no time left to give San Francisco a 7–3 victory over New York on "Monday Night Football." But Fagan has built a reputation as a clutch performer, dating back to his very first start in 1987 against Cincinnati; in that game, it was Fagan's fourth-down stop with just two seconds remaining that halted the Bengals and gave the ball back to the 49ers, who scored the game-winning touchdown on a Joe Montana pass on the next play.

Fagan plays the role of unsung hero on San Francisco's star-studded defensive line, and has developed an NFL reputation as a brawler in the trenches, impressing opponents with his lightning quickness and brute physical strength. In 1990, despite a short holdout, Fagan tallied 9 sacks on the season, and tied for the team's post-season sack lead (3). A highly effective player, Fagan is a consistent, all-around player. A great practice player and game hustler, Fagan is a self-made player.

HANK'S RATING: A

Clyde Simmons

Birthdate: August 4, 1964
College: Western Carolina
Height: 6-6
Weight: 275
How Acquired: Drafted in ninth round, 1986
Final 1990 Team: Philadelphia Eagles

Clyde Simmons is surrounded by such talented company, it's no wonder he so often gets overlooked when it comes to accolades. But his play is steady, and his 7.5 sacks in 1990 was another typical performance by the big defensive tackle—good for second best on a sack-heavy team. In a critical game against division rival Washington, the alert Simmons picked up a fumble after a bone-jarring sack by safety Wes Hopkins and rumbled 18 yards for a touchdown.

Simmons failed to make the Pro Bowl in 1989 after a career-high, 15.5-sack season, when he registered at least one sack in eleven games. "I think Clyde deserves more attention than he gets," says linemate Reggie White. "I think he's just as good as any defensive end in the league."

HANK'S RATING: A

Howie Long

Birthdate: January 6, 1960
College: Villanova
Height: 6-5
Weight: 270
How Acquired: Drafted in second round, 1981
Final 1990 Team: Los Angeles Raiders

Howie Long returned to the level of play that has made him a former Pro Bowler. He finished with 6 sacks, but more importantly, he showed the ability to dominate the line of scrimmage like he once did as a much younger man—much to the thrill of Raiders coaches. From the opening game, Long made it clear he would be a force to be reckoned with: He sacked Denver quarterback John Elway twice and generally harrassed the Broncos out-played offensive line. But some scouts note that he didn't seem to be playing "all out" in the manner of his younger years.

Although Long again missed several games due to injury (broken foot), he stayed healthy for the most part, proving once again that, when 100 percent, he is among the top defensive tackles in the game. Long made six Pro Bowls in seven years from 1982 to 1989, and routinely draws double teams. "He is without question one of the outstanding linemen in professional football," says a scout. "He has it all—speed, size, explosive quickness, strength, and still a good degree of intensity."

HANK'S RATING: A

William Perry

Birthdate: December 16, 1962
College: Clemson
Height: 6-2
Weight: 330
How Acquired: Drafted in first round, 1985
Final 1990 Team: Chicago Bears

William Perry, along with Steve McMichael and the retired Dan Hampton, split time at the two defensive tackle positions in 1990. Perry finished with 4 sacks, and played well in run situations. But Perry has yet to live up to expectations, largely due to his weight. Though popular among fans for being "The Refrigerator," Perry, and his annual weight problem, has been no laughing matter to the Bears, who have invested millions in the on-again, off-again lineman.

Perry was late to training camp in 1988 after reporting to an eating disorder clinic, then suffered a broken arm three weeks into the season and missed the rest of the year. In 1989, he ended up on injured reserve again with an injured left knee. Last season, he had another consistent season, forcing two fumbles, and carrying the ball in the offensive backfield once for a 1-yard loss. He had 70 tackles, but is often double-teamed to slow him down. Still a force that "must" be strongly blocked on every play. Amazing agility for a big, big man. It is sad, he could have been a Hall of Fame player.

HANK'S RATING: A

Fred Stokes

Birthdate: March 14, 1964
College: Georgia Southern
Height: 6-3
Weight: 262
How Acquired: Plan B free agent, 1989
Final 1990 Team: Washington Redskins

Fred Stokes might have been the surprise of the year among defensive tackles. A Plan B signee, he led the Redskins with 7.5 sacks, recovered a team-high 4 fumbles, forced 2 fumbles, and was third on the team with 8 quarterback pressures.

Used primarily in just pass-rush situations, Stokes had just 19 tackles, but fulfilled the wishes of the coaching staff. "The improved pass rush helped take pressure off the secondary," says head coach Joe Gibbs. "If the defensive line learns to work together, it could become one of the league's best."

Stokes, who never played football until his senior year in high school (his coach spotted him in the band and offered him a tryout), was an All-America offensive tackle in college. So he understands both sides of the ball. "Fred comes up with the big plays," says defensive coordinator Richie Petitbon. "We hope he'll pick up where he left off."

HANK'S RATING: A

Scott Davis

Birthdate: August 7, 1965
College: Illinois
Height: 6-7
Weight: 275
How Acquired: Drafted in first round, 1988
Final 1990 Team: Los Angeles Raiders

Defensive tackle Scott Davis quietly improved in 1990, upping his single-season sack total to a career-high 10, during a season that most critics openly thought Davis would never see. Coaches were disappointed with Davis in 1989, and angered by his off-season arrest for assaulting a former girlfriend in Chicago. When Los Angeles drafted Arizona lineman Anthony Smith in the first round, many believed the bell had tolled for Davis.

But Davis went to training camp in 1990 ready to play, and when given the opportunity, he made up for lost time with actions, not words. He attacked the season with a vengeance, moved back into the starting lineup, and solidified himself as a welcome addition alongside the constant presence of Howie Long and All-Pro Greg Townsend.

"Scott gives us a big, strong, talented defensive lineman who has great position skills," says head coach Art Shell. "He needs to continue to work hard to improve himself at his position." Smith will return from injury to challenge Davis again in 1991, but Davis has now worked for—and earned—the respect of the coaching staff. His wild, aggressive style of play flourishes in the Raiders system.

HANK'S RATING: A

Dean Hamel

Birthdate: July 7, 1961
College: Tulsa
Height: 6-3
Weight: 276
How Acquired: Trade, 1989
Final 1990 Team: Dallas Cowboys

Defensive tackle Dean Hamel, acquired prior to the 1990 season from the Washington Redskins, had just 1 sack last season, but Dallas coaches were quick to remind critics that rushing the passer wasn't his primary task. Hamel was called on to stuff the run, and he did an excellent job, showing great promise as Dallas went with a youth movement throughout the defensive line. "Hamel is a solid player, who adds a veteran's leadership with a youngster's zeal," says a scout.

"He's not going to make plays like a Charles Haley, but that's not his job title. He controls his man, reads well, and clogs things up." Consistency, we say, is what Hamel most gives the Cowboys highly-skilled defensive line.

HANK'S RATING: A

Steve McMichael

Birthdate: October 17, 1957
College: Texas
Height: 6-2
Weight: 268
How Acquired: Free Agent, 1981
Final 1990 Team: Chicago Bears

Defensive tackle Steve McMichael switched off starting assignments in 1990 with the retired Dan Hampton, and rotated during games with Hampton and William Perry. Though age and injuries have taken their toll on the veteran lineman, McMichael is still among the Bears most reliable players: Going into 1990, his string of 101 consecutive starts was the longest on the club.

McMichael is a strong, powerful run-stopper, who turns in a consistent performance week after week. He finished with 71 tackles last season, and defensed 4 passes. In 1989, he graded out higher than any other Bear lineman, and his 3 career safeties are a Chicago record. The former Pro Bowler is hoping to return to form in 1991, his twelfth NFL season after being waived by New England in 1981.

HANK'S RATING: A

Jeff Bryant

Birthdate: May 22, 1960
College: Clemson
Height: 6-5
Weight: 277
How Acquired: Drafted in first round, 1982
Final 1990 Team: Seattle Seahawks

Jeff Bryant, now in his tenth season, moved from right end, where he'd started since his rookie year in 1982, to right tackle, and had another solid season. He finished with 47 tackles and 5.5 sacks, which puts him second only to Jacob Green on the Seahawks career list.

Bryant is a dependable, consistent performer, having played in 127 games, starting 122 of those. The Seattle defensive line has been so durable over the years that starters Green, Bryant, and Joe Nash have started 101 of a possible 114 games together. Bryant personally has missed just 5 games in his career due to injury.

A skilled, intelligent worker, Bryant felt little pressure from newcomers, as he simply continued to work hard and play hard. But last year's first-round pick, Cortez Kennedy, is being groomed for right tackle. Look for Bryant, Nash, and Kennedy to all see action in 1991.

HANK'S RATING: A

Darryl Grant

Birthdate: November 22, 1959
College: Rice
Height: 6-1
Weight: 275
How Acquired: Drafted in ninth round, 1981
Final 1990 Team: Washington Redskins

Defensive tackle Darryl Grant started all sixteen games for the third straight year in 1990, the only Redskin defensive lineman who can claim such dependability. He also led the defensive linemen in tackles for the third straight season, finishing with 71, and added 6 quarterback hurries, a forced fumble, and a fumble recovery to his numbers.

Grant is considered the essential man in the middle for Washington, and is considered by Redskins' coaches as the "foundation" of the defense. He is a versatile, intelligent player; as a collegiate star, he played tackle, center, linebacker and nose tackle. He's also mentally alert—he has 3 career interceptions to his credit, including one he returned for a touchdown against Dallas in the 1982 NFC title game to put the Redskins in the Super Bowl. A consistent player, though some insiders question his production in "big game" situations.

HANK'S RATING: A

Tony Tolbert

Birthdate: December 29, 1967
College: Texas El-Paso
Height: 6-6
Weight: 241
How Acquired: Drafted in fourth round, 1989
Final 1990 Team: Dallas Cowboys

Third-year defensive tackle Tony Tolbert appears this high among the defensive linemen for one primary reason: Potential. This kid is good, and scouts say he is getting better with every rep. He finished the season with 6 sacks, third on the team, and made great strides throughout the 1990 season. Some scouts thought Tolbert improved more than any player on the Dallas defensive line in 1990, with the exception of rookie Jimmie Jones.

HANK'S RATING: A

Doug Smith

Birthdate: June 13, 1959
College: Auburn
Height: 6-6
Weight: 286
How Acquired: Drafted in first round, 1984
Final 1990 Team: Houston Oilers

Injuries plagued defensive tackle Doug Smith in 1990, and scouts attribute his constant health problems to his unwillingness to condition or train properly. "What Doug Smith does in the offseason is a mystery," says a team source. "We know he eats, doesn't lift weights, and doesn't condition. We wonder what he does do."

Smith is a dominating run-stopper who fuels his play with a nasty disposition and vicious tackling style. He respects no one, regardless of their tenure in the league or their ability. "If Smith gets leverage against you, he'll hurt you," says a scout from an opposing AFC team. "He's a scary player. He'll bite, spit, cuss, fall on the pile, he doesn't care. We file him under 'loose cannons.'"

The greatest disappointment, perhaps, is that Smith entered the league in 1985 with the potential to be among the best defensive tackles in the game. Though he has pure ability, his overall attitude, lifestyle and unwillingness to work have left his vast potential unfulfilled. "Do I respect Doug as a player, hell yes," says a teammate, who requested anonymity. "Do I respect him as a person, do I respect his lifestyle? Hell no. He could be twice the player he is. In just pure talent, he probably has more than anybody on the defensive line. But Sean [Jones] and Ray [Childress] work their asses off. That's the difference." In our Top 15, Smith could move higher if he improves his work habits.

HANK'S RATING: A

Tim Johnson

Birthdate: January 29, 1965
College: Penn State
Height: 6-3
Weight: 269
How Acquired: Plan B free agent, 1990
Final 1990 Team: Washington Redskins

Defensive tackle Tim Johnson joined the Redskins off Pittsburgh's Plan B list and earned a starting job, but still split time with second-year defensive tackle Tracy Rocker. The pair finished with similar stats: Johnson, 26 tackles, 3 sacks; Rocker, 35 tackles, 3 sacks. Johnson had 7 quarterback hurries, 3 passes defensed, forced a fumble, and recovered another.

Redskins coaches hold out a lot of faith for Johnson. He was consistent, and saved his best for last, when, in the playoffs against Philadelphia, he sacked quarterback Randall Cunningham twice, which changed the game's momentum. Scouts say Johnson isn't overly blessed with talent, but works extremely hard and makes few mistakes. He'll have to fend off the talented, hard-charging Rocker in 1991.

HANK'S RATING: A

Danny Noonan

Birthdate: July 14, 1965
College: Nebraska
Height: 6-4
Weight: 270
How Acquired: Drafted in first round, 1987
Final 1990 Team: Dallas Cowboys

Danny Noonan had 4.5 sacks in 1990 as he began to return to the form that once made him one of college football's most feared defensive linemen. Noonan, perhaps the strongest Cowboy, can bench press nearly 500 pounds and has incredible explosion off the line. But his production was all but nonexistent early in his career, evidence of his lack of overall skills.

"As Danny has acquired the skill it takes to play his position, he's proving he can be a major asset to this team," says head coach Jimmy Johnson. "He works hard and he wants to play. He's getting better." Noonan, at times, controlled his opponent, and like former Cowboy Randy White, has incredibly powerful hands and arms. He is without question a tremendous force against the run. Noonan is still gullible, however, to counter traps and more sophisticated line blocking. But his rapid improvement bodes well for the Cowboys.

HANK'S RATING: A

Cortez Kennedy

Birthdate: August 23, 1968
College: Miami
Height: 6-3
Weight: 293
How Acquired: Drafted in first round, 1990
Final 1990 Team: Seattle Seahawks

The forty-six-day holdout of rookie defensive lineman Cortez Kennedy virtually eliminated his 1990 season. His effectiveness was limited until the second half of the season, and even then, only appeared in erratic spurts. Kennedy contributed just 48 tackles and a single sack to the cause in 1990, and 10 of those tackles, along with his lone sack, occurred in a single game at Miami.

But scouts regard Kennedy as one of the brightest defensive line prospects in years, capable of playing the run and pass with equal effectiveness. "This kid can run (4.6), he's strong, he's physical," says an AFC East scout. "His huge size allows him to play the run extremely well, but his strength and speed make him an excellent pass rusher. It's seldom you find such a talented player in one package."

HANK'S RATING: A

Jimmie Jones

Birthdate: January 9, 1966
College: Miami
Height: 6-4
Weight: 284
How Acquired: Drafted in third round, 1990
Final 1990 Team: Dallas Cowboys

Rookie Jimmie Jones had an impressive freshman season from his defensive tackle position in 1990, recording 7.5 sacks his first time out of the gate. He made a strong case to become a full-time starter, and looks likely to earn the job in training camp this season. Jones displayed excellent quickness, good explosion, and sometimes stunning side-to-side movement. His ability to slip blocks "is something you don't really see from rookies with his lack of experience," says a scout. Jones, certainly a surprise last season, has given head coach Jimmy Johnson reason to smile. With the addition of first-round draft pick Russell Maryland, this could be the NFL's next overpowering defensive line, much like the Bears, Vikings, and Eagles of recent years.

HANK'S RATING: A

Joe Nash

Birthdate: October 11, 1960
College: Boston College
Height: 6-2
Weight: 269
How Acquired: Free Agent, 1982
Final 1990 Team: Seattle Seahawks

Left tackle Joe Nash, now in his eleventh season, moved over from nose tackle in 1990 to accomodate Seattle's new 4-3 defense. He made the switch comfortably, and finished with 53 quiet tackles and a lone sack. Nash has now played in 130 games, starting 111, in his career.

Seattle coaches say Nash, like Bryant, will be challenged in 1991 by the presence of talented youth like Cortez Kennedy, Bob Buczkowski and Eric Hayes, who was a fifth-round surprise for Seattle in 1990. Hayes started the season rotating at tackle and played some at end later in the year. But Nash remains a determined, dependable veteran, and don't expect him to leave quietly. A Top 25 tackle, Nash should enjoy the competition.

HANK'S RATING: A

Harvey Armstrong

Birthdate: December 29, 1959
College: SMU
Height: 6-3
Weight: 282
How Acquired: Free Agent, 1986
Final 1990 Team: Indianapolis Colts

Now in his sixth season, Harvey Armstrong has been more consistent and versatile than many of the Colts' higher-touted defensive linemen. He has played at end, tackle and nose, and at times came on as the team's most dominant lineman.

Against Miami in 1990, he had a team-high 8 tackles, and finished the year with 59 tackles. But he failed to register a sack, more evidence of the Colts' sagging pass rush. Armstrong is a quick, hard-working player with competent skills who is a dedicated team player.

HANK'S RATING: A

Marc Spindler

Birthdate: November 29, 1969
College: Pittsburgh
Height: 6-5
Weight: 277
How Acquired: Drafted in third round, 1990
Final 1990 Team: Detroit Lions

Defensive tackle Marc Spindler is rated low largely due to his few appearances during his rookie season of 1990. After a rowdy start, he missed the last twelve games with a knee injury, and Detroit coaches are hoping he can return to make an impact in 1991. "Spindler missed virtually the whole season," says defensive coordinator Woody Widenhofer. "But I know he's going to be healthy for 1991. I'm very excited about the defensive line."

But Spindler will be pushed by Detroit's youth movement along the line: Lawrence Pete, Jeff Hunter, and Mark Duckens are all making a move toward starting positions. But among these four, when healthy, Spindler is the best of the group.

HANK'S RATING: B

Rick Bryan

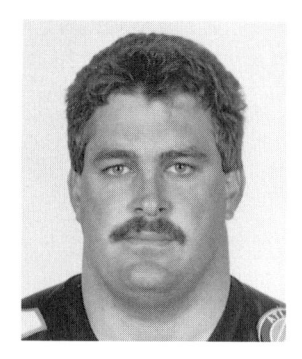

Birthdate: March 20, 1962
College: Oklahoma
Height: 6-4
Weight: 265
How Acquired: Drafted in first round, 1984
Final 1990 Team: Atlanta Falcons

Rick Bryan had a modest season in 1990, compiling 69 tackles, 1 sack, and 16 quarterback pressures in a less active role in Atlanta's new 3-4 defense. But the fact that Bryan was even on the field was testimony to his solid work habits—he suffered a neck injury in 1989 that would have ended most player's careers. And he tied for the team lead in batting down opponents' passes (3), and recovered 2 fumbles.

Though Bryan has lost a step, the eighth-year player gives 100 percent when on the field. He is a physical and emotional leader for the Falcons, and sets a glowing example to the team's younger players. But Bryan will be pressured by Atlanta's youth movement—namely cat-quick Oliver Barnett—in 1991.

HANK'S RATING: B

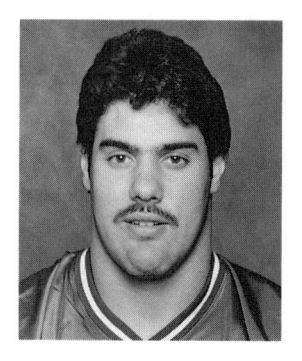

Mike Fox

Birthdate: August 5, 1967
College: West Virginia
Height: 6-6
Weight: 275
How Acquired: Drafted in second round, 1990
Final 1990 Team: New York Giants

Rookie Mike Fox showed an ability to collapse the pocket and was relentlessness that was a major factor in allowing the 3-4-oriented Giants the flexibility to play a 4-3. "By the end of the year, he was a rookie only in fact," says former head coach Bill Parcells. "Mike Fox played extremely hard, and enabled us to do a lot of different things defensively in the playoffs."

Fox is a big, talented player, and his rookie playing experience should reap big dividends for the Giants in coming seasons. He has strength, but lacks top speed and needs better pash rush skills. Insiders say he could earn a starting job if he can put together a productive training camp.

HANK'S RATING: B

Nose Tackles

Michael Dean Perry

Birthdate: August 27, 1965
College: Clemson
Height: 6-0
Weight: 280
How Acquired: Drafted in second round, 1988
Final 1990 Team: Cleveland Browns

For a short time, Michael Dean Perry was constantly labeled as the "younger brother of the Fridge." Times, however, have changed, and Michael Dean is now casting a formidable shadow of his own.

Perry's cocked stance, reminiscent of the retired Joe Klecko, gives him a unique advantage over most offensive linemen because of his explosiveness. "He has the ability to line up on one side and beat you to the other side," says Cincinnati tackle Bruce Reimers. "He puts relentless pressure on everybody he plays."

And for those of you who still think of Michael Dean as "the little brother," consider this: He recorded more sacks in his rookie year than brother William has ever had in a single season, and he tacked another 11.5 on during his 1990 Pro Bowl season. Our No. 1 ranked nose tackle.

HANK'S RATING: AAA

Michael Carter

Birthdate: October 29, 1960
College: SMU
Height: 6-2
Weight: 285
How Acquired: Drafted in fifth round, 1984
Final 1990 Team: San Francisco 49ers

Sheer determination made Michael Carter a force again among the NFL's dominant linemen after a devastating knee injury in 1990. "If he locks you up," says an opposing center, "you can forget it." Injuries sidelined Carter for much of 1989, giving him an appetite for the 1990 season. He responded with steady consistency.

Carter's job is to clog the middle and free up his teammates for the big plays. And, occasionally, he makes a big play himself. Against Washington in the playoffs, Charles Haley tipped a Mark Rypien pass into the hands of Carter, who promptly rumbled 61 yards for the 49ers fourth and deciding touchdown. "How's that for running time off the clock," 49er head coach George Seifert quipped afterward. In all seriousness, Seifert calls Carter "the ideal nose guard in the three-man front... Carter has great quickness, strength, and leverage. And he's very, very intense."

HANK'S RATING: AAA

Henry Thomas

Birthdate: January 12, 1965
College: LSU
Height: 6-2
Weight: 268
How Acquired: Drafted in third round, 1987
Final 1990 Team: Minnesota Vikings

Henry Thomas finished second on the Vikings in sacks with 8.5, and saw extensive playing time in the absence of veteran Keith Millard, who was injured. Thomas had 9 sacks in 1989, and has become a reliable contributor over his five-year career.

"What Thomas gives you at the nose is consistency," says a scout. "He plays hard every down, and most noticably, plays the two-gap with excellent quickness. He clogs running lanes, and in passing situations, he can get upfield and pressure the quarterback."

HANK'S RATING: AA

Jerry Ball

Birthdate: December 15, 1964
College: Southern Methodist
Height: 6-1
Weight: 298
How Acquired: Drafted in third round, 1987
Final 1990 Team: Detroit Lions

Defensive coordinator Woody Widenhofer may be single-handedly responsible for putting Jerry Ball back in the Pro Bowl at nose tackle: He fought for, and finally succeeded, in switching the Lions back to a more aggressive defensive scheme. He moved pass-rushing linebacker Mike Cofer to the line of scrimmage, then relieved Ball of his frustrating two-gap responsibilities. The result was a quicker, more aggressive Jerry Ball, one that wreaked havoc in the backfields of numerous opposing offenses when he was healthy.

But there was a flip-side. Ball missed all of the pre-season, then sprained an ankle. "We finally got [Ball] back toward the end of the year, but his late start was very disappointing," says Widenhofer. There were several players who felt Ball didn't deserve to be in the Pro Bowl: He finished the year tenth on the team in tackles with 50, and registered just 2 sacks and forced 1 fumble.

The bottom line: Ball is a highly talented nose tackle capable of single-handedly dominating games. Still has to improve on his consistency to become one of the league's premier defensive linemen. Many feel the only thing that can hold Ball back is Ball. Questions about his attitude and his weight worry scouts.

HANK'S RATING: AA

Dan Saleaumua

Birthdate: November 11, 1965
College: Arizona State
Height: 6-0
Weight: 289
How Acquired: Plan B free agent, 1989
Final 1990 Team: Kansas City Chiefs

Nose tackle Dan Saleaumua's omission from the Pro Bowl might have been a travesty in 1990. He was third on the team in sacks (7), was a constant force against the run, often dominated the line of scrimmage, and generally created havoc.

Saleaumua was always around the football. When linebacker Derrick Thomas forced a Dave Krieg fumble against Seattle, Saleaumua recovered the ball in the end zone for Kansas City's only touchdown. "Dan has been a pleasant surprise for us," says head coach Marty Schottenheimer. "We're pleased with his progress, and even more pleased that he's been able to maintain the consistency he showed he in 1989."

HANK'S RATING: AA

Erik Howard

Birthdate: November 12, 1964
College: Washington State
Height: 6-4
Weight: 268
How Acquired: Drafted in second round, 1986
Final 1990 Team: New York Giants

Nose tackle Erik Howard fills a Hercules-type role with the Giants. Primarily a run-stopper, Howard is one of the strongest Giants players ever, capable of bench-pressing a virtually unheard of 585 pounds (he has bench-pressed 225 pounds a staggering forty-four times). For his size, Howard possesses good agility and leaping ability, and is a key factor for New York in controlling the line of scrimmage. But he lacks nose tackle pass rush speed and quickness. He finished the season with only 3 sacks, but led Giant defensive linemen with 71 tackles.

In the playoffs against Chicago, Howard was credited by Giants coaches for playing the most critical role in holding the Bears without a rushing first down. He also forced the fumble that led to the game-winning field goal against the 49ers in the NFC title game.

HANK'S RATING: A

Brian Sochia

Birthdate: July 21, 1961
College: Northwest Oklahoma
Height: 6-3
Weight: 278
How Acquired: Free Agent, 1986
Final 1990 Team: Miami Dolphins

Nose tackle Brian Sochia had a beleagured 1990 season: He spent the first month on the reserve/nonfootball injury list for violating the NFL's steroid policy, then missed most of the year with a torn groin muscle. In his limited appearances, he recorded just 6 tackles and 1 sack on the year, but it was certainly not indicative of the talent he possesses (in 1989, Sochia started all sixteen games at nose and finished third on the team with 5 sacks).

Sochia made just his second start of the season against Indianapolis, and gave the Dolphins home-field advantage in the playoffs when he recovered a Jeff George fumble (forced by defensive end Jeff Cross) and returned it for a touchdown.

"We're hopeful Brian Sochia will regain his former Pro Bowl form," says head coach Don Shula.

HANK'S RATING: A

Greg Kragen

Birthdate: March 4, 1962
College: Utah State
Height: 6-3
Weight: 265
How Acquired: Free Agent, 1985
Final 1990 Team: Denver Broncos

Undersized nose tackle Greg Kragen had just 2 sacks in 1990, down from his Pro Bowl season numbers in 1989. Kragen first began to emerge as a Denver defensive leader in 1988, when he was one of only seven Broncos to start every game. During that season, he was named Defensive Player of the Game five times, including three times in a four-week stretch.

Kragen became a starter in 1986, when he moved into the nose tackle spot during the third week of the season and started every game thereafter through Super Bowl XXI. But Kragen's lack of size has really hurt him in recent years, as his body is beginning to show the wear of several bloody seasons in NFL trenches. Kragen plays the run with exceptional strength, and has great quickness in the two-gap. But, in a problem that has plagued Denver for several years, Kragen lacks the size at the point of attack to be consistently effective.

HANK'S RATING: A

Tory Epps

Birthdate: May 28, 1967
College: Memphis State
Height: 6-0
Weight: 280
How Acquired: Drafted in eighth round, 1990
Final 1990 Team: Atlanta Falcons

Nose tackle Tory Epps was an eighth-round find by Atlanta in 1990, earning all-rookie honors with 84 tackles, 3 sacks and 3 blocked kicks, including 2 in the same game against the World Champion 49ers.

A former linebacker, Epps bulked up and moved to nose tackle during his freshman season at Memphis State. His hard work during his rookie year in Atlanta began to pay dividends by the season's fourth week, and by the end of the year, he was in contention for the starting nose tackle job. "There is no question Glanville plays favorites," says a scout, "and he's attracted to hard work and balls-out effort. That's what Epps gives the defensive line. He doesn't have an ounce of Tony Casillas's talent. But he works harder than anybody up front, except Tim Green."

HANK'S RATING: A

Tim Krumrie

Birthdate: May 20, 1960
College: Wisconsin
Height: 6-2
Weight: 267
How Acquired: Drafted in tenth round, 1983
Final 1990 Team: Cincinnati Bengals

After suffering what might have been the second-most highly publicized broken leg during Super Bowl XXIII (The nod for the most-publicized broken leg goes to Joe Theismann, whose shin was shattered by Lawrence Taylor on "Monday Night Football."), Tim Krumrie bounced back in 1990 with his best year since the injury, but was still left on the Plan B unprotected list at season's end. But Krumrie re-signed with the Bengals, where he hopes to have another steady year in 1991.

"Cold, rain, snow . . . that's my kind of football," Krumrie says. "Getting the uniform dirty." Krumrie was modestly effective and had 2 sacks on the season, but he was no where near the player he was prior to the injury. Sadly, Krumrie has worked harder than virtually any player in the league to keep his job. He plays with a metal rod in his left leg that will remain there until he quits playing.

"When the rod comes out, I'll be done playing football," Krumrie says. "There is so much new bone formed around the rod that there would be too much trauma to the leg to take the rod out. I don't feel the rod anymore. It's all healed, there's no crack anymore. It's solid."

What plays Krumrie does make are the result of study and anticipation. "I'm a very good cheater," he says. "It's part of being a pro. The more you know about your opponent, the better off you'll be in a game." Though Krumrie still plays hard each down, he is not as consistently productive as he once was.

HANK'S RATING: A

Scott Mersereau

Birthdate: April 8, 1965
College: Southern Connecticut
Height: 6-3
Weight: 280
How Acquired: Free Agent, 1987
Final 1990 Team: New York Jets

Defensive end Scott Mersereau, a replacement player during the 1987 strike, continued to play with modest consistency in 1990. He finished with 4.5 sacks, and was aggressive, though unspectacular, against the run. Mersereau, who started at nose tackle in 1989, benefitted from new head coach Bruce Coslet's "attack" alignment. And though Mersereau is a talented spot player, he can't be considered an every-down player by NFL standards.

HANK'S RATING: A

Tony Casillas

Birthdate: October 26, 1963
College: Oklahoma
Height: 6-3
Weight: 280
How Acquired: Drafted in first round, 1986
Final 1990 Team: Atlanta Falcons

The production of Tony Casillas fell dramatically again in 1990, as the on-again, off-again nose tackle reported late, found himself in Jerry Glanville's doghouse, then failed to produce consistently in a limited role. Like teammate Aundrey Bruce, Casillas has been an enigma during his brief NFL career: loaded with talent, but lacking consistency and mental discipline.

Casillas, a millionaire and former first-round selection, had just 32 tackles and 1 sack, less than half the totals of rookie nose tackle Tory Epps, an eighth-round pick. He also had just 4 quarterback pressures, which ranked ahead of only three other players. His tackle total was dead last among all defensive linemen on the team.

Perhaps 1989 was a better indicator of Casillas' potential, when he made 152 tackles, had 16 quarterback hurries, 3 fumble recoveries, 2 forced fumbles and a pair of sacks. But until Casillas develops poise and consistency, he will not be considered among the league's finest at his position. In fact, he now faces a training camp battle with Epps for his starting job.

HANK'S RATING: A

Gerald Williams

Birthdate: September 8, 1963
College: Auburn
Height: 6-3
Weight: 279
How Acquired: Drafted in second round, 1986
Final 1990 Team: Pittsburgh Steelers

The defensive downfall of the Steelers in 1990 could largely be attributed to a lack of consistent play on the defensive line. The entire line recorded just 21.5 sacks in 1990, and gave up far too many yards rushing, especially in critical games; in two losses to Cincinnati, the Bengals rushed for 343 yards.

Gerald Williams had his best season at nose tackle and led the team with 6 sacks. Though he is beginning to emerge as one of the AFC's better and most consistent players, he must develop better skills against the run: quicker reaction time, better explosion, and more strength at the point of attack. But his growth as a pass rusher made him a much more complete player.

HANK'S RATING: A

Jeff Wright

Birthdate: June 13, 1963
College: Central Missouri State
Height: 6-2
Weight: 270
How Acquired: Drafted in eighth round, 1988
Final 1990 Team: Buffalo Bills

Nose tackle Jeff Wright is another product of Buffalo's fine scouting staff. Wright had 5 sacks in 1990, which is more than most scouts thought he would have as a little-known eighth-round draft pick in 1988 out of Central Missouri State. Wright is a stout, powerful nose tackle, with incredible hand and upper-body strength.

Despite his relatively small size for his position, Wright bench-presses 400 pounds and runs the 40 in 4.7. In addition to powerful explosion off the line of scrimmage, Wright also displays excellent lateral quickness—it was his sack to Dan Marino that ended the quarterback's sackless streak. An improving player.

HANK'S RATING: B

Tim Goad

Birthdate: February 28, 1966
College: North Carolina
Height: 6-3
Weight: 280
How Acquired: Drafted in fourth round, 1988
Final 1990 Team: New England Patriots

Nose tackle Tim Goad finished third on the Patriots with 89 tackles, including 2.5 sacks and 1 recovered fumble. He was perhaps the Patriots most consistent lineman in what was a horrible season for the defensive line, as New England surrendered more yards per play than any team in the NFL and finished dead last in total defense.

Goad, in his fourth season, will be given ample chance to earn a starting berth under the Patriots' new coaching staff, but he'll be tested by an assault of rookies and free agents. Goad is a strong, powerful nose tackle who, with help, is a steady player. No one questions his strength—Goad still holds the University of North Carolina's squat record of 705 pounds.

HANK'S RATING: B

Bob Nelson

Birthdate: March 3, 1959
College: Miami
Height: 6-4
Weight: 275
How Acquired: Free Agent, 1988
Final 1990 Team: Green Bay Packers

Nose tackle Bob Nelson, now in his fifth season, had a quiet, 56-tackle season in 1990. He became a starter in 1988, and has held down the nose tackle position since then. Though his play can hardly be considered spectacular, it is consistent. Last year was the first time in three years Nelson didn't lead the Green Bay defensive line in total tackles.

"Nelson has a great attitude and is a hard worker," says defensive line coach Greg Blache. "You always know you're going to get a day's work for a day's pay. It's hard to compare him to other nose tackles in the league, but he fills our need. He's able to two-gap, able to hold the middle. I think he fits what we need him to do, so he works well in our system. And he's a very intense, tough guy." But what sets Nelson apart, says Blache, is his awareness. "If you try to fool him, he's got a sense about it," he says. "He's very difficult to confuse."

HANK'S RATING: B

Who's Missing

Bob Golic

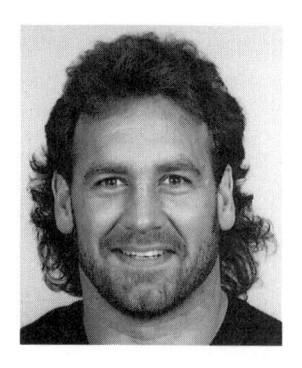

Birthdate: October 26, 1957
College: Notre Dame
Height: 6-2
Weight: 275
How Acquired: Plan B free agent, 1989
Position: Nose Tackle
Final 1990 Team: Los Angeles Raiders

Bob Golic played a familiar role in 1990 with the Los Angeles Raiders, as his steady, consistent play—despite being thirty-three years old—helped shape the Raiders defensive front into one of the league's finest units. But some questions exist as to how much more punishment his body can stand. Golic did have 4 sacks last season, blending well with the talent around him. Golic remains a strong, dynamic veteran, who boasts the savvy experience of a three-time Pro Bowler. If he doesn't have problems with injuries, look for Golic to remain a force.

HANK'S RATING: AA

Jim Jeffcoat

Birthdate: April 1, 1961
College: Arizona State
Height: 6-5
Weight: 256
How Acquired: Drafted in first round, 1983
Position: Defensive End
Final 1990 Team: Dallas Cowboys

The day of reckoning comes someday for even the game's best players, and that day has arrived for defensive end Jim Jeffcoat. He finished fourth on the team in 1990 with 3.5 sacks, but Jeffcoat's problem isn't so much what he can do, it's what he can't do—and that's match the speed, strength and size of the Cowboys' young, upstart defensive line. With the addition of first-round draft pick Russell Maryland, it's unlikely Jeffcoat will survive another year in Dallas—not with the likes of Noonan, Stubbs, Tolbert, and Jones already bidding for starting positions. But Jeffcoat is still capable of another productive year or two, and is surely of some value to another NFL club.

HANK'S RATING: B

Jim Skow

Birthdate: June 29, 1963
College: Nebraska
Height: 6-3
Weight: 243
How Acquired: Drafted in third round, 1986
Position: Defensive End
Final 1990 Team: Tampa Bay Buccaneers

One word comes up repeatedly among scouts during discussions about Jim Skow: Heart. "The guy has a big heart," says one. "He leaves everything he's got out on the field." Unfortunately, everything the former Bengal has—with all due respect to his work ethic and attitude—simply isn't enough for Tampa's beleaguered defensive line.

Skow played in twelve games in 1990 and started ten, but missed four games after suffering a dislocated elbow against the Saints. He had just 2 sacks on the season and several quarterback pressures, but was not the same player who had 14 sacks over a two-year period with the Bengals (1988 and 1989).

HANK'S RATING: B

Keith McCants

Birthdate: November 19, 1968
College: Alabama
Height: 6-3
Weight: 255
How Acquired: Drafted in first round, 1990
Position: Defensive End
Final 1990 Team: Tampa Bay Buccaneers

Keith McCants, Tampa Bay's brash first-round pick of 1990, was moved to defensive end during the 1991 offseason by new defensive coordinator Floyd Peters, a transformation Peters successfully used on former Minnesota linebacker Chris Doleman. McCants had a disappointing rookie season, although he did start the last four games of the year at linebacker.

He finished with 44 tackles, 2 sacks, 2 forced fumbles and 1 recovered fumble. McCants failed to adjust well to the pro game, where he was confused by the myriad of coverages and opponent tendencies he was forced to absorb. Loaded with natural ability, McCants wants to just chase the ball, like he did during his standout collegiate days at Alabama. The third youngest player in the NFL in 1990 (21), McCants must acquire maturity and good work habits to go with his God-given skills.

He is impossible to project as a defensive lineman, because, according to one scout, "we've only seen him at linebacker . . . and so far, he was limited at that. He's got a lot to learn, and before he learns anything, he has to want to learn." That may be Peters' biggest hurdle.

HANK'S RATING: B

Donald Evans

Birthdate: March 14, 1964
College: Winston-Salem
Height: 6-2
Weight: 262
How Acquired: Free Agent, 1990
Position: Defensive End
Final 1990 Team: Pittsburgh Steelers

Defensive end Donald Evans joined the Steelers as a free agent in 1990, and ended up a starter by opening day. The former linebacker struggled at times, but proved himself to Steeler coaches as a strong, intelligent, hard-working player. Coaches believe he has a future as a starter, but Pittsburgh has so many young defensive linemen vying for jobs there are serious questions whether he will retain his role.

HANK'S RATING: B

Ken Clarke

Birthdate: August 28, 1956
College: Syracuse
Height: 6-2
Weight: 281
How Acquired: Free Agent, 1989
Position: Defensive Tackle
Final 1990 Team: Minnesota Vikings

Ken Clarke, in his thirteenth season, finished with an impressive 7 sacks in 1990. But, there are many questions as to what role Clarke will play in 1991. He did impress head coach Jerry Burns with his willingness to work and his consistency after the team lost Keith Millard on the defensive front. "Ken was a steady player last season," says Burns. "He was a leader to the younger players."

HANK'S RATING: B

Anthony Smith

Birthdate: June 28, 1967
College: Arizona
Height: 6-3
Weight: 260
How Acquired: Drafted in first round, 1990
Position: Defensive End
Final 1990 Team: Los Angeles Raiders

Defensive end Anthony Smith missed his rookie season with a knee injury, but team doctors believe he should return in 1991 to challenge for playing time once again. Smith played every position on the defensive line during his college career at Arizona, and has all the qualities necessary to become a starting NFL defensive lineman: size, good strength, and 4.6 speed in the 40. But he will be hard-pressed to simply inherit a job in 1991, after the stalwart efforts turned in by the starting front four of Townsend, Long, Davis, and Golic. But, if healthy, there is little question that his time will come.

HANK'S RATING: B

Bob Buczkowski

Birthdate: May 5, 1964
College: Pittsburgh
Height: 6-5
Weight: 216
How Acquired: Free Agent, 1991
Position: Defensive Tackle
Final 1990 Team: Seattle Seahawks

Former first-round pick Bob Buczkowski is looking for a home, and he may have found one in Seattle. The once highly regarded draft pick has suffered through injuries, subsequent inconsistency and multiple trades, and has been unable to settle down, learn a scheme, and concentrate on his game. The Seahawks say they will give him that opportunity in 1991.

Buczkowski came to the Seahawks from Cleveland in exchange for a ninth-round draft pick. Now in his fourth season, the former Pitt standout was a first-round pick of the Raiders in 1986, but missed most of his first two seasons due to illnesses and injuries. As a member of the Cleveland Browns in 1990, he played in sixteen games, starting five, and was credited with 32 tackles. He remains an untested talent who possesses fine quickness, mobility, size, and strength.

HANK'S RATING: D

Best of Plan B

Bill Pickel

Birthdate: November 5, 1959
College: Rutgers
Height: 6-5
Weight: 260
Final 1990 Team: Los Angeles Raiders

When the New York Jets signed Bill Pickel off the Raiders' Plan B list, it was a homecoming of sorts for the Brooklyn native. Pickel, now in his ninth pro season, should give the Jets an instant boost on the defensive line. Pickel is an experienced, smart, aggressive player, who performs with intensity and productivity against both the pass or run.

Pickel has played in the Pro Bowl and led the Raiders in sacks in both 1984 and 1985, when he had back-to-back 12.5-sack seasons. "Though Pickel has lost a step, he has enough talent left to not only contribute to the New York line, but also teach their young players the kind of effort and dedication it takes to excel at that position," says a scout.

HANK'S RATING: B

Outside Linebackers

Lawrence Taylor

Birthdate: February 4, 1959
College: North Carolina
Height: 6-3
Weight: 243
How Acquired: Drafted in first round, 1981
Final 1990 Team: New York Giants

Lawrence Taylor, in what many considered an "off" year for the standout linebacker, still finished with 10.5 sacks in 1990, down 5 sacks from 1989. After a contract holdout that lasted until just four days before the season opener, Taylor, with only two days of practice, had 7 tackles, 3 sacks, and a forced fumble against the Eagles. At the age of thirty-one, Taylor already owns the NFL career record for sacks with 114.5. "Taylor still shows no signs of letting up," says former head coach Bill Parcells.

Off the field, Taylor has become much less controversial, but still conducts business as usual on the field. "Lawrence Taylor, as he has for years, still controls the game," says a scout. "He set the standards for all the young linebackers coming out of college today."

Taylor, despite the years of abuse on his body, is still a perennial do-everything player. Scouts say Taylor remains very effective in coverage and hasn't lost any speed. "Taylor is savvy and experienced now," says New York Jets GM Dick Steinberg. "He stuffs the run. He throws around tight ends. Sometimes he actually seems like he's getting better, rather than slipping."

Vikings scouts say that in every game of Taylor's they've graded, "he's never missed a tackle." Says one, "You don't block Lawrence Taylor. You pray."

HANK'S RATING: AAA

Derrick Thomas

Birthdate: January 1, 1967
College: Alabama
Height: 6-3
Weight: 234
How Acquired: Drafted in first round, 1989
Final 1990 Team: Kansas City Chiefs

Wow. That's what one scout said when asked to assess the awesome physical skills of right outside linebacker Derrick Thomas. Three years ago, linebacking was considered the Chiefs biggest weakness, a problem head coach Marty Schottenheimer quickly fixed. Now, arguably, it may the team's biggest strength—especially with the addition of the All-Pro Thomas.

Thomas is cut in the mold of Lawrence Taylor: incredible speed and strength, with the ability to run down just about any player in the league behind the line of scrimmage. Thomas led the NFL with 20 sacks, including an NFL-record 7 sacks against Seattle. In that game, Thomas dominated like few players ever have: He made 5 other tackles, and missed having 4 more sacks by literally inches. He forced two fumbles, one of which was recovered for a Chiefs' touchdown On the game's last play, Seattle quarterback Dave Krieg threw a 25-yard touchdown to Paul Skansi—but the battered Krieg was thankful he even got the pass away. "They could have called 'in the grasp,'" Krieg says. "Thomas had his hands around my hips."

HANK'S RATING: AAA

Darryl Talley

Birthdate: July 10, 1960
College: West Virginia
Height: 6-4
Weight: 235
How Acquired: Drafted in second round, 1983
Final 1990 Team: Buffalo Bills

Only one Buffalo linebacker started every game in 1989, and it wasn't Cornelius Bennett or Shane Conlan. It was little-known right outside linebacker Darryl Talley, in his seventh year out of West Virginia. That season, Talley made forty more tackles than either Bennett or Conlan (97), and had 6 sacks—more than Bennett and Conlan combined.

"Darryl may be the most underrated player in the game," says head coach Marv Levy. "He does it all." Talley added two blocked punts to his final numbers, as he quietly earned team MVP honors. "Darryl has positioned himself in a leadership role," Levy says.

The blue-collar Talley was equally outstanding in 1990, leading the Bills again with 123 tackles. When opponents neutralized standout defensive end Bruce Smith with double teams, it was Talley who stepped up with authority to punish runners on his side. In the deciding sixteenth week of the 1990 season, Talley had 10 tackles, 2 quarterback hurries, and a deflected pass in the Bills' 24–14 division-clinching victory over Miami.

HANK'S RATING: AAA

Pat Swilling

Birthdate: October 25, 1964
College: Maryland
Height: 6-3
Weight: 242
How Acquired: Drafted in third round, 1983
Final 1990 Team: New Orleans Saints

Pro Bowl pick Pat Swilling ironically finished last among Saints' starting linebackers in tackles (63), but recorded 11 sacks and forced 4 fumbles as the Saints' big-play maker. Still, Swilling's sacks were down from 16.5 in 1989. Swilling has tremendous speed (4.5), outstanding size, and great technique, making him virtually impossible to block with a lone running back when he takes a wide route to the quarterback. Unlike most pass-rushing linebackers, Swilling is strong at the point of attack and plays the run nearly as well as he plays the pass. "Swilling is a rare physical specimen," says a scout. "There are few players in the league that can do what he does."

HANK'S RATING: AA

James Francis

Birthdate: August 4, 1968
College: Baylor
Height: 6-4
Weight: 250
How Acquired: Drafted in first round, 1990
Final 1990 Team: Cincinnati Bengals

In his rookie year, Francis led the team in tackles (78), sacks (8), and returned an interception for a touchdown. He was consistently productive on an inconsistent defense, which saw lots of action in 1990, and will probably see more in 1991.

Francis proved to be a tremendous talent, capable of stuffing running backs and tight ends or whipping past offensive tackles for devastating sacks. His pass coverage still needs work, but Francis caught on quickly to the pro game; so quickly, in fact, that several scouts believe he's Pro Bowl material in 1991. We'll go out on a limb—he *will* be All-Pro in 1991.

HANK'S RATING: AA

Cornelius Bennett

Birthdate: August 25, 1966
College: Alabama
Height: 6-2
Weight: 235
How Acquired: Trade, 1987
Final 1990 Team: Buffalo Bills

When the Buffalo Bills sacrificed their 1988 first-round pick and 1989 first- and second-round picks for Cornelius Bennett, many NFL coaches thought the Bills had been buffaloed. But Bills general manager Bill Polian stands by his decision today, and with obvious reasons: the perennial Pro Bowl linebacker has been a consistent force in the Bills defensive resurgence.

"Cornelius, in his first full year [1989], helped take us to the division championship and the brink of the Super Bowl," he says. "And he's been a big reason for our defensive success, including last year's Super Bowl appearance." Head coach Marv Levy agrees. "I think Cornelius is incomparable as far as pursuit," Levy says. "No linebacker in the world ranges from sideline to sideline like Cornelius Bennett."

Bennett, in the fourth year of a five-year, $4 million contract, has earned every penny. He earned his first starting berth in the Pro Bowl in 1988, when he made 103 tackles and 9.5 sacks, and has since become a regular in the annual all-star game. "He's got the whole package—strength, speed, intelligence, and a love for the game," says Bills defensive coordinator Walt Corey. But insiders say Bennett does not always play within the defensive call coordination.

Scouts all agree on one thing: Bennett is a gamebreaker. Last year against Denver, Bennett made 8 tackles, broke up a pass, returned a blocked field goal 80 yards for a touchdown, and recovered a fumble to set up another score. A week later, Bennett made 10 tackles, including 2 sacks and 2 tackles for losses, forced 2 fumbles and recovered another to set up a field goal.

"He's a great cover guy, he can cover deep and has great reaction on the ball," says one scout. "Few linebackers can do that. He plays the run well, pursues extremely well." His only weakness, however, is that he struggles at the point of attack, and is occasionally manhandled when locked up with a tight end. But Buffalo plays him almost like a free safety, which seldom leaves him over a tight end. And in open space, Bennett is exceptional.

HANK'S RATING: AA

Carl Banks

Birthdate: August 29, 1962
College: Michigan State
Height: 6-4
Weight: 235
How Acquired: Drafted in first round, 1984
Final 1990 Team: New York Giants

Carl Banks missed seven games in 1990 with a broken wrist, but returned to full strength by season's end, when he had an outstanding Super Bowl. He finished the season with 51 tackles, outstanding totals considering his abbreviated season. Banks possesses sideline-to-sideline speed, can get upfield quickly, and has the excellent strength needed to control the league's better tight ends. He can run with any back or tight end in the league, and punishes receivers in the open field. A very skilled position player and a tremendous worker.

HANK'S RATING: AA

Tim Harris

Birthdate: September 10, 1964
College: Memphis State
Height: 6-5
Weight: 235
How Acquired: Drafted in fourth round, 1986
Final 1990 Team: Green Bay Packers

Ask Vikings assistant GM Bob Holloway about the abilities of Green Bay linebacker Tim Harris, and he doesn't hesitate. "Awesome is the closest word," he says. "He has a great under move on the blitz and simply overpowers anybody in his way. You have to block him with a tackle. He'll kill a back."

His 13.5 sacks in 1988 were the fifth-best total in the NFL, and his 19.5 sacks in 1989 were the best in the league. But opponents caught on in 1990, limiting him to just 7 sacks. Still, without his intensity and pass-rush abilities, the Packers might have been defenseless.

"On third downs, I look to myself to make the sack instead of asking someone else to do it," Harris says. "Harris is as good as a defensive player as there is in the NFL," says Chicago lineman Jimbo Covert. "He's big. He can run. And when you watch a guy who has fun playing football, it's him."

Harris can run down people down with his speed, and scouts say he's more effective running to the ball than at the point of attack. Harris' biggest weakness is against play-action, a problem that more film study could easily alleviate. "Harris," says Atlanta head coach Jerry Glanville, "is simply in a class by himself."

HANK'S RATING: AA

Rickey Jackson

Birthdate: March 20, 1958
College: Pittsburgh
Height: 6-2
Weight: 243
How Acquired: Drafted in second round, 1981
Final 1990 Team: New Orleans Saints

Rickey Jackson didn't get the accolades of some of his peers in 1990, but his numbers stood on their own: 68 tackles, 6 sacks, 7 fumble recoveries and 4 forced fumbles. Now in his eleventh year, Jackson patrols the perimeters of New Orleans base zone defense with bad intentions, delivers thunderous hits and dishes out lots of pain. Jackson is now the Saints' all-time leading sacker with 85.5, and is also the team leader in career fumble recoveries with 17.

HANK'S RATING: AA

Jessie Tuggle

Birthdate: February 14, 1965
College: Valdosta State
Height: 5-11
Weight: 230
How Acquired: Free Agent, 1987
Final 1990 Team: Atlanta Falcons

Jessie Tuggle may be the NFL's most underrated linebacker. His 201 tackles made him the first Falcon to have a 200-tackle season since Buddy Curry had 229 in 1983, and the fifth-year pro added 5 sacks and 10 quarterback pressures to his totals. Tuggle came to the Falcons as a free agent in 1987, and has since earned the respect of his teammates and coaches many times over.

He made his mark as a deadly hitter at both linebacker and on special teams; he demonstrated excellent speed last year with a 65-yard return of a fumble for a touchdown against Houston. Though not overly strong at the point of attack, Tuggle works hard, reacts well to what he sees, and avoids blocks. An unsung player.

HANK'S RATING: AA

Ken Harvey

Birthdate: May 6, 1965
College: California
Height: 6-2
Weight: 230
How Acquired: Drafted in first round, 1988
Final 1990 Team: Phoenix Cardinals

It shouldn't be too long before we see Ken Harvey in the Pro Bowl. He led the Cardinals with 10 sacks, largely due to the freedom he enjoyed while roaming around in Phoenix's new 3-4 defense. It was the second year in a row that Harvey led the team in sacks (7 in 1989), and he has proven that he is the team's finest athlete.

Harvey possesses a powerful combination of strength and speed, and at times offered dominating performances. In time, Harvey could develop into one of the NFL's most complete linebackers, but first must level his performance with more consistency.

HANK'S RATING: AA

Simon Fletcher

Birthdate: February 18, 1962
College: Houston
Height: 6-5
Weight: 240
How Acquired: Drafted in second round, 1985
Final 1990 Team: Denver Broncos

Simon Fletcher trapped opposing quarterbacks a career-high eleven times in 1990, which was also best among the Broncos, proof that his transformation to linebacker is finally complete. The former defensive end was moved to linebacker in 1986 to take advantage of his size and his ability to drop off into pass coverage. A lightning quick, agile player, Fletcher is the fastest of all Broncos linebackers.

Fletcher also benefits from playing opposite Karl Mecklenberg, who draws a lot of attention from opponents. "But right now, Fletcher is probably their best linebacker," says a scout. "He's probably passed Mecklenberg in ability, and is more of a threat because of his speed." The Broncos are in desperate need of another skilled linebacker to complement the one-two punch of Mecklenberg and Fletcher.

HANK'S RATING: AA

Junior Seau

Birthdate: January 19, 1969
College: USC
Height: 6-3
Weight: 243
How Acquired: Drafted in first round, 1990
Final 1990 Team: San Diego Chargers

In an impressive rookie season, Junior Seau finished second on the team with 85 tackles and started fifteen games. His efforts caught the attention of his NFL peers as they voted him a second alternate to the Pro Bowl. Called "an awesome physical specimen" by Charger scouts, Seau is a pure blitzer and has very polished skills in pass coverage. Timed at 4.61 in the 40, Seau also benches more than 440 pounds. "Junior plays with the kind of enthusiasm we like to have," says San Diego defensive coordinator Ron Lynn. "He's a reckless-type player, but not out of control."

HANK'S RATING: AA

Mike Cofer

Birthdate: April 7, 1960
College: Tennessee
Height: 6-5
Weight: 244
How Acquired: Drafted in third round, 1983
Final 1990 Team: Detroit Lions

Mike Cofer delivered his usual steady performance in 1990, finishing with 10 sacks, which tied for eighth in the NFC. Cofer, when healthy, is a tremendous talent, who brings a veteran's leadership to an unstable defensive unit. He still runs 4.6 in the 40, has tremendous power in hisupper body, and can cover any back in the league man-to-man.

Cofer played through the 1989 season despite being riddled with injuries, which caused him to sit out nine games. Team officials say shoulder and arch injuries have "limited his effectiveness" in recent years. But despite these setbacks, Cofer still had 9.5 sacks in 1989, which led the Lions for the second consecutive year.

Cofer will embrace the 1991 season as the Lions acquire new defensive talent to shore up one of the league's worst defenses. "I look for him to have a Pro Bowl season," says head coach Wayne Fontes. "He never complains, he never slacks up, he never gives you anything less than 110 percent."

HANK'S RATING: AA

Andre Tippett

Birthdate: December 17, 1959
College: Iowa
Height: 6-3
Weight: 241
How Acquired: Drafted in second round, 1982
Final 1990 Team: New England Patriots

It's no secret why Andre Tippett has been to the Pro Bowl so many times, and why he's expected to return with a vengeance after recovering from knee surgery. "He's probably as versatile as they come," says a scout. "If he's on the open side, you can't block him. He plays both sides in the 4–0 defense, and his excellent quickness makes him effective when he plays like a down lineman. He has no signs of weakness."

Except, say scouts, at the point of attack, when he's not as potent when there's a good tight end in front of him. Tippett never was as effective in pass coverage as when he rushed the passer, but he remains one of the league's best in big-play ability and pass-rush ability. "I look at what I'm doing and I want to be exceptional," Tippett says. "It's attitude. I don't want to be in the meeting room and hear someone say, 'You did a great job containing the tight end or stringing out that run.' I want to make a sack or cause a fumble. The NFL is filled with talent, but you must make something happen." Some feel his skill level is below his past performances.

HANK'S RATING: AA

Karl Mecklenberg

Birthdate: September 1, 1961
College: Minnesota
Height: 6-3
Weight: 240
How Acquired: Drafted in twelfth round, 1983
Final 1990 Team: Denver Broncos

Karl Mecklenberg made the Pro Bowl in 1989 for his fourth time in five years, and it was largely due to Denver's new defensive system under assistant coach Wade Phillips. In the new scheme, Mecklenberg was promised he wouldn't be called on to play five different positions (as he had been in the past).

The result: Mecklenberg led the team with 143 tackles, posted 7.5 sacks, 4 fumble recoveries and forced 2 fumbles. In 1990, during Denver's decline, Mecklenberg once again found himself up and down the defense, as he played both inside and outside linebacker, and, on occasion, did spot duty at defensive end. To make matters worse, chronic knee problems hurt his production.

Nevertheless, Mecklenberg's big-play ability remains his biggest asset. "Without Karl," says head coach Dan Reeves, "we're not the same team." When Mecklenberg missed nine weeks two years ago with a shattered thumb, it was the first time since his sophomore year at Minnesota that he had been sidelined by an injury. And he didn't take it lightly. "I'd much rather play than sit at home," says Mecklenberg, who in 1988 still posted a whopping 78 tackles in just seven games.

Scouts say Denver coaches study opponents' tendencies, then put Mecklenberg in a position to be productive. A smart player, Mecklenberg times his blitzes well. Capable of playing virtually anywhere as a linebacker or defensive lineman, Mecklenberg is most effective as a pass rusher from the linebacker position. But after eight years of double-teams and cut blocks, Mecklenberg is beginning to wear down. "He has played a lot of snaps," says a scout. "He still makes the key plays, but you have to wonder how long he can take the brunt of the punishment."

HANK'S RATING: AA

Chip Banks

Birthdate: September 18, 1959
College: USC
Height: 6-4

Weight: 245
How Acquired: Trade, 1989
Final 1990 Team: Indianapolis Colts

Now entering his third season with the Colts (and ninth in the NFL), Chip Banks, it appears, has quieted his off-the-field troubles and focused on playing football. He tallied 69 tackles and 4.5 sacks in 1990, his best numbers as a Colt, and forced 2 fumbles. Banks is a highly skilled veteran whose personal problems seem to keep him from his potential.

The former Charger has above-average speed, good lateral quickness, and good recognition of opposing formations. Scouts wonder what this physical talent—and former Pro Bowler—could do in a full season without any outside distractions. With his abilities, he could have been in the NFL Hall of Fame.

HANK'S RATING: AA

Clay Matthews

Birthdate: March 15, 1956
College: USC
Height: 6-2
Weight: 245
How Acquired: Drafted in first round, 1978
Final 1990 Team: Cleveland Browns

In an era of specialization, Clay Matthews is a throwback to old times: he plays every down defensively, regardless of down and distance, and still volunteers for special teams. He finished last seasons with 102 tackles, proving that this fourteen-year veteran can still run with his younger peers. A very smart player.

Matthews may be the NFL's last ironman, capable of doing it all defensively. Two years ago, in a 17–7 victory over Seattle, Matthews played in a team-high fifty-nine plays and returned an interception 25 yards to set up the winning score. He also added 3.5 sacks and 3 forced fumbles in 1990, giving the Browns something to smile about in an otherwise dull season. And with Brian Bosworth retired, Matthews can also claim the NFL's best haircut.

HANK'S RATING: AA

Kevin Greene

Birthdate: July 31, 1962
College: Auburn
Height: 6-3
Weight: 250
How Acquired: Drafted in fifth round, 1985
Final 1990 Team: Los Angeles Rams

An aggressive pass rusher who lines up on the left side of the Los Angeles defense, Kevin Greene started slow in 1990 after a summer-long contract dispute, but finished with a respectable 52 tackles, recovered 4 fumbles and registered a team-high 13 sacks (third in the NFC). Though his pass rush ability was "down" in 1990, it was a solid answer to critics who doubted his performance of 1988 and 1989, when he had back-to-back 16-sack seasons.

Greene was voted to his first Pro Bowl in 1989 as he blossomed into the team's only consistent pass-rushing threat. But despite his powerfully muscled frame and bull-rushing form, Greene still struggled when opponents singled him out with double- and triple-team blocking schemes. When co-starters Frank Stams and Fred Strickland ended the season early with injuries, it only increased the pressure on Greene, who often seemed like the lone life preserver on a quickly sinking defense. The only player we've listed twice (also as a lineman). Scouts say he can truly play both positions.

HANK'S RATING: AA

Andre Collins

Birthdate: May 4, 1968
College: Penn State
Height: 6-1
Weight: 230
How Acquired: Drafted in second round, 1990
Final 1990 Team: Washington Redskins

After quietly joining the Redskins as a second-round pick in 1990, Andre Collins quickly made himself heard on the field, rolling up 6 sacks—good for second on the team—and finishing fifth in tackles with 92. "I think, in the years to come, he's going to remind people of Jack Ham," says Washington linebacker coach Larry Peccatiello. "I'm not saying he'll be Jack Ham, I'm just saying he has that kind of ability." Always in the thick of things, Collins runs very well to the action.

HANK'S RATING: AA

Aaron Wallace

Birthdate: April 17, 1967
College: Texas A&M
Height: 6-3
Weight: 240
How Acquired: Drafted in second round, 1990
Final 1990 Team: Los Angeles Raiders

Aaron Wallace finished second on the Raiders in sacks (9) in his 1990 rookie campaign at outside linebacker, making Los Angeles coaches optimistic about the youngster's bright future. Wallace has powerful explosion in his legs and tremendous upper body strength, as well as impressive lateral quickness. His biggest weakness is technique, as he learns the finer nuances of the pro game.

HANK'S RATING: AA

Mike Merriweather

Birthdate: November 26, 1960
College: Pacific
Height: 6-2
Weight: 219
How Acquired: Trade, 1989
Final 1990 Team: Minnesota Vikings

For Mike Merriweather, 1987 seems like a long, long time ago. It was in 1987 when Merriweather was a perennial Pro Bowl performer for the Pittsburgh Steelers; he has been unable to duplicate that performance during his two-year stint in Minnesota. Merriweather finished with just 2.5 sacks in 1990, far off his potential—and that despite the fact that Minnesota returned him to the weakside position, where he's most comfortable. To his credit, however, Merriweather never really fit into the scheme of departed defensive coordinator Floyd Peters.

But Merriweather remains a threat, and Minnesota management still raves about him. His finest game in 1990 was against Chicago, when he made 13 tackles, had a sack and a half, stole the ball from Neal Anderson and carried it 33 yards for a touchdown, and forced another fumble. "He stays injury free, and is a big-play guy," says Minnesota assistant GM Bob Holloway. "He still has some trouble with tight end blocks, but has everything else you want in an outside guy." Merriweather is an attacker, swatting down passes, blindsiding quarterbacks, running down receivers from behind.

"Merriweather understands leverage," says Buffalo director of personnel John Butler. "He has great balance, and is a great blitzer." But his biggest weakness is at the point of attack, where his light 219-pound frame forces him to give ground. A great athlete, Merriweather can run with any back or tight end. But his size hampers him in direct confrontations. May lack the "toughness" needed to be a top linebacker again.

HANK'S RATING: AA

Duane Bickett

Birthdate: December 1, 1962
College: USC
Height: 6-5
Weight: 251
How Acquired: Drafted in first round, 1985
Final 1990 Team: Indianapolis Colts

Duane Bickett has heard the criticism before. Not enough speed to make the big play. Doesn't play special teams. Too stiff. "Just to look at the kid, you don't think much of him," says a scout. "But I like his attitude. He sets an example with his style of play, he busts his butt on every snap."

Bickett is good news to Indianapolis head coach Ron Meyer, who calls Bickett "the very heart and soul" of the Colts defense. Bickett finished second on the Colts with 117 tackles in 1990, the first time in three years he didn't lead the team. He also tacked on 4.5 sacks and 2 fumble recoveries.

"I rate him as a top combination outside linebacker," says an NFC scout. "He can play the run, he can play the pass, and they often use him as the nickel pass rusher. In my book, he's a critical big-play player." The key, perhaps, to Bickett's success is classroom study and good technique. Bickett doesn't run well, a fact he acknowledges, but he recognizes routes immediately and has great reaction and anticipation. But some still question if his athletic skill level will allow him to become a "top" linebacker.

HANK'S RATING: AA

Ken Norton, Jr.

Birthdate: September 29, 1966
College: UCLA
Height: 6-2
Weight: 234
How Acquired: Drafted in second round, 1988
Final 1990 Team: Dallas Cowboys

Ken Norton has dramatically improved his play during the past two seasons, and the Cowboys are hoping he will return at full strength in 1991 from offseason surgery to remove torn cartilage in his right knee. Norton benefitted from the presence of veteran Eugene Lockhart, who has since been traded, and in 1991 the Cowboys will expect him to come into his own. Norton, considered by some scouts as too rigid, is a decent athlete with great run-stopping skills. His cover technique needs work, however. His improvement in 1990 can be traced to his playing tougher.

HANK'S RATING: AA

David Griggs

Birthdate: February 5, 1967
College: Virginia
Height: 6-3
Weight: 239
How Acquired: Free Agent, 1989
Final 1990 Team: Miami Dolphins

David Griggs moved into the Dolphins starting lineup in 1990 with flair, finishing fifth on the team with 62 tackles and 5.5 sacks. "With a year behind him, Griggs should continue to improve and hopefully develop into a top NFL outside linebacker."

Griggs joined the Dolphins as a free agent in 1989, and showed his versatility by playing both linebacker and tight end. But his speed, range and size impressed coaches, and he was given the opportunity to prove himself and performed admirably. While his technique still needs work, Griggs covers well and is an occasional force as an outside pass rusher. Griggs possesses raw skills and outstanding work habits, a combination that could make him a great player.

HANK'S RATING: A

Ron Rivera

Birthdate: January 7, 1962
College: California
Height: 6-3
Weight: 240
How Acquired: Drafted in second round, 1984
Final 1990 Team: Chicago Bears

Ron Rivera became a starter midway through the 1987 season, and though he hasn't become a dominating player, he has evolved into one of the Bears steadiest defensive players. Rivera finished with just 64 tackles in 1990, down from his 96 stops in 1989. Over his eight-year career, Rivera has demonstrated an ability to play hurt, play consistent, and play hard. Like several other Bear players, Rivera's style of play and personality fit well within Chicago's scheme.

HANK'S RATING: A

Hugh Green

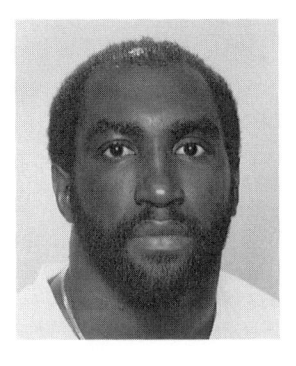

Birthdate: July 27, 1959
College: Pittsburgh
Height: 6-2
Weight: 228
How Acquired: Trade, 1985
Final 1990 Team: Miami Dolphins

Hugh Green had another dependable season, finishing with 56 tackles and 2 sacks. "Hugh gives us reliable play at outside linebacker," says head coach Don Shula. Green, once the most decorated linebackers in college history, still has the speed and agility to make him a threat as a pass rusher and pass-cover specialist. Green struggles, however, at the point of attack, but is still above-average against the run. More than one "expert" felt Green had lost the skill level he once had.

HANK'S RATING: A

Lamar Lathon

Birthdate: December 23, 1967
College: Houston
Height: 6-3
Weight: 250
How Acquired: Drafted in first round, 1990
Final 1990 Team: Houston Oilers

Lamar Lathon impressed scouts around the league in his first NFL season, as he moved his unbelievable size around with dazzling speed (4.5). A hard-hitting tackler, Lathon forced the fumble against Pittsburgh's Tim Worley in the season finale that turned the momentum in favor of Houston. Lathon had trouble with injuries early, but came on toward the season's end with intensity. Without question, Lathon is a future impact player capable of turning a game around. Great pass rush potential.

HANK'S RATING: A

Wilber Marshall

Birthdate: April 18, 1962
College: Florida
Height: 6-1
Weight: 230
How Acquired: Free Agent, 1988
Final 1990 Team: Washington Redskins

Wilbur Marshall finally had what many opposing coaches believed was a Pro Bowl season, but was overlooked for more high-profile players. After enduring several years of criticism for not dominating as he once did in Chicago, Marshall finally responded with his best season as the Redskins right linebacker.

Marshall finished with 5 sacks and 8 quarterback hurries, but most importantly was third on the team in tackles with 107. He was equally effective in pass coverage, defensing 2 passes, intercepting 1, and forcing 2 fumbles, both of which he recovered. He also responded with big games, including a tremendous effort against Super Bowl-bound Buffalo, when he made 7 tackles, 1 sack, forced 2 fumbles, and recovered another.

HANK'S RATING: A

Darion Conner

Birthdate: September 28, 1967
College: Jackson State
Height: 6-2
Weight: 256
How Acquired: Drafted in second round, 1990
Final 1990 Team: Atlanta Falcons

Darion Conner finished 1990 with 83 tackles, 2 sacks and 22 quarterback pressures—second-best on the team, giving Atlanta brass their most pleasant surprise of the season. Conner, the team's second-round pick out of Jackson State, demonstrated outstanding speed (4.5 in the 40) for such a huge man, and proved to be an active, aggressive hitter. "Conner is a borderline trained killer," says head coach Jerry Glanville.

HANK'S RATING: A

David Wyman

Birthdate: March 31, 1964
College: Stanford
Height: 6-2
Weight: 242
How Acquired: Drafted in second round, 1987
Final 1990 Team: Seattle Seahawks

The Seahawks tried to trade David Wyman to the 49ers in 1987, but the trade was nullified because of a shoulder injury. That bad news in 1987 became good news for Seattle over the past few seasons, as Wyman seems to be one of the team's few linebackers who has played consistently and stayed healthy. Wyman, though unspectacular, is a steady performer, and led the team in tackles in 1989 with 98.

He is slow in the flat when mismatched against faster running backs, but plays very tough against the run. Like many of the other Seattle defensive players, Wyman is an overachiever with limited ability, but plays within his limitations.

HANK'S RATING: A

Darrin Comeaux

Birthdate: April 15, 1960
College: Arizona State
Height: 6-1
Weight: 239
How Acquired: Free Agent, 1988
Final 1990 Team: Seattle Seahawks

Darrin Comeaux came to the Seahawks on waivers from the 49ers in 1988, and has since worked his way into the starting lineup after the departure of injured wanna-be Brian Bosworth. He had an outstanding 1989 season, and was consistent again in 1990 when rookies Ned Bolcar and Terry Wooden missed games with injuries. Seahawk coaches are hoping that some of the team's younger players emerge to push Comeaux, but don't be surprised to see this overachiever continue to fight his way back into the middle of things.

HANK'S RATING: A

Greg Lloyd

Birthdate: May 26, 1965
College: Fort Valley State
Height: 6-2
Weight: 222
How Acquired: Drafted in sixth round, 1987
Final 1990 Team: Pittsburgh Steelers

Greg Lloyd has quietly become the Steelers big-play linebacker, though his number of big plays dropped off in 1990. The team's best athlete on defense, Lloyd matured into a more complete player last season as he learned to control his fiery emotion. Blazing speed and his fierce competitiveness set Lloyd apart in the Steelers defensive backfield. He has Pro Bowl potential.

HANK'S RATING: A

Seth Joyner

Birthdate: November 18, 1964
College: Texas-El Paso
Height: 6-2
Weight: 248
How Acquired: Drafted in eighth round, 1986
Final 1990 Team: Philadelphia Eagles

Seth Joyner upped his sack total in 1990 to 7.5 from 4.5 in 1989, evidence of his rapid improvement since becoming a starter three years ago. Joyner's strengths include his quick recognition of offensive formations, and he is a smart, aggressive player.

In the Eagles' scheme, the left linebacker has to be a solid rush linebacker and be able to control the tight end; Joyner does both with consistency. Joyner is the only starting linebacker the Eagles routinely leave in the game in nickel situations, proof of his pass-coverage ability. A very productive player who is capable of making big plays.

HANK'S RATING: A

Jerry Robinson

Birthdate: December 18, 1956
College: UCLA
Height: 6-2
Weight: 225
How Acquired: Trade, 1985
Final 1990 Team: Los Angeles Raiders

Now in his thirteenth season, Jerry Robinson still has the impressive versatility that made him NFL rookie of the year in 1979. The former Pro Bowler was an anchor on the renegade Los Angeles defense, playing tough run and pass defense, at both inside and outside positions. Though years of punishment have taken the edge off his quickness, Robinson is still fast enough to cover running backs. A steady veteran.

HANK'S RATING: A

Bill Romanowski

Birthdate: April 2, 1966
College: Boston College
Height: 6-4
Weight: 231
How Acquired: Drafted in third round, 1985
Final 1990 Team: San Francisco 49ers

After pressing for more playing time for several years, Bill Romanowski made his point in 1990: He led the team with a career-high 79 tackles, including 68 solo stops from his inside linebacker position. An emerging star, Romanowski is regarded as one of the 49ers' biggest hitters and has the speed to play inside or outside. Scouts like his lateral quickness and agility, but question his strength at the point of attack. He covers well, is physical against the run, and is difficult to block. An excellent player within the 49ers scheme.

HANK'S RATING: A

John Roper

Birthdate: October 4, 1965
College: Texas A&M
Height: 6-1
Weight: 228
How Acquired: Drafted in second round, 1989
Final 1990 Team: Chicago Bears

John Roper and 1990 second-round pick Ron Cox split playing time with Chicago veteran Jim Morrissey at the right linebacker spot last season, and with mixed results. Expect Cox to severely push Roper, once a full-time starter, for the job. After a spectacular rookie year in 1989, when he finished with 68 tackles and 4.5 sacks, Roper dropped way off in production in 1990, with just 21 tackles and 1 sack. Cox, meanwhile, had 28 tackles, 3 sacks, and demonstrated strength, power and incredible mobility as a pass rusher. Cox has 4.5 speed and bench-presses more than 400 pounds; Roper will have his hands full trying to stave off this hard-charging challenge.

HANK'S RATING: A

Jessie Small

Birthdate: November 30, 1966
College: Eastern Kentucky
Height: 6-3
Weight: 239
How Acquired: Drafted in second round, 1989
Final 1990 Team: Philadelphia Eagles

Only in his third season, Jessie Small has successfully become an NFL linebacker after being a stand-up defensive end in college. In his first two seasons, the Eagles used him almost exclusively as a speed pass-rush player, then carefully taught him coverages and pass-drop technique. The result, at first, was a tentative, hesitant, thinking linebacker.

But as 1990 wore on, Small began to relax and play with a vengeance. His education complete, Small is now in a position to be as productive "as any linebacker taken in the first round of the 1989 draft," according to one scout.

HANK'S RATING: A

Rufus Porter

Birthdate: May 18, 1965
College: Southern University
Height: 6-1
Weight: 221
How Acquired: Free Agent, 1988
Final 1990 Team: Seattle Seahawks

It's hard to believe that Rufus Porter came to Seattle in 1988 as a free-agent signee who weighed just 207 pounds. Now bulked up to a "stout" 221 pounds, Porter led Seattle linebackers with 5 sacks in 1990, half his total of 1989. But Seattle used Porter primarily as a "designated" pass-rushing end in 1989, and he was exclusively an outside linebacker in 1990. Though he handled the transformation well, Porter is still a bit undersized for the position, and he gives ground when mismatched against better running teams. But he is outstanding in pass coverage, and has big-play capability.

Porter is also an exceptional special teams player, which earned him a spot in the Pro Bowl in 1988 and 1989. Constantly double-teamed on special teams, Porter still finds his way to the bottom of the pile while dishing out thunderous hits.

HANK'S RATING: A

Chris Martin

Birthdate: December 19, 1960
College: Auburn
Height: 6-2
Weight: 232
How Acquired: Free Agent, 1988
Final 1990 Team: Kansas City Chiefs

Chris Martin had 5.5 sacks in 1990, up from 4.5 in 1989, and continued to play with consistency as the AFC's most unheralded left outside linebacker. Kansas City coaches say that Martin actually graded out higher than Derrick Thomas during Thomas's 10-sack rookie season in 1989. Martin breaks down well against the run, and is an efficient blitzer; Thomas gets so much attention that it opens lanes for Martin. He has good quickness and also excels in pass coverage.

HANK'S RATING: A

Leon White

Birthdate: October 4, 1963
College: Brigham Young
Height: 6-3
Weight: 237
How Acquired: Drafted in fifth round, 1989
Final 1990 Team: Cincinnati Bengals

Leon White is an often outstanding veteran outside linebacker who leads by actions, not words, according to the Bengal coaching staff. A bright and articulate player, White became a starter in 1988 after impressing Bengals coaches with outstanding special teams play.

White's toughness is perhaps his biggest credo, a principal reason that the Bengals typically move him inside in goalline situations. "Leon is a steady, strong linebacker," says head coach Sam Wyche. But several scouts wonder about his pass defense ability. A humble performer, White isn't into praise, either. "Almost every time someone like me makes a big play, it's because someone else did something earlier," he says.

HANK'S RATING: B

Johnny Meads

Birthdate: June 25, 1961
College: Nicholls State
Height: 6-2
Weight: 232
How Acquired: Drafted in third round, 1984
Final 1990 Team: Houston Oilers

Johnny Meads is an above-average player whose biggest contribution is consistency. Meads has never been a dominating player, but performs at a reliable, workman-like pace, making few mistakes and directing traffic. Meads reacts well to what he sees, and relies on his veteran experience when his physical skills fail him. A tireless worker, Meads is a team player who works hard on the field and in the weight room.

Against New Orleans last season, Meads demonstrated his all-around skills in his finest game of the season. He made 14 tackles, forced 3 fumbles, returned an interception 32 yards, broke up a pass, had a sack-and-a-half, and made 3 other tackles for losses. "Having a guy like Meads is always a positive," says a scout. "He can't throw the tight end and run down the quarterback every play, but he is a steady contributor. He helps in more ways than just one."

HANK'S RATING: B

Larry Kelm

Birthdate: November 29, 1964
College: Texas A&M
Height: 6-4
Weight: 240
How Acquired: Drafted in fourth round, 1987
Final 1990 Team: Los Angeles Rams

Larry Kelm had an average, but decent, season in 1990, in light of all the defensive problems suffered by the Rams. Scouts say Kelm possesses good lateral movement and excellent burst, but is often slow in recognizing defenses and often appears confused against certain formations. He has also been troubled by minor injuries throughout his four-year career, but has managed to play through all but the most serious. A physical player, Kelm is capable of man-handling a tight end, but has trouble shedding blocks in traffic.

HANK'S RATING: B

Fred Strickland

Birthdate: August 15, 1966
College: Purdue
Height: 6-2
Weight: 250
How Acquired: Drafted in second round, 1988
Final 1990 Team: Los Angeles Rams

A brilliant third-year player in 1990, promising Fred Strickland was lost for the season after suffering a broken leg against Chicago on October 14. His loss devastated Rams coaches, who were counting on his development. Strickland is a rangy, explosive sprinter with 4.5 speed and possesses great upper-body power, enabling him to rush the passer and stuff the run.

But Strickland's weakness has been his inability to stay healthy: his rookie year was marred by a fractured index finger; he missed six games in 1989 with ankle and right knee (lateral cartilage) problems. It's easy to understand Strickland's frustration at yet another injury—not to mention head coach John Robinson's. "If we can get our linebackers back . . ." Robinson says, "we can get this football team back where it belongs."

HANK'S RATING: B

Broderick Thomas

Birthdate: February 20, 1967
College: Nebraska
Height: 6-4
Weight: 245
How Acquired: Drafted in first round, 1989
Final 1990 Team: Tampa Bay Buccaneers

Tampa Bay's first-round pick in 1989, Broderick Thomas was drafted ahead of his namesake, Derrick Thomas, but so far has failed to match Derrick's production. Broderick finished with 7.5 sacks in 1990 (Derrick had 7 against Seattle alone), the best pass-rushing season ever by a Buc linebacker, but struggled throughout the season with his inconsistent play.

But when Thomas played well, he offered flashes of brilliance. He finished the season with 72 tackles and 33 quarterback pressures, while starting fifteen of sixteen games at outside linebacker. His best game came against Dallas, when he posted 3 sacks, including 2 on successive plays in the second quarter.

The nephew of Bears standout Mike Singletary, Thomas displays work habits very similar to those of the perennial Chicago All-Pro. "We feel Broderick will really come into his own this year," says new Tampa Bay head coach Richard Williamson. "He's a conscientious, hard-working player with a lot of natural ability. We expect big things from him."

HANK'S RATING: B

Dennis Gibson

Birthdate: February 8, 1964
College: Iowa State
Height: 6-2
Weight: 243
How Acquired: Drafted in eighth round, 1987
Final 1990 Team: Detroit Lions

Although Dennis Gibson missed the last four games with a foot injury, he was still a picture of consistency in 1990 as he continued to live up to his billing as one of the NFL's most underrated linebackers. Gibson has been among the Lions' most solid players in the past three seasons, as he contributes with consistent, solid play. Scouts credit Gibson with an uncanny ability to read blocks and has "a good feeling" for pass drops. He is a very intelligent player who does a great job playing the running game with gap control. A heady, though unspectacular, player.

HANK'S RATING: B

Ray Berry

Birthdate: October 28, 1963
College: Baylor
Height: 6-2
Weight: 230
How Acquired: Drafted in second round, 1987
Final 1990 Team: Minnesota Vikings

With the retirement of veteran Scott Studwell, Ray Berry and Mike Merriweather will be left to shoulder the load for the Vikings at linebacker in 1991. And it could be a grim situation: Of the two, only Merriweather has big-play potential, as Berry has battled injuries and inconsistency throughout his five-year career. A strong, rangy player, Berry possesses all the physical tools, but thus far has been unable to develop as a professional. With defensive coordinator Floyd Peters gone to Tampa Bay, don't be surprised to see defensive end Chris Doleman—a former linebacker—moved back to his old position. Among eight linebackers listed on Minnesota's training camp roster, only Merriweather and Berry have more than two years professional experience. Scary.

HANK'S RATING: B

George Jamison

Birthdate: September 30, 1962
College: Cincinnati
Height: 6-1
Weight: 228
How Acquired: Chosen in supplemental draft, 1984
Final 1990 Team: Detroit Lions

George Jamison made his move on a starting job in 1988, when he took advantage of a unfortunate opportunity—starter Jimmy Williams went down to injury. But Jamison made the most of his chance, demonstrating excellent quickness, superb pass coverage, and the ability to make big plays. His effort impressed Detroit coaches, who moved him into the starting lineup, where he has been entrenched ever since.

HANK'S RATING: B

Kevin Murphy

Birthdate: September 8, 1963
College: Oklahoma
Height: 6-2
Weight: 235
How Acquired: Drafted in second round, 1986
Final 1990 Team: Tampa Bay Buccaneers

Kevin Murphy, in his sixth season last year, continued to develop as a solid player at both outside linebacker positions, though he is expected to start this year at the left outside spot. A physical, hard-nosed player, Murphy played extensively in every game in 1990, and finished third among Tampa Bay linebackers with 77 tackles. He also finished third in sacks with 4, and had 2 quarterback pressures. Considered Tampa Bay's top "blue-collar" player, Murphy is nicknamed "The Champ" by his teammates.

HANK'S RATING: B

Scott Stephen

Birthdate: June 18, 1964
College: Arizona State

Height: 6-2
Weight: 232
How Acquired: Drafted in third round, 1987
Final 1990 Team: Green Bay Packers

Backed up by hard-charging second-year man Tony Bennett, outside linebacker Scott Stephen will be hard-pressed to hold onto his job in 1991, despite a decent year last season. Stephen finished fourth on the team in tackles with 97, defensed 6 passes, and forced 2 fumbles. Though not a gamebreaking player in the mold of superstar Tim Harris, Stephen is consistent and dependable.

"Scott is a very strong player at the point," says Green Bay outside linebackers coach Dick Mosely. "He plays strong over the tight end, and he has the ability to rush the passer. But it's going to be a very competitive position."

HANK'S RATING: B

Frank Stams

Birthdate: July 17, 1965
College: Notre Dame
Height: 6-2
Weight: 240
How Acquired: Drafted in second round, 1989
Final 1990 Team: Los Angeles Rams

After a solid rookie season, Ram officials placed high hopes on former Notre Dame standout Frank Stams for 1990. But like linebacking mate Fred Strickland, Stams' 1990 season came to a premature end. On December 20 against San Francisco, he suffered a knee injury that required arthroscopic surgery.

Stams played primarily on special teams his rookie year, but displayed good physical skills: excellent body control, powerful hips and chest, and good pass-cover technique. Though he has yet to register a sack in his two seasons, Stams, when healthy, is believed to be a big part of the Rams linebacking future. But several scouts questioned whether he has NFL-linebacker talent level. He has been pushed by Brett Faryniarz, a former free agent now in his third year, and George Bethune, a seventh-round draft pick in 1989—both of whom have also shown promise.

HANK'S RATING: B

Chris Singleton

Birthdate: February 20, 1967
College: Arizona
Height: 6-2
Weight: 247
How Acquired: Drafted in first round, 1990
Final 1990 Team: New England Patriots

Chris Singleton wasted little time in his 1990 rookie season to establish himself as the club's future at outside linebacker. He played in thirteen games, starting four, and finished with 28 tackles and 3 quarterback sacks. His best game came against Cincinnati, when he tallied 6 tackles and 2 sacks.

Despite his limited playing time, Singleton made every minute count, impressing the New England front office with his strength against the run. He is still very raw against the pass, however, but possesses great football instincts. "Chris has a bright future with the Patriots," says Joe Mendes, Patriots' vice president of player operations.

HANK'S RATING: B

Anthony Bell

Birthdate: July 2, 1964
College: Michigan State
Height: 6-3
Weight: 235
How Acquired: Drafted in first round, 1986
Final 1990 Team: Phoenix Cardinals

Like the other Phoenix starting linebackers, Anthony Bell is a former first-round pick, and in the past two years has enjoyed the two best seasons of his five-year career. But that's still not saying much: Phoenix coaches openly expressed disappointment in the mediocre numbers posted by the fifth overall pick of the 1986 draft.

Yes, Bell is consistent, but not much more than that; he has yet to develop into the big-play performer Phoenix scouts once believed he would be. Just not a *solid* NFL player. The acquisition of first-round defensive end Eric Swann gave head coach Joe Bugel the freedom to convert defensive end Freddie Joe Nunn back to linebacker, his natural position. Expect Nunn, a lightning-quick, physical player to remove Bell from the Cardinals starting lineup.

HANK'S RATING: B

Inside Linebackers

Vaughan Johnson

Birthdate: March 24, 1962
College: North Carolina State
Height: 6-3
Weight: 235
How Acquired: Chosen in supplemental draft, 1984
Final 1990 Team: New Orleans Saints

"Very few linebackers can dominate from inside like Vaughan Johnson," says an NFC personnel man. "Outside guys can control games, but inside players are limited by the scheme." Which is exactly why Vaughan Johnson, who had 102 tackles last year with the Saints, is so unique. For the past three years, Johnson has controlled several games single-handedly, and for two seasons (1988 and 1989) he led the Saints in tackles.

An example of Johnson's overwhelming dominance occurred in a game two years ago against Los Angeles: On the Rams opening series he batted down a third-down pass intended for Greg Bell. On the second L.A. series, on a fourth-and-three attempt, he stuffed Charles White at the line of scrimmage. No gain. Late in the game, with the Rams mounting a comeback, he swatted down a would-be touchdown pass.

"Johnson is well coached; he's an excellent technician," says New York GM Dick Steinberg. "He lacks the athleticism of some of the other guys, but he makes up for it with hard work." New Orleans coaches say Johnson, who made the Pro Bowl last season, has been the best inside linebacker for the past three years. His potential is scary—and unlimited.

HANK'S RATING: AAA

John Offerdahl

Birthdate: August 17, 1964
College: Western Michigan
Height: 6-3
Weight: 240
How Acquired: Drafted in second round, 1986
Final 1990 Team: Miami Dolphins

John Offerdahl made his fifth consecutive Pro Bowl in 1990, much to the debate of his peers. Some scouts say he's overrated, while others say he's still underrated. But we did seem to get everybody to agree that while Offerdahl lacks good cover skills and lateral movement, he is a tremendous run-stopper and reacts with amazing quickness to a thrown ball.

"John Offerdahl is the most instinctive kid I've ever seen," says Buffalo personnel man John Butler. "He's always at the football. You block him. You send the tight end after him. You double-team him. Then you look at the bottom of the pile, and there's No. 56."

Offerdahl's biggest strength is against the run. In fact many feel he is "only" effective against the run. When the Dolphins do blitz him, "he gets cut a lot and sometimes fills the wrong hole," says a scout. But he's still outstanding as a run-down player at the point of attack. You can live with him against the pass, but that's probably the biggest area where he needs more improvement."

HANK'S RATING: AA

Pepper Johnson

Birthdate: June 29, 1964
College: Ohio State
Height: 6-3
Weight: 248
How Acquired: Drafted in second, 1986
Final 1990 Team: New York Giants

Inside linebacker Pepper Johnson led the Giants in 1990 with 119 tackles, earning his first spot in the Pro Bowl. Johnson also forced 3 fumbles and had 3.5 sacks. But it was Johnson's versatility that made New York's 3–4 defense so dominant throughout the season. Johnson's speed allows him to perform a variety of tasks, from covering running backs and tight ends to occasionally blitzing to keeping an eye out for draw plays. He has above-average strength, which allows him to handle running backs and tight ends and adequately take on offensive linemen. Johnson is an impact player.

HANK'S RATING: AA

Chris Spielman

Birthdate: October 11, 1965
College: Ohio State
Height: 6-0
Weight: 244
How Acquired: Drafted in second round, 1988
Final 1990 Team: Detroit Lions

Scouts call Chris Spielman an "ultimate effort guy," a linebacker who excels through drive and desire, not just talent and ability. Spielman, despite missing four games after shoulder surgery early in the season, led the team in tackles for the third consecutive season. Prior to the surgery, and in extreme pain, Spielman made 12 tackles, 1 sack and recovered a fumble to help beat the Falcons. He had surgery three days later; exactly four weeks after arthroscopic surgery, Spielman had 10 more tackles and an interception against the Saints.

When Spielman was drafted, several scouts openly wondered if the short, stiff Spielman even belonged in the NFL. "Chris has proven that not only does he belong in the NFL, but he might be one of the best middle linebackers in the game," says Detroit head coach Wayne Fontes. Spielman has great instincts and has improved his pass coverage dramatically since entering the league.

HANK'S RATING: AA

Mike Singletary

Birthdate: October 9, 1958
College: Baylor
Height: 6-0
Weight: 230
How Acquired: Drafted in second round, 1981
Final 1990 Team: Chicago Bears

One of very few players in the NFL who continues to be unanimous All-Pro selections last year, Mike Singletary, now in his eleventh season, continues to prove critics wrong. "There are people who don't think I can maintain this pace," he says. "Bring them on." Singletary finished 1990 with 151 tackles, down from his career-high of 170 tackles in 1989. He has finished first or second in tackles for the past nine seasons, and was voted to his ninth Pro Bowl. He also set a new personal-best with 20 tackles at Denver, where he also recovered a fumble to set up a field goal.

Singletary stuffs the run, plays the pass with exceptional ability, and simply puts fear in the opposition. His fierce tackling style broke the helmets of sixteen opposing players during his college days at Baylor. He has cracked four more in the NFL, including Eric Dickerson's in the NFC Championship in 1986. "It scares me when I think about it," he says. "I look around and I don't see anybody else breaking helmets. I hope there's nothing wrong with me."

But some NFL scouts agree that Singletary's ability is slipping. According to one source, Singletary was rated No. 1 in 1984 and 1985, No. 2 in 1986 and 1987, but No. 21 in 1988. "You look at scouting reports, and it hints that his best days may be behind him," the scout says. "But then you look at his leadership and his work habits. What a player." Others have also commented that he is not the player he has been in the past. But he is still entrenched in our Top 10.

HANK'S RATING: AA

Gary Plummer

Birthdate: January 26, 1960
College: California
Height: 6-2
Weight: 240
How Acquired: Free Agent, 1986
Final 1990 Team: San Diego Chargers

Inside linebacker Gary Plummer led the San Diego Chargers with 111 tackles in 1990—a feat he's recorded every year since joining the team as a free agent in 1986. Plummer has 535 tackles in five seasons at inside linebacker, more than any San Diego player in history over a five-year period.

Plummer, who played three USFL seasons and two college seasons under San Diego defensive coordinator Ron Lynn, excels through toughness, determination, and intelligence. He thoroughly understands the San Diego defensive system and makes it play to his strengths.

HANK'S RATING: AA

Sam Mills

Birthdate: June 5, 1959
College: Montclair State
Height: 5-9
Weight: 225
How Acquired: Free Agent, 1986
Final 1990 Team: New Orleans Saints

A classic over-achiever, Sam Mills was given no chance to make the NFL when he left tiny Montclair State in 1980, and was even waived by Cleveland in 1981. But after a brilliant three-year career in the defunct USFL under current Saints head coach Jim Mora, Mills proved his worth—he led his team in tackles all three years. Mora brought him to New Orleans, and he responded by making two Pro Bowls in his first four seasons as a Saint.

Mills has started in all but three games since his arrival to New Orleans, and makes up for his lack of size with aggressiveness, quickness, and intelligence. He led the Saints again last year with 112 tackles. Alongside Vaughan Johnson, another Pro Bowl inside linebacker, Mills helps give the Saints one of the most formidable linebacking corps anywhere.

HANK'S RATING: AA

David Little

Birthdate: January 3, 1959
College: Florida
Height: 6-1
Weight: 233
How Acquired: Drafted in seventh round, 1981
Final 1990 Team: Pittsburgh Steelers

David Little made the Pro Bowl in 1990 from his left inside position, where he has been a fixture the past seven years. The Steeler's leading tackler the past four years, many opposing coaches call Little the best inside linebacker in the league. Despite his age, Little's productivity has maintained an even keel. The team's defensive captain, Little is an extremely intelligent player with great leadership qualities, and hasn't missed a nonstrike game in his ten-year career.

HANK'S RATING: AA

Billy Ray Smith

Birthdate: August 10, 1961
College: Arkansas
Height: 6-3
Weight: 236
How Acquired: Drafted in first round, 1983
Final 1990 Team: San Diego Chargers

Billy Ray Smith is one of the most respected linebackers in the NFL, largely due to his unselfish, mistake-free level of play. Smith has mastered all four linebacking positions, but is at his best at one of the two outside linebacker spots, where he can roam the field and react to what he sees.

A three-time Pro Bowler, Smith is a strong, intelligent player who can take on tight ends or rush the passer with equal ability. With the emergence of San Diego pass rushers Leslie O'Neal and Burt Grossman, Smith doesn't get asked to rush the passer too often any more, but he doesn't complain about his less visible role in pass-cover schemes.

HANK'S RATING: AA

Dino Hackett

Birthdate: June 28, 1964
College: Appalachian State
Height: 6-3
Weight: 238
How Acquired: Drafted in second round, 1986
Final 1990 Team: Kansas City Chiefs

Dino Hackett lacks technique, control, discipline—all the things most coaches demand. "But Dino Hackett is all football player," says New York Jets GM Dick Steinberg. "He hasn't realized his potential yet. He does everything on competitiveness; he doesn't fit in with a structured defense."

Which should make 1991 another interesting year for Kansas City coach Marty Schottenheimer, a great believer in structured defenses. Hackett continues to roll up tackles, despite injuries to his knees, shoulders, and arms. His penchant for full-speed tackles often caused burning and numbing sensations in both arms. "I hit people with my head," says Hackett. "I take on blocks with my head, and it's scary when I get the burners and have numbness in my arms. But I'm out there to get the job done, and I'll do anything to get that job done."

Scouts say Hackett is more effective away from the ball. He runs sideline to sideline, attacks the football, and will run through walls to get to the football. "Dino is a very determined player," says Schottenheimer. "In spite of his style of play, he fits in very well with what we do." Imagine how he'd fit in if he started playing smart?

HANK'S RATING: AA

Shane Conlan

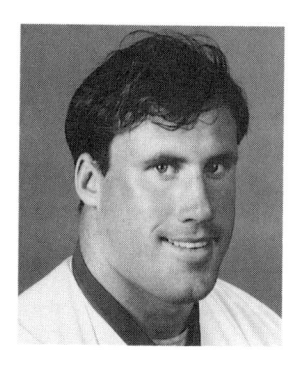

Birthdate: April 3, 1964
College: Penn State
Height: 6-3
Weight: 235
How Acquired: Drafted in first round, 1987
Final 1990 Team: Buffalo Bills

Although Shane Conlan was a Pro Bowl choice again in 1990, he has received mixed reviews. Despite occasional brilliant play, Conlan continues to be injury prone and one dimensional: A great run-stopper, but average in pass coverage. "When Conlan is completely healthy, he's a great player," says a scout. "But I think there are some doubts around the league because he's been dinged up a little. But I really like him at the point of attack—he'll stand in there." And, critics are quick to point out, while Conlan helps out on a lot of plays, "he doesn't make a great deal of big plays."

Toughness, perhaps, is Conlan's biggest asset. He suffered a concussion two years ago against Green Bay, but returned to play the second half. In another test of courage, he stayed in the game despite a deep bruise that discolored his right lower leg. Conlan is an unorthodox player who doesn't fit a mold. He often plays reckless football, but has great pursuit and good drive in zone coverage. His unpredictability is hard to prepare for, but scouts say Conlan needs to be more in control to be a truly great linebacker.

HANK'S RATING: A

Mike Johnson

Birthdate: November 26, 1962
College: Virginia Tech
Height: 6-1
Weight: 225
How Acquired: Drafted in first round, 1989
Final 1990 Team: Cleveland Browns

A powerful middle linebacker, Mike Johnson earned his first Pro Bowl spot in 1989—then things unraveled for the Cleveland franchise in 1990. But not because Johnson didn't try—he led the team in tackles with 161, the third time in four years. A tenacious, vicious tackler, Johnson is a bit undersized for his position by modern standards, but makes up for it with outstanding speed. Johnson breaks down well against the run, covers well, and is capable of rushing the passer. A talented player who should adapt well to new coach Bill Belichick's linebacker-strong system.

HANK'S RATING: A

Hardy Nickerson

Birthdate: September 1, 1965
College: California
Height: 6-2
Weight: 231
How Acquired: Drafted in fifth round, 1987
Final 1990 Team: Pittsburgh Steelers

Hardy Nickerson won the starting job at right inside linebacker in 1988, but missed eight starts in 1989 due to a broken leg. He was replaced by then-rookie Jerry Olsavsky, who will continue to push Nickerson for playing time. Steeler coaches praise Nickerson's intensity, and are high on his physical style of play. But Nickerson has suffered injuries in every season since he became a starter.

HANK'S RATING: A

Jack Del Rio

Birthdate: April 4, 1963
College: USC
Height: 6-4
Weight: 236
How Acquired: Free Agent, 1989
Final 1990 Team: Dallas Cowboys

A free agent who moved into the Cowboys starting lineup, Del Rio is a steady athlete with average agility, who makes up for his shortcomings with desire, intelligence, and determination. Del Rio compensates for his lack of speed by coordinating well with his teammates in pass coverage.

Del Rio is a competitive tackler and is a superb player against the run. An above-average linebacker who lacks big-play ability but often excels through heart, hustle, and excellent instincts.

HANK'S RATING: A

Riki Ellison

Birthdate: August 15, 1960
College: USC
Height: 6-2
Weight: 225
How Acquired: Plan B free agent
Final 1990 Team: Los Angeles Raiders

The Los Angeles Raiders were quick to grab Riki Ellison when the San Francisco 49ers made him an unprotected Plan B player in 1989, and Ellison quickly worked his way into the starting lineup. Ellison missed all of 1989 with an injury after being hurt in the preseason, but as a Raider, he has rebounded with rugged intensity.

In the season's fifteenth week, Ellison made 11 tackles, broke up a pass and set up the Raider' first touchdown with an interception as Los Angeles defeated Cincinnati 24–7. He is tough against the run and is an intense competitor. A heady player Ellison makes few mistakes, but struggles when mismatched against quicker running backs or tight ends.

HANK'S RATING: A

John Rade

Birthdate: August 31, 1960
College: Boise State
Height: 6-1
Weight: 240
How Acquired: Drafted in eighth round, 1983
Final 1990 Team: Atlanta Falcons

Nicknamed "Radar" by his teammates for his innate ability to zoom in on a ballcarrier, John Rade put in another fine season for Atlanta under new head coach Jerry Glanville. He tallied 145 tackles and 5 quarterback pressures, giving him six 100-tackle NFL seasons. A steady player who makes few mistakes and is capable of making the big play, Rade also plays hurt and maintains a year-round conditioning program.

HANK'S RATING: A

Jeff Herrod

Birthdate: July 29, 1966
College: Mississippi
Height: 6-0
Weight: 246
How Acquired: Drafted in ninth round, 1988
Final 1990 Team: Indianapolis Colts

Jeff Herrod has made his presence felt at left inside linebacker since earning a starting job with the Colts during training camp in 1989. He started fourteen of fifteen games in 1989, then enjoyed the best season of his career in 1990, piling up a team-high 155 tackles, also a personal best. He had 4 sacks and an incredible three 16-tackle games, and reached double-digits in tackles in nine of thirteen games.

The first cousin of actor Mr. T, Herrod earned his spot on the Colts' A-team through tremendous desire, hard work, and discipline. Scouts praise his ability against the run, but add that he needs work in pass coverage and pass-rush situations. "With some refinement, he can become an all-around solid player," says one. "But his technique is still a problem. He's still a little rough around the edges."

HANK'S RATING: A

Kurt Gouveia

Birthdate: September 14, 1964
College: Brigham Young
Height: 6-1
Weight: 227
How Acquired: Drafted in eighth round, 1986
Final 1990 Team: Washington Redskins

In his fourth pro season, Kurt Gouveia stepped into the Redskins starting lineup in 1990 at middle linebacker, with modest results. Gouveia had 76 tackles, 1 sack, and returned a recovered fumble 39 yards for a touchdown against New England. His biggest contribution may have been on special teams, where he recorded 24 tackles—many of which were first hits. Many scouts believe Gouveia is too rigid and lacks the ability to maintain his starting position ahead of hard-charging youngster Greg Manusky. But Gouveia is a disciplined, consistent player with a solid work ethic—don't be surprised if he proves the critics wrong again in 1991.

HANK'S RATING: A

Johnny Holland

Birthdate: March 11, 1965
College: Texas A&M
Height: 6-2
Weight: 221
How Acquired: Drafted in second round, 1987
Final 1990 Team: Green Bay Packers

Inside linebacker Johnny Holland had the most productive season of his career in 1989 with 121 tackles, then followed that performance with 110 tackles in 1990. Prior to 1990, nagging injuries and contract holdouts had distracted the four-year veteran, but coaches feel he finally began to live up to his potential last season.

"Johnny's been a victim of circumstance [prior to 1990]," says defensive coordinator Hank Bullough. "He has a lot of ability, but he hasn't been 100 percent because of injuries and because of holdouts." Scouts point to Holland's uncanny ability to find the ball in traffic as his greatest asset, a factor that led to his nickname of "Mr. Anywhere" during his collegiate career at Texas A&M.

HANK'S RATING: A

Eugene Seale

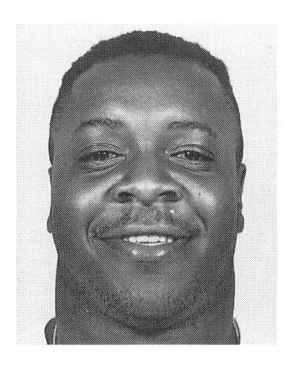

Birthdate: June 3, 1964
College: Lamar
Height: 5-10
Weight: 250
How Acquired: Free Agent, 1987
Final 1990 Team: Houston Oilers

The Houston Oilers found Eugene Seale operating a jackhammer in Beaumont, Texas, during the 1987 players strike, and Seale's improvement since that time has marveled coaches. After the strike, he made his mark originally as a headhunting member of former head coach Jerry Glanville's kamikaze special teams, but most scouts thought he was too small—and too overweight—to be taken seriously as a linebacker.

But Seale has proven the critics wrong, and saw his most action in 1990, and at times played brilliantly. He stuffed the run with authority and showed decent speed in the flat. He's not an every-down player, but he is a tremendous hitter, which often results in big plays. Some scouts consider him the NFL's most feared special teams player. He bites, scratches, punches—and splatters ballcarriers, which is why his teammates call him "The One-Man Gang." On an opening kickoff against the Raiders two years ago, Seale exploded into the return man. When his opponent started to get up, Seale decked him again with a right cross and was ejected, six seconds into the game. As far as we know, that's a record that still stands.

Though the potential is there, Seale must lose weight to become an every-down player.

HANK'S RATING: A

Keith DeLong

Birthdate: August 14, 1967
College: Tennessee
Height: 6-2
Weight: 235
How Acquired: Drafted in first round, 1989
Final 1990 Team: San Francisco 49ers

Keith DeLong continued his quiet emergence in 1990 with 51 tackles, proving his willingness to become a vital element in the 49ers' defense. DeLong, though still unproven, has great lateral movement and strong football instincts, but scouts say he must improve his physical skills in hand-to-hand confrontations to become an every-down player.

HANK'S RATING: A

Percy Snow

Birthdate: November 5, 1967
College: Michigan State
Height: 6-2
Weight: 244
How Acquired: Drafted in first round, 1990
Final 1990 Team: Kansas City Chiefs

First-round draft pick Percy Snow moved into the Chiefs starting lineup during his rookie year, and demonstrated monster potential. Snow is a low-slung, hard-driving middle linebacker with outstanding instincts and quickness. His addition to the Kansas City linebacking corps gives the Chiefs perhaps the best trio of linebackers in the AFC. Snow still needs to work on his pass coverage, however.

HANK'S RATING: A

Byron Evans

Birthdate: February 23, 1964
College: Arizona
Height: 6-2
Weight: 235
How Acquired: Drafted in fourth round, 1987
Final 1990 Team: Philadelphia Eagles

Byron Evans earned the starting job in training camp in 1989, and has rapidly improved since. "When he came to camp," says former Eagles head coach Buddy Ryan, "I wasn't sure he could handle the defense. But he did an excellent job. In fact, he was the team's most improved player, and he's the hardest-hitting linebacker in the NFL."

Evans has always had the physical tools, but in the past two seasons he has really grasped the mental part of the game. He makes the checks and adjustments on the Eagle defense, and dramatically improved in pass coverage. He has strength, speed, and durability, and needs only to refine his technique. Evans is also a valuable team leader. "His enthusiasm carries over to the rest of the team, and tends to motivate people," says a Philadelphia assistant.

HANK'S RATING: A

Al Smith

Birthdate: November 26, 1964
College: Utah State
Height: 6-1
Weight: 240

How Acquired: Drafted in sixth round, 1987
Final 1990 Team: Houston Oilers

Al Smith may be the most underrated linebacker in the league, but his frequent injuries and unwillingness to play hurt have hurt his reputation around the league. Former coach Jerry Glanville was amazed several years ago when Smith, a standout in pass coverage and a physical run stopper, refused to play after injuring his big toe. "I've never seen a guy that dominating who missed so many weeks with a sore toe," chagrined Glanville at the time.

But when Smith does play, he has Pro Bowl abilities, but has never really played up to his full potential. He is quick, aggressive, and mean, and sometimes is virtually unblockable. If he can resolve the inconsistency question, Smith could be one of the AFC's best linebackers.

HANK'S RATING: B

Eugene Marve

Birthdate: August 14, 1960
College: Saginaw Valley State
Height: 6-2
Weight: 240
How Acquired: Trade, 1988
Final 1990 Team: Tampa Bay Buccaneers

Eugene Marve finished his third year as Tampa Bay's starter at inside linebacker since his acquisition from Buffalo in 1988. Marve provided the young Tampa defense with a veteran's leadership, starting all sixteen games for the third year in a row. His 111 tackles was good for third on the team, and marked the seventh time in his nine-year career that he has topped more than 100 tackles. Though Marve lacks the physical skills of his youth, he still adds stability, tenacity, and mistake-free play to the Buc defense.

HANK'S RATING: B

Johnny Rembert

Birthdate: January 19, 1961
College: Clemson
Height: 6-3
Weight: 234
How Acquired: Drafted in fourth round, 1983
Final 1990 Team: New England Patriots

Johnny Rembert made the Pro Bowl in his first season as a starter (1988), but, like many of his teammates, has lacked the consistency he displayed that season. Rembert excels in pass coverage—he once deflected three long passes against Buffalo in the same game. Though never considered a big pass rusher, Rembert plays the run well and knows his limitations. New Patriot coaches plan to push him back to Pro Bowl form.

HANK'S RATING: B

Ed Reynolds

Birthdate: September 23, 1961
College: Virginia
Height: 6-5
Weight: 242
How Acquired: Free Agent, 1983
Final 1990 Team: New England Patriots

Ed Reynolds became a starter in 1988 at the left inside linebacker position, and impressed then-Patriot coaches with his outstanding intelligence and anticipation. Reynolds may be one of the league's best classroom workers, spending hours studying film and opponents' tendencies. A former collegiate defensive lineman, Reynolds is an aggressive tackler and has decent speed in pass coverage. Reynolds is at his best around the hashmarks, however, and lacks the range to go sideline-to-sideline.

HANK'S RATING: B

Burnell Dent

Birthdate: March 16, 1963
College: Tulane
Height: 6-1
Weight: 236
How Acquired: Drafted in sixth round, 1986
Final 1990 Team: Green Bay Packers

Although his 50 tackles and 1 sack weren't exactly headlines after the 1990 season, Burnell Dent did exactly what the Packers asked of him: Be a consistent, productive player at the inside linebacker spot in the Packers' 3-4 defense. He replaced Brian Noble when the veteran went down in December with a season-ending injury, and his solid play solidified his role. Dent has further enhanced his value by making outstanding plays on special teams for the past three years.

Dent had his first crack as a starter in 1989 while replacing injured Johnny Holland, where he quickly impressed Packer coaches. "I would feel very comfortable if Burnell had to be a starter at either [inside linebacker] position," says defensive coordinator Hank Bullough. "I feel very comfortable about him as a football player."

HANK'S RATING: B

Eric Hill

Birthdate: November 14, 1966
College: LSU
Height: 6-1
Weight: 248
How Acquired: Drafted in first round, 1989
Final 1990 Team: Phoenix Cardinals

After a promising season in 1989, middle linebacker Eric Hill went through the motions in 1990 in what coaches thought was a less-than-expected effort from the third-year player. Hill was a first-round draft pick in 1989, and lived up to his billing with a 91-tackle season, earning numerous postseason media honors. He started fourteen games his rookie year, then became a full-time starter in 1990. But nagging injuries and inconsistent play marred his season, and scouts criticized Hill for his inability to take punishment at the point of attack. A physically blessed athlete, Hill, like the other Cardinal linebackers, must develop consistency.

HANK'S RATING: B

Ervin Randle

Birthdate: October 12, 1962
College: Baylor
Height: 6-1
Weight: 250
How Acquired: Drafted in third round, 1985
Final 1990 Team: Tampa Bay Buccaneers

Ervin Randle saw action in all sixteen games last year, while starting seven at right inside linebacker. Randle appeared to be loaded with promise after a spectacular 1987 season, but injuries have curtailed his development. He led the Bucs in 1989 with 114 tackles, but finished second in 1990 among linebackers with 78 tackles. He improved markedly as a pass rusher, however, recording 5.5 sacks—up from 2.5 sacks in his previous five seasons. Though Randle is a versatile, aggressive player, he is being pushed for playing time by Winston Moss, who in a backup role had 71 tackles.

HANK'S RATING: B

Robert Lyles

Birthdate: March 21, 1961
College: Texas Christian
Height: 6-1
Weight: 230
How Acquired: Drafted in fifth round, 1984
Final 1990 Team: Atlanta Falcons

Robert Lyles is perhaps best known for coining the Houston Astrodome "The House of Pain" during his Oilers tenure under current Atlanta coach Jerry Glanville. But when Glanville added Lyles to the Falcons roster in 1990, he brought some pain with him, and dished it out in large doses to Atlanta's opponents.

In his eleven games with Atlanta, Lyles finished with 51 tackles in giving the Falcons the same steady play he was noted for in Houston. His bone-jarring hits and error-free play make him a Glanville favorite; it's unlikely Lyles would excel in any other system.

HANK'S RATING: B

Who's Missing

Freddie Joe Nunn

Birthdate: April 9, 1962
College: Mississippi
Height: 6-4
Weight: 255
How Acquired: Drafted in first round, 1985
Positions: Outside Linebaker
Final 1990 Team: Phoenix Cardinals

Perhaps the Cardinals' biggest defensive problem in 1990 was a small defensive line, a primary reason the team drafted huge end Eric Swann and swtiched from the 3-4 to the 4-3. And, despite a stockpile of former first-round picks at linebacker, that position was still listed as a "need" by season's end.

In 1991, coaches will turn to Freddie Joe Nunn to help resolve two problems: One, by removing him from the defensive line, they add size up front, which should offer some relief to a defense that gave up an average of 144.9 rushing yards a game last season. And two, by playing him at linebacker, they add a lightning quick pass-rusher who recorded 9 sacks as a defensive end last season.

Nunn has long been considered as potentially one of the NFL's finest pass rushers, but his progress has lagged due to personal problems and puzzling inconsistency. He suffered a four-game drug suspension in 1989—the only four games he hasn't started during his seventy-two-game NFL career. After being drafted as an outside linebacker in 1985, he beefed up from 228 to 255 pounds in 1987, and in fifty-six games as a defensive end, piled up 39 sacks. But despite his outstanding quickness for such a large man, he often gets pushed around at the point of attack.

HANK'S RATING: AA

Brian Noble

Birthdate: September 6, 1962
College: Arizona State
Height: 6-3
Weight: 252
How Acquired: Drafted in fifth round, 1985
Position: Inside Linebacker
Final 1990 Team: Green Bay Packers

A consistent, intense performer in Green Bay's 3-4 scheme, Brian Noble posted 113 tackles in 1990, good for second-best on the team—and good for his average of more than 100 tackles a year for the duration of his six-year career. Noble had the best year of his career in 1989, when he led the team with 138 tackles. He put up those numbers after a brutal off-season conditioning program that saw him lose fifteen pounds to gain greater mobility.

He was a valuable asset to the Packer defense in 1990 until the first week of December, when he went down with a season-ending injury. Noble will have to battle to regain his starting role, but should do so with relative ease. "Brian knows what he's doing," says defensive coordinator Hank Bullough. "He's a smart, intelligent guy."

HANK'S RATING: A

Carl Zander

Birthdate: March 23, 1963
College: Tennessee
Height: 6-2
Weight: 235
How Acquired: Drafted in second round, 1985
Position: Inside Linebacker
Final 1990 Team: Cincinnati Bengals

Carl Zander, who called Cincinnati's defensive signals in 1990, remains one of the NFL's most intelligent and determined linebackers. But Zander's productivity has fallen in recent years, and Bengals coaches have intentionally pressured Zander, who, despite his zeal, might be fading. If he is, however, it has nothing to do with his work ethic.

Zander makes few errors, is very quick, and is tough and aggressive. But Cincinnati brass are seeking more competition at the linebacker position. "We created a lot of competition in this area—purposely," says general manager Paul Brown. But don't be surprised if the zealous Zander responds with new life.

HANK'S RATING: A

Tony Bennett

Birthdate: July 1, 1967
College: Mississippi
Height: 6-1
Weight: 234
How Acquired: Drafted in first round, 1990
Position: Outside Linebacker
Final 1990 Team: Green Bay Packers

Remember this kid's name. Tony Bennett's thunderous tackles and big-play ability made him Green Bay's number-one selection in 1990, and turned the heads of several veterans. Fullback Michael Haddix says watching Tony Bennett reminds him of another Bennett—Cornelius, the Bills' talented All-Pro performer. "It's been a long time since I've seen a linebacker with his speed, quickness, and strength," says Haddix. Bennett, in a limited 1990 role, finished with 13 tackles and 3 sacks. Expect him to become a big-play bookend opposite of gun-twirling veteran Tim Harris.

HANK'S RATING: B

Aundray Bruce

Birthdate: April 30, 1966
College: Auburn
Height: 6-5
Weight: 248
How Acquired: Drafted in first round, 1988
Position: Outside Linebacker
Final 1990 Team: Atlanta Falcons

Despite being blessed with God-given abilities, Aundray Bruce has had an enigmatic professional career, and 1990 was no exception. Bruce opened the season with an incredible 6 quarterback pressures and a thunderous sack of Warren Moon, but his season, for all practical purposes, ended there. His bad attitude and poor work habits put him into Jerry Glanville's doghouse, and he remained there the rest of the season.

His 40 tackles and 4 sacks were off his mark of 66 tackles and 6 sacks in 1989; those are hardly the kind of numbers the Falcons had in mind when they made Bruce the number-one overall pick of the 1988 draft. "Aundray may be one of the most gifted players I've ever seen," says a former Detroit scout. "But when you watch him on film, his shortcomings are obvious: When he can simply chase the ball, he's virtually unstoppable. But when you put him in a complex situation, where he has to stop and think, he quits reacting and starts thinking. He's purely a reaction, go-find-the-ball player."

HANK'S RATING: B

Best of Plan B

Jim Morrissey

Birthdate: December 24, 1962
College: Michigan State
Height: 6-3
Weight: 227
How Acquired: Drafted in eleventh round, 1985
Position: Outside Linebacker
Final 1990 Team: Chicago Bears

The Bears baffled opposing scouts when they didn't protect Jim Morrissey, who many believed was an up-and-coming linebacker. Morrissey started all eighteen games at right linebacker and finished fourth on the team with 109 tackles in 1990. His 12 stops at Denver tied his career high. Prior to 1990, he had started fifteen of the seventeen games that he played in over the previous two years (1988–89). A capable run-stopper with basic skills in pass coverage, Morrissey fits in the Bears scheme extremely well. Nobody signed him off Plan B, so don't be surprised if the unsung Morrissey ends up starting again over inconsistent but improving third-year man John Roper.

HANK'S RATING: A

Matt Millen

Birthdate: March 12, 1958
College: Penn State
Height: 6-2
Weight: 245
How Acquired: Free Agent, 1989
Position: Inside Linebacker
Final 1990 Team: San Francisco 49ers

Matt Millen joined the 49ers only five days before the 1989 season started, but became a starter almost instantly. He gave San Francisco strength on the inside like the team had seldom had in the past, stuffing the run with authority and offering unparalleled—often savage—leadership. Millen finished fifth on the 49ers' last year with 62 tackles, giving the Redskins hope that the old dog can still hunt for a few more punishing, violent years. Millen thinks so, but admits the end is quickly approaching.

Fred Smerlas, Millen's roommate in San Francisco, said recently that when the 49ers younger players would head out to party, "Matt and I would go in our room, turn on the air conditioner, and just lie down. We just can't run around like the young guys anymore." But Millen has to be praised for his courage and level of play at this stage of his career: He's an intelligent veteran who will have an immediate impact on Washington's run defense, if only for a season.

HANK'S RATING: A

O'Brien Alston

Birthdate: December 21, 1965
College: Maryland
Height: 6-6
Weight: 241
How Acquired: Drafted in tenth round, 1988
Position: Outside Linebacker
Final 1990 Team: Indianapolis Colts

O'Brien Alston spent most of 1989 and all of 1990 on the Colts' injured reserve list, after having reconstructive surgery on his left knee and arthroscopic surgery on his right knee. But the Raiders took a chance on Alston, who once was thought to have an outstanding NFL future. Alston earned a starting job in 1988 at left outside linebacker, and at times played brilliantly. His speed is average, but his strength against the run is excellent. A longshot to make the Raiders, Alston might surprise everyone; he works extremely hard in the weight room and is a dedicated player. A perfect Raider.

HANK'S RATING: C

Cornerbacks

Rod Woodson

Birthdate: March 10, 1965
College: Purdue
Height: 6-0
Weight: 196
How Acquired: Drafted in first round, 1987
Final 1990 Team: Pittsburgh Steelers

Few corners have ever had the season Rod Woodson had for the Pittsburgh Steelers in 1990. On top of being a Pro Bowl player and perhaps the league's most consistent corner, Woodson was also a scoring threat on special teams, capable of scoring from anywhere on the field. His presence on defense literally cut the field in half for opposing offenses.

Time and again Woodson proved himself. He had 6 solo tackles, broke up a pass, and returned a punt 52 yards for a touchdown in the Steelers' 20–9 win over division-rival Houston. In a Monday night game against the Rams, Woodson intercepted a pass and returned two kickoffs 49 and 45 yards. Woodson led the team with 5 interceptions, ranked fifth in tackles and second in passes defensed.

Woodson has been consistent, too. A tenacious tackler, brilliant cover man, and heads-up kick returner, Woodson represents one of the AFC's biggest threats. And don't forget that it was his crushing textbook hit on Houston tailback Lorenzo White in the playoffs that forced the fumble that led to Gary Anderson's winning overtime field goal.

HANK'S RATING: AAA

Deion Sanders

Birthdate: August 9, 1967
College: Florida State
Height: 6-0
Weight: 187
How Acquired: Drafted in first round, 1989
Final 1990 Team: Atlanta Falcons

When 50,000 fans filled Atlanta-Fulton County Stadium to watch the Braves in April—and flashy outfielder Deion Sanders, there was speculation in the hallways of the Falcons organization that Neon Deion was finished as a football player. "He won't be back," confided a Falcons source in April. "The Braves love him. If things don't change, we're going to need two corners, not just one."

But one month in the NFL can be an eternity. By late May, the Braves were demoting Sanders to Richmond, and no sooner had the spotlight left the multi-talented athlete than football—and the Falcons—was once again his focus. That came as a relief to Atlanta, which couldn't afford his loss at right cornerback.

Sanders might be the most naturally gifted corner in the game. He has tremendous speed and good instincts, as well as perfect technique in man-to-man coverage. The 1990 season marked his second-consecutive season with 1,000-plus combined return yards. With 2,133 yards the past two seasons, Sanders is just 29 yards shy of breaking the team's career return-yardage mark. Sanders also tied for the team lead with interceptions with 3. "Sanders gives everything he has," says head coach Jerry Glanville. "He works as hard as anybody on the field."

Sanders finished with 50 tackles, and maintained his excellence in man-to-man coverage. His biggest weaknesses, simply, are his inability to keep his head in the game and his poor tackling form; at San Francisco, 49er tight end Brent Jones embarrassed Sanders, dragging the cornerback 15 yards into the end zone.

HANK'S RATING: AAA

Kevin Ross

Birthdate: January 16, 1962
College: Temple
Height: 5-9
Weight: 182
How Acquired: Drafted in seventh round, 1984
Final 1990 Team: Kansas City Chiefs

Kevin Ross has been Kansas City's starting right cornerback from the day he joined the team in 1984, and with good reason: He is a hard-hitting, fleet-footed talent—the kind that doesn't come along every season. Scouts rave about Ross's hitting ability. "He may be the hardest hitter, pound for pound, in the NFL," says one. "But he doesn't give up anything speedwise, either. He's as talented in coverage as anyone, too."

Ross made his second consecutive trip to the Pro Bowl in 1990, and was a critical performer at critical times. In a 17–3 victory over Green Bay, Ross showed his versatility: He intercepted a pass, forced a fumble to stop a drive at the Chiefs' 1-yard line, recovered another fumble, made two tackles and held Sterling Sharpe to just three catches.

HANK'S RATING: AAA

Wayne Haddix

Birthdate: July 23, 1965
College: Liberty
Height: 6-1
Weight: 205
How Acquired: Free Agent, 1990
Final 1990 Team: Tampa Bay Buccaneers

Cornerback Wayne Haddix earned a Pro Bowl spot in 1990 with 7 interceptions, and, get this, was actually the Buccaneers fifth-leading scorer with 18 points. Haddix proved himself as a big-play performer several times during the season, and showed coaches he could be relied on for tight bump and run coverage and disciplined run support.

Haddix intercepted two Don Majkowski passes and returned one for a touchdown to help Tampa Bay upset Green Bay 26–14. Haddix was the only bright spot against San Francisco later in the season, when he scored his third touchdown on a 65-yard interception return.

HANK'S RATING: AA

Albert Lewis

Birthdate: October 6, 1960
College: Grambling
Height: 6-2
Weight: 198
How Acquired: Drafted in third round, 1983
Final 1990 Team: Kansas City Chiefs

Thirty-one-year-old Albert Lewis made yet another Pro Bowl trip in 1990, as the crafty veteran continued his dominance against the best receivers the AFC had to offer. Lewis excels in bump-and-run coverage, is a brutally physical player, and seldom misses a game with an injury. An example of his game-dominating talent occurred in week nine against the Raiders, when Lewis recovered a fumble to set up a field goal, stopped a drive with an interception, made two tackles, and broke up two passes in Kansas City's 9–7 victory.

But perhaps the most nervous players who faced Lewis were opposing punters, as he continued to harrass opponents' kicking games throughout the season. Against Cleveland, Lewis blocked his third punt in three weeks and helped set up another block—both of them led to touchdowns. Lewis has nine blocks in his career. "You have to account for him," says Kansas City special teams coach Kurt Schottenheimer. "He prepares to do it. He looks at the protection and the guy snapping the ball and knows where the punter is going to strike the ball." Former Cleveland coach Bud Carson says Lewis "has a great knack for escaping blockers."

HANK'S RATING: AA

Issiac Holt

203

Birthdate: October 4, 1962
College: Alcorn State
Height: 6-2
Weight: 202
How Acquired: Trade, 1989
Final 1990 Team: Dallas Cowboys

Something good came out of the Herschel Walker trade, only it had less to do with Walker and more to do with left cornerback Ike Holt, who at the time of the trade, seemed like another nameless player thrown in for good measure.

Wrong. Holt has bloomed in Dallas, becoming the best and by far the most consistent defensive player on the Cowboys. He only picked off 3 passes in 1990, but that was because very few teams were willing to test him by throwing in his direction. And he played tough on special teams, blocking two punts, returning one for a touchdown, and returned one of his picks for a score. Scouts call Holt an impact player, "a guy who really makes few mistakes, has his own style of technique, and understands how to use his body in coverage."

Holt made 2 tackles and intercepted 2 passes, returning the second 64 yards for a touchdown in the fourth quarter, to help Dallas beat Tampa Bay.

HANK'S RATING: AA

Don Griffin

Birthdate: March 17, 1964
College: MTSU
Height: 6-0
Weight: 176
How Acquired: Drafted in twelfth round, 1989
Final 1990 Team: San Francisco 49ers

Cornerback Don Griffin had what many considered a Pro Bowl season in 1990, but was overlooked in favor of more marquee names. He intercepted 3 passes and played the run with a vengeance. Griffin is a rapidly improving player who is an extremely efficient cover corner and a vicious hitter. The biggest earmark of his career has been consistency, and he is only now beginning to receive the recognition he deserves. He makes our Top 10 list for cornerbacks.

HANK'S RATING: AA

Mark Collins

Birthdate: January 16, 1964
College: Cal State-Fullerton
Height: 5-10
Weight: 190
How Acquired: Drafted in second round, 1986
Final 1990 Team: New York Giants

Left cornerback Mark Collins was an exceptional cover man in 1990, and performed well in the Giants' zone coverage. Collins, along with teammate Everson Walls, was a large reason New York allowed only 171.7 yards per game through the air during the regular season, the league's sixth-lowest total. Many players believed Collins, also a tenacious hitter, was overlooked in Pro Bowl voting.

Collins has excellent anticipation, outstanding vision, and breaks on a thrown ball with good judgment and unique quickness. He is a position player who studies hard and understands where he should be in given situations against given formations. Collins had just 2 interceptions in 1990, but he proved himself time and again, as opponents threw away from Walls.

HANK'S RATING: A

Carl Lee

Birthdate: April 6, 1961
College: Marshall
Height: 5-11
Weight: 184

How Acquired: Drafted in seventh round, 1983
Final 1990 Team: Minnesota Vikings

Carl Lee's 1990 season paralleled that of the rest of the Minnesota Vikings as he battled inconsistency and personality conflicts, but he was still one of the best cover corners in the NFL and earned a starting berth in the Pro Bowl.

Lee has excellent speed, closes like gangbusters on a thrown ball, and though not overly physical, is still very tough in the open field. If the Vikings are to return to their playoff form of years past, defensive backs Lee and Browner will have to play a big role.

HANK'S RATING: A

Everson Walls

Birthdate: December 28, 1959
College: Grambling State
Height: 6-1
Weight: 194
How Acquired: Free Agent, 1990
Final 1990 Team: New York Giants

The old man can still do it, and he did it with style in 1990. The Giants eagerly signed their old nemesis when Dallas left him unprotected, and Walls wasted little time proving the Cowboys moved too soon. Scouts love Walls, who always seems to be in the right place at exactly the right time. But Walls has an unorthodox coverage attitude—does not play the coverage exactly as taught by the coaching staff.

He started all sixteen games for New York at right cornerback, and led the team with 6 interceptions and 17 passes defensed. He also provided tremendous leadership to a relatively young secondary that is quicky becoming one of the NFL's best. And Walls also made it clear that, when called on, he could still change the outcome of a game. Against the Redskins, he set up a touchdown with his first interception, returned his second interception 28 yards for the clinching touchdown, and made 3 tackles in the Giants' 21–10 victory over arch-rival Washington.

HANK'S RATING: A

Nate Odomes

Birthdate: August 25, 1965
College: Wisconsin
Height: 5-10
Weight: 188
How Acquired: Drafted in second round, 1987
Final 1990 Team: Buffalo Bills

Nate Odomes was considered the best defensive back in the country during his senior year at Wisconsin, and since joining the Bills in 1987, he hasn't disappointed them. A brilliant corner, Odomes plays with intelligence and poise, and breaks on the ball as well as anybody in football. The 4.37 speedster was an integral part of Buffalo's pass defense, and few quarterbacks were willing to test Odomes too often. He had only 1 interception in 1990, but that was due to opposing quarterbacks being unwilling to throw repeatedly at Odomes.

HANK'S RATING: A

Darrell Green

Birthdate: February 15, 1960
College: Texas A&I
Height: 5-8
Weight: 170
How Acquired: Drafted in first round, 1983
Final 1990 Team: Washington Redskins

Cornerback Darrell Green often virtually single-handedly neutralized the opposition's best receiver. Green returned from a 1989 wrist injury with a passion, leading the team with 17 passes defensed. Green was so good at times that opposing quarterbacks often refused to even throw his way. "Big play people are hard to find," says Washington head coach Joe Gibbs. "Darrell always gives you that threat."

Green picked off 4 passes in 1990 and made 78 tackles. Some insiders feel he may be slipping a bit, but he's still in our Top 15.

HANK'S RATING: A

Gill Byrd

Birthdate: February 20, 1961
College: San Jose State
Height: 5-11
Weight: 198
How Acquired: Drafted in first round, 1983
Final 1990 Team: San Diego Chargers

Cornerback Gill Byrd is repeatedly overlooked for postseason honors. Over the past three seasons, Byrd has intercepted more passes than any corner in the NFL, but has yet to make the Pro Bowl in one of those three years. In 1990, he picked off 7 passes, which made him San Diego's career interception leader.

Byrd also continues to be a big-play performer, as he displayed in San Diego's win over Tampa Bay, when he intercepted two passes, the first setting up a touchdown, and made two tackles. Byrd is cat-quick, intelligent, understands leverage and position, and has damn near perfect technique. He is also durable, missing just five games in eight NFL seasons. Teammates praise Byrd for his unselfish style of play and tremendous work ethic.

HANK'S RATING: A

Terry McDaniel

Birthdate: February 8, 1965
College: Tennessee
Height: 5-10
Weight: 175
How Acquired: Drafted in first round, 1988
Final 1990 Team: Los Angeles Raiders

Cornerback Terry McDaniel had what many believed was a Pro Bowl season in 1990, demonstrating outstanding man-to-man coverage and vicious tackling. McDaniel picked off only three passes as more and more AFC quarterbacks elected to throw in other directions.

McDaniel can change directions on a dime, has incredible speed (4.5), and in the open field exhibits great range, quickness, and closing ability. And when the opportunity arises, he plays with the physical toughness that is a Raiders trademark. Scouts believe McDaniel will soon rank among the league's top five cornerbacks.

HANK'S RATING: A

Eric Allen

Birthdate: November 22, 1965
College: Arizona State
Height: 5-10
Weight: 188
How Acquired: Drafted in second round, 1988
Final 1990 Team: Philadelphia Eagles

Cornerback Eric Allen, in only his second pro season, was selected to the 1989 Pro Bowl after becoming one of the NFL's top cover corners. Though his interception total fell from 8 to 3 in 1990, Allen remains one of the league's fifteen best. Scouts say his strong suits are speed and recovery ability. "You can get a lot of garbage interceptions—overthrows, etc." says one scout. "But just about every pick Eric gets is because he had perfect position on the receiver and played the ball perfectly."

HANK'S RATING: A

J.B. Brown

Birthdate: January 5, 1967
College: Maryland
Height: 6-1
Weight: 192
How Acquired: Drafted in twelfth round, 1989
Final 1990 Team: Miami Dolphins

Miami head coach Don Shula doesn't hesitate to talk about why the Dolphins secondary's play picked up in 1990. Of course, he got consistent big plays from his veteran safety tandem of Louis Oliver and Jarvis Williams. But the biggest surprise came from the play of second-year man J.B. Brown, who came on in 1990 like gangbusters. Shula couldn't have been happier.

"His outstanding play really helped us improve our pass coverage," Shula says. Brown started at corner in all sixteen games and defensed 12 passes, good for second on the team. He also had 48 tackles, which was good for third on the team. Brown is an outstanding leaper with tremendous acceleration, and is steadily acquiring the confidence and technique to become a standout NFL cornerback.

HANK'S RATING: A

Mark Lee

Birthdate: March 20, 1958
College: Washington
Height: 5-11
Weight: 189
How Acquired: Drafted in second round, 1980
Final 1990 Team: Green Bay Packers

Left cornerback Mark Lee will enter his twelfth season in 1991, and he vows that he won't face the same fate as long-time Packer veteran Dave Brown, who was forced out last year as he headed into his sixteenth season. Lee has been called "the finest bump-and-run corner in the league" by his position coach, Dick Jauron, but opposing scouts are amazed that Lee has survived this far at the NFL's most visible and vulnerable position.

Lee finished the year with just 44 tackles, but defensed a team-high 15 passes. "Mark can cover anybody in the league one-on-one," says Jauron. "He has tremendous physical toughness. He not only plays well against the pass, but he can go out there and really put the wood to people in the running game."

HANK'S RATING: A

Eric Davis

Birthdate: January 28, 1968
College: Jacksonville State
Height: 5-11
Weight: 178
How Acquired: Drafted in second round, 1990
Final 1990 Team: San Francisco 49ers

The 49ers drafted cornerback Eric Davis in the second round with the intention of him becoming a starter—they just didn't expect him to make such a dramatic move on the job. But good work habits, solid form, and great man cover skills earned him the job before season's end, and now 49er coaches are hoping Davis can improve on his solid rookie campaign.

Davis is an aggressive corner, and his physical style is often borderline. He got away with one in the playoffs against Washington, while covering Redskins star Gary Clark. Clark got past Davis, but Davis managed to fend off Clark's facemask with his right hand and deflect the ball with his left.

HANK'S RATING: A

Darryl Pollard

Birthdate: May 11, 1965
College: Weber State
Height: 5-11
Weight: 187
How Acquired: Free Agent, 1988
Final 1990 Team: San Francisco 49ers

Cornerback Darryl Pollard, like teammate Don Griffin, is a rapidly improving player whose talent far exceeds the recognition he's received. The former free agent possesses tremendous desire, works hard in the weight room, and is a polished, skilled performer on the field. The 49ers are quickly recognizing Pollard as a big-play talent, a fact he solidified in the NFC playoffs when he intercepted a second-half Mark Rypien pass to help protect the 49ers 21–10 lead.

HANK'S RATING: B

Reggie Rutland

Birthdate: June 20, 1964
College: Georgia Tech
Height: 6-1
Weight: 195
How Acquired: Drafted in fourth round, 1987
Final 1990 Team: Minnesota Vikings

Cornerback Reggie Rutland has the ability to be an outstanding player, but Vikings coaches keep waiting for him to step up and live up to his potential. Rutland, in his fifth season, now has the experience and savvy to go with his God-given speed, quickness, and vision. Rutland has shown signs of excellence in the past, but must acquire more consistency to become a consummate player. Finished 1990 with just 2 interceptions.

HANK'S RATING: B

Richard Johnson

Birthdate: September 16, 1963
College: Wisconsin
Height: 6-1
Weight: 195
How Acquired: Drafted in first round, 1985
Final 1990 Team: Houston Oilers

Cornerback Richard Johnson might have been the happiest person in Houston when Jerry Glanville left for the Falcons. Johnson's attitude and work habits two years ago put him in Glanville's doghouse, and he wasted two seasons of his career trying to worm his way out of it. But new coach Jack Pardee gave Johnson a new start, and he flourished in the Oilers' new 4–3 zone defense. Johnson has good speed, and is highly regarded by scouts as a hitter and zone cover man. He'd lose a footrace, however, with many of the AFC's faster receivers, but is a disciplined, determined player. And it is those qualities that will make him a fine NFL cornerback.

HANK'S RATING: B

Patrick Hunter

Birthdate: October 24, 1964
College: Nevada-Reno
Height: 5-11
Weight: 186
How Acquired: Drafted in third round, 1986
Final 1990 Team: Seattle Seahawks

Right cornerback Patrick Hunter played reasonably well in his fifth season, intercepting 1 pass and making 56 tackles, a career high. But Hunter's inconsistent play caused the Seahawks to look for help at his position after the 1989 season, but he earned his job back with a steady training camp and went on to start all sixteen games. Hunter will be challenged by fifth-round pick Harlan Davis, a 4.3 speedster.

HANK'S RATING: B

Eugene Daniel

Birthdate: May 4, 1961
College: LSU
Height: 5-11
Weight: 188
How Acquired: Drafted in eighth round, 1984
Final 1990 Team: Indianapolis Colts

Right cornerback Eugene Daniel made his presence felt in 1990 with 59 tackles, but failed to intercept a pass. Opposing receivers found the eight-year veteran easier to beat than in years past, and coaches openly questioned Daniel's consistency. Scouts say Daniel faces the biggest test in his career in the 1991 season, as he tries to maintain the 4.4 speed and cover ability that helped him become Indianapolis's ninth all-time interceptor.

HANK'S RATING: B

Cris Dishman

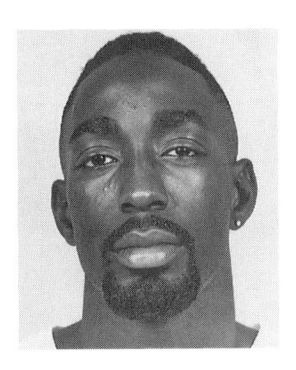

Birthdate: August 13, 1965
College: Purdue
Height: 6-0
Weight: 178
How Acquired: Drafted in fifth round, 1988
Final 1990 Team: Houston Oilers

Cris Dishman earned himself a starting cornerback spot in 1990, but also showed at times that he still needs to match his outstanding raw talent with a veteran's maturity. He embarrassed himself in a preseason game by intercepting a pass, taunting would-be tacklers on what appeared to be a certain touchdown return, then fumbling the ball back to the opposition.

Dishman has speed, intelligence, great acceleration, and quick lateral movement—an excellent corner athlete. "He's everything you're looking for in a pure corner," says Atlanta coach Jerry Glanville. But it's a lack of common sense, not ability, that keeps Dishman in the doghouse. With all his skills, some scouts question whether Dishman has the mental toughness to be a prime-time coverge man.

HANK'S RATING: B

Kirby Jackson

Birthdate: February 2, 1965
College: Mississippi State
Height: 5-10
Weight: 180
How Acquired: Free Agent, 1987
Final 1990 Team: Buffalo Bills

Kirby Jackson missed action due to injury in 1990, but was back in time for the Super Bowl. But Bills coaches are expecting him to compete for his job this year with second-year player James Williams, a talented and lightning-quick player out of Fresno State.

A former free agent, Jackson was waived by two other teams before earning a job on the Bills roster. His determination and discipline impressed Buffalo coaches, and his level of play has improved each year. Kirby's greatest asset is experience. He led the Bills in interceptions in 1990 with three.

HANK'S RATING: B

Ben Smith

Birthdate: May 14, 1967
College: Georgia
Height: 5-11
Weight: 183
How Acquired: Drafted in first round, 1990
Final 1990 Team: Philadelphia Eagles

Ben Smith, the Eagles first-round pick in 1990, was moved from free safety to left cornerback, where he experienced growing pains. Smith had 3 interceptions last season, and impressed Philadelphia coaches with his speed and recovery ability once a pass was in the air. Problem was he was often recovering because he was not a smart-coverage corner. Relies on his speed rather than his brain, leading to inconsistency. With maturity, though, scouts believe Smith could develop into one of the league's better cornerbacks.

HANK'S RATING: B

Donnell Woolford

Birthdate: January 6, 1966
College: Clemson
Height: 5-9
Weight: 187
How Acquired: Drafted in first round, 1989
Final 1990 Team: Chicago Bears

Chicago coaches knew left cornerback Donnell Woolford was a gutty player with solid tackling and cover skills. But after injuring his right leg midway through the 1990 season, Woolford impressed them again with his toughness, as he played through his second pro season despite hindering injuries.

As a rookie in 1989, Woolford survived sharp criticism from head coach Mike Ditka, when he stepped into the starting lineup under adverse circumstances and was given the task of covering receivers like Sterling Sharpe, Henry Ellard, Mark Carrier, and Gary Clark. And he did it with flair. He held Sharpe to two catches and shut out Ellard, and survived a separated shoulder, a broken hand, a staph infection in his left eye, and several deep muscle bruises. If he can continue to stay healthy, Woolford is an impressive cover corner.

HANK'S RATING: B

Ronnie Lippett

Birthdate: December 10, 1960
College: Miami

Height: 5-11
Weight: 180
How Acquired: Drafted in eighth round, 1983
Final 1990 Team: New England Patriots

Cornerback Ronnie Lippett intercepted 4 passes in 1990 to move into seventh place on the Patriots' all-time interception list, with 22 career picks. Lippett's quickness and acceleration are surprising this late in his career. Injuries have taken their toll on his body, however, as Lippett has missed all or parts of the past three seasons with serious health problems.

When healthy, Lippett is a cat-quick corner with the hands and mind of a burglar. Scouts point to his technique and sure tackling ability as two of Lippett's biggest assets. He played three years with Patriot teammate Fred Marion at Miami, giving the pair eleven years of experience together.

HANK'S RATING: B

Cedric Mack

Birthdate: September 14, 1960
College: Baylor
Height: 6-0
Weight: 185
How Acquired: Drafted in second round, 1983
Final 1990 Team: Phoenix Cardinals

The NFL days of cornerback Cedrick Mack could well be numbered: Coaches feel he simply doesn't shut down enough receivers, despite his ingenuity. Trailing Indianapolis 17–13 with about ten minutes to play, Mack intercepted Jeff George at the Colts' 35. He returned the ball 14 yards to the 21, then lateraled to Turner, who dashed the last 21 yards for the winning touchdown. "I wasn't surprised when Cedric tossed me the ball," Turner says. "We've been doing it so much in practice that it just seemed the natural thing to do."

Turner might be surprised, however, when coaches give him Mack's starting job in 1991.

HANK'S RATING: B

Frank Minnifield

Birthdate: January 1, 1960
College: Louisville
Height: 5-9
Weight: 180
How Acquired: Free Agent, 1984
Final 1990 Team: Cleveland Browns

Cornerback Frank Minnifield missed four games in 1990 before signing his contract, then missed several more due to injuries. In what little time he played, Minnifield offered little help in the Browns' porous pass defense. His 25 tackles ranked among his worst, and his 2 interceptions were also unspectacular. And more than one insider feels he's lost his "fire" to be a competitive man coverage man.

Minnifield has reached a crossroad in his career; either he pulls himself back up to his former Pro Bowl caliber, or he retires. AFC receivers no longer fear him, and new coach Bill Belichick won't tolerate his bad attitude.

HANK'S RATING: B

Garry Lewis

Birthdate: August 25, 1967
College: Alcorn State
Height: 5-11
Weight: 180
How Acquired: Drafted in seventh round, 1990
Final 1990 Team: Los Angeles Raiders

Cornerback Garry Lewis, a seventh-round pick in 1990, was a pleasant surprise for the Raiders during his rookie year. He started early in the year, and appeared in every game in nickel and dime situations. Coaches expect him to become a full-time starter in 1991.

Lewis is a versatile defensive back who can play safety or corner, and possesses good speed and quickness. His greatest shortcoming is technique, an area that Lewis has worked hard on in the 1990 offseason. "This kid is loaded with potential," says an AFC scout, who scouted Lewis while he was still in college. "This year will be a big year for him. He's either going to be great, or he's going to fall short. And from what [Raider] coaches have told me, it's really up to him and how hard he works."

HANK'S RATING: B

Marcus Turner

Birthdate: January 13, 1966
College: UCLA
Height: 6-0
Weight: 191
How Acquired: Waivers, 1989
Final 1990 Team: Phoenix Cardinals

Cornerback Marcus Turner was originally signed to the club's developmental squad in 1989, elevated to the active roster later that season, and became a part-time starter in 1990. Coaches are eager to see how he progresses in the 1991 season. A former UCLA star, Turner responds well to fierce competiton and also excels on special teams. He is a bright player with good speed, and breaks well on the ball.

HANK'S RATING: B

Jerry Holmes

Birthdate: December 22, 1957
College: West Virginia
Height: 6-2
Weight: 175
How Acquired: Plan B free agent, 1990
Final 1990 Team: Green Bay Packers

The fact that Jerry Holmes is still playing is testimony to his role as a survivor in professional football. Holmes finished 1990 with 56 tackles, including 12 defensed passes and 3 interceptions, another solid season for the thirty-three-year-old former Plan B acquisition. A former starter for both the Lions and the Jets, Holmes is a steady player who occasionally gives up the big play but offers steady man cover skills.

Holmes was originally signed by the Packers as insurance, and ended up a starter through injuries and poor play by other players. The Packers had hoped second-year speedster LeRoy Butler would take over the left corner position, but Butler's inconsistency put him on the bench watching the veteran Holmes.

HANK'S RATING: B

Toi Cook

Birthdate: December 3, 1967
College: Stanford
Height: 5-11
Weight: 188
How Acquired: Drafted in eighth round, 1987
Final 1990 Team: New Orleans Saints

In just his second year as a starting cornerback, Toi Cook had a borderline season in 1990. He led the Saints with a whopping 20 passes defensed, but that was largely due to the fact that opposing offenses loved to pick on him. He finished with 66 tackles, 1 sack, and 2 interceptions. Cook is a powerful tackler, but he lacks speed in the open field and must learn to limit his mistakes in coverage. He will be challenged by Vince Buck for the starting job.

HANK'S RATING: B

Alan Grant

Birthdate: October 1, 1966
College: Stanford
Height: 5-10
Weight: 187
How Acquired: Drafted in fourth round, 1990
Final 1990 Team: Indianapolis Colts

The Colts finally solved the revolving door situation at left cornerback when they drafted Alan Grant last year. Grant instantly brought speed, determination, and savvy to the position. If he can answer the questions scouts have about his desire to cover aggressively, he will only get better. He had his best day in week sixteen against the Redskins: After Washington held the ball for nearly forty minutes, outgained the Colts by 218 yards, and rolled up nearly 200 yards rushing, Grant picked off a Mark Rypien pass with fifty seconds left and returned it 25 yards for the winning touchdown.

HANK'S RATING: B

Robert Massey

Birthdate: February 17, 1967
College: North Carolina Central
Height: 5-10
Weight: 182
How Acquired: Drafted in second round, 1989
Final 1990 Team: New Orleans Saints

Saints coaches were pleased with Robert Massey in his second season. He finished third on the team with 65 tackles, and defensed 12 passes, second only to Toi Cook's 20 defensed passes. Massey proved himself as a fierce hitter who closes well on the run. He has outstanding quickness and excellent leaping ability, but he does not challenge receivers enough in man coverage exposure.

Massey's biggest weakness is keeping his head in the game, and he often falls prey to the errors typical of young players. In the playoffs against Chicago, Massey made a game-changing mistake: trailing 10–3, defensive end Renaldo Turnbull blocked a field-goal attempt, and rookie cornerback Vince Buck returned it for the apparent tying touchdown. Except that Massey had lined up offsides, and the play was nullified and the Bears were given a first down.

Nevertheless, Massey has shown outstanding pro potential, and should develop into a steady player.

HANK'S RATING: B

Ray Crockett

Birthdate: November 5, 1967
College: Baylor
Height: 5-9
Weight: 181
How Acquired: Drafted in fourth round, 1989
Final 1990 Team: Detroit Lions

Cornerback Ray Crockett was a mild surprise in 1990, in just his second NFL season. Scouts say Crockett lacks polished cover skills, but they like his aggressiveness and his knack for always being around the football. He finished the season with 3 interceptions, and had a critical fumble return for a touchdown in the Detroit's late-season upset of Green Bay.

"Ray really came along at the corner position and probably was our best defensive back last year at the end of the year," says defensive coordinator Woody Widenhofer. "He played very steady, tackled very well, was aggressive and made some real big plays for us the last four or five games. I'm looking for him to become an even better player this year."

HANK'S RATING: B

Dwayne Harper

Birthdate: March 29, 1966
College: South Carolina
Height: 5-11
Weight: 174
How Acquired: Drafted in eleventh round, 1988
Final 1990 Team: Seattle Seahawks

Left cornerback Dwayne Harper turned in another solid season, starting all sixteen games and making 71 tackles, third on the team. He intercepted 3 passes, but the fourth-year player was picked on often by opposing quarterbacks, largely due to his relative inexperience; going into 1990, he had only one season of extensive action under his belt. His durability, however, has never been in question—he's played in all forty-six games since he became a Seahawk.

Harper had excellent straight-ahead speed coming out of college, and has worked hard as a pro to refine his technique and overall cover ability. Many scouts believe 1991 could be Harper's finest season. "He's got the experience now to be a great player," says one. "By the fourth year, most corners either level out and play real well at that level for several years, or they move on to their life's work." Seattle defensive coordinator Tom Catlin calls Harper "a rising star ... good, and getting better."

HANK'S RATING: B

David Johnson

Birthdate: April 14, 1966
College: Kentucky
Height: 6-0
Weight: 185
How Acquired: Drafted in seventh round, 1989
Final 1990 Team: Pittsburgh Steelers

Steelers coaches were pleasantly surprised with David Johnson, who in just his second season claimed a starting role in Pittsburgh's talented secondary. He improved even more as the season progressed, defensing a team-high 18 passes, as most quarterbacks opted to test Johnson as opposed to Rod Woodson.

Johnson has excellent speed, quick feet, and is a disciplined worker. He excels in zone coverage, but is very capable in man-to-man coverage, as well. Barring injury, Johnson should become a fixture in the Pittsburgh secondary for many years.

HANK'S RATING: B

Jerry Gray

Birthdate: December 2, 1962
College: Texas
Height: 6-0
Weight: 185
How Acquired: Drafted in first round, 1985
Final 1990 Team: Los Angeles Rams

Cornerback Jerry Gray, once considered among the league's most potent defensive backs, never regained his Pro Bowl form after returning from September arthroscopic knee surgery last season. Gray missed the season's first three games, and played at far less than 100 percent the rest of the way. While he returned with the same work ethics, and showed tremendous toughness and determination, he lost some quickness and failed to produce at the level his position requires.

Rams coaches are undecided about Gray's future as a starter, and training camp will go a long way in making their decisions.

HANK'S RATING: B

Lemuel Stinson

Birthdate: May 10, 1966
College: Texas Tech

Height: 5-9
Weight: 159
How Acquired: Drafted in sixth round, 1988
Final 1990 Team: Chicago Bears

Lemuel Stinson finished the 1990 season on injured reserve, but he'll be back in the Chicago starting lineup by the start of the 1991 season. He won the starting cornerback job in training camp, and was leading the conference with 6 interceptions before injuring his knee on the second play at Denver. Prior to the injury, Stinson showed outstanding potential on several occasions, including a 2-interception performance at Atlanta.

After leading the Bears in interceptions in 1989 with 4 interceptions, Stinson suffered an injury to his right knee which required arthroscopic surgery and forced him to miss the final month of that season. A former collegiate wide receiver, Stinson has excellent straight-ahead speed, and is still relatively new to his position. He has shown dramatic improvement over the past few seasons in his pass cover technique.

HANK'S RATING: B

Martin Mayhew

Birthdate: October 8, 1965
College: Florida State
Height: 5-8
Weight: 172
How Acquired: Free Agent, 1989
Final 1990 Team: Washington Redskins

Martin Mayhew became the starting corner opposite Darrell Green when Redskins coaches believed A.J. Johnson would miss the season with a knee injury. Mayhew was burned early, but improved dramatically as the season progressed, and kept his job after Johnson returned sooner than expected. The second-year player led the team with 7 interceptions. Johnson's return immensely helped Mayhew and the defensive secondary. Will be plenty of competition between Mayhew and Johnson this season.

HANK'S RATING: B

Sam Seale

Birthdate: October 6, 1962
College: Western State Colorado
Height: 5-9
Weight: 185
How Acquired: Free Agent, 1988
Final 1990 Team: San Diego Chargers

Cornerback Sam Seale led the Chargers with 8 defensed passes in 1990, and added 2 interceptions and 38 tackles. But he split time with free-agent Donald Frank, who is expected to pose a stiff challenge for the improving Seale in 1991.

Seale had his best season in 1989, intercepting 4 passes and knocking down 12 more. His 9.4 speed in the 100 is among the Chargers' fastest times, and he is capable of running with any receiver in the NFL. His technique and inconsistency, however, are his weaknesses. "Seale can be as good as he wants to be," says a scout. "Like it does with so many defensive backs, it will probably come down to how hard he wants to work at his trade."

HANK'S RATING: B

Tony Stargell

Birthdate: August 7, 1966
College: Tennessee State
Height: 5-11
Weight: 190
How Acquired: Drafted in third round, 1990
Final 1990 Team: New York Jets

Cornerback Tony Stargell was an unlikely hero in 1990, after being the team's third-round selection. After several early torchings, Stargell settled down and displayed excellent potential. Stargell has positive man cover potential; his greatest shortcomings were a lack of technique and experience. He must also learn body control and position. But he possesses superb raw skills, and with another mini-camp and training camp behind him, Stargell could have a promising 1991.

HANK'S RATING: B

James Hasty

Birthdate: May 23, 1965
College: Washington State
Height: 6-0
Weight: 197
How Acquired: Drafted in third round, 1988
Final 1990 Team: New York Jets

Cornerback James Hasty was thrilled when new defensive coordinator Pete Carroll, who worked as Minnesota's secondary coach for five years, added bump-and-run coverage to New York's new defensive scheme. Although the high-risk defense exposed New York's youthful secondary in 1990, it also brought maturity to a group of rapidly improving defensive backs, namely Hasty.

Carroll credits Hasty for having the "speed and the instincts it takes to play this position." He runs the 40 in 4.5, has excellent leaping ability, and "is still learning," Carroll says. Now in his fourth season, Hasty will feel the heat from Jets coaches this season, who believe it's time to show more improvement if he is to blossom into one of the AFC's better corners.

HANK'S RATING: C

Vince Buck

Birthdate: January 12, 1968
College: Central State Ohio
Height: 6-0
Weight: 198
How Acquired: Drafted in second round, 1990
Final 1990 Team: New Orleans Saints

Cornerback Vince Buck lived up to his press clippings in 1990 after the Saints made him their second-round pick. But New Orleans lack of secondary help left Saints coaches in a quandry. "Vince has the ability to be a real good safety, but that doesn't mean we're going to do it, because our corner position isn't strong enough," says head coach Jim Mora. "We need all the help we can get at corner." Translation: Although Buck is a natural safety, and lacks the blazing speed to be a legitimate every-down corner, he will stay at that position because New Orleans has few other options. Buck is an athletic player who needs work to become an impact player that you'd like from a second-round pick. Scouts feel he has the skills, but that he is not a smart "coverage system" player.

HANK'S RATING: C

Raymond Clayborn

Birthdate: January 2, 1955
College: Texas
Height: 6-1
Weight: 186
How Acquired: Plan B Free Agent, 1990
Final 1990 Team: Cleveland Browns

Raymond Clayborn found himself in the worst position of his career in 1990 after the Plan B free agent signed with Cleveland. His $1.8 million contract divided the team, as other veterans younger than Clayborn—including team leader Hanford Dixon—were snubbed by management. Dixon eventually retired, cornerback Frank Minnifield missed four games in a contract dispute, and almost before it started, Cleveland's season was over.

Clayborn still possesses a brilliant mind, good technique, and strong tackling ability, but age, again, is a serious question: Can a thirty-six-year-old cornerback who has lost his coverage speed survive in the NFL? Only Clayborn can answer that question, and new coach Bill Belichick will be watching with interest.

HANK'S RATING: C

Safeties

David Fulcher

Birthdate: September 28, 1964
College: Arizona State
Height: 6-3
Weight: 234
How Acquired: Drafted in third round, 1986
Final 1990 Team: Cincinnati Bengals

When scouts describe David Fulcher, they all say the same thing: It's amazing that somebody that size (6-3, 234) has that kind of speed. Built like a linebacker, Fulcher plays strong safety with the dexterity of a much smaller man.

"There are days when David has not only played over his own head, but over the heads of his opponents," says head coach Sam Wyche. "He has not only made the big plays, but he's been such a force on defense that he has forced opponents to change their game plans completely."

One of those days came last year against the Jets, when Fulcher made 10 tackles, sacked Ken O'Brien for a safety and ended the Jets' final scoring threat with a leaping interception in the end zone to lead the Bengals' to a 25–20 victory. Nine of his tackles were unassisted. Although Fulcher once again fell prey to injury, missing four weeks last season with a separated shoulder, his peers saw enough of him to vote him into the Pro Bowl.

"We have to have an attitude that, whatever team we play, we're mad at them and want to kill them," Fulcher says. "We've got that attitude against Cleveland, Houston, and Pittsburgh, but we've got to have it against teams we don't play as often, too."

HANK'S RATING: AAA

Joey Browner

Birthdate: May 15, 1960
College: USC
Height: 6-2
Weight: 212
How Acquired: Drafted in first round, 1983
Final 1990 Team: Minnesota Vikings

It was once again easy to determine that safety Joey Browner was Minnesota's best overall player in 1990. Opposing coaches credited him with being a major reason for the Vikings' six-game winning streak, and despite the shortcomings of several teammates, Browner played with dedication and heart.

Scouts say Browner may be the craftiest, nastiest safety in the game. "Joey is a vicious tackler," says former defensive coordinator Floyd Peters. "Few people run through one of his tackles." Not even Barry Sanders, the NFC's leading rusher. Two years ago Sanders burst through the line of scrimmage, skirted two linebackers, and burst into the secondary, where Browner applied a hit that sounded like a gunshot. "I hadn't seen anybody stop Barry one-on-one," says former Detroit assistant Mouse Davis. "But Browner drilled him, he just nailed his ass. It was impressive."

HANK'S RATING: AA

Steve Atwater

Birthdate: October 28, 1966
College: Arkansas
Height: 6-3
Weight: 213
How Acquired: Drafted in first round, 1989
Final 1990 Team: Denver Broncos

Safety Steve Atwater made his first Pro Bowl in 1990, finishing second on the Broncos with 173 tackles and playing some of the most physical football ever seen in the Denver secondary. Atwater missed playing time due to injuries for the first time in his brief two-year career, but the time he spent on the field made up for any time he missed.

Atwater started every game as a rookie, led the Bronco defense with 86 first hits, was second on the squad with 129 total tackles, and intercepted 3 passes. "I can't say enough about Steve's contributions to our football team during his rookie year," says head coach Dan Reeves.

HANK'S RATING: AA

Bubba McDowell

Birthdate: November 4, 1966
College: Miami
Height: 6-1
Weight: 195
How Acquired: Drafted in third round, 1989
Final 1990 Team: Houston Oilers

Bubba McDowell had another Pro Bowl-worthy season in 1990, finishing with 81 tackles and 2 interceptions. A fearless leader, McDowell improved rapidly last season, as he gained recognition of opposing offenses and developed better instincts in the pro passing game.

McDowell was disappointed after being a third-round pick in 1989, and set out to prove scouts wrong. He ended up as one of just nine drafted rookies to start all sixteen games that year, led the Oilers in solo tackles a team-best seven times, and forced 4 fumbles. In addition to being a force at safety, he dominated on special teams, blocking two punts and forcing a fumble on a kickoff against Cincinnati that led to victory.

McDowell is an impact player who is still learning. His best years are still ahead of him, and his potential is unlimited.

HANK'S RATING: AA

Scott Case

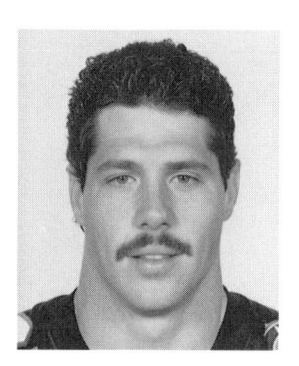

Birthdate: May 17, 1962
College: Oklahoma
Height: 6-0
Weight: 178
How Acquired: Drafted in second round, 1984
Final 1990 Team: Atlanta Falcons

Ernest Givens. Roger Craig and Jerry Rice. Flipper Anderson. The list was long and distinguished, as each week of the 1990 season saw new stars inducted into the ERHPC (Ears Ringing and Head Pounding Club), courtesy of Atlanta safety Scott Case. A quick poll around the league reveals that Case is either the NFL's fiercest or nastiest player, depending on whom you believe.

Case's brutal hit on Craig—which violently snapped back the runner's head and lifted him off his feet—was especially memorable. "I don't believe," says Craig, "that I've ever been hit like that." It took new coach Jerry Glanville no time to fall in love with his latest mercenary. "Scott plays hurt, he plays hard, and he never complains," Glanville says. "You just point him at the target and he destroys it."

In 1988, Case led the NFL with 10 interceptions, which set a new club record. The only Falcon defensive back of the 1980s voted into the Pro Bowl, Case has led the Atlanta secondary in tackles four of his last six years. His 8 interceptions in 1983 at the University of Oklahoma set a school record.

Case's emergence under Glanville took no one by surprise. "I demand a lot of my safeties in run support, and our scheme requires a guy that will rock you," says Glanville, who frequently refers to his safeties as "trained killers." Case prepared for his new mission with elbow pads, neck rolls, a larger face mask, and heavier shoulder pads. Against the Rams on December 22, Case played perhaps his finest game, compiling 8 bone-jarring tackles, a sack, and returned an interception 36 yards for the winning touchdown. Afterward, quarterback Jim Everett had nothing but respect for the low-flying Falcon. "He's amazing," Everett said.

HANK'S RATING: AA

Louis Oliver

Birthdate: March 9, 1966
College: Florida
Height: 6-2
Weight: 226
How Acquired: Drafted in first round, 1989
Final 1990 Team: Miami Dolphins

Free safety Louis Oliver tied for third in the AFC and tied for tenth in the NFL with 5 interceptions in 1990, as he continued to improve and excel as one of the league's brightest young defensive stars.

Ironically, Oliver's five picks tied with teammate and Miami strong safety Jarvis Williams, and together they set new single-season career highs. He also is a proven asset in run support, and finished fourth on the team in tackles with 65. Oliver is a brutal hitter, solid tackler, and breaks well on the ball. Like Williams, his defensive backfield mate, he has superstar ability.

HANK'S RATING: AA

Mark Carrier

Birthdate: April 28, 1968
College: USC
Height: 6-1
Weight: 180
How Acquired: Drafted in first round, 1990
Final 1990 Team: Chicago Bears

Safety Mark Carrier had a brilliant rookie season, as he was everything and more that head coach Mike Ditka had hoped he would be. He finished third on the team with 122 tackles, defensing a team-high 20 passes, forcing a team-high 5 fumbles, and intercepting a league-high 10 passes. His outstanding play earned him Defensive Rookie of the Year honors, and he was one of just three rookies voted to the Pro Bowl.

Few rookie defensive backs ever dominate a game, but Carrier was an exception, not once, but several times. Against Tampa Bay, Carrier intercepted 2 passes to set up 10 points, made 11 tackles, and tipped a pass that led to another interception.

Carrier came out of USC as a highly regarded safety, but many scouts didn't think he was talented enough to warrant being taken in the first round. But the Bears made him the sixth player picked, and he quickly proved critics wrong. Though Carrier runs a 4.6 in the 40, not blazing fast among defensive backs, he exhibits tremendous body control and is a heady, instinctive player.

HANK'S RATING: AA

Carnell Lake

Birthdate: July 15, 1967
College: UCLA
Height: 6-1
Weight: 205
How Acquired: Drafted in second round, 1989
Final 1990 Team: Pittsburgh Steelers

In just two seasons at strong safety, Carnell Lake has developed at a rapid pace. He tied for third on the team in tackles with 67, and was also third in passes defensed, with 11. His intelligence and versatility make him one of the finer defensive backs in the game, but with the presence of superstar cornerback Rod Woodson, Lake is easily overlooked in the Pittsburgh secondary. He started fifteen games as a rookie in 1989 and impressed coaches with a relatively mistake-free season. Scouts say Lake is a budding star in his own right.

HANK'S RATING: AA

Mark Murphy

Birthdate: April 22, 1958
College: West Liberty
Height: 6-2
Weight: 201
How Acquired: Free Agent, 1984
Final 1990 Team: Green Bay Packers

Strong safety Mark Murphy once again led the Packers in tackles with 128, including 103 solo efforts, intercepted 3 passes, forced a fumble, and defensed 11 passes. For Murphy, it was just another routine season of production.

Murphy is a model of consistency, routinely finishing among the team's top tacklers and interceptors and delivering thunderous hits that have earned the respect of the NFC Central's best receivers. Coaches keep mentioning Murphy's age—he'll be thirty-three this season—but his production continues to increase. "You'd like to have forty-seven Mark Murphys," says head coach Lindy Infante. "You could line up and play anybody. You'd like to clone him."

Murphy isn't the most gifted safety in the NFL, "but I doubt there are any who are more professional," Infante says. "He's a leader. When you put Mark Murphy on the field, you can turn your back and not worry about that position."

HANK'S RATING: AA

Eddie Anderson

Birthdate: July 22, 1963
College: Fort Valley State
Height: 6-1
Weight: 200
How Acquired: Free Agent, 1987
Final 1990 Team: Los Angeles Raiders

Free safety Eddie Anderson won the hearts of Raiders' brass in 1987 when he broke six ribs on former Denver wide receiver Steve Watson—with one hit. The former replacement player, who can bench press more than 500 pounds, is a ferocious tackler. Raiders coaches have ignored his frequent coverage mistakes to allow him to grow into the position. A great extra effort type player and savage hitter.

HANK'S RATING: AA

Jarvis Williams

Birthdate: May 16, 1965
College: Florida
Height: 5-11
Weight: 198
How Acquired: Drafted in second round, 1988
Final 1990 Team: Miami Dolphins

It's only been a few years since fans and pundits alike were criticizing the Miami pass defense. Times have changed, though, as the Dolphins now boast one of the best secondaries in the NFL. Jarvis Williams and Louis Oliver were arguably one of the best safety tandems in 1990, and improved noticably with the improved play of second-year corner J.B. Brown.

Williams finished third on the Dolphins in tackles with 76, and tied for the team lead in interceptions with 5, a career high. Williams, like Oliver, is a ferocious hitter who, unlike many safeties, still has the speed to cover any receiver opposing offenses throw at him.

After surprising coaches by starting all sixteen games in 1988 as a rookie, Williams has still yet to miss a game. "Our coverage in the secondary is only getting better as those two guys [Oliver and Williams] continue to play together," says head coach Don Shula. Williams and Oliver played together at the University of Florida, and 1991 will give them six years of experience in the same defensive backfield. "It's safe to say we understand each other," says

Williams. "It's also pretty safe to say we complement each other."

HANK'S RATING: A

Erik McMillan

Birthdate: May 3, 1965
College: Missouri
Height: 6-2
Weight: 197
How Acquired: Drafted in third round, 1988
Final 1990 Team: New York Jets

Erik McMillan had lots of critics when the Jets made the free safety their third-round pick in 1988. But nobody was talking after 1989, when McMillan made his second consecutive Pro Bowl. His nasty disposition and intimidating scowl puts fear in the hearts of receivers across the AFC. "He is a big-time player," says Buffalo's Andre Reed.

McMillan has had success trying to do it on his own. In 1989, with the Jets mired in a thirteen-quarter slump when they failed to score a touchdown, McMillan scored three on defense by himself. But his youthful recklessness backfired last year against the Colts, when he intercepted a Jeff George pass, returned it 24 yards, attempted a lateral to a teammate, only to have the Colts recover. George threw a touchdown on the next play.

But McMillan does more right than wrong, and is an unselfish player. Against Dallas last year, teammate Terance Mathis caught a punt at his own 2-yard line, started up the middle of the field, cut to the right sideline, and—boom—it was McMillan's crushing block at midfield that sprung him for a 98-yard touchdown, which tied an NFL record.

McMillan did not play up to his 1989 standards in 1990. Some scouts report that McMillan would sometimes fail to play the defense called, but rather freelance it. The Jets are hoping he'll return to his old form.

HANK'S RATING: A

Dennis Smith

Birthdate: February 3, 1959
College: USC
Height: 6-3
Weight: 200
How Acquired: Drafted in first round, 1981
Final 1990 Team: Denver Broncos

Safety Dennis Smith is entering the twilight of his brilliant twelve-year career. He intercepted just 2 passes in 1990, and suffered injuries that forced him to miss playing time. But Smith, a veteran weekend warrior, still deserves his place among the NFL's better safeties. The respect felt for him around the league was evident when peers voted him to the Pro Bowl.

Rookie safety Alton Montgomery, who ended 1990 with 2 interceptions, is the obvious future at free safety, but he couldn't pick a better player to study under than Smith, who has started in the Denver secondary since 1982. His athleticism, versatility, and jumping ability put him into two Pro Bowls in the mid-1980s, and at one time, Denver coaches utilized him as a receiver to take advantage of his speed and leaping ability. But age has robbed Smith of most of his ability, except for his heart and determination. But Smith is still a necessary ingredient in the Denver secondary, especially with the question mark of talented left corner Tyrone Braxton, who suffered a potentially career-ending knee injury last season and is coming off major surgery.

Smith can still play well on pure instinct, but his heroics, with few exceptions, are all but over. A veteran leader that the game will sorely miss when he retires.

HANK'S RATING: A

William White

Birthdate: February 19, 1966
College: Ohio State
Height: 5-10
Weight: 191
How Acquired: Drafted in fourth round, 1988
Final 1990 Team: Detroit Lions

Strong safety William White performed his job quietly and capably in 1990. While other Lions defenders could claim better years or better stats, White simply did his job for sixteen games, made few errors, led the team in interceptions (5) and finished second in tackles with 106.

"William White was probably our best tackler," says defensive coordinator Woody Widenhofer. "He was our most steady player back there."

But Widenhofer adds that White will have to work for his job in 1991, as he expects competition to come from recent free-agent signees Melvin Jenkins and Sean Van Horse.

HANK'S RATING: A

Mark Kelso

Birthdate: July 23, 1963
College: William & Mary
Height: 5-11
Weight: 185
How Acquired: Free Agent, 1986
Final 1990 Team: Buffalo Bills

As free safeties go, Mark Kelso has to be considered among the league's toughest, though not the swiftest. Kelso hits so hard it's hard to believe (forgive us) he played at William & Mary, and this former free agent has earned the respect of his peers through hard, disciplined play. Kelso originally made his mark as a special teamer, then worked his way into the starting lineup by impressing coaches with intelligence and crushing hits.

Kelso lacks the footspeed to run with the league's faster wideouts, and is beatable if locked up in a rare man-to-man situation. But in Buffalo's hard-hitting zone coverage, Kelso is the primary reason opposing receivers keep their heads on a swivel.

HANK'S RATING: A

Tim McDonald

Birthdate: January 6, 1965
College: USC
Height: 6-2
Weight: 209
How Acquired: Drafted in first round, 1987
Final 1990 Team: Phoenix Cardinals

Phoenix coaches felt strong safety Tim McDonald had a subpar year, despite leading the team in tackles (141) and interceptions (4). McDonald is among the NFL's top fifteen safeties, so in his case, outstanding statistics don't always count. "An average season for Tim would probably be an outstanding year for most safeties," says head coach Joe Bugel. But make no mistake, Phoenix needs for McDonald to have a better than average season.

HANK'S RATING: A

Barney Bussey

Birthdate: May 20, 1962
College: South Carolina State
Height: 6-0
Weight: 206
How Acquired: Drafted in fifth round, 1984
Final 1990 Team: Cincinnati Bengals

After spending several years as David Fulcher's backup, Barney Bussey moved into the starting free safety spot and produced surprising results. Bussey, a physical, aggressive player who makes few mistakes and plays with intelligence, experienced a rebirth during the 1990 season. Bussey made a number of big plays, including 4 interceptions, 2 sacks and a fumble recovery.

Bussey proved, too, that Fulcher wasn't the only safety who could change a game by himself. Against Pittsburgh, for instance, he returned a fumble 70 yards for a touchdown, made 3 tackles, and broke up a pass to help the Bengals overpower the Steelers, 27–3. With time running out in the second quarter, he tackled Pittsburgh holder Jim Stryzinski inches from the goal line on a fake field goal.

HANK'S RATING: A

Leonard Smith

Birthdate: September 2, 1960
College: McNeese State

Height: 5-11
Weight: 202
How Acquired: Trade, 1988
Final 1990 Team: Buffalo Bills

Leonard Smith spent a lot of time in 1990 at free safety after Mark Kelso suffered a broken ankle in mid-season, but was able to return to strong safety when Kelso returned for the Super Bowl. Smith is a savage hitter, whose tenacity and aggressiveness in recent years has created big plays for the opportunistic Bills defense. Smith finished with 2 interceptions on the year, and added another in the playoffs against the Raiders, but his presence was felt more on run support and while punishing receivers over the middle. Smith lacks the speed he once had, but he can still be counted on for consistent, steady, heads-up play.

HANK'S RATING: A

Bennie Blades

Birthdate: September 3, 1966
College: Miami
Height: 6-1
Weight: 221
How Acquired: Drafted in first round, 1988
Final 1990 Team: Detroit Lions

The Lions made Bennie Blades a full-time free safety in 1990, and Blades continued to flourish as a big-league hitter but still failed to develop the cover skills that Lions coaches thought he would learn by now. He also missed six games with injury.

"He should become one of the better free safeties in the NFL," says head coach Wayne Fontes. "He can play either safety position, but we're starting him at free where we think he can make more plays and be more intimidating. But it's time for him to step up and be the player he's capable of being. There's no reason he shouldn't be an All-Pro player."

Blades' coverage may be suspect, but his heart isn't. Fans still remember two years ago against the Vikings, when Minnesota receiver Anthony Carter split the seam down the middle. Blades crushed Carter, sending his helmet bouncing down the field. "I thought I ripped his head off," Blades said later.

HANK'S RATING: A

Brian Jordan

Birthdate: March 29, 1967
College: Richmond
Height: 5-11
Weight: 202
How Acquired: Free Agent, 1989
Final 1990 Team: Atlanta Falcons

Brian Jordan's aggressive play quickly made him a Glanville favorite, as he threw his 202-pound body around with reckless abandon and played brilliantly in pass coverage. He was also second on the team with 193 tackles, and continued to get better and better as the season wore on.

Nicknamed "bazeball" by Glanville, Jordan, like teammate Deion Sanders, also plays professional baseball in the offseason. Were it not for the presence of Sanders, Jordan's blazing 4.4 speed would make him the fastest player in the defensive backfield. His pass cover technique improved dramatically by season's end, and all that remains for Jordan to become a star is consistency.

HANK'S RATING: A

Shaun Gayle

Birthdate: March 8, 1962
College: Ohio State
Height: 5-11
Weight: 194
How Acquired: Drafted in tenth round, 1984
Final 1990 Team: Chicago Bears

Shaun Gayle made the switch from free to strong safety in 1990 to make room for rookie Mark Carrier, and started all sixteen games for the first time in his career. He was second in tackles (125) and forced fumbles (4), and recorded the first sack of his career.

Gayle is a versatile athlete capable of playing any position in the secondary, which he's done since becoming a Bear in 1984. A tough, physical performer, Gayle has played in numerous games despite injuries. But injuries have also forced him to miss several games—he's been on IR during three of his seven pro seasons.

HANK'S RATING: A

Mark Robinson

Birthdate: September 13, 1962
College: Penn State
Height: 5-11
Weight: 200
How Acquired: Trade, 1988
Final 1990 Team: Tampa Bay Buccaneers

Mark Robinson moved into the starting strong safety spot almost the day Tampa Bay acquired him in 1988 from Kansas City. Robinson is consistent, dependable, and has proven big-play ability. In a critical divisional game last year with Minnesota, Robinson had 14 tackles, including 1 for a loss, and also broke up 3 passes as the Buccaneers surprised the Vikings 23–20 in overtime.

HANK'S RATING: A

Lloyd Burruss

Birthdate: October 31, 1957
College: Maryland
Height: 6-0
Weight: 205
How Acquired: Drafted in third round, 1981
Final 1990 Team: Kansas City Chiefs

Lloyd Burruss continued to perform well in his strong safety role, but don't tell him he will be thirty-four years old this year. Burruss is going to be severely tested in 1991 by fourth-year player Kevin Porter, who Chiefs coaches believe is a future star. Porter played well in a limited role in 1990, as did Burruss, who has been a steady player throughout his storied career. But Burruss also gave up his share of big plays, a contributing factor to the the fact Kansas City surrendered an average of 202.6 yards passing a game last year.

HANK'S RATING: B

Mike Harden

Birthdate: February 16, 1959
College: Michigan
Height: 6-1
Weight: 195
How Acquired: Free Agent, 1989
Final 1990 Team: Los Angeles Raiders

Strong safety Mike Harden had 3 interceptions in 1990, but more importantly he gave the Raiders secondary more than a decade of professional experience. As has happened with so many players in the past, joining the silver and black [in 1989] revived the career of Harden, who seemed to be fading during his last few seasons in Denver.

Harden is a tough, versatile veteran who hits with bone-crushing force. Harden has played both corner and safety, but lacks the speed that once made him a talented corner. Harden can be beaten deep, but he relies on savvy and experience to overcome his slipping skills. Harden fits perfectly in the Raiders scheme.

HANK'S RATING: B

Thomas Everett

Birthdate: November 21, 1964
College: Baylor
Height: 5-9
Weight: 184
How Acquired: Drafted in fourth round, 1987
Final 1990 Team: Pittsburgh Steelers

Free safety Thomas Everett has been a starter since his rookie season, but seldom survives a season without injuries. A talented, quick player, Everett is a vicious hitter, which often results in numerous self-inflicted injuries due to his relatively small size. Coaches praise his intelligence and respect his intensity level. Everett is at his best when providing thunderous hits in run support.

HANK'S RATING: B

Nesby Glasgow

Birthdate: April 15, 1957
College: Washington
Height: 5-10
Weight: 187
How Acquired: Free Agent, 1988
Final 1990 Team: Seattle Seahawks

Based on his age (thirty-three) and the challenge of younger players, Nesby Glasgow had a feeling he might not be in the Seahawks plans for 1990. At the outset of the season, he was right, but he moved into the starting lineup during the season's third game and wound up as Seattle's most consistent defensive player.

Glasgow led the team in tackles (83) and shared the lead in forced fumbles (three). He also was an emotional locker room leader to a defense plagued by injuries and backbreaking mistakes. His best outing came in an overtime win against San Diego, when he made 7 unassisted tackles and forced the fumble that set up Norm Johnson's winning 40-yard field goal in overtime.

Glasgow has aged, and lacks the speed that once made him a perennial starter. It's unlikely he can repeat his 1990 heroics, but don't count him out. He's a savvy, experienced veteran, who relies on brains to be successful. Great tackler versus middle receivers.

HANK'S RATING: B

Terry Kinard

Birthdate: November 24, 1959
College: Clemson
Height: 6-1
Weight: 198
How Acquired: Plan B Free Agent, 1990
Final 1990 Team: Houston Oilers

Safety Terry Kinard had a dramatic impact in his first season with the Houston Oilers, tying for the lead in the secondary with 4 interceptions and making several big plays. Against the Browns, his 47-yard interception return set up Houston's first touchdown, and his 72-yard fumble return scored the team's third. Kinard fell victim to minor injuries during the season, but for the most part was a reliable cog in the Houston "Air Patrol." Scouts say Kinard is a rigid, predictable player, but makes the most of his limited skills, and his vicious hitting often creates big plays.

HANK'S RATING: B

Deron Cherry

Birthdate: September 12, 1959
College: Rutgers
Height: 5-11
Weight: 202
How Acquired: Free Agent, 1981
Final 1990 Team: Kansas City Chiefs

Long regarded as one of the best free safeties in the NFL, Deron Cherry went to six consecutive Pro Bowls from 1983 to 1988, and ranks fifth among active players in interceptions. He picked off three more in 1990, and once again gave the Chiefs steady, consistent play. But Cherry's biggest obstacle is Father Time: He will be thirty-two next season.

Cherry's resumé ranks among the NFL's most unique. He joined the Chiefs in 1981 as a free-agent punter, but was moved to defensive back, where he became one of the NFL's most productive interceptors since earning a starting job in 1983. Cherry is intelligent, makes few mistakes, and is a perfectionist in man coverage. He's lost a step, but still has a few years left in him.

HANK'S RATING: B

Keith Taylor

Birthdate: December 21, 1964
College: Illinois
Height: 5-11
Weight: 206
How Acquired: Free Agent, 1988
Final 1990 Team: Indianapolis Colts

Strong safety Keith Taylor started all sixteen games for the Colts in 1990, finishing with 104 tackles, 2 interceptions, and 10 defensed passes. A former free agent, Taylor worked his way into the Colts starting lineup in 1988 after excelling in nickel and dime situations.

Taylor has quick feet, recognizes formations quickly, and reacts well to what he sees. His durability has been excellent, and Taylor is a savage hitter, despite having suffered a broken neck in a car accident while in college (1984). His vertical speed is questionable, as is his pure cover ability in man situations. But he is a capable veteran.

HANK'S RATING: B

Harry Hamilton

Birthdate: November 29, 1962
College: Penn State
Height: 6-0
Weight: 195
How Acquired: Free Agent, 1988
Final 1990 Team: Tampa Bay Buccaneers

Free safety Harry Hamilton has given the young Buccaneer secondary consistency and leadership. He led the team in 1990 with 119 tackles, making him the first non-linebacker ever to lead the Bucs in tackles. He also led the Bucs with 4 forced fumbles, while recovering 2, and finished second on the club with 5 interceptions. Hamilton has quick feet, good vision, and excellent play recognition. He can be outstanding at times, but even on his average days he doesn't hurt the team. A big hitter.

HANK'S RATING: B

Vince Albritton

Birthdate: July 23, 1962
College: Washington
Height: 6-2
Weight: 214
How Acquired: Free Agent, 1984
Final 1990 Team: Dallas Cowboys

Safety Vince Albritton has been a consistent, though not sensational, player in the Cowboys defense in recent years. He is liked by defensive coaches for his steady play, seldom making mistakes and showing the ability to find the football, bring strong run support, and offer steady coverage. Albritton is not an overly talented player, but relies on hard work and discipline to maintain his starting role.

HANK'S RATING: B

Alvin Walton

Birthdate: March 14, 1964
College: Kansas
Height: 6-0
Weight: 180
How Acquired: Drafted in third round, 1986
Final 1990 Team: Washington Redskins

Strong safety Alvin Walton led the Redskins in tackles with 143 in 1990, and continued the steady play that has endeared him to head coach Joe Gibbs. He also added 2 interceptions to his numbers, and returned one 57 yards for a touchdown against Phoenix. "Alvin does about all you can ask of your strong safety," says defensive coordinator Richie Petitbon. "He hits, he doesn't miss tackles, and he makes interceptions. I really think he's a Pro Bowl-caliber player."

HANK'S RATING: B

Tiger Greene

Birthdate: February 15, 1962
College: Western Carolina
Height: 6-0
Weight: 194
How Acquired: Free Agent, 1986
Final 1990 Team: Green Bay Packers

Another aging veteran in the Green Bay secondary, free safety Tiger Greene finished 1990 with 41 tackles and defensed 2 passes. Greene has been used for years by the Packers as a tough utility defensive back, who keeps winding up as a starter. A reckless tackler, Greene is a steady player, though not overly talented. Green Bay coaches keep hoping that daredevil third-year player Chuck Cecil can stay healthy long enough to win the starting job, but Cecil has spent more time on injured reserve than on the field in recent years.

HANK'S RATING: B

Eugene Robinson

Birthdate: May 28, 1963
College: Colgate
Height: 6-0
Weight: 186
How Acquired: Free Agent, 1985
Final 1990 Team: Seattle Seahawks

Free safety Eugene Robinson was second on the Seahawks in tackles with 82, after leading the team in 1988 and 1989. He also led the club in interceptions with 3, including 2 that led to offensive touchdowns. Robinson, now in his seventh season, has been one of Seattle's most consistent defensive backs, and remarkably hasn't missed a game since joining the team as a free agent in 1985. Long on intelligence, savvy and experience, Robinson is short on footspeed, but is a sure tackler. A respectable veteran.

HANK'S RATING: B

James Washington

Birthdate: January 10, 1965
College: UCLA
Height: 6-1
Weight: 195
How Acquired: Plan B free agent, 1990
Final 1990 Team: Dallas Cowboys

Safety James Washington gave head coach Jimmy Johnson reason to smile in 1990, as he showed steady improvement and proved he was ready for a full-time defensive role. He also showed big-play ability, intercepting 2 passes and recovering a fumble to set up 3 touchdowns as Dallas crushed Phoenix, 41–10. He also made 4 tackles and forced the fumble that he recovered. Washington has good speed, good hands, and good quickness. The Cowboys are hoping Washington can pull himself up to the next level.

HANK'S RATING: B

Wes Hopkins

Birthdate: September 26, 1961
College: Southern Methodist
Height: 6-1
Weight: 215
How Acquired: Drafted in second round, 1983
Final 1990 Team: Philadelphia Eagles

The play of Wes Hopkins has vastly improved since he was sidelined for most of the 1986 and 1987 seasons with a serious knee injury. He led the Eagles in 1990 with 5 interceptions, and provided tremendous run support from his safety position, finishing once again among the Eagles top tacklers. Scouts say Hopkins is capable of "contributing in a lot of ways . . . he can make the defensive calls and really understands the system."

HANK'S RATING: B

Fred Marion

Birthdate: January 2, 1959
College: Miami
Height: 6-2
Weight: 191
How Acquired: Drafted in fifth round, 1982
Final 1990 Team: New England Patriots

Free safety Fred Marion led the Patriots in tackles with 119, evidence that little tackling was going on in front of him. Marion, now in his ninth season, is still a talented zone safety, as well as a ferocious hitter. He is more consistent than spectacular, but coaches praise his work habits and effectiveness in the clutch.

HANK'S RATING: B

Gene Atkins

Birthdate: November 22, 1964
College: Florida A&M
Height: 6-1
Weight: 200
How Acquired: Drafted in seventh round, 1987
Final 1990 Team: New Orleans Saints

Gene Atkins moved from strong to free safety in 1990, and produced respectable numbers in his new freewheeling position. He made 54 tackles, including 3 sacks, while intercepting 2 passes. But his presence was felt most on his thunderous run support, where he forced a team-high 5 fumbles and recovered three. Atkins has good speed, is very aggressive, and loves to hit—the main reason coaches decided to utilize him at free safety. But he is known to bite early on play action, and can be beaten deep.

HANK'S RATING: B

Myron Guyton

Birthdate: August 26, 1967
College: Eastern Kentucky
Height: 6-1
Weight: 205
How Acquired: Drafted in eighth round, 1989
Final 1990 Team: New York Giants

Myron Guyton played capable football in 1990 during his second pro season, making 76 tackles and defensing 10 passes, but the year made a huge difference in Guyton's level of experience, exposure, and playing ability. Guyton earned his spot at free safety after playing strong safety during his rookie year in 1989. Coaches like his speed and toughness, but Guyton made very few big plays.

HANK'S RATING: B

Brett Maxie

Birthdate: January 13, 1962
College: Texas Southern
Height: 6-2
Weight: 194
How Acquired: Free Agent, 1985
Final 1990 Team: New Orleans Saints

Brett Maxie flipped from free to strong safety in 1990, with modest results. He finished the year with 58 tackles and 2 interceptions. Scouts like Maxie's anticipation and quickness, but most believe him to be more of a free safety than strong safety. "I don't think his body can hold up at strong safety," says a scout. "He's not that big, but he's exceptionally quick."

HANK'S RATING: B

Vince Newsome

Birthdate: January 22, 1961
College: Washington
Height: 6-1
Weight: 185
How Acquired: Drafted in fourth round, 1983
Final 1990 Team: Los Angeles Rams

Veteran safety Vince Newsome will be tested to keep his job in 1991, after the entire Rams defense fell under close scrutiny during a miserable 1990 season. "I think when you play like this, everyone has to question whether their job is secure," Newsome says. "Obviously, it isn't. Let the cards fall where they may."

Newsome led the team in tackles in 1989 with 89. He has

started 110 games for the Rams, and has typically been a steady, reliable performer in the Los Angeles defense. Newsome drops well in coverage, has quick recognition of opposing offenses, and breaks well on the ball. Newsome still is capable of several more excellent seasons.

HANK'S RATING: B

Johnny Jackson

Birthdate: January 11, 1967
College: Houston
Height: 6-1
Weight: 204
How Acquired: Drafted in fifth round, 1989
Final 1990 Team: San Francisco 49ers

Johnny Jackson was drafted in the fifth round and waived by the 49ers in 1989, but quickly re-signed, and Jackson hasn't disappointed his employers. An instinctive, error-free player, Jackson plays "with a maturity beyond his years," says a 49er coach. Jackson always seems to be around the football, and is developing big-play qualities. In 1989, he returned a blocked field goal for a touchdown, started at safety and corner, and recovered an onside kick. An outstanding young talent with excellent potential.

HANK'S RATING: B

Greg Jackson

Birthdate: August 20, 1966
College: LSU
Height: 6-1
Weight: 200
How Acquired: Free Agent, 1989
Final 1990 Team: New York Giants

Strong safety Greg Jackson came of age in 1990 during his second pro season, finishing with 87 tackles and 5 interceptions, both numbers good for second on the team, and defensed 11 passes.

The strong safety position was wide open during training camp last season, but Jackson won the job on the basis of his solid technique, speed, and cover ability. As the season progressed, Jackson gave New York coaches even more to smile about with his occasional game-breaking form: In the Giants' 24-20 nipping of Washington, Jackson made 7 tackles, 6 of them solos, intercepted 2 passes to break up a pair of drives, and deflected another pass. A talented up and coming safety.

HANK'S RATING: B

Mike Prior

Birthdate: November 14, 1964
College: Illinois State
Height: 6-0
Weight: 210
How Acquired: Free Agent, 1987
Final 1990 Team: Indianapolis Colts

Free safety Mike Prior once again paced the Colts in interceptions in 1990 with 3 picks and defensed 15 passes, but the former free agent's lack of speed was a liability in zone coverage. However, Prior is an enforcer in the Colts secondary, dishing out punishment as well as anybody in the league.

He finished the season with 113 tackles, tops among defensive backs, and still proved his worth in run support. He reached double-figures in tackles four times, including two 10-tackle efforts against AFC champion Buffalo and an 11-tackle effort against Washington. Prior plays well within his limitations, works hard, never complains, and is steady and reliable. Those are the positives; the only negative is a lack of footspeed, but certainly not a lack of effort.

HANK'S RATING: B

Michael Ball

Birthdate: August 5, 1964
College: Southern University
Height: 6-0
Weight: 217
How Acquired: Drafted in fourth round, 1988
Final 1990 Team: Indianapolis Colts

Strong safety Michael Ball, in a word, is inconsistent. Scouts have said that Ball can look like a Pro Bowler on one play and a rookie the next, but speed and potential kept him active in 1990, his third year in the Colts lineup.

Though not a starter, he played in all sixteen games, but registered just 23 tackles. At times, Ball flashes the dominating, physical style that made him an all-conference player at Southern University. Coaches are tired of waiting, however, and 1991 will be a critical year.

HANK'S RATING: B

Thane Gash

Birthdate: September 1, 1965
College: East Tennessee State
Height: 5-11
Weight: 200
How Acquired: Drafted in seventh round, 1988
Final 1990 Team: Cleveland Browns

In a dismal season in Cleveland, free safety Thane Gash finished second on the Browns in tackles with 134, and led the team in tackles in seven different games. He also picked off a pass and defensed 7 passes, and was effective as a back-side blitzer. Entering his fourth season, Gash is well liked by the new coaching staff for his kamikaze style of play.

Gash needs to improve his technique and play recognition. Though Gash isn't helped by the fact that Cleveland has some gaping holes in it, he has to improve himself if he ever wants to be considered a top safety.

HANK'S RATING: C

Who's Missing

Eric Thomas

Birthdate: September 11, 1964
College: Tulane
Height: 5-11
Weight: 181
How Acquired: Drafted in second round, 1987
Position: Cornerback
Final 1990 Team: Cincinnati Bengals

Starting right cornerback Eric Thomas missed the 1990 season when he suffered a serious knee injury in a pickup basketball game. It remains to be seen whether he will be physically able to return to form in 1991; when healthy, Thomas was among the most talented corners in the AFC.

HANK'S RATING: A

Lewis Billups

Birthdate: October 10, 1963
College: North Alabama
Height: 5-11
Weight: 179
How Acquired: Drafted in second round, 1986
Position: Cornerback
Final 1990 Team: Cincinnati Bengals

Lewis Billups lost his starting job at cornerback in 1990, and he had nobody but himself to blame. The Bengals have put up with his off-the-field problems for years, but appear to finally have run out of patience. It's unlikely he'll win his job back in 1991; Billups will miss most of training camp while serving a thirty-day jail sentence for pointing a gun at a police officer. And don't forget, he skipped the 1990 mini-camp altogether. Billups is a quick, talented player, whose lack of focus and dedication is costing him his career.

HANK'S RATING: A

Darryl Henley

Birthdate: October 30, 1966
College: UCLA
Height: 5-9
Weight: 170
How Acquired: Drafted in second round, 1989
Position: Cornerback
Final 1990 Team: Los Angeles Rams

Cornerback Darryl Henley saw his rookie season in 1990 cut short by injury, but Rams coaches hold out high hopes for him if he can return to form. Henley, a former UCLA star, has tremendous speed, excellent lateral movement, and great burst on the football. The biggest question, however, is his size, or the lack of it: Henley is just 5-9, 170 pounds. But don't be surprised to see him starting on opening day.

HANK'S RATING: B

Tim McKyer

Birthdate: September 5, 1963
College: Texas-Arlington
Height: 6-1
Weight: 177
Position: Cornerback
Final 1990 Team: Miami Dolphins

Former Miami cornerback Tim McKyer draws the ire of opponents because he does a lot of talking—but unfortunately for so many receivers, he can still, on occasion, back it up. In a late-season victory against Seattle that kept Miami in the hunt for a division title, McKyer killed two Seattle drives with back-to-back interceptions. Against Pittsburgh, he picked off Bubby Brister twice, giving him three two-pick games in his career.

He finished as the Dolphin leader in passes defensed with 17, and tacked on 4 interceptions. McKyer has been bothered in recent years by a recurring groin injury, but gave the Dolphins steady veteran leadership in the secondary. However, head coach Don Shula tired of McKyer's constant mouthing, which occasionally caused opposing quarterbacks to single him out. Should contribute in Philadelphia if he allows himself to be coached.

HANK'S RATING: B

Bobby Butler

Birthdate: May 28, 1959
College: Florida State

Height: 5-11
Weight: 175
How Acquired: Drafted in first round, 1981
Position: Cornerback
Final 1990 Team: Atlanta Falcons

Veteran Bobby Butler came off the bench with four games remaining to stabilize the left corner when Falcons coaches finally gave up on Charles Dimry, who failed miserably in his trial-by-fire test. During his one month as a starter, Butler made 36 tackles and intercepted 3 passes, and used his savvy experience to make up for his lack of speed. He still has tremendous quickness and outstanding agility. "Bobby is similar to [Redskin] Darrell Green," says 49er receiver Jerry Rice. "He's so quick that if the ball's not there, he can recover."

The Falcons hope to find a young corner to become an every-down player and use Butler strictly in nickel and dime situations. Too inconsistent as a starter, but he is a reliable athlete whom Glanville can depend on in emergency situations.

HANK'S RATING: B

James Williams

Birthdate: March 30, 1967
College: Fresno State
Height: 5-10
Weight: 172
How Acquired: Drafted in first round, 1990
Position: Cornerback
Final 1990 Team: Buffalo Bills

The Bills knew they had something when they drafted James Williams in the first round of the 1989 draft; Buffalo scouts had marveled when Williams set a then-combine record by running the 40 in 4.45. Williams is a blazing fast, quick-footed defensive back who should take over one of the Bills starting corner spots this season. He performed well in nickel situations last year, as Bills coaches used his rookie season to polish his pass cover technique.

Williams breaks well on a thrown ball, has tremendous hand-eye coordination, and is a fearless hitter. "This kid has a chance to be a superstar in this league," says a scout. "He has all the tools, and he works at his job. Now he just has to put it all together." Superstar potential may be a little optimistic, but he can be a steady contributor.

HANK'S RATING: B

Dave Waymer

Birthdate: July 1, 1958
College: Notre Dame
Height: 6-1
Weight: 188
How Acquired: Plan B free agent, 1990
Position: Safety
Final 1990 Team: San Francisco 49ers

Dave Waymer will soon be thirty-two years old, a fact not lost on the 49ers coaching staff, yet he will enter 1991 as one of the starting safeties on the depth chart. Waymer proved his versatility and durability in the 1990 season, when he played both safety positions, filled in well while others were injured, and occasionally came up with the big play. Waymer, now in his twelfth season, can play corner if necessary, but is mostly considered a dependable, error-free safety at this stage of his career. Waymer is a tremendous hitter, but gives up a lot of ground against young, speedy, vertical receivers.

HANK'S RATING: B

Best of Plan B

Todd Bowles

Birthdate: November 18, 1963
College: Temple
Height: 6-2
Weight: 203
Position: Safety
Final 1990 Team: Washington Redskins

Washington coaches called free safety Todd Bowles a coach on the field, and with good reason. "He understands the game," says head coach Joe Gibbs. "He gets people in the right places. When we had all the young guys in the game, he kept the secondary together." Bowles is consistent, works hard, and makes few errors. A better weak safety than strong safety, San Francisco will try him at both spots.

HANK'S RATING: A

Ronnie Lott

Birthdate: May 8, 1959
College: USC
Height: 6-0
Weight: 200
Position: Safety
Final 1990 Team: San Francisco 49ers

During the 1991 Pro Bowl, Miami tight end Ferrell Edmunds was just looking for a routine catch in a routine game until Ronnie Lott laid him prone with a fierce helmet-to-chin blow that sounded like a gunshot. "I play like that every week," Lott says. "Pro Bowl, Super Bowl, it doesn't matter. I'm just an intense player. You catch the ball, you get hit."

Nobody brings such determined leadership to the game as safety Ronnie Lott. "Players like Ronnie Lott win Super Bowls," says George Seifert. "He's dedicated to his job." And, like Minnesota's Joey Browner, he will take your head off if the opportunity presents itself (it's hard to believe, but Lott and Browner were once teammates at Southern Cal).

Lott suffered the first serious injuries of his career in 1990, when both his knees began deteriorating. He played against the Giants with two sprained knees, a feat few players would be tough enough to manage. But he still managed to play, and excel, down the stretch, particularly the playoffs. Though scouts believe he has lost the speed and quickness to make "normal" interceptions, Lott is a money player, a big hitter, who will make a sudden impact in the Raiders secondary.

HANK'S RATING: A

Jeff Donaldson

Birthdate: April 19, 1962
College: Colorado
Height: 6-0
Weight: 190
Position: Safety
Final 1990 Team: Kansas City Chiefs

In what may be his last NFL season, Donaldson, in the words of head coach Jerry Glanville, "may be the the last of the trained killers." Donaldson's thunderous hits earned him the nickname "Lethal Weapon" when he played for Glanville in Houston, and he lived up to his reputation during his one-year stint in 1990 with Kansas City. Now reunited with Glanville, Donaldson will bring tremendous leadership to a young Falcon secondary, and his savage tackles will bring Atlanta fans to their feet.

Donaldson, who weighs just 190, has played the past seven years like he weighs 220. In Houston's scheme, Donaldson was responsible for run support on both corners; his thunderous hits on running backs are still legend in the Astrodome.

HANK'S RATING: B

Felix Wright

Birthdate: June 22, 1959
College: Drake
Height: 6-2
Weight: 195
Position: Safety
Final 1990 Team: Cleveland Browns

Strong safety Felix Wright led the NFL in 1989 with 9 interceptions, but his production fell off dramatically in 1990. The Vikings took him from Cleveland as a Plan B prospect, but most NFL scouts believe Wright's 1989 season was overrated. "Half of his interceptions," says one, "were overthrown passes that fell in his lap." Wright has lost the footspeed to cover deep, and his recovery ability is seriously in question. Not reliable because he doesn't keep his head in the game.

HANK'S RATING: B

William Frizzell

Birthdate: September 8, 1962
College: North Carolina Central
Height: 6-3
Weight: 206
Position: Safety
Philadelphia Eagles

William Frizzell played virtually every position in the Philadelphia secondary in 1990, and intercepted 3 passes, good for second on the team. He is a very versatile player, who can "match up with virtually any receiver in the league without hurting you," says a scout. A fine nickel back who could challenge for a starting spot on certain teams.

HANK'S RATING: B

Terry Hoage

Birthdate: April 11, 1962
College: Georgia
Height: 6-3
Weight: 201
Position: Safety
Final 1990 Team: Philadelphia Eagles

Strong safety Terry Hoage had a disappointing season in 1990, finishing with just 1 interception. But the Eagles counted on him for much more than just coverage, and in the past used him as an undersized linebacker in run support. A vicious hitter, Hoage is a very intelligent safety capable of calling defenses, and is very disruptive to opposing offenses. The Redskins lost safety Todd Bowles to San Francisco, so by adding Hoage they have a veteran who lacks Bowles coverage speed, but adds a more physical aspect to their secondary.

HANK'S RATING: B

Best of the 1991 Rookie Class

Quarterbacks

Brett Favre

Team: Atlanta Falcons
Round: Second
Overall: 33rd
HW: 6-2, 212
College: Southern Mississippi

Jim Kelly mentality. Lost thirty inches of intestines in a car accident before the season, yet came back to play well. Brought Southern Mississippi back to beat Auburn; teammates rally around him. Scouts rave over his arm strength, quick release, poise, and gutty performances.

Browning Nagle

Team: New York Jets
Round: Second
Overall: 34th
HW: 6-2, 230
College: Louisville

A rising star. Arm strength falls in the same category as San Diego's Billy Joe Tolliver. Really became comfortable in the latter part of the season, doesn't force the ball. Needs to develop more touch. Scouts like his cockiness, but question whether his volatileness will adversely effect his play. Playing for Howard Schnellenberger and his pro style offense should help his transition to the NFL.

Craig Erickson

Team: Philadelphia Eagles
Round: Fifth
Overall: 131st
HW: 6-2, 196
College: Miami

Post-season injury has made some scouts skeptical. The knee injury seems to be severe. Sufficient arm strength, but must improve accuracy and reads. Is very mobile—possesses 4.75 speed and likes to run. A fearless quarterback.

Dan McGwire

Team: Seattle Seahawks
Round: First
Overall: 16th
HW: 6-8, 237
College: San Diego State

Steadily improved through his senior season. Tremendous arm strength—impressed scouts with his ability to throw different routes. Throws a very accurate deep ball, but lacks mobility. A classic drop-back passer. Scouts are scared by his slow release and erratic performances.

Todd Marinovich

Team: Los Angeles Raiders
Round: First
Overall: 24th
HW: 6-4, 200
College: USC

Unfortunately needs more time for development. Not the greatest arm strength, but makes things happen off broken routes. Scouts question whether he has top passing touch. A proven winner with definite raw skills—his biggest obstacle is immaturity.

Running Backs

Harvey Williams

Team: Kansas City Chiefs
Round: First
Overall: 21st
HW: 6-1, 208
College: LSU

Outstanding speed (4.45) with great slashing ability. Has tremendous vision; can find a crease and go. Needs to develop tougher inside running skills, but has the quickness to bounce outside. Above-average hands as a receiver. Developed some mental maturity as a senior, but scouts still have questions about his stability.

Nick Bell

Team: Los Angeles Raiders
Round: Second
Overall: 43rd
HW: 6-3, 256
College: Iowa

A track man in the 55 meters, Bell has been called "unbelievable in the open field" by scouts. A real workhorse in the Christian Okoye mold, Bell has the body to hold up under a 30-carry-a-game workload, but scouts question whether he will handle it mentally. Has unique speed for his size (4.55); can turn the corner. Scouts say his biggest asset is his hands; biggest weakness is a lack of blocking skills. Somewhat of a surprise that he slipped to second round.

Eric Bieniemy

Team: San Diego Chargers
Round: Second
Overall: 39th
HW: 5-7, 190
College: Colorado

Sneaky speed at 4.50, but has powerful burst between the tackles and runs with great balance. Possesses great line of scrimmage quickness. Protects the ball. Always makes the first man miss. Catching ability is a question mark, but is a tough, physical runner with tremendous potential and talent. Size prevents him from being an every-down back.

Jarrod Bunch

Team: New York Giants
Round: First
Overall: 27th
HW: 6-0, 245
College: Michigan

Bunch will push starter Maurice Carthon for playing time; Carthon, a punishing blocker, has never been much of a runner. Bunch excels at both and fits perfectly in the "bigger is better" scheme of the Giants.

Leonard Russell

Team: New England Patriots
Round: First
Overall: 14th
HW: 6-2, 235
College: Arizona State

The Patriots passed on quarterbacks with their first two picks and instead looked to upgrade the running back. Russell isn't a can't-miss pick, but has excellent potential. But scouts doubt he's a 1,000-yard-per-season type player. "He needs work," says one. "We didn't have him rated as a first-round pick, that's for sure."

Wide Receivers

Alvin Harper

Team: Dallas Cowboys
Round: First
Overall: 12th
HW: 6-2, 205
College: Tennessee

Seven-foot-plus high jumper with deceiving speed (4.45). A big receiver who has no problems releasing against the press. Scouts say he can power release, swim release, or simply run past bump and run coverage. Runs excellent routes, will catch in a crowd, and has tremendous ability after the catch. Has the size to take punishment and dish it out on smaller defensive backs. A positive draft choice who has the skills to be a *dominating* receiver. Will instantly help a Dallas passing attack that ranked twenty-seventh.

Randall Hill

Team: Miami Dolphins
Round: First
Overall: 23rd
HW: 5-10, 175
College: Miami

A polished wideout with great quickness, Hill ran 4.3 in the 40 at the college combine. He possesses excellent side-to-side explosion, and catches the ball in traffic. But he is also a cocky, talkative showboat in the mold of Tim McKyer, who Shula traded to Atlanta.

Mike Pritchard

Team: Atlanta Falcons
Round: First
Overall: 13th
HW: 5-11, 190
College: Colorado

You had to guess that June Jones would leap on the first 4.4 guy he could get his hands on, and Pritchard was the man. The Falcons will field one of the fastest four-wide sets in football in 1991, and with Jones' run-and-shoot influence, Pritchard could develop into a deadly scoring threat.

Willie Jake Reed

Team: Minnesota Vikings
Round: Third
Overall: 68th
HW: 6-3, 215
College: Grambling

Deceiving speed (4.48), but great size and athletic ability. Reed has raw skills, but big play potential. Ran the ball out of the wingback position at Grambling, so he can play halfback. Must develop softer hands.

Reggie Barrett

Team: Detroit Lions
Round: Third
Overall: 58th
HW: 6-2, 215
College: Texas-El Paso

Deceptive speed (4.55), but not as polished as he should be. Needs to understand the passing game more, but will catch the ball in a crowd. Al Toon size a tremendous asset.

Derek Russell

Team: Denver Broncos
Round: Fourth
Overall: 89th
HW: 6-0, 175
College: Arkansas

Runs excellent routes, displays tremendous concentration. Exciting player with modest speed (4.49), who needs more reps. Could be a steal for Denver.

Tight Ends

Reggie Johnson

Team: Denver Broncos
Round: Second
Overall: 30th
HW: 6-2, 255
College: Florida State

Tenacious blocker, with the speed (4.7) to run the seam. Could be more consistent catching the ball, but is very coachable. Needs more dedication. Scouts question his off-season work ethic, but has unlimited tools. Johnson already has great run blocking skills.

Chris Smith

Team: Cincinnati Bengals
Round: Eleventh
Overall: 295th
HW: 6-4, 230
College: BYU

A little light, which is evident in his blocking. Scouts question whether he can effectively run block in the NFL. Catches everything. Runs well (4.75), comes from a passing offense, and understands coverage. A Todd Christiansen-type player, only not as tenacious.

Adrian Cooper

Team: Pittsburgh Steelers
Round: Fourth
Overall: 103rd
HW: 6-4, 255
College: Oklahoma

Cooper will make the tough catch, and has decent speed (4.85). Must improve his blocking to play in the NFL. Doesn't seem to be a *natural* tight end, but is a solid selection who can also play special teams.

Jerry Evans

Team: Phoenix Cardinals
Round: Eighth
Overall: 204th
HW: 6-3, 245
College: Toledo

It took Phoenix coaches little time to fall in love with Evans, who quickly impressed teammates in minicamp with his speed, strength, and quickness. A prototype tight end, Evans could earn a starting job by September. "He catches the ball well, he works extremely hard, and he's one of the most physical tight ends I've ever seen," says head coach Joe Bugel. "We're hoping he continues the progress we've seen so far."

Offensive Linemen

Charles McRae

Team: Tampa Bay Buccaneers
Round: First
Overall: 7th
HW: 6-7, 300
College: Tennessee

Good speed (5.22). Transplanted defensive lineman who brings an aggressive mentality to the other side of the ball. Must learn to pass protect and use his hands, but has shown tremendous improvement in last two seasons. Will play opposite Paul Gruber at tackle. Most complete lineman in draft. Future All-Pro.

Pat Harlow

Team: New England Patriots
Round: First
Overall: 11th
HW: 6-6, 285
College: USC

Outstanding lineman that will play tackle for the Patriots. Excellent speed (5.12), good body control and long, powerful arms. Some scouts felt his pass protection skills were good for a college player, while others question whether he has the agility for it.

Antone Davis

Team: Philadelphia Eagles
Round: First
Overall: 8th
HW: 6-4, 315
College: Tennessee

Runs exceptionally well (5.12). Can play guard or tackle. A dominating run blocker who also has quick feet on pass protection. Struggles with quick counter moves inside, but that can be coached. Occasionally takes a play off, must learn to play every snap hard. Has all the tools to be a Pro Bowler, but some insiders question his consistency. Philadelphia gave up a lot to grab him.

Stan Thomas

Team: Chicago Bears
Round: First
Overall: 22nd
HW: 6-5, 290
College: Texas

Plays right tackle, can also play guard. Decent speed (5.34), but his agility is in question. Tenacious, hard-nose football player who has destroyed opponents on both run and pass. Must learn more patience in pass protection in the NFL—may have trouble against NFL pass rush moves. Has a hard time playing under control. Adds needed depth for Bears line.

Eugene Williams

Team: Miami Dolphins
Round: Fifth
Overall: 121st
HW: 6-2, 315
College: Iowa State

Played both guard and tackle in college, will probably play guard in the NFL due to height. Modest speed (5.3), with solid recover ability on both run and pass. Understands blocking angles and pass protection. Well-coached.

Defensive Linemen

Ted Washington

Team: San Francisco 49ers
Round: First
Overall: 25th
HW: 6-5, 300
College: Louisville

Outstanding quickness (5.15). Breaks down well for a large man. Very difficult to knock off his feet, with great burst on pass rush. Could play either 40 tackle or 30 end in the NFL. Some questions about weight. Could be best NFL player in the draft.

Russell Maryland

Team: Dallas Cowboys
Round: First
Overall: 1st
HW: 6-1, 270
College: Miami

Will play defensive tackle for the Cowboys. Productive football player who goes all out and gets upfield with great speed (4.90). Everybody who plays against him double-teams him. "If you single block him," says a scout, "he beats you." Size, strength, and speed reminiscent of Michael Dean Perry. Two biggest positives are his effort and his rush quickness.

Huey Richardson

Team: Pittsburgh Steelers
Round: First
Overall: 15th
HW: 6-5, 245
College: Florida

Tremendous speed (4.75) and strength, gets great upfield surge. Originally a linebacker, but coaches put his hand down last year—with great success. Scouts have questions about whether he has the weight to be a defensive end in the NFL; must bulk up to handle the point of attack and tight ends. A surprise pick for Pittsburgh, a team that needed receivers, Richardson was too good to pass up.

Bobby Wilson

Team: Washington Redskins
Round: First
Overall: 17th
HW: 6-2, 280
College: Michigan State

Played nose and tackle in college, could play end in the NFL. A power bull-rusher on the pass; maintains constant pressure. Has the speed (4.90) to chase people down. A junior-college transfer who has improved each year. Look for Wilson to develop rapidly. First number one for Washington since 1983 (Darrell Green).

Eric Swann

Team: Phoenix Cardinals
Round: First
Overall: 6th
HW: 6-4, 303
College: None

Highly recruited out of high school, but never passed college requirements to attend North Carolina State. Tremendous raw potential: twenty years old, 4.85 speed, benches 400 pounds. Scouts say he's a physical specimen, but "mentally needs more time to learn the game." Insiders question his toughness. Not enough positive evidence to be sixth pick in the draft. One insider labeled this a "typical senseless Phoenix pick." Injury during minicamp sets him back even further.

Linebackers

Mike Croel

Team: Denver
Round: First
Overall: 4th
HW: 6-3, 235
College: Nebraska

Tenacious, runs the field exceptionally well. Good speed (4.5) and positive quicks. Sheds blockers well, but needs to get stronger at the point of attack. Great wrap-up tackler. Will play outside for the Broncos, who are desperate for linebacker help. Has All-Pro potential.

Dixon Edwards

Team: Dallas Cowboys
Round: Second
Overall: 37th
HW: 6-1, 221
College: Michigan State

Size and strength are what prevented Edwards from being a first-rounder; scouts question his strength versus run blockers. Has the speed (4.65) to play outside in the NFL. Great instincts, makes big plays. An excellent blitzer on the open side of coverage. May only be effective as a weak side linebacker.

Alfred Williams

Team: Cincinnati Bengals
Round: First
Overall: 18th
HW: 6-6, 240
College: Colorado

Williams was a surprisingly high pick for Cincinnati—certainly not a can't miss prospect. Has the tools to play outside in the NFL. Has great upfield burst (4.75). Needs to take his intensity up another level; athleticism alone won't cut it in the NFL. Cincinnati hopes Williams can help defense that managed league-low 25 sacks.

Roman Phifer

Team: Los Angeles Rams
Round: Second
Overall: 31st
HW: 6-1, 225
College: UCLA

A very athletic outside linebacker whose stock rose after an outstanding senior year. Very quick (4.70). Recognizes run or pass quickly, and very effective against both. Needs to gain another ten pounds.

Keith Traylor

Team: Denver Broncos
Round: Third
Overall: 61st
HW: 6-2, 253
College: Central State Oklahoma

Great size and speed (4.73) for an inside player. Had an injury plagued senior year. Must concentrate more and treat football as a year-round sport. Good gamble for Broncos.

Defensive Backs

Todd Lyght

Team: Los Angeles Rams
Round: First
Overall: 5th
HW: 6-0, 180
College: Notre Dame

Will play corner for the Rams. Tough, great burst (4.51), with tremendous man to man cover skills. Tried to do too much in college, struggled with nagging injuries. The most skillful corner available in the draft. Not the fastest guy around, but is very intelligent and is an expert at knocking a receiver off his route. Has All-Pro potential, and it may not take him long to show it.

Bruce Pickens

Team: Atlanta Falcons
Round: First
Overall: 3rd
HW: 5-10, 185
College: Nebraska

Pickens wowed scouts at the combine when he smoked through a 4.4 40, and Atlanta coach Jerry Glanville is praying he's the answer opposite right corner Deion Sanders. Pickens is a strong man-cover-type player, and a vicious hitter. A Glanville special, actually.

Eric Turner

Team: Cleveland Browns
Round: First
Overall: 2nd
HW: 6-1, 207
College: UCLA

New Cleveland coach Bill Belichick is hoping Turner does for the Browns what Mark Carrier did for Chicago last year as a rookie. That's possible, but unlikely. Turner is an outstanding run stopper, excellent zone cover man, and a big hitter. But don't expect him to wow you in man coverage.

Jessie Campbell

Team: Philadelphia Eagles
Round: Second
Overall: 48th
HW: 6-2, 225
College: North Carolina State

Can play either strong or free safety in the NFL. Possesses great cover ability for a safety. An enforcer as a run stopper, loves contact. Must learn to play within a scheme and not just play his own game.

Henry Jones

Team: Buffalo Bills
Round: First
Overall: 26th
HW: 6-0, 197
College: Illinois

The Bills drafted corners in the first round the past two years, an obvious need they're hoping Jones will quickly fill. Scouts say he's certainly capable. Had a steady career for the Illini. Some scouts question his man-to-man coverage skills.

Special Teams

For slug-mouth fans, here's two defensive backs who will play as rookies for one reason—they are devastating special teams

Mike Dumas

Team: Houston Oilers
Round: Second
Overall: 28th
HW: 5-10, 175
College: Indiana

An outstanding kick blocker—has blocked nine in his career. Will make an instant impact on special teams. Former All-Big 10 corner, moved to safety his senior year. Had a 100-yard interception against Purdue but didn't score, perhaps an indication that his speed could improve (4.55). Has great ball awareness and is an intimidating run supporter. Most insiders feel that his only chance to be a regular is at strong safety.

Steve Jackson

Team: Houston Oilers
Round: Second
Overall: 71st
HW: 5-8, 180
College: Purdue

A 4.5 kick returner, Jackson throws his body around on kickoff coverage and run support. Outstanding kick blocker. Will chase people down from across the field for touchdown-saving tackles. Effective bumping receivers at the line of scrimmage, but question whether he has man coverage ability.

Who's Missing

Here's what scouts are saying about seven players who during their college careers were either underrated or overrated.

Shawn Moore

Team: Denver
Round: Eleventh
Overall: 284th
HW: 6-1, 213
College: Virginia

"Good runner, decent arm, but terribly inconsistent. When I worked him out, he couldn't hit his ass with a banjo." Scouts also point to his poor mechanics.

Ricky Watters

Team: San Francisco 49ers
Round: Second
Overall: 45th
HW: 6-2, 220
College: Notre Dame

"Great athletic ability, but must learn to play within his own limitations. Physical skills are there, but Watters has yet to show the mental discipline it takes to play at a higher level." San Francisco needs a back. Watters could end up a fine NFL runner and receiver.

Jeff Graham

Team: Pittsburgh Steelers
Round: Second
Overall: 46th
HW: 6-1, 195
College: Ohio State

"Lacks blazing speed (4.54), but he's a strider that will be on top of you before you know it. Catches in a crowd. Outstanding punt return ability—to the tune of about 12 yards a return." Pittsburgh gambled that a quality receiver would be there in the second. May well have found one.

Eric Moten

Team: San Diego Chargers
Round: Second
Overall: 47th
HW: 6-3, 300
College: Michigan State

"Modest speed (5.2). Tries to maul you, very tenacious, really gets into linebackers well. Needs improvement on pass protection, but has the size and athletic ability to pick it up." Chargers' GM Bobby Beathard has a proven drafting record. Some coaches question 100 percent hustle.

Chris Zorich

Team: Chicago Bears
Round: Second
Overall: 49th
HW: 6-0, 268
College: Notre Dame

"Really has a problem with a lack of height and size. He probably won't get any bigger, he's reached his max. He's all football player, but his body just can't hold up for sixteen games." With Perry and McMichael, Bears need Zorich for depth, not as a starter. Always gives extra effort.

Michael Stonebreaker

Team: Chicago Bears
Round: Ninth
Overall: 245th
HW: 6-0, 226
College: Notre Dame

"Very instinctive, runs well (4.77), reacts well. Again, his problem is size. He physically collapses under mismatches. Scouts wonder if he has strength to handle run blockers. He'll probably be moved outside in the NFL, because physically, he doesn't match up well anywhere."

Dexter Davis

Team: Phoenix Cardinals
Round: Fourth
Overall: 86th
HW:
College: Clemson

"Good cover guy, plays both zone and man. Physically wants to mix it up. Plays hard, is very active, but lacks discipline, both mentally and physically. Experience should take care of that."

Statistics

Individual Statistics

Passing—NFC

	Team	Att.	Comp.	Comp. Pct.	Yds.	TD	TD Pct.	Lg.	Int.	Int. Pct.	Avg. Gain	Rating
Simms	N.Y.G.	311	184	59.2	2,284	15	4.8	80	4	1.3	7.34	92.7
Cunningham	Phil.	465	271	58.3	3,466	30	6.5	95	13	2.8	7.45	91.6
Montana	S.F.	520	321	61.7	3,944	26	5.0	78	16	3.1	7.58	89.0
Harbaugh	Chi.	312	180	57.7	2,178	10	3.2	80	6	1.9	6.98	81.9
Peete	Det.	271	142	52.4	1,974	13	4.8	68	8	3.0	7.28	79.8
Everett	LA.Rm	554	307	55.4	3,989	23	4.2	55	17	3.1	7.20	79.3
Miller	Atl.	388	222	57.2	2,735	17	4.4	75	14	3.6	7.05	78.7
Rypien	Wash.	304	166	54.6	2,070	16	5.3	53	11	3.6	6.81	78.4
Testaverde	T.B.	365	203	55.6	2,818	17	4.7	89	18	4.9	7.72	75.6
Majkowski	G.B.	264	150	56.8	1,925	10	3.8	76	12	4.5	7.29	73.5
Rosenbach	Phx.	437	237	54.2	3,098	16	3.7	68	17	3.9	7.09	72.8
Gannon	Minn.	349	182	52.1	2,278	16	4.6	78	16	4.6	6.53	68.9
Walsh	N.O.	336	179	53.3	2,010	12	3.6	58	13	3.9	5.98	67.2
Aikman	Dall.	399	226	56.6	2,579	11	2.8	61	18	4.5	6.46	66.6

Non-qualifiers

	Team	Att.	Comp.	Comp. Pct.	Yds.	TD	TD Pct.	Lg.	Int.	Int. Pct.	Avg. Gain	Rating
Byars	Phil.	4	4	100.0	53	4	100.0	18	0	0.0	13.25	158.3
McGee	LA.Rm	2	2	100.0	23	1	50.0	22	0	0.0	11.50	154.2
Byner	Wash.	2	1	50.0	31	1	50.0	31	0	0.0	15.50	135.0
Bailey	Chi.	1	1	100.0	22	0	0.0	22	0	0.0	22.00	118.8
Green	Phx.	1	1	100.0	20	0	0.0	20	0	0.0	20.00	118.8
Young	S.F.	62	38	61.3	427	2	3.2	34	0	0.0	6.89	92.6
Wills	Chi.	13	9	69.2	106	1	7.7	18	1	7.7	8.15	87.3
McMahon	Phil.	9	6	66.7	63	0	0.0	21	0	0.0	7.00	86.8
Hostetler	N.Y.G.	87	47	54.0	614	3	3.4	44	1	1.1	7.06	83.2
Rutledge	Wash.	68	40	58.8	455	2	2.9	40	1	1.5	6.69	82.4
Millen	Atl.	63	34	54.0	427	1	1.6	53	0	0.0	6.78	80.6
Wilson	Minn.	146	82	56.2	1,155	9	6.2	75	8	5.5	7.91	79.6
Kiel	G.B.	85	51	60.0	504	2	2.4	22	2	2.4	5.93	74.9
Gagliano	Det.	159	87	54.7	1,190	10	6.3	44	10	6.3	7.48	73.6
Dilweg	G.B.	192	101	52.6	1,267	8	4.2	59	7	3.6	6.60	72.1
Mitchell	Wash.	6	3	50.0	40	0	0.0	18	0	0.0	6.67	71.6
Campbell	Atl.	76	36	49.3	527	3	4.1	70	4	5.5	7.22	61.7
Humphries	Wash.	156	91	58.3	1,015	3	1.9	44	10	6.4	6.51	57.5
Fourcade	N.O.	116	50	43.1	785	3	2.6	68	8	6.9	6.77	46.1
Ware	Det.	30	13	43.3	164	1	3.3	33	2	6.7	5.47	44.3
Tomczak	Chi.	104	39	37.5	521	3	2.9	48	5	4.8	5.01	43.8
Chandler	T.B.	83	42	50.6	464	1	1.2	68	6	7.2	5.59	41.4
Long	LA.Rm	5	1	20.0	4	0	0.0	4	0	0.0	.80	39.6
Laufenberg	Dall.	67	24	35.8	279	1	1.5	27	6	9.0	4.16	16.9

Passing—AFC

	Team	Att.	Comp.	Comp. Pct.	Yds.	TD	TD Pct.	Lg.	Int.	Int. Pct.	Avg. Gain	Rating
Kelly	Buff.	346	219	63.3	2,829	24	6.9	71	9	2.6	8.18	101.2
Moon	Hou.	584	362	62.0	4,689	33	5.7	87	13	2.2	8.03	96.8
DeBerg	K.C.	444	258	58.1	3,444	23	5.2	90	4	.9	7.76	96.3
Schroeder	LA.Rd	334	182	54.5	2,849	19	5.7	68	9	2.7	8.53	90.8
Marino	Mia.	531	306	57.6	3,563	21	4.0	69	11	2.1	6.71	82.6
Brister	Pitt.	387	223	57.6	2,725	20	5.2	90	14	3.6	7.04	81.6
Elway	Denv.	502	294	58.6	3,526	15	3.0	66	14	2.8	7.02	78.5
O'Brien	N.Y.J.	411	226	55.0	2,855	13	3.2	69	10	2.4	6.95	77.3
Esiason	Cin.	402	224	55.7	3,031	24	6.0	53	22	5.5	7.54	77.0
George	Ind.	334	181	5.2	2,152	16	4.8	75	13	3.9	6.44	73.9
Krieg	Sea.	448	265	59.2	3,194	15	3.3	63	20	4.5	7.13	73.6
Tolliver	S.D.	410	216	52.7	2,574	16	3.9	45	16	3.9	6.28	68.9
Kosar	Clev.	423	230	54.4	2,562	10	2.4	50	15	3.5	6.06	65.7
Wilson	N.E.	265	139	52.5	1,625	6	2.3	36	11	4.2	6.13	61.6

Non-qualifiers

	Team	Att.	Comp.	Comp. Pct.	Yds.	TD	TD Pct.	Lg.	Int.	Int. Pct.	Avg. Gain	Rating
Johnson	Cin.	1	1	100.0	4	1	100.0	4	0	0.0	4.00	122.9
Francis	Clev.	2	2	100.0	26	0	0.0	17	0	0.0	13.00	118.8
Evans	L.A.Rd	1	1	100.0	36	0	0.0	36	0	0.0	36.00	118.8
Jensen	Mia.	1	1	100.0	31	0	0.0	31	0	0.0	31.00	118.8
Stark	Ind.	1	1	100.0	40	0	0.0	40	0	0.0	40.00	118.8
Taylor	N.Y.J.	10	7	70.0	49	1	10.0	15	0	0.0	4.90	114.2
Carlson	Hou.	55	37	67.3	383	4	7.3	53	2	3.6	6.96	96.3
Herrmann	Ind.	1	1	100.0	6	0	0.0	45	0	0.0	6.00	91.7
Reich	Buff.	63	36	57.1	469	2	3.2	43	0	0.0	7.44	91.3
Wilhelm	Cin.	19	12	63.2	117	0	0.0	19	0	0.0	6.37	80.4
Trudeau	Ind.	144	84	58.3	1,078	6	4.2	73	6	4.2	7.49	78.4
Grogan	N.E.	92	50	54.3	615	4	4.3	48	3	3.3	6.68	76.1
Gilbert	Buff.	15	8	53.3	106	2	13.3	23	2	13.3	7.07	76.0
Strom	Pitt.	21	14	66.7	162	0	0.0	22	1	4.8	7.71	69.9
Hodson	N.E.	156	85	54.5	968	4	2.6	56	5	3.2	6.21	68.5
Friesz	S.D.	22	11	50.0	98	1	4.5	17	1	4.5	4.45	58.5
Eason	N.Y.J.	28	13	46.4	155	0	0.0	31	1	3.6	5.54	49.0
Pagel	Clev.	148	69	46.6	819	3	2.0	32	8	5.4	5.53	48.2
Vlasic	S.D.	40	19	47.5	168	1	2.5	27	2	5.0	4.20	46.7
Humphrey	Denv.	2	0	0.0	0	0	0.0	0	0	0.0	0.00	39.6
Toon	N.Y.J.	2	0	0.0	0	0	0.0	0	0	0.0	0.00	39.6
D. Smith	Buff.	1	0	0.0	0	0	0.0	0	0	0.0	0.00	39.6
James	Cin.	1	0	0.0	0	0	0.0	0	0	0.0	0.00	39.6
Sewell	Denv.	1	0	0.0	0	0	0.0	0	0	0.0	0.00	39.6
Kubiak	Denv.	22	11	50.0	145	0	0.0	36	4	18.2	6.59	31.6
Secules	Mia.	7	3	42.9	17	0	0.0	8	1	14.3	2.43	10.7
Pelluer	K.C.	5	2	40.0	14	0	0.0	11	1	20.0	2.80	8.3
Ferguson	Ind.	8	2	25.0	21	0	0.0	13	2	25.0	2.63	0.0
Philcox	Cin.	2	0	0.0	0	0	0.0	0	1	50.0	0.00	0.0
Allen	L.A.Rd	1	0	0.0	0	0	0.0	0	1	100.0	0.00	0.0
Stephens	N.E.	1	0	0.0	0	0	0.0	0	1	100.0	0.00	0.0

Rushing—NFC

	Team	Att.	Yds.	Avg.	Lg.	TD		Team	Att.	Yds.	Avg.	Lg.	TD
B. Sanders	Det.	255	1,304	5.1	45	13	Johnson	Atl.	30	106	3.5	12	3
Byner	Wash.	297	1,219	4.1	22	6	Humphries	Wash.	23	106	4.6	17	2
Anderson	Chi.	260	1,078	4.1	52	10	Miller	Atl.	26	99	3.8	18	1
Cunningham	Phil.	118	942	8.0	52	5	Bailey	Chi.	26	86	3.3	9	0
E. Smith	Dall.	241	937	3.9	48	11	Dupard	Wash.	19	85	4.5	11	0
Johnson	Phx.	234	926	4.0	41	5	Flagler	Phx.	13	85	6.5	29	1
Gary	L.A.Rm	204	808	4.0	48	14	Mitchell	Wash.	15	81	5.4	21	2
Anderson	N.Y.G.	225	784	3.5	28	11	Wilson	Minn.	12	79	6.6	24	0
Walker	Minn.	184	770	4.2	58	5	Fourcade	N.O.	15	77	5.1	12	1
Sherman	Phil.	164	685	4.2	36	1	Fontenot	G.B.	17	76	4.5	18	0
Rozier	Atl.	153	675	4.4	67	3	Rice	Minn.	22	74	3.4	13	0
Muster	Chi.	141	664	4.7	28	6	Dupree	L.A.Rm	19	72	3.8	13	0
G. Anderson	T.B.	166	646	3.9	22	3	Chandler	T.B.	13	71	5.5	18	1
Heyward	N.O.	129	599	4.6	47	4	Ware	Det.	7	64	9.1	30	0
Mayes	N.O.	138	510	3.7	18	7	Simms	N.Y.G.	21	61	2.9	20	1
Cobb	T.B.	151	480	3.2	17	2	Monk	Wash.	7	59	8.4	26	0
Riggs	Wash.	123	475	3.9	20	6	Vick	Phil.	16	58	3.6	17	1
Rosenbach	Phx.	86	470	5.5	25	3	Rouse	Chi.	16	56	3.5	10	0
D. Carter	S.F.	114	460	4.0	74	1	Delpino	L.A.Rm	13	52	4.0	13	0
Hampton	N.Y.G.	109	455	4.2	41	2	Wilder	Det.	11	51	4.6	13	0
Broussard	Atl.	126	454	3.6	50	4	Workman	G.B.	8	51	6.4	31	0
Toney	Phil.	132	452	3.4	20	1	Clark	Minn.	16	49	3.1	11	0
Craig	S.F.	141	439	3.1	26	1	Highsmith	Dall.	19	48	2.5	7	0
Thompson	Phx.	106	390	3.7	40	4	Dixon	Dall.	11	43	3.9	18	0
Fenney	Minn.	87	376	4.3	27	2	Gentry	Chi.	11	43	3.9	11	0
Peete	Det.	48	365	7.6	37	6	Tomczak	Chi.	12	41	3.4	14	2
Fenerty	N.O.	73	355	4.9	60	2	Query	G.B.	3	39	13.0	18	0
Harbaugh	Chi.	51	322	6.3	17	4	Campbell	Atl.	9	38	4.2	20	0
Rathman	S.F.	101	318	3.1	22	7	Perkins	T.B.	13	36	2.8	9	0
Haddix	G.B.	98	311	3.2	13	0	Johnston	Dall.	10	35	3.5	8	1
Hilliard	N.O.	90	284	3.2	17	0	Drummond	Phil.	8	33	4.1	9	1
Testaverde	T.B.	38	280	7.4	48	1	Jones	Phx.	4	33	8.3	15	0
Gannon	Minn.	52	268	5.2	27	1	Everett	L.A.Rm	20	31	1.5	15	1
Thompson	G.B.	76	264	3.5	37	1	Wright	Dall.	3	26	8.7	14	0
Green	L.A.Rm	68	261	3.8	31	0	Morris	Chi.	2	26	13.0	16	0
McGee	L.A.Rm	44	234	5.3	19	1	Walsh	N.O.	20	25	1.3	18	0
Tillman	N.Y.G.	84	231	2.8	17	1	Lang	Atl.	9	24	2.7	9	0
Agee	Dall.	53	213	4.0	28	0	Bryant	Wash.	6	24	4.0	12	0
Sanders	Phil.	56	208	3.7	39	1	Ellard	L.A.Rm	2	21	10.5	13	0
Anderson	Minn.	59	207	3.5	14	2	Williams	Phil.	2	20	10.0	18	0
Hostetler	N.Y.G.	39	190	4.9	30	2	Saxon	Dall.	1	20	20.0	20	0
Majkowski	G.B.	29	186	6.4	24	1	Smith	Minn.	9	19	2.1	7	0
Jones	Atl.	49	185	3.8	22	0	Sanders	Wash.	4	17	4.3	12	0
Woodside	G.B.	46	182	4.0	21	1	Settle	Atl.	9	16	1.8	4	0
Aikman	Dall.	40	172	4.3	20	1	A. Carter	Minn.	3	16	5.3	11	0
Sydney	S.F.	35	166	4.7	19	2	Henderson	S.F.	6	14	2.3	9	0
Meggett	N.Y.G.	22	164	7.4	51	0	Rouson	N.Y.G.	3	14	4.7	6	0
Montana	S.F.	40	162	4.1	20	1	Sharpe	G.B.	2	14	7.0	10	0
Young	S.F.	15	159	10.6	31	0	Barnett	Phil.	2	13	6.5	12	0
Gagliano	Det.	46	145	3.1	22	0	Anderson	L.A.Rm	1	13	13.0	13	0
Carthon	N.Y.G.	36	143	4.0	12	0	Dozier	Minn.	6	12	2.0	4	0
Byars	Phil.	37	141	3.8	23	0	Rutledge	Wash.	4	12	3.0	12	1
Warner	L.A.Rm	49	139	2.8	9	1	Kiel	G.B.	5	9	1.8	4	1
Green	Chi.	27	126	4.7	14	0	Pringle	Atl.	2	9	4.5	9	0
Fullwood	G.B.	44	124	2.8	16	1	Sikahema	Phx.	3	8	2.7	4	0
Dilweg	G.B.	21	114	5.4	22	0	T. Smith	Dall.	6	6	1.0	3	0
Harvey	T.B.	27	113	4.2	14	0	C. Carter	Minn.	2	6	3.0	8	0

	Team	Att.	Yds.	Avg.	Lg.	TD		Team	Att.	Yds.	Avg.	Lg.	TD
Laufenberg	Dall.	2	6	3.0	5	0	Hill	T.B.	1	0	0.0	0	0
L. Tate	Chi.	3	5	1.7	4	0	Mojsiejenko	Wash.	1	0	0.0	0	0
Goodburn	Wash.	1	5	5.0	5	0	Tupa	Phx.	1	0	0.0	0	0
Rypien	Wash.	15	4	.3	8	0	Walsh	Dall.	1	0	0.0	0	0
Bates	Dall.	1	4	4.0	4	0	Kemp	G.B.	1	−1	−1.0	−1	0
Ingram	N.Y.G.	1	4	4.0	4	0	Perry	Chi.	1	−1	−1.0	−1	0
J.T. Smith	Phx.	1	4	4.0	4	0	Martin	Dall.	4	−2	−.5	3	0
Proehl	Phx.	1	4	4.0	4	0	Newsome	Minn.	2	−2	−1.0	0	0
Feagles	Phil.	2	3	1.5	3	0	H. Jones	Minn.	1	−7	−7.0	−7	0
Wolfley	Phx.	2	3	1.5	2	0	McKinnon	Dall.	1	−8	−8.0	−8	0
Baker	N.Y.G.	1	3	3.0	3	0	Buford	Chi.	1	−9	−9.0	−9	0
McMahon	Phil.	3	1	.3	3	0	Camarillo	Phx.	1	−11	−11.0	−11	0
Clark	Wash.	1	1	1.0	1	0	Millen	Atl.	7	−12	−1.7	2	0
Rice	S.F.	2	0	0.0	2	0	English	L.A.Rm	2	−19	−9.5	−8	0
Carlson	T.B.	1	0	0.0	0	0							

Rushing—AFC

	Team	Att.	Yds.	Avg.	Lg.	TD		Team	Att.	Yds.	Avg.	Lg.	TD
Thomas	Buff.	271	1,297	4.8	80	11	Esiason	Cin.	50	157	3.1	21	0
Butts	S.D.	265	1,225	4.6	52	8	Hoard	Clev.	58	149	2.6	42	3
Humphrey	Denv.	288	1,202	4.2	37	7	Stradford	Mia.	37	138	3.7	15	1
Word	K.C.	204	1,015	5.0	53	4	Winder	Denv.	42	120	2.9	19	2
Brooks	Cin.	195	1,004	5.1	56	5	Krieg	Sea.	32	115	3.6	25	0
Fenner	Sea.	215	859	4.0	36	14	Adams	N.E.	28	111	4.0	13	0
Smith	Mia.	226	831	3.7	33	8	Perryman	N.E.	32	97	3.0	13	1
Stephens	N.E.	212	808	3.8	26	2	Paige	Mia.	32	95	3.0	11	2
Okoye	K.C.	245	805	3.3	32	7	Bratton	Denv.	27	82	3.0	10	3
Hoge	Pitt.	203	772	3.8	41	7	D. Smith	Buff.	20	82	4.1	13	2
Williams	Sea.	187	714	3.8	25	3	Schroeder	L.A.Rd	37	81	2.2	17	0
White	Hou.	168	702	4.2	22	8	Gainer	Clev.	30	81	2.7	9	1
Mack	Clev.	158	702	4.4	26	5	Ezor	Denv.	23	81	3.5	15	0
Jackson	L.A.Rd	125	698	5.6	88	5	Hodson	N.E.	12	79	6.6	23	0
Allen	L.A.Rd	179	682	3.8	28	12	V. Jones	Hou.	14	75	5.4	14	0
Dickerson	Ind.	166	677	4.1	43	4	Ball	Cin.	22	72	3.3	15	1
Thomas	N.Y.J.	123	620	5.0	41	1	O'Brien	N.Y.J.	21	72	3.4	15	0
Bernstine	S.D.	124	589	4.8	40	4	Higgs	Mia.	10	67	6.7	27	0
Bentley	Ind.	137	556	4.1	26	4	Givins	Hou.	3	65	21.7	31	0
Baxter	N.Y.J.	124	539	4.3	28	6	Brister	Pitt.	25	64	2.6	11	0
McNeil	N.Y.J.	99	458	4.6	29	6	Kelly	Buff.	22	63	2.9	15	0
Worley	Pitt.	109	418	3.8	38	0	McNair	K.C.	14	61	4.4	13	0
W. Williams	Pitt.	68	389	5.7	70	3	Tatupu	N.E.	16	56	3.5	15	0
Hector	N.Y.J.	91	377	4.1	22	2	Carlson	Hou.	11	52	4.7	16	0
Harmon	S.D.	66	363	5.5	41	0	Kubiak	Denv.	9	52	5.8	18	0
Green	Cin.	83	353	4.3	39	1	B. Jones	K.C.	10	47	4.7	14	0
Smith	L.A.Rd	81	327	4.0	17	2	Sewell	Denv.	17	46	2.7	8	3
Logan	Mia.	79	317	4.0	17	2	Jennings	Cin.	12	46	3.8	13	1
K. Davis	Buff.	64	302	4.7	47	4	Mueller	L.A.Rd	13	43	3.3	12	0
Pinkett	Hou.	66	268	4.1	19	0	Rozier	Hou.	10	42	4.2	11	0
Woods	Cin.	64	268	4.2	32	6	Gardner	Buff.	15	41	2.7	14	0
Elway	Denv.	50	258	5.2	21	3	Secules	Mia.	8	34	4.3	17	0
Metcalf	Clev.	80	248	3.1	17	1	Marino	Mia.	16	29	1.8	15	0
Allen	N.E.	63	237	3.8	29	1	Eason	N.Y.J.	7	29	4.1	24	0
Taylor	Cin.	51	216	4.2	24	2	Slaughter	Clev.	5	29	5.8	17	0
Moon	Hou.	55	215	3.9	17	2	Trudeau	Ind.	10	28	2.8	9	0
Mueller	Buff.	59	207	3.5	20	2	Jackson	Denv.	5	28	5.6	16	1
Foster	Pitt.	36	203	5.6	38	1	McCallum	L.A.Rd	10	25	2.5	6	0
Bell	L.A.Rd	47	164	3.5	21	1	Lewis	S.D.	4	25	6.3	10	1

	Team	Att.	Yds.	Avg.	Lg.	TD		Team	Att.	Yds.	Avg.	Lg.	TD
Reich	Buff.	15	24	1.6	9	0	Jensen	Mia.	4	6	1.5	2	0
Reed	Buff.	3	23	7.7	26	0	Goodburn	K.C.	1	5	5.0	5	0
Beebe	Buff.	1	23	23.0	23	0	Morris	N.E.	2	4	2.0	3	0
Tolliver	S.D.	14	22	1.6	14	0	Plummer	S.D.	2	3	1.5	2	1
Jones	Sea.	5	20	4.0	5	0	Banks	Mia.	1	3	3.0	3	0
Taylor	N.Y.J.	2	20	10.0	15	1	Friesz	S.D.	1	3	3.0	3	0
Blades	Sea.	3	19	6.3	12	0	Porter	Denv.	1	3	3.0	3	0
Kinnebrew	Buff.	9	18	2.0	4	1	George	Ind.	11	2	.2	6	1
Bell	Pitt.	5	18	3.6	12	0	Prokop	N.Y.J.	3	2	.7	8	0
Stryzinski	Pitt.	3	17	5.7	9	0	McNeal	Sea.	1	2	2.0	2	0
Saxon	K.C.	3	15	5.0	8	0	Gannon	N.E.	1	0	0.0	0	0
Limbrick	Mia.	5	14	2.8	5	0	Hansen	N.E.	1	0	0.0	0	0
Nelson	S.D.	3	14	4.7	5	0	Vlasic	S.D.	1	0	0.0	0	0
Kosar	Clev.	10	13	1.3	5	0	Wilson	S.D.	1	0	0.0	0	0
A. Miller	S.D.	3	13	4.3	10	0	Pagel	Clev.	3	−1	−.3	0	0
Loville	Sea.	7	12	1.7	4	0	F. Jones	K.C.	1	−1	−1.0	−1	0
Warren	Sea.	6	11	1.8	4	1	Redden	Clev.	1	−1	−1.0	−1	0
James	Cin.	1	11	11.0	11	0	Evans	L.A.Rd	1	−2	−2.0	−2	0
Clark	Ind.	7	10	1.4	11	0	T. Jones	Hou.	1	−2	−2.0	−2	0
Strom	Pitt.	4	10	2.5	10	0	Chadwick	Sea.	1	−3	−3.0	−3	0
Fernandez	L.A.Rd	3	10	3.3	9	0	Wellsandt	N.Y.J.	1	−3	−3.0	−3	0
Hester	Ind.	4	9	2.3	10	0	Fryar	N.E.	2	−4	−2.0	−1	0
Mathis	N.Y.J.	2	9	4.5	10	0	Moore	N.Y.J.	2	−4	−2.0	4	0
Overton	N.E.	5	8	1.6	6	0	DeBerg	K.C.	21	−5	−.2	6	0
Brown	N.Y.J.	1	8	8.0	8	0	Grogan	N.E.	4	−5	−1.3	0	0
Martin	Mia.	1	8	8.0	8	0	Lipps	Pitt.	1	−5	−5.0	−5	0
Wilson	N.E.	5	7	1.4	6	0	Stone	Pitt.	2	−6	−3.0	10	0
Wilhelm	Cin.	6	6	1.0	4	0	Edmunds	Mia.	1	−7	−7.0	−7	0
Pelluer	K.C.	5	6	1.2	5	0	Barber	Cin.	1	−13	−13.0	−13	0

Receiving—NFC

	Team	No.	Yds.	Avg.	Lg.	TD		Team	No.	Yds.	Avg.	Lg.	TD
Rice	S.F.	100	1,502	15.0	64	13	McGee	L.A.Rm	47	388	8.3	25	4
Rison	Atl.	82	1,208	14.7	75	10	Jordan	Minn.	45	636	14.1	38	3
Byars	Phil.	81	819	10.1	54	3	Kemp	G.B.	44	527	12.0	29	2
Ellard	L.A.Rm	76	1,294	17.0	50	4	Jones	Phx.	43	724	16.8	68	4
Clark	Wash.	75	1,112	14.8	53	8	Hill	T.B.	42	641	15.3	48	5
A. Carter	Minn.	70	1,008	14.4	56	8	Anderson	Chi.	42	484	11.5	50	3
Monk	Wash.	68	770	11.3	44	5	Davis	Chi.	39	572	14.7	51	3
Sharpe	G.B.	67	1,105	16.5	76	6	Meggett	N.Y.G.	39	410	10.5	38	1
Martin	Dall.	64	732	11.4	45	0	Cobb	T.B.	39	299	7.7	17	0
Johnson	Det.	64	727	11.4	44	6	G. Anderson	T.B.	38	464	12.2	74	2
E. Martin	N.O.	63	912	14.5	58	5	Dixon	Atl.	38	399	10.5	34	4
Novacek	Dall.	59	657	11.1	41	4	Williams	Phil.	37	602	16.3	45	9
Proehl	Phx.	56	802	14.3	45	4	Barnett	Phil.	36	721	20.0	95	8
Jones	S.F.	56	747	13.3	67	5	Perriman	N.O.	36	386	10.7	29	2
Sanders	Wash.	56	727	13.0	38	3	B. Sanders	Det.	35	462	13.2	47	3
Clark	Det.	53	932	17.6	57	8	Walker	Minn.	35	315	9.0	32	4
Green	Phx.	53	797	15.0	54	4	Collins	Atl.	34	503	14.8	61	2
Anderson	L.A.Rm	51	1,097	21.5	55	4	Query	G.B.	34	458	13.5	47	2
H. Jones	Minn.	51	810	15.9	75	7	Bavaro	N.Y.G.	33	393	11.9	61	5
Kei. Jackson	Phil.	50	670	13.4	37	6	Weathers	G.B.	33	390	11.8	29	1
Carrier	T.B.	49	813	16.6	68	4	Hampton	N.Y.G.	32	274	8.6	27	2
Taylor	S.F.	49	748	15.3	78	7	Hall	T.B.	31	464	15.0	54	2
Holohan	L.A.Rm	49	475	9.7	28	2	Haynes	Atl.	31	445	14.4	60	0
Rathman	S.F.	48	327	6.8	28	0	Morris	Chi.	31	437	14.1	67	3
Muster	Chi.	47	452	9.6	48	0	Fontenot	G.B.	31	293	9.5	59	1

	Team	No.	Yds.	Avg.	Lg.	TD		Team	No.	Yds.	Avg.	Lg.	TD
Byner	Wash.	31	279	9.0	19	1	Quick	Phil.	9	135	15.0	39	1
Matthews	Det.	30	349	11.6	52	1	Williams	S.F.	9	54	6.0	9	0
Agee	Dall.	30	272	9.1	30	1	Pillow	T.B.	8	118	14.8	23	0
Gary	L.A.Rm	30	150	5.0	22	1	Phillips	Det.	8	112	14.0	29	0
C. Carter	Minn.	27	413	15.3	78	3	Cross	N.Y.G.	8	106	13.3	21	0
West	G.B.	27	356	13.2	50	5	Perkins	T.B.	8	85	10.6	34	2
Baker	N.Y.G.	26	541	20.8	80	4	Scales	N.O.	8	64	8.0	20	1
Ingram	N.Y.G.	26	499	19.2	57	5	Carter	L.A.Rm	8	58	7.3	16	0
Bryant	Wash.	26	248	9.5	37	1	Tillman	N.Y.G.	8	18	2.3	16	0
Johnson	Phx.	25	241	9.6	35	0	Drewrey	T.B.	7	182	26.0	89	1
D. Carter	S.F.	25	217	8.7	26	0	Wilson	S.F.	7	89	12.7	34	0
Craig	S.F.	25	201	8.0	31	0	Wilson	G.B.	7	84	12.0	18	0
E. Smith	Dall.	24	228	9.5	57	0	Kozlowski	Chi.	7	83	11.9	32	0
Woodside	G.B.	24	184	7.7	25	0	Riggs	Wash.	7	60	8.6	18	0
Broussard	Atl.	24	160	6.7	18	0	Sikahema	Phx.	7	51	7.3	13	0
Gentry	Chi.	23	320	13.9	80	2	Turner	N.Y.G.	6	69	11.5	18	0
Sherman	Phil.	23	167	7.3	26	3	Peebles	T.B.	6	50	8.3	18	1
Turner	N.O.	21	396	18.9	68	4	J. Anderson	T.B.	5	77	15.4	52	0
Irvin	Dall.	20	413	20.7	61	5	Lewis	S.F.	5	44	8.8	14	0
Greer	Det.	20	332	16.6	68	3	Drummond	Phil.	5	39	7.8	29	0
Thornton	Chi.	19	254	13.4	32	1	Walls	S.F.	5	27	5.4	11	0
Campbell	Det.	19	236	12.4	51	2	Kyles	N.Y.G.	4	77	19.3	35	0
Thomas	Atl.	18	383	21.3	72	1	Alphin	N.O.	4	57	14.3	17	0
J.T. Smith	Phx.	18	225	12.5	45	2	Rice	Minn.	4	46	11.5	24	0
Fenerty	N.O.	18	209	11.6	28	0	Bailey	Atl.	4	44	11.0	13	0
Shuler	Phil.	18	190	10.6	25	0	Henderson	S.F.	4	35	8.8	9	0
Milling	Atl.	18	161	8.9	24	1	Workman	G.B.	4	30	7.5	9	1
Anderson	N.Y.G.	18	139	7.7	18	0	Green	Chi.	4	26	6.5	10	1
Reeves	Phx.	18	126	7.0	16	0	Howard	Wash.	3	36	12.0	17	0
Heyward	N.O.	18	121	6.7	12	0	Hill	N.O.	3	35	11.7	13	0
A. Cox	L.A.Rm	17	266	15.7	32	0	Faison	L.A.Rm	3	27	9.0	12	1
Sherrard	S.F.	17	264	15.5	43	2	Mrosko	N.Y.G.	3	27	9.0	16	1
Brenner	N.O.	17	213	12.5	31	2	Fullwood	G.B.	3	17	5.7	10	0
Toney	Phil.	17	133	7.8	32	3	Highsmith	Dall.	3	13	4.3	7	0
Fenney	Minn.	17	112	6.6	17	0	Thompson	G.B.	3	1	.3	1	1
J. Johnson	Wash.	15	218	14.5	35	2	Waddle	Chi.	2	32	16.0	23	0
Delpino	L.A.Rm	15	172	11.5	42	4	Dixon	Dall.	2	26	13.0	21	0
Warren	Wash.	15	123	8.2	18	1	Green	L.A.Rm	2	23	11.5	16	1
McKinnon	Dall.	14	172	12.3	28	1	Sanders	Phil.	2	20	10.0	12	0
Carthon	N.Y.G.	14	151	10.8	63	0	Smith	Chi.	2	20	10.0	12	0
Johnston	Dall.	14	148	10.6	26	1	Stanley	Wash.	2	15	7.5	12	0
Hilliard	N.O.	14	125	8.9	20	1	Robinson	N.Y.G.	2	13	6.5	7	0
Awalt	Dall.	13	133	10.2	25	0	Thompson	Phx.	2	11	5.5	6	0
Flagler	Phx.	13	130	10.0	21	1	Jordan	Phx.	2	10	5.0	6	0
Rozier	Atl.	13	105	8.1	24	0	Mitchell	Wash.	2	5	2.5	5	0
Jones	Atl.	13	103	7.9	16	0	Ken. Jackson	Phil.	1	43	43.0	43	0
Haddix	G.B.	13	94	7.2	28	2	Hargrove	Phil.	1	34	34.0	34	1
Anderson	Minn.	13	80	6.1	17	0	Hobbs	Wash.	1	18	18.0	18	1
Wilkins	Atl.	12	175	14.6	37	2	Dozier	Minn.	1	12	12.0	12	0
Farr	Det.	12	170	14.2	44	0	Rouson	N.Y.G.	1	12	12.0	12	0
J. Harris	G.B.	12	157	13.1	26	0	Hilgenberg	N.O.	1	9	9.0	9	0
Mayes	N.O.	12	121	10.1	66	0	Le Bel	Phil.	1	9	9.0	9	0
Johnson	L.A.Rm	12	66	5.5	11	3	Lewis	Minn.	1	9	9.0	9	0
Manuel	N.Y.G.	11	169	15.4	19	0	Wilder	Det.	1	8	8.0	8	1
Boso	Chi.	11	135	12.3	25	1	Coley	Chi.	1	7	7.0	7	0
Tice	N.O.	11	113	10.3	19	0	Lang	Atl.	1	7	7.0	7	0
Wright	Dall.	11	104	9.5	20	0	Tomczak	Chi.	1	5	5.0	5	0
Harvey	T.B.	11	86	7.8	18	1	Clark	Minn.	1	4	4.0	4	0
Sydney	S.F.	10	116	11.6	23	1	Testaverde	T.B.	1	3	3.0	3	0
Johnson	Atl.	10	79	7.9	16	1	Sharpe	Phx.	1	1	1.0	1	1

Receiving—AFC

	Team	No.	Yds.	Avg.	Lg.	TD		Team	No.	Yds.	Avg.	Lg.	TD
Jeffires	Hou.	74	1,048	14.2	87	8	Chadwick	Sea.	27	478	17.7	54	4
Hill	Hou.	74	1,019	13.8	57	5	Brooks	Cin.	26	269	10.4	35	4
Williams	Sea.	73	699	9.6	60	0	Sewell	Denv.	26	268	10.3	36	0
Givins	Hou.	72	979	13.6	80	9	Hill	Pitt.	25	391	15.6	66	0
Reed	Buff.	71	945	13.3	56	8	Humphrey	Denv.	24	152	6.3	26	0
Bentley	Ind.	71	664	9.4	73	2	Morgan	Ind.	23	364	15.8	42	5
Duncan	Hou.	66	785	11.9	37	1	Newsome	Clev.	23	240	10.4	38	2
Paige	K.C.	65	1,021	15.7	86	5	Walker	S.D.	23	240	10.4	23	1
A. Miller	S.D.	63	933	14.8	31	7	Skansi	Sea.	22	257	11.7	25	2
Brooks	Ind.	62	823	13.3	75	5	McMurtry	N.E.	22	240	10.9	26	0
Slaughter	Clev.	59	847	14.4	50	4	Jones	N.E.	21	301	14.3	26	0
Jackson	Denv.	57	926	16.2	66	4	D. Smith	Buff.	21	225	10.7	39	0
Toon	N.Y.J.	57	757	13.3	46	6	Thomas	N.Y.J.	20	204	10.2	55	1
Metcalf	Clev.	57	452	7.9	35	1	Woods	Cin.	20	162	8.1	22	0
Hester	Ind.	54	924	17.1	64	6	Stone	Pitt.	19	332	17.5	90	1
Fryar	N.E.	54	856	15.9	56	4	Mathis	N.Y.J.	19	245	12.9	23	0
Johnson	Denv.	54	747	13.8	49	3	B. Jones	K.C.	19	137	7.2	19	5
Fernandez	L.A.Rd	52	839	16.1	66	5	Nattiel	Denv.	18	297	16.5	52	2
Duper	Mia.	52	810	15.6	69	5	T. Brown	L.A.Rd	18	265	14.7	51	3
Kane	Sea.	52	776	14.9	63	4	Dickerson	Ind.	18	92	5.1	17	0
Cook	N.E.	51	455	8.9	35	5	Winder	Denv.	17	145	8.5	17	0
Gault	L.A.Rd	50	985	19.7	68	3	Fenner	Sea.	17	143	8.4	50	1
Lipps	Pitt.	50	682	13.6	37	3	McNeil	N.Y.J.	16	230	14.4	59	0
Thomas	Buff.	49	532	10.9	63	2	Adams	N.E.	16	146	9.1	28	1
Blades	Sea.	49	525	10.7	24	3	Butts	S.D.	16	117	7.3	26	0
Harmon	S.D.	46	511	11.1	36	2	Mueller	Buff.	16	106	6.6	30	1
Langhorne	Clev.	45	585	13.0	39	2	Birden	K.C.	15	352	23.5	90	3
Brennan	Clev.	45	568	12.6	28	2	Early	S.D.	15	238	15.9	45	1
Brown	Cin.	44	706	16.0	50	9	Allen	L.A.Rd	15	189	12.6	30	1
Moore	N.Y.J.	44	692	15.7	69	6	Perryman	N.E.	15	88	5.9	15	0
Jensen	Mia.	44	365	8.3	18	1	Burkett	N.Y.J.	14	204	14.6	46	0
McGee	Cin.	43	737	17.1	52	1	Barber	Cin.	14	196	14.0	28	1
Mack	Clev.	42	360	8.6	30	2	Lewis	S.D.	14	192	13.7	40	1
R. Thomas	K.C.	41	545	13.3	47	4	Verdin	Ind.	14	178	12.7	45	1
Harry	K.C.	41	519	12.7	60	2	Cox	S.D.	14	93	6.6	12	1
Holman	Cin.	40	596	14.9	53	5	Harris	Hou.	13	172	13.2	42	3
McNair	K.C.	40	507	12.7	65	2	Heller	Sea.	13	157	12.1	23	1
Hoge	Pitt.	40	342	8.6	27	3	Banks	Mia.	13	131	10.1	23	0
Boyer	N.Y.J.	40	334	8.4	25	1	Pruitt	Mia.	12	216	18.0	35	3
White	Hou.	39	368	9.4	29	4	Bell	Pitt.	12	137	11.4	43	1
Lofton	Buff.	35	712	20.3	71	4	Beach	Ind.	12	124	10.3	21	1
Paige	Mia.	35	247	7.1	17	4	Green	Cin.	12	90	7.5	22	1
Dykes	N.E.	34	549	16.2	35	2	Beebe	Buff.	11	221	20.1	49	1
McKeller	Buff.	34	464	13.7	43	5	Kattus	Cin.	11	145	13.2	31	2
Green	Pitt.	34	387	11.4	46	7	Smith	Mia.	11	134	12.2	53	1
Clayton	Mia.	33	425	12.9	43	3	Roberts	K.C.	11	119	10.8	27	0
Horton	L.A.Rd	33	404	12.2	36	3	Pinkett	Hou.	11	85	7.7	38	0
Mularkey	Pitt.	32	365	11.4	28	3	McNeal	Sea.	10	143	14.3	30	0
Edmunds	Mia.	31	446	14.4	35	1	Calloway	Pitt.	10	124	12.4	20	1
T. Jones	Hou.	30	409	13.6	47	6	Ford	Hou.	10	98	9.8	24	1
Stradford	Mia.	30	257	8.6	23	0	Wilson	S.D.	10	87	8.7	20	0
Martin	Mia.	29	388	13.4	45	2	Hoard	Clev.	10	73	7.3	17	0
McEwen	S.D.	29	325	11.2	32	3	Metzelaars	Buff.	10	60	6.0	12	1
Kay	Denv.	29	282	9.7	22	0	Hayes	K.C.	9	83	9.2	21	1
Bratton	Denv.	29	276	9.5	63	1	K. Davis	Buff.	9	78	8.7	16	1
Young	Denv.	28	385	13.8	42	4	Riggs	Cin.	8	79	9.9	21	0
Stephens	N.E.	28	196	7.0	43	1	Sievers	N.E.	8	77	9.6	25	0

	Team	No.	Yds.	Avg.	Lg.	TD		Team	No.	Yds.	Avg.	Lg.	TD
Baxter	N.Y.J.	8	73	9.1	22	0	Word	K.C.	4	28	7.0	10	0
Hector	N.Y.J.	8	72	9.0	25	0	Jennings	Cin.	4	23	5.8	13	0
Worley	Pitt.	8	70	8.8	27	0	Limbrick	Mia.	4	23	5.8	9	0
Mobley	Ind.	8	41	5.1	9	0	Okoye	K.C.	4	23	5.8	8	0
Bernstine	S.D.	8	40	5.0	11	0	Dyal	L.A.Rd	3	51	17.0	29	0
Sharpe	Denv.	7	99	14.1	33	1	A. Brown	Mia.	3	49	16.3	24	0
Mandley	K.C.	7	97	13.9	24	0	James	Cin.	3	36	12.0	16	0
Gainer	Clev.	7	85	12.1	20	0	Taylor	Cin.	3	22	7.3	20	1
Logan	Mia.	7	54	7.7	12	0	Verhulst	Denv.	3	13	4.3	6	0
Smith	Cin.	7	45	6.4	11	0	Rolle	Buff.	3	6	2.0	3	3
Joines	Clev.	6	86	14.3	24	0	Ball	Cin.	2	46	23.0	48	1
Jackson	L.A.Rd	6	68	11.3	18	0	Tasker	Buff.	2	44	22.0	24	2
Mowatt	N.E.	6	67	11.2	16	0	Talley	Clev.	2	28	14.0	19	0
Dressel	N.Y.J.	6	66	11.0	21	0	Caravello	S.D.	2	21	10.5	17	1
Schwedes	Mia.	6	66	11.0	19	1	Overton	N.E.	2	19	9.5	15	0
Allen	N.E.	6	48	8.0	19	0	Whitaker	K.C.	2	17	8.5	16	1
Timpson	N.E.	5	91	18.2	42	0	Edwards	Buff.	2	11	5.5	6	0
Dawkins	N.Y.J.	5	68	13.6	31	0	Tatupu	N.E.	2	10	5.0	6	0
McNeil	Hou.	5	63	12.6	16	0	Graddy	L.A.Rd	1	47	47.0	47	1
Wellsandt	N.Y.J.	5	57	11.4	20	0	Prior	Ind.	1	40	40.0	40	0
Rozier	Hou.	5	46	9.2	24	0	Jones	Sea.	1	22	22.0	22	0
W. Williams	Pitt.	5	42	8.4	13	1	Kauric	Clev.	1	21	21.0	21	0
Johnson	Ind.	5	32	6.4	15	2	O'Shea	Pitt.	1	13	13.0	13	0
Clark	Ind.	5	23	4.6	11	0	Hendrickson	S.D.	1	12	12.0	12	0
Martin	N.E.	4	65	16.3	19	1	Bell	L.A.Rd	1	7	7.0	7	0
Galbraith	Clev.	4	62	15.5	28	0	F. Jones	K.C.	1	5	5.0	5	0
Townsell	N.Y.J.	4	57	14.3	18	0	Saxon	K.C.	1	5	5.0	5	0
Porter	Denv.	4	44	11.0	16	0	Foster	Pitt.	1	2	2.0	2	0
Simmons	Ind.	4	33	8.3	12	0	Plummer	S.D.	1	2	2.0	2	1
Smith	L.A.Rd	4	30	7.5	17	3	Lanier	Denv.	1	−4	−4.0	−4	0
Nelson	S.D.	4	29	7.3	10	0	Krieg	Sea.	1	−6	−6.0	−6	0

Sacks—NFC

	Team	Sacks		Team	Sacks		Team	Sacks
Haley	S.F.	16.0	Collins	Wash.	6.0	Saddler	Phx.	4.0
White	Phil.	15.0	Green	Atl.	6.0	Strauthers	Minn.	4.0
Greene	L.A.Rm	13.0	Holt	S.F.	6.0	Gann	Atl.	3.5
Dent	Chi.	12.0	Jackson	N.O.	6.0	Jeffcoat	Dall.	3.5
Doleman	Minn.	11.0	Noga	Minn.	6.0	Johnson	N.Y.G.	3.5
Swilling	N.O.	11.0	Tolbert	Dall.	6.0	Moss	T.B.	3.5
Taylor	N.Y.G.	10.5	Mann	Wash.	5.5	Small	Phil.	3.5
Armstrong	Chi.	10.0	Randle	T.B.	5.5	Atkins	N.O.	3.0
Cofer	Det.	10.0	Wilks	N.O.	5.5	Bell	Phx.	3.0
Harvey	Phx.	10.0	Marshall	Wash.	5.0	Bennett	G.B.	3.0
Fagan	S.F.	9.0	Piel	L.A.Rm	5.0	Brown	G.B.	3.0
Nunn	Phx.	9.0	Tuggle	Atl.	5.0	Browner	Minn.	3.0
Turnbull	N.O.	9.0	Marshall	N.Y.G.	4.5	Case	Atl.	3.0
Thomas	Minn.	8.5	Noonan	Dall.	4.5	Coleman	Wash.	3.0
Jones	Dall.	7.5	Brock	G.B.	4.0	Cox	Chi.	3.0
Joyner	Phil.	7.5	Bruce	Atl.	4.0	Duckens	Det.	3.0
Simmons	Phil.	7.5	Hayworth	Det.	4.0	Epps	Atl.	3.0
Stokes	Wash.	7.5	Jackson	N.Y.G.	4.0	Ferguson	Det.	3.0
Stubbs	Dall.	7.5	W. Martin	N.O.	4.0	Geathers	Wash.	3.0
Thomas	T.B.	7.5	McMichael	Chi.	4.0	Hawkins	L.A.Rm	3.0
Clarke	Minn.	7.0	Murphy	T.B.	4.0	Howard	N.Y.G.	3.0
T. Harris	G.B.	7.0	Patterson	G.B.	4.0	Hunter	Det.	3.0
Brown	S.F.	6.0	Perry	Chi.	4.0	Jax	Phx.	3.0

	Team	Sacks		Team	Sacks		Team	Sacks
T. Johnson	Wash.	3.0	Del Rio	Dall.	1.5	Hoage	Phil.	1.0
Newton	T.B.	3.0	Fox	N.Y.G.	1.5	Holmes	G.B.	1.0
Owens	Det.	3.0	Frizzell	Phil.	1.5	Jackson	S.F.	1.0
Pitts	Phil.	3.0	Hill	Phx.	1.5	Johnson	N.O.	1.0
Reid	Atl.	3.0	Lyles	Atl.	1.5	V. Jones	Det.	1.0
Rocker	Wash.	3.0	Banks	N.Y.G.	1.0	Lockhart	Dall.	1.0
Williams	Wash.	3.0	Blades	Det.	1.0	Mack	Phx.	1.0
J. Williams	Det.	3.0	Bowles	Wash.	1.0	Murphy	G.B.	1.0
Merriweather	Minn.	2.5	Brooks	Det.	1.0	Nelson	G.B.	1.0
Norton	Dall.	2.5	Brown	Phil.	1.0	Noble	G.B.	1.0
Wahler	Phx.	2.5	Bryan	Atl.	1.0	Osborne	Phx.	1.0
White	T.B.	2.5	Caldwell	Wash.	1.0	Pruitt	Chi.	1.0
Ball	Det.	2.0	Cannon	T.B.	1.0	Randle	Minn.	1.0
Bethune	L.A.Rm	2.0	M. Carter	S.F.	1.0	Roberts	S.F.	1.0
Burt	S.F.	2.0	Casillas	Atl.	1.0	Romanowski	S.F.	1.0
Conner	Atl.	2.0	Chapura	Phil.	1.0	Roper	Chi.	1.0
Faryniarz	L.A.Rm	2.0	Cline	Det.	1.0	Simmons	N.O.	1.0
Golic	Phil.	2.0	Cook	N.O.	1.0	Singletary	Chi.	1.0
Hopkins	Phil.	2.0	Cooks	N.Y.G.	1.0	Smith	L.A.Rm	1.0
Jamison	Det.	2.0	Crockett	Det.	1.0	Solomon	Dall.	1.0
Jones	Chi.	2.0	Davis	T.B.	1.0	Spindler	Det.	1.0
Koch	Wash.	2.0	Dent	G.B.	1.0	Stephen	G.B.	1.0
Marve	T.B.	2.0	Evans	Phil.	1.0	Thompson	N.Y.G.	1.0
McCants	T.B.	2.0	Fullington	Minn.	1.0	Turner	S.F.	1.0
Millard	Minn.	2.0	Gayle	Chi.	1.0	Wilcher	L.A.Rm	1.0
Reed	L.A.Rm	2.0	Gouveia	Wash.	1.0	Wright	L.A.Rm	1.0
Skow	T.B.	2.0	Grant	Wash.	1.0	Gray	Phil.	.5
Spielman	Det.	2.0	Hairston	Phx.	1.0	Mills	N.O.	.5
Woolford	Chi.	2.0	Hamel	Dall.	1.0			

Sacks—AFC

	Team	Sacks		Team	Sacks		Team	Sacks
D. Thomas	K.C.	20.0	Griggs	Mia.	5.5	Nichols	N.Y.J.	3.5
B. Smith	Buff.	19.0	Maas	K.C.	5.5	Pleasant	Clev.	3.5
O'Neal	S.D.	13.5	Martin	K.C.	5.5	Rolling	S.D.	3.5
Byrd	N.Y.J.	13.0	Davis	N.Y.J.	5.0	Tippett	N.E.	3.5
Green	Sea.	12.5	Mecklenburg	Denv.	5.0	Baker	Clev.	3.0
S. Jones	Hou.	12.5	Porter	Sea.	5.0	Bayless	S.D.	3.0
Townsend	L.A.Rd	12.5	Willis	Pitt.	5.0	Evans	Pitt.	3.0
Cross	Mia.	11.5	Wright	Buff.	5.0	Hackett	K.C.	3.0
Perry	Clev.	11.5	Banks	Ind.	4.5	Hand	Ind.	3.0
Fletcher	Denv.	11.0	Bickett	Ind.	4.5	Hobby	N.E.	3.0
Davis	L.A.Rd	10.0	Lloyd	Pitt.	4.5	Hobley	Mia.	3.0
Grossman	S.D.	10.0	Mersereau	N.Y.J.	4.5	Holmes	Denv.	3.0
Smith	K.C.	9.5	Tuatagaloa	Cin.	4.5	Singleton	N.E.	3.0
Wallace	L.A.Rd	9.0	M. Washington	N.Y.J.	4.5	Woods	Sea.	3.0
Childress	Hou.	8.0	Bennett	Buff.	4.0	Agnew	N.E.	2.5
Francis	Cin.	8.0	Golic	L.A.Rd	4.0	Braggs	Clev.	2.5
Fuller	Hou.	8.0	Herrod	Ind.	4.0	Brown	N.E.	2.5
Clancy	Ind.	7.5	Lageman	N.Y.J.	4.0	Goad	N.E.	2.5
Williams	S.D.	7.5	Powers	Denv.	4.0	E. Johnson	Hou.	2.5
Saleaumua	K.C.	7.0	Seals	Buff.	4.0	Meads	Hou.	2.5
Junior	Mia.	6.0	Talley	Buff.	4.0	Oglesby	Mia.	2.5
Long	L.A.Rd	6.0	Wilson	Mia.	4.0	Bailey	Buff.	2.0
B. Williams	N.E.	6.0	Davidson	Pitt.	3.5	Brooks	Denv.	2.0
G. Williams	Pitt.	6.0	Griffin	K.C.	3.5	Burnett	Clev.	2.0
Bryant	Sea.	5.5	Matthews	Clev.	3.5	Bussey	Cin.	2.0

	Team	Sacks		Team	Sacks		Team	Sacks
Cooper	K.C.	2.0	Atwater	Denv.	1.0	Siragusa	Ind.	1.0
Faulkner	Ind.	2.0	Bell	K.C.	1.0	A. Smith	Hou.	1.0
Galloway	Denv.	2.0	Blaylock	Clev.	1.0	Smith	S.D.	1.0
Glasgow	Sea.	2.0	Brown	Mia.	1.0	Sochia	Mia.	1.0
Green	Mia.	2.0	Comeaux	Sea.	1.0	Stallworth	N.Y.J.	1.0
Hammerstein	Cin.	2.0	Conlan	Buff.	1.0	Team	S.D.	1.0
Hinkle	Pitt.	2.0	Dennison	Denv.	1.0	Townsend	Denv.	1.0
Jenkins	Pitt.	2.0	Freeman	Pitt.	1.0	Turner	Mia.	1.0
M. Johnson	Clev.	2.0	Fulcher	Cin.	1.0	Walker	Cin.	1.0
A. Jones	Pitt.	2.0	Gibson	Clev.	1.0	B. Washington	N.Y.J.	1.0
Kragen	Denv.	2.0	Glenn	Mia.	1.0	White	Cin.	1.0
Krumrie	Cin.	2.0	Grant	Cin.	1.0	J. Williams	Pitt.	1.0
Lodish	Buff.	2.0	Grayson	Clev.	1.0	Wise	L.A.Rd	1.0
McClendon	Cin.	2.0	Hicks	Buff.	1.0	Wyman	Sea.	1.0
McDaniel	L.A.Rd	2.0	Johnson	N.Y.J.	1.0	Alm	Hou.	.5
McSwain	N.E.	2.0	Kennedy	Sea.	1.0	Buck	Cin.	.5
Nickerson	Pitt.	2.0	Lake	Pitt.	1.0	Buczkowski	Clev.	.5
Robinson	L.A.Rd	2.0	Lucas	Denv.	1.0	Clifton	N.Y.J.	.5
Robinson	S.D.	2.0	McElroy	Sea.	1.0	Elder	S.D.	.5
D. Smith	Hou.	2.0	Meisner	K.C.	1.0	Gannon	N.E.	.5
Snow	K.C.	2.0	L. Miller	S.D.	1.0	Garner	Buff.	.5
Veris	N.E.	2.0	Nash	Sea.	1.0	Hinkle	S.D.	.5
Williams	Mia.	2.0	Odom	Mia.	1.0	McDowell	Hou.	.5
E. Williams	N.E.	2.0	Offerdahl	Mia.	1.0	Gl. Montgomery	Hou.	.5
Lee	Mia.	1.5	Oliver	Mia.	1.0	Patton	Buff.	.5
Pickel	L.A.Rd	1.5	Rembert	N.E.	1.0	Phillips	S.D.	.5
Smith	N.E.	1.5	Reynolds	N.E.	1.0	Walters	Clev.	.5
Thompson	Ind.	1.5	Seau	S.D.	1.0			

Interceptions—NFC

	Team	No.	Yds.	Lg.	TD		Team	No.	Yds.	Lg.	TD
Carrier	Chi.	10	39	14	0	Allen	Phil.	3	37	35	1
Haddix	T.B.	7	231	65	3	Griffin	S.F.	3	32	23	0
Browner	Minn.	7	103	31	1	Everett	T.B.	3	28	23	0
Waymer	S.F.	7	64	24	0	Lott	S.F.	3	26	15	0
Mayhew	Wash.	7	20	15	0	Washington	Dall.	3	24	13	0
Walls	N.Y.G.	6	80	40	1	Dent	Chi.	3	21	15	0
Stinson	Chi.	6	66	30	0	McMillian	Minn.	3	20	20	0
White	Det.	5	120	48	1	Woolford	Chi.	3	18	9	0
Hopkins	Phil.	5	45	21	0	Crockett	Det.	3	17	9	0
Hamilton	T.B.	5	39	27	0	Dimry	Atl.	3	16	13	0
Jackson	N.Y.G.	5	8	5	0	Jordan	Atl.	3	14	14	0
Robinson	T.B.	4	81	27	0	Reasons	N.Y.G.	3	13	10	0
McDonald	Phx.	4	63	38	0	Murphy	G.B.	3	6	4	0
Humphery	L.A.Rm	4	52	44	1	P. Williams	N.Y.G.	3	4	4	0
Newsome	L.A.Rm	4	47	22	0	B. Smith	Phil.	3	1	1	0
Green	Wash.	4	20	18	1	Butler	Atl.	3	0	0	0
Sanders	Atl.	3	153	82	2	Walton	Wash.	2	118	61	1
Merriweather	Minn.	3	108	73	0	Maxie	N.O.	2	88	50	1
Frizzell	Phil.	3	91	37	1	Cook	N.O.	2	55	50	0
Bowles	Wash.	3	74	43	0	Mack	Phx.	2	53	39	0
Holt	Dall.	3	72	64	1	Paul	Chi.	2	49	26	0
Reynolds	T.B.	3	70	46	0	Edwards	Wash.	2	33	33	0
Taylor	Phx.	3	50	34	0	Lee	Minn.	2	29	25	0
Butler	G.B.	3	42	28	0	Stephen	G.B.	2	26	26	0
Holmes	G.B.	3	39	24	0	Blades	Det.	2	25	21	0
Case	Atl.	3	38	36	1	Rutland	Minn.	2	21	16	0

	Team	No.	Yds.	Lg.	TD		Team	No.	Yds.	Lg.	TD
Mitchell	Atl.	2	16	16	0	Golic	Phil.	1	12	12	0
Atkins	N.O.	2	15	15	0	Spielman	Det.	1	12	12	0
Rivera	Chi.	2	13	13	0	Taylor	N.Y.G.	1	11	11	1
Morrissey	Chi.	2	12	12	0	Fullington	Minn.	1	10	10	0
Brim	Minn.	2	11	11	0	Joyner	Phil.	1	9	9	0
Young	Phx.	2	8	5	0	Patterson	G.B.	1	9	9	1
Rice	T.B.	2	7	4	0	Millen	S.F.	1	8	8	0
Gayle	Chi.	2	5	5	0	Marshall	Wash.	1	6	6	0
Jax	Phx.	2	5	4	0	Terrell	L.A.Rm	1	6	6	0
Collins	N.Y.G.	2	0	0	0	Bates	Dall.	1	4	4	0
Newman	L.A.Rm	2	0	0	0	A. Johnson	Wash.	1	0	0	0
Thompson	N.O.	2	0	0	0	Bell	Phx.	1	0	0	0
Turner	Phx.	1	70	47	2	Cecil	G.B.	1	0	0	0
Jackson	Chi.	1	45	45	1	Cofer	Det.	1	0	0	0
Evans	Phil.	1	43	22	1	Coleman	Wash.	1	0	0	0
McNorton	Det.	1	33	33	0	Duerson	N.Y.G.	1	0	0	0
White	Phil.	1	33	33	0	Guyton	N.Y.G.	1	0	0	0
Holland	G.B.	1	32	32	0	Hendrix	Dall.	1	0	0	0
Moss	T.B.	1	31	31	0	Henley	L.A.Rm	1	0	0	0
Doleman	Minn.	1	30	30	0	Hoage	Phil.	1	0	0	0
Lewis	S.F.	1	28	28	0	Horton	Dall.	1	0	0	0
Oldham	Det.	1	28	28	0	Johnson	N.Y.G.	1	0	0	0
Gant	Dall.	1	26	26	0	Lee	G.B.	1	0	0	0
Noga	Minn.	1	26	26	1	Pitts	G.B.	1	0	0	0
Zordich	Phx.	1	25	25	0	Pollard	S.F.	1	0	0	0
Irvin	Det.	1	22	22	0	V. Jones	Det.	1	0	0	0
Welch	Det.	1	16	16	0	Williams	Dall.	1	0	0	0
Davis	S.F.	1	13	13	0						

Interceptions—AFC

	Team	No.	Yds.	Lg.	TD		Team	No.	Yds.	Lg.	TD
R. Johnson	Hou.	8	100	35	1	Donaldson	K.C.	3	28	14	0
Byrd	S.D.	7	63	24	0	B. Washington	N.Y.J.	3	22	13	0
Ross	K.C.	5	97	40	0	McDaniel	L.A.Rd	3	20	15	0
McMillan	N.Y.J.	5	92	25	0	Harden	L.A.Rd	3	19	15	0
Oliver	Mia.	5	87	35	0	Jackson	Buff.	3	16	14	0
Williams	Mia.	5	82	42	1	Everett	Pitt.	3	2	2	0
Woodson	Pitt.	5	67	34	0	Henderson	Denv.	2	71	49	1
Lippett	N.E.	4	94	73	0	Johnson	Pitt.	2	60	34	1
Griffin	Pitt.	4	75	36	0	Talley	Buff.	2	60	60	1
Kinard	Hou.	4	75	47	0	Taylor	Ind.	2	51	40	0
Hurst	N.E.	4	61	36	0	Blaylock	Clev.	2	45	45	0
Dishman	Hou.	4	50	42	0	Curtis	N.Y.J.	2	45	23	0
McKyer	Mia.	4	40	21	0	Montgomery	Denv.	2	43	24	0
Bussey	Cin.	4	37	18	0	L. Smith	Buff.	2	39	39	1
Fulcher	Cin.	4	20	18	0	Atwater	Denv.	2	32	27	0
Marion	N.E.	4	17	16	0	Glenn	Mia.	2	31	31	1
Woodruff	Pitt.	3	110	59	0	Wyman	Sea.	2	24	22	0
Robinson	Sea.	3	89	39	0	Hagy	Buff.	2	23	23	0
Harper	Sea.	3	69	47	0	Rembert	N.E.	2	22	11	0
Prior	Ind.	3	66	36	0	Lewis	K.C.	2	15	15	0
Wright	Clev.	3	56	36	0	Seale	S.D.	2	14	14	0
Anderson	L.A.Rd	3	49	31	0	Braggs	Clev.	2	13	11	0
Clifton	N.Y.J.	3	49	39	0	Smith	S.D.	2	12	12	0
Cherry	K.C.	3	40	21	0	McDowell	Hou.	2	11	11	0
Billups	Cin.	3	39	29	0	Frank	S.D.	2	8	4	0
Petry	K.C.	3	33	33	1	Hasty	N.Y.J.	2	0	0	0

	Team	No.	Yds.	Lg.	TD		Team	No.	Yds.	Lg.	TD
Kelso	Buff.	2	0	0	0	Lloyd	Pitt.	1	9	9	0
Minnifield	Clev.	2	0	0	0	Ellison	L.A.Rd	1	7	7	0
Williams	Buff.	2	0	0	0	Fuller	S.D.	1	5	5	0
Stargell	N.Y.J.	2	-3	0	0	Kumerow	Mia.	1	5	5	0
Rolling	S.D.	1	67	67	0	Lang	Denv.	1	5	5	0
M. Johnson	Clev.	1	64	64	1	Robinson	L.A.Rd	1	5	5	1
Little	Pitt.	1	35	35	0	Willis	Pitt.	1	5	5	0
Meads	Hou.	1	32	32	0	Grayson	Clev.	1	3	3	0
Offerdahl	Mia.	1	28	28	0	Jones	Pitt.	1	3	3	0
Allen	Hou.	1	27	27	0	Washington	L.A.Rd	1	2	2	0
Grant	Ind.	1	25	25	1	Bayless	S.D.	1	0	0	0
White	Cin.	1	21	21	0	Bolcar	Sea.	1	0	0	0
Hinkle	Pitt.	1	19	19	0	Elder	S.D.	1	0	0	0
Lyles	S.D.	1	19	19	0	Glenn	S.D.	1	0	0	0
Francis	Cin.	1	17	17	1	Hall	Pitt.	1	0	0	0
Gash	Clev.	1	16	16	0	Hicks	Buff.	1	0	0	0
Plummer	Denv.	1	16	16	0	Hunter	Sea.	1	0	0	0
Hobley	Mia.	1	15	15	0	Jefferson	Sea.	1	0	0	0
Waiters	Clev.	1	15	15	0	Jenkins	Sea.	1	0	0	0
Burruss	K.C.	1	14	14	0	Knight	Hou.	1	0	0	0
Bentley	Buff.	1	13	13	0	Lake	Pitt.	1	0	0	0
Porter	K.C.	1	13	13	0	Mayes	N.Y.J.	1	0	0	0
Smith	Denv.	1	13	13	0	Odomes	Buff.	1	0	0	0
Herrod	Ind.	1	12	12	0	Pool	Buff.	1	0	0	0
Zander	Cin.	1	12	12	0	Price	Cin.	1	0	0	0
Braxton	Denv.	1	10	10	0	Seals	Buff.	1	0	0	0
Goode	Ind.	1	10	10	0	Snow	K.C.	1	0	0	0
Pearson	K.C.	1	10	10	0	Townsend	L.A.Rd	1	0	0	0
Bickett	Ind.	1	9	9	0						

Scoring—NFC

	Team	TD	XP/att.	FG/att.	Saf.	Pts.		Team	TD	XP/att.	FG/att.	Saf.	Pts.
Lohmiller	Wash.	0	41/41	30/40	0	131	Barnett	Phil.	8	0/0	0/0	0	48
Butler	Chi.	0	36/37	26/37	0	114	Clark	Det.	8	0/0	0/0	0	48
Cofer	S.F.	0	39/39	24/36	0	111	Clark	Wash.	8	0/0	0/0	0	48
Ruzek	Phil.	0	45/48	21/29	0	108	Byner	Wash.	7	0/0	0/0	0	42
Davis	Atl.	0	40/40	22/33	0	106	H. Jones	Minn.	7	0/0	0/0	0	42
Jacke	G.B.	0	28/29	23/30	0	97	Mayes	N.O.	7	0/0	0/0	0	42
B. Sanders	Det.	16	0/0	0/0	0	96	Rathman	S.F.	7	0/0	0/0	0	42
Christie	T.B.	0	27/27	23/27	0	96	Taylor	S.F.	7	0/0	0/0	0	42
Andersen	N.O.	0	29/29	21/27	0	92	Johnson	Det.	6	0/0	0/0	0	36
Gary	L.A.Rm	15	0/0	0/0	0	90	Kel. Jackson	Phil.	6	0/0	0/0	0	36
Lansford	L.A.Rm	0	42/43	15/24	0	87	Muster	Chi.	6	0/0	0/0	0	36
Del Greco	Phx.	0	31/31	17/27	0	82	Peete	Det.	6	0/0	0/0	0	36
Bahr	N.Y.G.	0	29/30	17/23	0	80	Riggs	Wash.	6	0/0	0/0	0	36
Willis	Dall.	0	26/26	18/25	0	80	Sharpe	B.G.	6	0/0	0/0	0	36
Anderson	Chi.	13	0/0	0/0	0	78	Bavaro	N.Y.G.	5	0/0	0/0	0	30
Rice	S.F.	13	0/0	0/0	0	78	Cunningham	Phil.	5	0/0	0/0	0	30
Murray	Det.	0	34/34	13/19	0	73	E. Martin	N.O.	5	0/0	0/0	0	30
Anderson	N.Y.G.	11	0/0	0/0	0	66	G. Anderson	T.B.	5	0/0	0/0	0	30
E. Smith	Dall.	11	0/0	0/0	0	66	Hill	T.B.	5	0/0	0/0	0	30
Igwebuike	Minn.	0	19/19	14/16	0	61	Ingram	N.Y.G.	5	0/0	0/0	0	30
Rison	Atl.	10	0/0	0/0	0	60	Irvin	Dall.	5	0/0	0/0	0	30
Walker	Minn.	9	0/0	0/0	0	54	Johnson	Phx.	5	0/0	0/0	0	30
Williams	Phil.	9	0/0	0/0	0	54	Jones	S.F.	5	0/0	0/0	0	30
Reveiz	Minn.	0	19/20	11/12	0	52	McGee	L.A.Rm	5	0/0	0/0	0	30
A. Carter	Minn.	8	0/0	0/0	0	48	Monk	Wash.	5	0/0	0/0	0	30

	Team	TD	XP/att.	FG/att.	Saf.	Pts.		Team	TD	XP/att.	FG/att.	Saf.	Pts.
West	G.B.	5	0/0	0/0	0	30	Sherrard	S.F.	2	0/0	0/0	0	12
Anderson	L.A.Rm	4	0/0	0/0	0	24	Thompson	G.B.	2	0/0	0/0	0	12
Baker	N.Y.G.	4	0/0	0/0	0	24	Tomczak	Chi.	2	0/0	0/0	0	12
Broussard	Atl.	4	0/0	0/0	0	24	Turner	Phx.	2	0/0	0/0	0	12
Carrier	T.B.	4	0/0	0/0	0	24	Wilkins	Atl.	2	0/0	0/0	0	12
Delpino	L.A.Rm	4	0/0	0/0	0	24	Agee	Dall.	1	0/0	0/0	0	6
Dixon	Atl.	4	0/0	0/0	0	24	Aikman	Dall.	1	0/0	0/0	0	6
Ellard	L.A.Rm	4	0/0	0/0	0	24	Allen	Phil.	1	0/0	0/0	0	6
Green	Phx.	4	0/0	0/0	0	24	Bailey	Chi.	1	0/0	0/0	0	6
Hampton	N.Y.G.	4	0/0	0/0	0	24	Boso	Chi.	1	0/0	0/0	0	6
Harbaugh	Chi.	4	0/0	0/0	0	24	Browner	Minn.	1	0/0	0/0	0	6
Heyward	N.O.	4	0/0	0/0	0	24	Bryant	Wash.	1	0/0	0/0	0	6
Johnson	Atl.	4	0/0	0/0	0	24	Case	Atl.	1	0/0	0/0	0	6
Jones	Phx.	4	0/0	0/0	0	24	Chandler	T.B.	1	0/0	0/0	0	6
Karlis	Det.	0	12/12	4/7	0	24	Craig	S.F.	1	0/0	0/0	0	6
Novacek	Dall.	4	0/0	0/0	0	24	Crockett	Det.	1	0/0	0/0	0	6
Proehl	Phx.	4	0/0	0/0	0	24	D. Carter	S.F.	1	0/0	0/0	0	6
Sherman	Phil.	4	0/0	0/0	0	24	Dent	Chi.	1	0/0	0/0	0	6
Thompson	Phx.	4	0/0	0/0	0	24	Drewrey	T.B.	1	0/0	0/0	0	6
Toney	Phil.	4	0/0	0/0	0	24	Drummond	Phil.	1	0/0	0/0	0	6
Turner	N.O.	4	0/0	0/0	0	24	Duerson	N.Y.G.	1	0/0	0/0	0	6
Allegre	N.Y.G.	0	9/9	4/5	0	21	Evans	Phil.	1	0/0	0/0	0	6
Byars	Phil.	3	0/0	0/0	0	18	Everett	L.A.Rm	1	0/0	0/0	0	6
C. Carter	Minn.	3	0/0	0/0	0	18	Faison	L.A.Rm	1	0/0	0/0	0	6
Davis	Chi.	3	0/0	0/0	0	18	Fontenot	G.B.	1	0/0	0/0	0	6
Greer	Det.	3	0/0	0/0	0	18	Fourcade	N.O.	1	0/0	0/0	0	6
Haddix	T.B.	3	0/0	0/0	0	18	Frizzell	Phil.	1	0/0	0/0	0	6
Johnson	L.A.Rm	3	0/0	0/0	0	18	Fullwood	G.B.	1	0/0	0/0	0	6
Jordan	Minn.	3	0/0	0/0	0	18	Gannon	Minn.	1	0/0	0/0	0	6
Morris	Chi.	3	0/0	0/0	0	18	Gouveia	Wash.	1	0/0	0/0	0	6
Query	G.B.	3	0/0	0/0	0	18	Green	Chi.	1	0/0	0/0	0	6
Rosenbach	Phx.	3	0/0	0/0	0	18	Green	Wash.	1	0/0	0/0	0	6
Rozier	Atl.	3	0/0	0/0	0	18	Greene	G.B.	1	0/0	0/0	0	6
Sanders	Atl.	3	0/0	0/0	0	18	Hargrove	Phil.	1	0/0	0/0	0	6
Sanders	Wash.	3	0/0	0/0	0	18	Harvey	T.B.	1	0/0	0/0	0	6
Sydney	S.F.	3	0/0	0/0	0	18	Hilliard	N.O.	1	0/0	0/0	0	6
Anderson	Minn.	2	0/0	0/0	0	12	Hobbs	Wash.	1	0/0	0/0	0	6
Brenner	N.O.	2	0/0	0/0	0	12	Holt	Dall.	1	0/0	0/0	0	6
Butler	Atl.	2	0/0	0/0	0	12	Humphery	L.A.Rm	1	0/0	0/0	0	6
Campbell	Det.	2	0/0	0/0	0	12	J. Williams	Det.	1	0/0	0/0	0	6
Cobb	T.B.	2	0/0	0/0	0	12	Jackson	Chi.	1	0/0	0/0	0	6
Collins	Atl.	2	0/0	0/0	0	12	Jones	Atl.	1	0/0	0/0	0	6
Fenerty	N.O.	2	0/0	0/0	0	12	Kiel	G.B.	1	0/0	0/0	0	6
Fenney	Minn.	2	0/0	0/0	0	12	Majkowski	G.B.	1	0/0	0/0	0	6
Flagler	Phx.	2	0/0	0/0	0	12	Matthews	Det.	1	0/0	0/0	0	6
Gentry	Chi.	2	0/0	0/0	0	12	Maxie	N.O.	1	0/0	0/0	0	6
Green	L.A.Rm	2	0/0	0/0	0	12	McKinnon	Dall.	1	0/0	0/0	0	6
Haddix	G.B.	2	0/0	0/0	0	12	Merriweather	Minn.	1	0/0	0/0	0	6
Hall	T.B.	2	0/0	0/0	0	12	Miller	Atl.	1	0/0	0/0	0	6
Holohan	L.A.Rm	2	0/0	0/0	0	12	Milling	Atl.	1	0/0	0/0	0	6
Hostetler	N.Y.G.	2	0/0	0/0	0	12	Mitchell	Wash.	1	0/0	0/0	0	6
Humphries	Wash.	2	0/0	0/0	0	12	Montana	S.F.	1	0/0	0/0	0	6
J. Johnson	Wash.	2	0/0	0/0	0	12	Mrosko	N.Y.G.	1	0/0	0/0	0	6
J. Smith	Phx.	2	0/0	0/0	0	12	Patterson	G.B.	1	0/0	0/0	0	6
Johnston	Dall.	2	0/0	0/0	0	12	Peebles	T.B.	1	0/0	0/0	0	6
Kemp	G.B.	2	0/0	0/0	0	12	Quick	Phil.	1	0/0	0/0	0	6
Meggett	N.Y.G.	2	0/0	0/0	0	12	Rutledge	Wash.	1	0/0	0/0	0	6
Noga	Minn.	2	0/0	0/0	0	12	Sanders	Phil.	1	0/0	0/0	0	6
Perkins	T.B.	2	0/0	0/0	0	12	Scales	N.O.	1	0/0	0/0	0	6
Perriman	N.O.	2	0/0	0/0	0	12	Sharpe	Phx.	1	0/0	0/0	0	6

	Team	TD	XP/att.	FG/att.	Saf.	Pts.		Team	TD	XP/att.	FG/att.	Saf.	Pts.
Simmons	Phil.	1	0/0	0/0	0	6	Warren	Wash.	1	0/0	0/0	0	6
Simms	N.Y.G.	1	0/0	0/0	0	6	Weathers	G.B.	1	0/0	0/0	0	6
Taylor	N.Y.G.	1	0/0	0/0	0	6	White	Det.	1	0/0	0/0	0	6
Testaverde	T.B.	1	0/0	0/0	0	6	Wilder	Det.	1	0/0	0/0	0	6
Thomas	Atl.	1	0/0	0/0	0	6	Woodside	G.B.	1	0/0	0/0	0	6
Thornton	Chi.	1	0/0	0/0	0	6	Workman	G.B.	1	0/0	0/0	0	6
Tillman	N.Y.G.	1	0/0	0/0	0	6	Wright	Dall.	1	0/0	0/0	0	6
Tuggle	Atl.	1	0/0	0/0	0	6	Coleman	Wash.	0	0/0	0/0	1	2
Vick	Phil.	1	0/0	0/0	0	6	Doleman	Minn.	0	0/0	0/0	1	2
Walls	N.Y.G.	1	0/0	0/0	0	6	Dusbabek	Minn.	0	0/0	0/0	1	2
Walton	Wash.	1	0/0	0/0	0	6	Green	Atl.	0	0/0	0/0	1	2
Warner	L.A.Rm	1	0/0	0/0	0	6	Turner	S.F.	0	0/0	0/0	1	2
							team	Wash.	0	0/0	0/0	1	2

Scoring—AFC

	Team	TD	XP/att.	FG/att.	Saf.	Pts.		Team	TD	XP/att.	FG/att.	Saf.	Pts.
Lowery	K.C.	0	37/38	34/37	0	139	Brooks	Ind.	5	0/0	0/0	0	30
Norwood	Buff.	0	50/52	20/29	0	110	Cook	N.E.	5	0/0	0/0	0	30
Treadwell	Denv.	0	34/36	25/34	0	109	Duper	Mia.	5	0/0	0/0	0	30
Johnson	Sea.	0	33/34	23/32	0	102	Fernandez	L.A.Rd	5	0/0	0/0	0	30
Leahy	N.Y.J.	0	32/32	23/26	0	101	Hill	Hou.	5	0/0	0/0	0	30
Stoyanovich	Mia.	0	37/37	21/25	0	100	Holman	Cin.	5	0/0	0/0	0	30
Anderson	Pitt.	0	32/32	20/25	0	92	Jackson	Denv.	5	0/0	0/0	0	30
Breech	Cin.	0	41/44	17/21	0	92	Jackson	L.A.Rd	5	0/0	0/0	0	30
Fenner	Sea.	15	0/0	0/0	0	90	K. Davis	Buff.	5	0/0	0/0	0	30
Jaeger	L.A.Rd	0	40/42	15/20	0	85	McKeller	Buff.	5	0/0	0/0	0	30
Carney	S.D.	0	27/28	19/21	0	84	Morgan	Ind.	5	0/0	0/0	0	30
Biasucci	Ind.	0	32/33	17/24	0	83	Paige	K.C.	5	0/0	0/0	0	30
Allen	L.A.Rd	13	0/0	0/0	0	78	Smith	L.A.Rd	5	0/0	0/0	0	30
Thomas	Buff.	13	0/0	0/0	0	78	Bernstine	S.D.	4	0/0	0/0	0	24
White	Hou.	12	0/0	0/0	0	72	Bratton	Denv.	4	0/0	0/0	0	24
Garcia	Hou.	0	26/28	14/20	0	68	Chadwick	Sea.	4	0/0	0/0	0	24
Staurovsky	N.E.	0	19/19	16/22	0	67	Dickerson	Ind.	4	0/0	0/0	0	24
Kauric	Clev.	0	24/27	14/20	0	66	Fryar	N.E.	4	0/0	0/0	0	24
Hoge	Pitt.	10	0/0	0/0	0	60	Kane	Sea.	4	0/0	0/0	0	24
Brooks	Cin.	9	0/0	0/0	0	54	Lofton	Buff.	4	0/0	0/0	0	24
Brown	Cin.	9	0/0	0/0	0	54	McNeil	N.Y.J.	6	0/0	0/0	0	24
Givins	Hou.	9	0/0	0/0	0	54	Metcalf	Clev.	4	0/0	0/0	0	24
Smith	Mia.	9	0/0	0/0	0	54	R. Thomas	K.C.	4	0/0	0/0	0	24
Butts	S.D.	8	0/0	0/0	0	48	Slaughter	Clev.	4	0/0	0/0	0	24
Jeffires	Hou.	8	0/0	0/0	0	48	W. Williams	Pitt.	4	0/0	0/0	0	24
Reed	Buff.	8	0/0	0/0	0	48	Word	K.C.	4	0/0	0/0	0	24
A. Miller	S.D.	7	0/0	0/0	0	42	Young	Denv.	4	0/0	0/0	0	24
Green	Pitt.	7	0/0	0/0	0	42	Birden	K.C.	3	0/0	0/0	0	18
Humphrey	Denv.	7	0/0	0/0	0	42	Blades	Sea.	3	0/0	0/0	0	18
Mack	Clev.	7	0/0	0/0	0	42	Clayton	Mia.	3	0/0	0/0	0	18
Okoye	K.C.	7	0/0	0/0	0	42	Elway	Denv.	3	0/0	0/0	0	18
Zendejas	Hou.	0	20/21	7/12	0	41	Gault	L.A.Rd	3	0/0	0/0	0	18
Baxter	N.Y.J.	6	0/0	0/0	0	36	Harris	Hou.	3	0/0	0/0	0	18
Bentley	Ind.	6	0/0	0/0	0	36	Hoard	Clev.	3	0/0	0/0	0	18
Hester	Ind.	6	0/0	0/0	0	36	Horton	L.A.Rd	3	0/0	0/0	0	18
Moore	N.Y.J.	6	0/0	0/0	0	36	Johnson	Denv.	3	0/0	0/0	0	18
Paige	Mia.	6	0/0	0/0	0	36	Lewis	S.D.	3	0/0	0/0	0	18
T. Jones	Hou.	6	0/0	0/0	0	36	Lipps	Pitt.	3	0/0	0/0	0	18
Toon	N.Y.J.	6	0/0	0/0	0	36	McEwen	S.D.	3	0/0	0/0	0	18
Woods	Cin.	6	0/0	0/0	0	36	Mueller	Buff.	3	0/0	0/0	0	18
B. Jones	K.C.	5	0/0	0/0	0	30	Mularkey	Pitt.	3	0/0	0/0	0	18

	Team	TD	XP/att.	FG/att.	Saf.	Pts.		Team	TD	XP/att.	FG/att.	Saf.	Pts.
Pruitt	Mia.	3	0/0	0/0	0	18	Glenn	Mia.	1	0/0	0/0	0	6
Rolle	Buff.	3	0/0	0/0	0	18	Goode	Ind.	1	0/0	0/0	0	6
Sewell	Denv.	3	0/0	0/0	0	18	Graddy	L.A.Rd	1	0/0	0/0	0	6
Stephens	N.E.	3	0/0	0/0	0	18	Grant	Ind.	1	0/0	0/0	0	6
T. Brown	L.A.Rd	3	0/0	0/0	0	18	Hayes	K.C.	1	0/0	0/0	0	6
Taylor	Cin.	3	0/0	0/0	0	18	Heller	Sea.	1	0/0	0/0	0	6
Williams	Sea.	3	0/0	0/0	0	18	Henderson	Denv.	1	0/0	0/0	0	6
Reveiz	S.D.	0	7/8	2/7	0	13	Higgs	Mia.	1	0/0	0/0	0	6
Ball	Cin.	2	0/0	0/0	0	12	Jennings	Cin.	1	0/0	0/0	0	6
Brennan	Clev.	2	0/0	0/0	0	12	Jensen	Mia.	1	0/0	0/0	0	6
D. Smith	Buff.	2	0/0	0/0	0	12	Johnson	Pitt.	1	0/0	0/0	0	6
Dykes	N.E.	2	0/0	0/0	0	12	Kinard	Hou.	1	0/0	0/0	0	6
Green	Cin.	2	0/0	0/0	0	12	Kinnebrew	Buff.	1	0/0	0/0	0	6
Harmon	S.D.	2	0/0	0/0	0	12	L. Smith	Buff.	1	0/0	0/0	0	6
Harry	K.C.	2	0/0	0/0	0	12	M. Johnson	Clev.	1	0/0	0/0	0	6
Hector	N.Y.J.	2	0/0	0/0	0	12	Martin	K.C.	1	0/0	0/0	0	6
Hodson	N.E.	2	0/0	0/0	0	12	Martin	N.E.	1	0/0	0/0	0	6
Johnson	Ind.	2	0/0	0/0	0	12	Mathis	N.Y.J.	1	0/0	0/0	0	6
Kattus	Cin.	2	0/0	0/0	0	12	McDaniel	L.A.Rd	1	0/0	0/0	0	6
L. Miller	S.D.	2	0/0	0/0	0	12	McGee	Cin.	1	0/0	0/0	0	6
Langhorne	Clev.	2	0/0	0/0	0	12	Metzelaars	Buff.	1	0/0	0/0	0	6
Logan	Mia.	2	0/0	0/0	0	12	Odom	Mia.	1	0/0	0/0	0	6
Martin	Mia.	2	0/0	0/0	0	12	Odomes	Buff.	1	0/0	0/0	0	6
McNair	K.C.	2	0/0	0/0	0	12	Perryman	N.E.	1	0/0	0/0	0	6
Moon	Hou.	2	0/0	0/0	0	12	Petry	K.C.	1	0/0	0/0	0	6
Nattiel	Denv.	2	0/0	0/0	0	12	Price	Cin.	1	0/0	0/0	0	6
Newsome	Clev.	2	0/0	0/0	0	12	R. Johnson	Hou.	1	0/0	0/0	0	6
Plummer	S.D.	2	0/0	0/0	0	12	Robinson	L.A.Rd	1	0/0	0/0	0	6
Skansi	Sea.	2	0/0	0/0	0	12	Robinson	Sea.	1	0/0	0/0	0	6
Tasker	Buff.	2	0/0	0/0	0	12	Ross	K.C.	1	0/0	0/0	0	6
Thomas	N.Y.J.	2	0/0	0/0	0	12	Saleaumua	K.C.	1	0/0	0/0	0	6
Winder	Denv.	2	0/0	0/0	0	12	Schwedes	Mia.	1	0/0	0/0	0	6
Francis	Cin.	1	0/0	0/0	1	8	Sharpe	Denv.	1	0/0	0/0	0	6
Mecklenburg	Denv.	1	0/0	0/0	1	8	Sochia	Mia.	1	0/0	0/0	0	6
Adams	N.E.	1	0/0	0/0	0	6	Stone	Pitt.	1	0/0	0/0	0	6
Allen	N.E.	1	0/0	0/0	0	6	Stradford	Mia.	1	0/0	0/0	0	6
B. Williams	N.E.	1	0/0	0/0	0	6	Talley	Buff.	1	0/0	0/0	0	6
Barber	Cin.	1	0/0	0/0	0	6	Taylor	N.Y.J.	1	0/0	0/0	0	6
Beach	Ind.	1	0/0	0/0	0	6	Taylor	S.D.	1	0/0	0/0	0	6
Beebe	Buff.	1	0/0	0/0	0	6	Townsend	L.A.Rd	1	0/0	0/0	0	6
Bell	L.A.Rd	1	0/0	0/0	0	6	Verdin	Ind.	1	0/0	0/0	0	6
Bell	Pitt.	1	0/0	0/0	0	6	Walker	S.D.	1	0/0	0/0	0	6
Bennett	Buff.	1	0/0	0/0	0	6	Warren	Sea.	1	0/0	0/0	0	6
Blaylock	Clev.	1	0/0	0/0	0	6	Whitaker	K.C.	1	0/0	0/0	0	6
Boyer	N.Y.J.	1	0/0	0/0	0	6	Williams	Buff.	1	0/0	0/0	0	6
Bussey	Cin.	1	0/0	0/0	0	6	Williams	Mia.	1	0/0	0/0	0	6
Calloway	Pitt.	1	0/0	0/0	0	6	Woodson	Pitt.	1	0/0	0/0	0	6
Caravello	S.D.	1	0/0	0/0	0	6	Byrd	N.Y.J.	0	0/0	0/0	1	2
Cox	S.D.	1	0/0	0/0	0	6	Childress	Hou.	0	0/0	0/0	1	2
Davis	N.Y.J.	1	0/0	0/0	0	6	Fletcher	Denv.	0	0/0	0/0	1	2
Duncan	Hou.	1	0/0	0/0	0	6	Fulcher	Cin.	0	0/0	0/0	1	2
Early	S.D.	1	0/0	0/0	0	6	Grossman	S.D.	0	0/0	0/0	1	2
Edmunds	Mia.	1	0/0	0/0	0	6	Maas	K.C.	0	0/0	0/0	1	2
Ford	Hou.	1	0/0	0/0	0	6	Stowe	Pitt.	0	0/0	0/0	1	2
Foster	Pitt.	1	0/0	0/0	0	6	Team	Denv.	0	0/0	0/0	1	2
Gainer	Clev.	1	0/0	0/0	0	6	Team	Mia.	0	0/0	0/0	1	2
George	Ind.	1	0/0	0/0	0	6							

Punting—NFC

	Team	No.	Yds.	Lg.	Gross Avg.	TB	Ins. 20	Blk.	Ret.	Ret. Yds.	Net Avg.
Camarillo	Phx.	67	2,865	63	42.8	5	16	0	41	258	37.4
Landeta	N.Y.G.	75	3,306	67	44.1	11	24	0	41	291	37.3
Barnhardt	N.O.	70	2,990	65	42.7	6	20	1	43	302	36.2
Fulhage	Atl.	70	2,913	59	41.6	4	15	0	39	314	36.0
Saxon	Dall.	79	3,413	62	43.2	8	20	0	43	438	35.6
Feagles	Phil.	72	3,026	60	42.0	3	20	2	37	338	35.5
Arnold	Det.	63	2,560	59	40.6	5	10	0	29	233	35.3
Mojsiejenko	Wash.	43	1,687	53	39.2	0	17	1	25	182	34.2
Royals	T.B.	72	2,902	62	40.3	5	8	0	39	352	34.0
Buford	Chi.	76	3,073	59	40.4	7	22	2	39	322	33.5
Newsome	Minn.	78	3,299	61	42.3	8	19	1	44	513	33.2
Bracken	G.B.	64	2,431	59	38.0	2	17	1	34	266	32.7
English	L.A.Rm	68	2,663	58	39.2	2	8	1	46	420	31.9
Helton	S.F.	69	2,537	56	36.8	8	15	1	30	215	30.9

Non-qualifiers

	Team	No.	Yds.	Lg.	Gross Avg.	TB	Ins. 20	Blk.	Ret.	Ret. Yds.	Net Avg.
Goodburn	Wash.	11	377	48	34.3	1	6	0	5	23	30.4

Punting—AFC

	Team	No.	Yds.	Lg.	Gross Avg.	TB	Ins. 20	Blk.	Ret.	Ret. Yds.	Net Avg.
Horan	Denv.	58	2,575	67	44.4	6	14	1	22	159	38.9
Stark	Ind.	71	3,084	61	43.4	3	24	1	42	334	37.4
Kidd	S.D.	61	2,442	59	40.0	2	14	1	28	131	36.6
Roby	Mia.	72	3,022	62	42.0	3	20	0	40	397	35.6
Prokop	N.Y.J.	59	2,363	58	40.1	3	18	0	33	257	34.7
Donnelly	Sea.	67	2,722	54	40.6	8	18	0	29	254	34.4
Johnson	Cin.	64	2,705	70	42.3	8	12	0	36	352	34.3
Tuten	Buff.	53	2,107	55	39.8	4	12	0	26	214	34.2
Stryzinski	Pitt.	65	2,454	51	37.8	5	18	1	16	105	34.1
Hansen	N.E.	90	3,752	69	41.7	8	18	2	50	503	33.6
Gossett	L.A.Rd	60	2,315	57	38.6	4	18	2	24	153	33.6
Barker	K.C.	64	2,479	56	38.7	1	16	0	38	324	33.4
Wagner	Clev.	74	2,879	65	38.9	2	13	4	41	425	30.9

Non-qualifiers

	Team	No.	Yds.	Lg.	Gross Avg.	TB	Ins. 20	Blk.	Ret.	Ret. Yds.	Net Avg.
Gr. Montgomery	Hou.	34	1,530	60	45.0	5	7	0	23	186	36.6
Goodburn	K.C.	17	653	58	38.4	2	6	0	6	87	30.9
Nies	Buff.	5	174	39	34.8	0	0	0	5	37	27.4
Elway	Denv.	1	37	37	37.0	1	0	0	0	0	17.0
Breech	Cin.	1	34	34	34.0	1	0	0	0	0	14.0
Leahy	N.Y.J.	1	12	12	12.0	0	0	0	0	0	12.0
O'Brien	N.Y.J.	1	23	23	23.0	0	0	0	3	18	5.0

Kickoff Returns—NFC

	Team	No.	Yds.	Avg.	Lg.	TD		Team	No.	Yds.	Avg.	Lg.	TD
Meggett	N.Y.G.	21	492	23.4	58	0	Smith	Minn.	1	16	16.0	16	0
Gray	Det.	41	939	22.9	65	0	Walls	S.F.	1	16	16.0	16	0
Wilson	G.B.	35	798	22.8	36	0	Hobbs	Wash.	6	92	15.3	21	0
Green	L.A.Rm	25	560	22.4	99	1	Workman	G.B.	14	210	15.0	26	0
Walker	Minn.	44	966	22.0	64	0	Broussard	Atl.	3	45	15.0	23	0
Sanders	Atl.	39	851	21.8	50	0	Green	Phx.	1	15	15.0	15	0
Dixon	Dall.	36	736	20.4	47	0	Griffin	S.F.	1	15	15.0	15	0
Fenerty	N.O.	28	572	20.4	58	0	McDonald	L.A.Rm	1	15	15.0	15	0
Sikahema	Phx.	27	544	20.1	32	0	Stepnoski	Dall.	1	15	15.0	15	0
Howard	Wash.	24	467	19.5	35	0	Bland	G.B.	7	104	14.9	24	0
Delpino	L.A.Rm	20	389	19.5	38	0	Rice	Minn.	12	176	14.7	24	0
D. Carter	S.F.	42	783	18.6	35	0	Anderson	Minn.	3	44	14.7	24	0
Hampton	N.Y.G.	20	340	17.0	33	0	Morse	N.O.	4	56	14.0	18	0
Bailey	Chi.	23	363	15.8	30	0	Ingram	N.Y.G.	3	42	14.0	26	0
							Jenkins	Phil.	1	14	14.0	14	0

Non-qualifiers

	Team	No.	Yds.	Avg.	Lg.	TD		Team	No.	Yds.	Avg.	Lg.	TD
Gordon	Atl.	1	43	43.0	43	0	Pringle	Atl.	1	14	14.0	14	0
Thompson	G.B.	3	103	34.3	76	1	Proehl	Phx.	4	53	13.3	15	0
Jones	Atl.	8	236	29.5	76	1	Lewis	Minn.	3	39	13.0	15	0
Fontenot	G.B.	3	88	29.3	50	0	Case	Atl.	1	13	13.0	13	0
Atkins	N.O.	19	471	24.8	50	0	V. Buck	N.O.	3	38	12.7	17	0
Wright	Dall.	12	276	23.0	90	1	Edwards	Phil.	3	36	12.0	14	0
Harris	Phil.	2	44	22.0	44	0	Andolsek	Det.	1	12	12.0	12	0
Sanders	Wash.	1	22	22.0	22	0	Heyward	N.O.	1	12	12.0	12	0
Gentry	Chi.	18	388	21.6	59	0	Gouveia	Wash.	2	23	11.5	15	0
Phillips	Det.	2	43	21.5	23	0	Vick	Phil.	2	22	11.0	13	0
Ken. Jackson	Phil.	6	125	20.8	30	0	Cross	N.Y.G.	1	10	10.0	10	0
Peebles	T.B.	18	369	20.5	55	0	Coleman	T.B.	1	9	9.0	9	0
G. Anderson	T.B.	6	123	20.5	37	0	Jax	Phx.	2	17	8.5	9	0
Mitchell	Wash.	18	365	20.3	37	0	Middleton	Wash.	1	7	7.0	7	0
Cobb	T.B.	11	223	20.3	45	0	Wilkins	Atl.	1	7	7.0	7	0
Sanders	Phil.	15	299	19.9	37	0	Hillary	Minn.	1	6	6.0	6	0
Campbell	Det.	12	238	19.8	38	0	Rouse	Chi.	3	17	5.7	10	0
Stanley	Wash.	9	177	19.7	37	0	Schreiber	Minn.	1	5	5.0	5	0
Mayes	N.O.	2	39	19.5	21	0	Williams	S.F.	2	7	3.5	7	0
Shepard	Dall.	4	75	18.8	22	0	Allen	Phil.	1	2	2.0	2	0
Berry	L.A.Rm	17	315	18.5	29	0	Johnson	Atl.	2	2	1.0	6	0
Tillman	S.F.	6	111	18.5	30	0	Dupard	Wash.	2	0	0.0	0	0
Oldham	Det.	13	234	18.0	42	0	Bowles	Wash.	1	0	0.0	0	0
Lang	Atl.	1	18	18.0	18	0	Dixon	Atl.	1	0	0.0	0	0
Hargrove	Phil.	19	341	18.0	30	0	Hager	Phil.	1	0	0.0	0	0
Drewrey	T.B.	14	244	17.4	29	0	Hall	T.B.	1	0	0.0	0	0
Harvey	T.B.	12	207	17.3	27	0	Haynes	Atl.	1	0	0.0	0	0
Centers	Phx.	16	272	17.0	26	0	L. Tate	Chi.	1	0	0.0	0	0
Bellamy	Phil.	1	17	17.0	17	0	McKnight	Det.	1	0	0.0	0	0
Mack	N.O.	1	17	17.0	17	0	Roper	Chi.	1	0	0.0	0	0
Flagler	Phx.	10	167	16.7	27	0	West	G.B.	1	0	0.0	0	0
Sydney	S.F.	2	33	16.5	19	0	Whitmore	N.Y.G.	1	0	0.0	0	0
Barnett	Phil.	4	65	16.3	22	0	Guyton	N.Y.G.	0	0	0.0	0	0
Green	Chi.	7	112	16.0	20	0	Ryan	Chi.	1	−1	−1.0	−1	0
							Jordan	Minn.	1	−3	−3.0	−3	0

Kickoff Returns—AFC

	Team	No.	Yds.	Avg.	Lg.	TD
Clark	Denv.	20	505	25.3	75	0
Elder	S.D.	24	571	23.8	90	0
Woodson	Pitt.	35	764	21.8	49	0
Warren	Sea.	23	478	20.8	71	0
Martin	N.E.	25	515	20.6	38	0
Holland	L.A.Rd	32	655	20.5	87	0
McNeil	Hou.	27	551	20.4	64	0
Metcalf	Clev.	52	1,052	20.2	101	2
Jennings	Cin.	29	584	20.1	33	0
D. Smith	Buff.	32	643	20.1	38	0
R. Brown	L.A.Rd	30	575	19.2	34	0
Mathis	N.Y.J.	43	787	18.3	35	0
Logan	Mia.	20	357	17.9	35	0

Non-qualifiers

	Team	No.	Yds.	Avg.	Lg.	TD
Brown	N.Y.J.	1	63	63.0	63	0
James	Cin.	1	43	43.0	43	0
Schwedes	Mia.	2	52	26.0	30	0
Jefferson	Sea.	4	96	24.0	26	0
Edwards	Buff.	11	256	23.3	54	0
Ball	Cin.	16	366	22.9	38	0
Pinkett	Hou.	4	91	22.8	28	0
Townsell	N.Y.J.	7	158	22.6	38	0
Lewis	S.D.	17	383	22.5	39	0
Frank	S.D.	8	172	21.5	31	0
Higgs	Mia.	10	210	21.0	30	0
Johnson	Denv.	6	126	21.0	39	0
Timpson	N.E.	3	62	20.7	26	0
Worthen	K.C.	11	226	20.5	32	0
Montgomery	Denv.	14	286	20.4	59	0
Loville	Sea.	18	359	19.9	29	0
Beebe	Buff.	6	119	19.8	27	0
Fullwood	Clev.	6	119	19.8	27	0
F. Jones	K.C.	9	175	19.4	46	0
Verdin	Ind.	18	350	19.4	44	0
Bentley	Ind.	11	211	19.2	36	0
Robinson	N.E.	11	211	19.2	27	0
Price	Cin.	10	191	19.1	33	0
Overton	N.E.	10	188	18.8	23	0
Grant	Ind.	15	280	18.7	29	0
Stradford	Mia.	3	56	18.7	21	0
Morris	N.E.	11	202	18.4	22	0
Simmons	Ind.	19	348	18.3	34	0
Stone	Pitt.	5	91	18.2	24	0
Jackson	Denv.	1	18	18.0	18	0
Paige	Mia.	1	18	18.0	18	0
Odegard	N.Y.J.	5	89	17.8	25	0
Smith	Cin.	2	35	17.5	20	0
Ezor	Denv.	13	214	16.5	50	0
McNair	K.C.	14	227	16.2	23	0
Saxon	K.C.	5	81	16.2	23	0
Green	Pitt.	1	16	16.0	16	0
Kinchen	Mia.	1	16	16.0	16	0
Taylor	Cin.	1	16	16.0	16	0
Ford	Hou.	14	219	15.6	23	0
Allen	N.E.	11	168	15.3	34	0
Collins	Mia.	2	30	15.0	30	0
Barnett	Clev.	1	15	15.0	15	0
McNeal	Sea.	2	29	14.5	17	0
Barber	Cin.	1	14	14.0	14	0
Birden	K.C.	1	14	14.0	14	0
Boyer	N.Y.J.	1	14	14.0	14	0
Winder	Denv.	4	55	13.8	24	0
A. Miller	S.D.	1	13	13.0	13	0
Orr	S.D.	1	13	13.0	13	0
Mandley	K.C.	4	51	12.8	23	0
Bratton	Denv.	3	37	12.3	18	0
Jones	N.E.	2	24	12.0	13	0
Rolle	Buff.	2	22	11.0	11	0
Jones	Sea.	2	21	10.5	13	0
J. Williams	Pitt.	3	31	10.3	20	0
Kattus	Cin.	1	10	10.0	10	0
Word	K.C.	1	10	10.0	10	0
Adams	Mia.	5	49	9.8	15	0
Foster	Pitt.	3	29	9.7	13	0
Nelson	S.D.	4	36	9.0	26	0
Coleman	N.E.	2	18	9.0	12	0
Hoard	Clev.	2	18	9.0	10	0
Lipps	Pitt.	1	9	9.0	9	0
Mobley	Ind.	1	9	9.0	9	0
Sims	Mia.	1	9	9.0	9	0
E. Johnson	Clev.	2	17	8.5	11	0
Griffin	Pitt.	2	16	8.0	14	0
Duffy	N.Y.J.	1	8	8.0	8	0
Adams	N.E.	1	7	7.0	7	0
Dressel	N.Y.J.	1	7	7.0	7	0
McCallum	L.A.Rd	1	7	7.0	7	0
Riggs	Cin.	1	7	7.0	7	0
Graf	Mia.	1	6	6.0	6	0
Talley	Clev.	1	6	6.0	6	0
Galbraith	Clev.	3	16	5.3	10	0
Kay	Denv.	2	10	5.0	7	0
Glasgow	Sea.	1	2	2.0	2	0
Nichols	N.Y.J.	2	3	1.5	3	0
Atwater	Denv.	1	0	0.0	0	0
Ball	Ind.	1	0	0.0	0	0
Gainer	Clev.	1	0	0.0	0	0
Jarvis	Ind.	1	0	0.0	0	0
McSwain	N.E.	1	0	0.0	0	0
Nattiel	Denv.	1	0	0.0	0	0
Norgard	Hou.	1	0	0.0	0	0
Roberts	K.C.	1	0	0.0	0	0
Turk	L.A.Rd	1	0	0.0	0	0
Martin	Mia.	0	0	0.0	0	0
Olsansky	Pitt.	0	0	0.0	0	0

Punt Returns—NFC

	Team	No.	FC	Yds.	Avg.	Lg.	TD		Team	No.	FC	Yds.	Avg.	Lg.	TD
Bailey	Chi.	36	13	399	11.1	95	1	Sutton	L.A.Rm	14	3	136	9.7	22	0
Meggett	N.Y.G.	43	12	467	10.9	68	1	Jordan	Atl.	2	4	19	9.5	10	0
Gray	Det.	34	7	361	10.6	39	0	Martin	Dall.	5	3	46	9.2	17	0
Query	G.B.	32	7	308	9.6	25	0	Mitchell	Wash.	12	4	107	8.9	26	0
Sanders	Atl.	29	13	250	8.6	79	1	Davis	S.F.	5	3	38	7.6	24	0
Sikahema	Phx.	36	6	306	8.5	20	0	Edwards	Phil.	8	7	60	7.5	13	0
V. Buck	N.O.	37	8	305	8.2	33	0	Ellard	L.A.Rm	2	0	15	7.5	8	0
Taylor	S.F.	26	5	212	8.2	30	0	Hargrove	Phil.	12	2	83	6.9	13	0
Drewrey	T.B.	23	15	184	8.0	16	0	Griffin	S.F.	16	8	105	6.6	20	0
Harris	Phil.	28	8	214	7.6	30	0	Green	Wash.	1	1	6	6.0	6	0
Stanley	Wash.	24	8	176	7.3	32	0	Hillary	Minn.	8	4	45	5.6	12	0
Lewis	Minn.	33	22	236	7.2	30	0	Harris	Dall.	12	6	63	5.3	12	0
Shepard	Dall.	20	1	121	6.1	13	0	Rison	Atl.	2	0	10	5.0	8	0
								Proehl	Phx.	1	1	2	2.0	2	0

Non-qualifiers

	Team	No.	FC	Yds.	Avg.	Lg.	TD		Team	No.	FC	Yds.	Avg.	Lg.	TD
								Wilson	S.F.	1	0	1	1.0	1	0
Morse	N.O.	8	1	95	11.9	18	0	Campbell	Det.	1	0	0	0.0	0	0
J. Smith	Phx.	3	0	34	11.3	16	0	Mitchell	Atl.	1	0	0	0.0	0	0
Bellamy	Phil.	2	0	22	11.0	22	0	Reid	Atl.	1	0	0	0.0	0	0
Henley	L.A.Rm	19	4	195	10.3	26	0	Thomas	Wash.	1	0	0	0.0	0	0
McKinnon	Dall.	2	1	20	10.0	20	0	A. Carter	Minn.	0	5	0	0.0	0	0
Howard	Wash.	10	3	99	9.9	21	0	Pitts	G.B.	0	2	0	0.0	0	0
								Williams	Phil.	2	0	−1	−.5	0	0

Punt Returns—AFC

	Team	No.	FC	Yds.	Avg.	Lg.	TD		Team	No.	FC	Yds.	Avg.	Lg.	TD
Verdin	Ind.	31	3	396	12.8	36	0	Hale	Buff.	10	4	76	7.6	25	0
Woodson	Pitt.	38	8	398	10.5	52	1	Birden	K.C.	10	3	72	7.2	22	0
Warren	Sea.	28	16	269	9.6	39	0	L. Lewis	Clev.	8	7	56	7.0	18	0
T. Brown	L.A.Rd	34	8	295	8.7	39	0	Adams	Clev.	13	4	81	6.2	25	0
Price	Cin.	29	14	251	8.7	66	1	Edwards	Buff.	14	5	92	6.1	16	0
Clark	Denv.	21	1	159	7.6	32	0	Nattiel	Denv.	1	0	5	5.0	5	0
Worthen	K.C.	25	3	180	7.2	37	0	Mays	S.D.	7	4	30	4.3	17	0
McNeil	Hou.	30	20	172	5.7	26	0	Smith	Cin.	1	0	4	4.0	4	0
Martin	Mia.	26	9	140	5.4	35	0	Grant	Ind.	2	0	6	3.0	6	0
Fryar	N.E.	28	10	133	4.8	17	0	Harry	K.C.	1	0	2	2.0	2	0
								Stradford	Mia.	3	2	4	1.3	4	0

Non-qualifiers

	Team	No.	FC	Yds.	Avg.	Lg.	TD		Team	No.	FC	Yds.	Avg.	Lg.	TD
								Martin	N.E.	1	0	1	1.0	1	0
Taylor	S.D.	6	3	112	18.7	55	1	Prior	Ind.	2	6	0	0.0	0	0
Mathis	N.Y.J.	11	7	165	15.0	98	1	Daniel	Ind.	1	0	0	0.0	0	0
Nelson	S.D.	3	0	44	14.7	33	0	Hasty	N.Y.J.	1	0	0	0.0	0	0
Townsell	N.Y.J.	17	4	154	9.1	20	0	Hill	Pitt.	1	0	0	0.0	0	0
N. Lewis	S.D.	13	8	117	9.0	63	1	Lyles	S.D.	1	0	0	0.0	0	0
Odomes	Buff.	1	0	9	9.0	9	0	Odegard	N.Y.J.	1	0	0	0.0	0	0
Schwedes	Mia.	14	3	122	8.7	23	0	Waiters	Clev.	1	0	0	0.0	0	0
Jefferson	Sea.	8	0	68	8.5	14	0	Whitaker	K.C.	1	0	0	0.0	0	0
Johnson	Denv.	11	11	92	8.4	29	0	Williams	Mia.	1	5	0	0.0	0	0
Brennan	Clev.	9	4	72	8.0	15	0	Duncan	Hou.	0	1	0	0.0	0	0

Team Statistics

Offense—NFC

	Atl.	Chi.	Dall.	Det.	G.B.	L.A.Rm	Minn.	N.O.	N.Y.G.	Phil.	Phx.	S.F.	T.B.	Wash.
GAMES (W-L-T)	5-11-0	11-5-0	7-9-0	6-10-0	6-10-0	5-11-0	6-10-0	8-8-0	13-3-0	10-6-0	5-11-0	14-2-0	6-10-0	10-6-0
FIRST DOWNS	274	295	250	278	276	311	288	254	273	325	270	324	238	327
Rushing	85	142	88	112	72	89	106	107	120	132	115	107	83	117
Passing	168	134	135	152	183	191	164	134	135	170	135	201	142	193
Penalty	21	19	27	14	21	31	18	13	18	23	20	16	13	17
TOTAL YDS. GAINED	5055	4980	4081	4977	4675	5430	5034	4476	4805	5700	4745	5895	4475	5562
Avg. Per Game	315.9	311.3	255.1	311.1	292.2	339.4	314.6	279.8	300.3	356.3	296.6	368.4	279.7	347.6
RUSHING (NET)	1594	2436	1500	1927	1369	1612	1867	1850	2049	2556	1915	1718	1626	2083
Avg. Per Game	99.6	152.3	93.8	120.4	85.6	100.8	116.7	115.6	128.1	159.8	119.7	107.4	101.6	130.2
PASSING (NET)	3461	2544	2581	3050	3306	3818	3167	2626	2756	3144	2830	4177	2849	3479
Avg. Per Game	216.3	159.0	161.3	190.6	206.6	238.6	197.9	164.1	172.3	196.5	176.9	261.1	178.1	217.4
RUSHES	420	551	393	366	350	422	455	464	541	540	451	454	410	515
Avg. Yards	3.8	4.4	3.8	5.3	3.9	3.8	4.1	4.0	3.8	4.7	4.2	3.8	4.0	4.0
PASSES ATTEMPTED	528	430	475	460	541	561	497	447	398	479	439	583	448	536
Completed	293	229	254	242	302	310	265	226	231	281	238	360	245	301
Pct. Comp.	55.5	53.3	53.5	52.6	55.8	55.3	53.3	50.6	58.0	58.7	54.2	61.7	54.7	56.2
Tackled	46	43	43	44	62	30	49	20	29	50	44	37	53	22
Yards Lost	265	283	317	278	390	198	278	131	142	438	288	194	433	132
Had Intercepted	18	12	24	20	21	17	24	23	5	13	18	16	24	22
Yards Opp. Ret.	368	164	353	346	293	204	260	283	54	88	201	176	346	271
Opp. Tds on Int.	2	0	4	3	2	2	1	0	1	0	1	1	2	5
PUNTS	70	78	79	63	65	69	79	71	75	74	67	70	72	55
Gross Avg.	41.6	39.4	43.2	40.6	37.4	38.6	41.8	42.1	44.1	41.0	42.8	36.2	40.3	37.5
Touchbacks	4	7	8	5	2	2	8	6	11	3	5	8	5	1
Net Avg.	36.0	33.1	35.6	35.3	32.3	31.5	32.8	36.2	37.3	34.7	37.4	30.9	34.0	32.8
Blocked	0	1	0	0	1	1	1	0	0	2	0	0	0	1
PUNT RETURNS	35	36	39	35	32	35	33	45	43	40	40	48	23	48
Avg. Ret.	8.0	11.1	6.4	10.3	9.6	9.9	6.8	8.9	10.9	7.9	8.6	7.4	7.8	8.1
Ret. for Td	1	1	0	0	0	0	0	0	1	0	0	0	0	0
KICKOFF RETURNS	58	54	54	70	63	63	66	58	46	54	60	53	63	61
Avg. Ret	21.2	16.3	20.4	20.9	20.7	20.3	18.9	20.8	19.2	17.9	17.8	18.2	18.7	18.2
Ret. for Td	1	0	1	0	1	1	0	0	0	0	0	0	0	0
PENALTIES	125	75	98	88	84	87	83	108	83	120	96	104	77	102
Yards	1004	615	729	711	674	632	565	829	655	981	883	828	651	824
FUMBLES	40	29	27	29	37	25	30	29	21	32	25	24	38	14
Fumbles Lost	21	14	9	16	22	14	13	16	9	15	14	14	19	6
Opp. Fumbles	26	38	32	31	26	32	25	35	28	32	28	21	33	24
Opp. Fumbles Rec.	18	14	19	18	14	19	11	19	11	11	11	14	17	12
THIRD DOWN ATTEMPTS	208	221	197	164	197	204	215	208	207	219	192	232	204	219
Converted to First Down	78	75	67	53	75	76	81	83	80	90	76	113	77	103
Third Down Efficiency	37.5	33.9	34.0	32.3	38.1	37.3	37.7	39.9	38.6	41.1	39.6	48.7	37.7	47.0
FOURTH DOWN ATTEMPTS	21	13	10	13	12	18	15	9	17	12	16	9	19	14
Converted to First Down	9	5	5	7	5	6	6	5	8	9	7	7	9	7
Fourth Down Efficiency	42.9	38.5	50.0	53.8	41.7	33.3	40.0	55.6	47.1	75.0	43.8	77.8	47.4	50.0
TOUCHDOWNS	40	39	27	46	29	43	39	30	39	48	31	40	28	41
Rushing	11	22	13	19	5	17	10	14	17	10	13	12	7	16
Passing	21	14	12	24	20	24	25	15	18	34	16	28	18	22
Returns	8	3	2	3	4	2	4	1	4	4	2	0	3	3
EXTRA POINTS ATT.	40	39	27	46	29	43	39	30	39	48	31	40	27	41
Extra Points	40	36	26	46	28	42	38	29	38	45	31	39	27	41
FG/FGA	22/33	26/37	18/25	17/26	23/30	15/24	25/28	21/27	21/28	21/29	17/27	24/36	23/27	30/40
Total Points	348	348	244	373	271	345	351	274	335	396	268	353	264	381

Offense—AFC

	Buff.	Cin.	Clev.	Denv.	Hou.	Ind.	K.C.	L.A.Rd	Mia.	N.E.	N.Y.J.	Pitt.	S.D.	Sea.
GAMES (W-L-T)	13-3-0	9-7-0	3-13-0	5-11-0	9-7-0	7-9-0	11-5-0	12-4-0	12-4-0	1-15-0	6-10-0	9-7-0	6-10-0	9-7-0
FIRST DOWNS	302	277	259	323	376	245	280	258	303	239	295	263	272	284
Rushing	123	107	74	126	97	81	115	110	90	65	128	93	112	111
Passing	161	151	167	170	251	142	142	133	190	156	143	150	142	155
Penalty	18	19	18	27	28	22	23	15	23	18	24	20	18	18
TOTAL YDS. GAINED	5276	5063	4367	5213	6222	4155	5215	4716	5047	4163	4886	4525	4940	4583
Avg. Per Game	329.8	316.4	272.9	325.8	388.9	259.7	325.9	294.8	315.4	260.2	305.4	282.8	308.8	286.4
RUSHING (NET)	2080	2120	1220	1872	1417	1282	1948	2028	1535	1398	2127	1880	2257	1749
Avg. Per Game	130.0	132.5	76.3	117.0	88.6	80.1	121.8	126.8	95.9	87.4	132.9	117.5	141.1	109.3
PASSING (NET)	3196	2943	3147	3341	4805	2873	3267	2688	3512	2765	2759	2645	2683	2834
Avg. Per Game	199.8	183.9	196.7	208.8	300.3	179.6	204.2	168.0	219.5	172.8	172.4	165.3	167.7	177.1
RUSHES	479	485	345	462	328	335	504	496	420	383	476	456	484	457
Avg. Yards	4.3	4.4	3.5	4.1	4.3	3.8	3.9	4.1	3.7	3.7	4.5	4.1	4.7	3.8
PASSES ATTEMPTED	425	425	573	527	639	488	449	336	539	514	451	408	472	448
Completed	263	237	301	305	399	269	260	183	310	274	246	237	246	265
Pct. Comp.	61.9	55.8	52.5	57.9	62.4	55.1	57.9	54.5	57.5	53.3	54.5	58.1	52.1	59.2

264

	Buff.	Cin.	Clev.	Denv.	Hou.	Ind.	K.C.	L.A.Rd	Mia.	N.E.	N.Y.J.	Pitt.	S.D.	Sea.
Tackled	27	33	42	46	39	51	22	29	16	58	40	33	20	40
Yards Lost	208	209	260	330	267	424	191	197	99	443	300	242	157	360
Had Intercepted	11	23	23	18	15	21	5	10	12	20	11	15	19	20
Yards Opp. Ret.	156	233	422	169	237	221	86	100	184	143	186	124	310	252
Opp. Tds on Int.	0	1	3	3	2	1	0	0	0	0	0	0	1	0
PUNTS	58	65	78	60	34	72	81	62	72	92	61	66	62	67
Gross Avg.	39.2	42.1	36.9	43.5	49.3	42.8	35.7	37.3	42.0	40.8	39.3	37.2	39.4	40.6
Touchbacks	4	9	2	7	5	2	3	4	3	7	3	5	2	7
Net Avg.	33.5	34.0	29.8	38.5	40.9	37.1	29.8	32.5	35.6	33.1	33.9	33.6	36.1	34.7
Blocked	0	0	3	0	0	1	0	2	0	2	0	1	1	0
PUNT RETURNS	25	30	31	33	30	36	37	34	39	29	30	39	35	36
Avg. Ret.	7.1	8.5	6.7	7.8	5.7	11.2	6.8	8.7	6.0	4.6	10.6	10.2	9.6	9.4
Ret. for Td	0	1	0	0	0	0	0	0	0	0	1	1	2	0
KICKOFF RETURNS	51	62	71	66	47	66	46	64	43	77	61	50	55	50
Avg. Ret.	20.2	20.4	18.0	19.1	18.5	18.0	17.0	19.3	18.1	18.1	18.5	19.2	21.6	19.8
Ret. for Td	0	0	2	0	0	0	0	0	0	0	0	0	0	0
PENALTIES	92	83	122	108	135	78	111	97	64	99	101	110	103	89
Yards	683	627	922	775	1009	590	886	682	486	742	848	928	886	746
FUMBLES	17	25	37	30	34	23	30	24	33	33	28	40	24	32
Fumbles Lost	10	12	23	14	21	10	14	14	15	16	13	17	13	16
Opp. Fumbles	33	32	24	36	22	25	38	21	23	25	29	33	26	32
Opp. Fumbles Rec.	17	16	9	15	12	15	25	9	8	18	11	18	11	18
THIRD DOWN ATTEMPTS	184	194	208	207	181	181	221	178	206	227	193	188	224	200
Converted to First Down	81	78	81	86	96	55	91	85	88	89	71	74	101	86
Third Down Efficiency	44.0	40.2	38.9	41.5	53.0	30.4	41.2	47.8	42.7	39.2	36.8	39.4	45.1	43.0
FOURTH DOWN ATTEMPTS	11	19	19	14	12	19	10	8	13	12	21	10	18	7
Converted to First Down	5	12	8	7	3	11	7	2	10	2	5	4	6	6
Fourth Down Efficiency	45.5	63.2	42.1	50.0	25.0	57.9	70.0	25.0	76.9	16.7	23.8	40.0	33.3	85.7
TOUCHDOWNS	53	44	27	36	49	33	38	42	39	19	32	33	36	34
Rushing	20	16	10	19	10	9	11	20	13	4	16	11	14	18
Passing	28	25	13	15	37	22	23	19	21	14	14	20	18	15
Returns	5	3	4	2	2	2	4	3	5	1	2	2	4	1
EXTRA POINTS ATT.	53	44	27	36	49	33	38	42	38	19	32	33	36	34
Extra Points	50	41	24	34	46	32	37	40	37	19	32	32	34	33
FG/FGA	20/29	17/22	14/20	25/34	21/32	17/24	34/37	15/20	21/25	16/22	23/26	20/25	21/28	23/32
Total Points	428	360	228	331	405	281	369	337	336	181	295	292	315	306

Defense—NFC

	Atl.	Chi.	Dall.	Det.	G.B.	L.A.Rm	Minn.	N.O.	N.Y.G.	Phil.	Phx.	S.F.	T.B.	Wash.
OPP. POINTS	365	280	308	413	347	412	326	275	211	299	396	239	367	301
OPP. FIRST DOWNS	300	256	281	334	286	287	257	279	245	251	306	250	313	267
Rushing	79	102	110	141	113	93	107	91	90	59	140	77	129	77
Passing	179	136	153	174	160	176	136	167	139	169	146	157	168	166
Penalty	42	18	18	19	13	18	14	21	16	23	20	16	16	24
OPP. YDS. GAINED	5270	4492	4615	5734	5442	5411	4717	4878	4206	4660	5216	4273	5479	4730
Avg. Per Game	329.4	280.8	288.4	358.4	340.1	338.2	294.8	304.9	262.9	291.3	326.0	267.1	342.4	295.6
RUSHING (NET)	1357	1572	1976	2388	2059	1649	2074	1559	1459	1172	2318	1258	2223	1587
Avg. Per Game	84.8	98.3	123.5	149.3	128.7	103.1	129.6	97.4	91.2	73.3	144.9	78.6	138.9	99.2
PASSSING (NET)	3913	2920	2639	3346	3383	3762	2643	3319	2747	3488	2898	3015	3256	3143
Avg. Per Game	244.6	182.5	164.9	209.1	211.4	235.1	165.2	207.4	171.7	218.0	181.1	188.4	203.5	196.4
OPP. RUSHES	413	391	482	532	475	418	503	410	388	336	521	353	496	382
Avg. Yards	3.3	4.0	4.1	4.5	4.3	3.9	4.1	3.8	3.8	3.5	4.4	3.6	4.5	4.2
OPP. PASSES	537	495	470	507	479	501	422	534	496	566	402	522	471	514
Completed	297	258	271	319	256	296	218	316	278	273	233	265	263	281
Pct. Comp.	55.3	52.1	57.7	62.9	53.4	59.1	51.7	59.2	56.0	48.2	58.0	50.8	55.8	54.7
Tackled	33	41	36	41	27	30	47	42	30	46	36	44	34	45
Yards Lost	214	300	292	279	172	180	277	265	186	283	232	263	204	340
Intercepted By	17	31	11	17	16	12	22	8	23	19	16	17	25	21
Yards Ret.	237	268	126	273	154	105	358	158	116	271	274	171	487	271
Ret. for Td	3	1	1	1	1	1	2	1	2	3	2	0	3	2
OPP. PUNTS	74	74	70	62	69	66	77	74	76	86	63	82	55	76
Gross Avg.	40.1	37.9	40.6	40.8	39.1	41.4	39.4	40.9	41.3	40.3	43.6	40.0	40.5	43.3
Touchbacks	7	6	4	6	9	5	4	2	4	10	4	6	4	5
Net Avg.	34.0	32.7	34.9	35.1	31.6	33.5	35.4	36.2	34.1	34.1	36.9	35.9	35.8	39.2
Blocked	1	0	2	0	1	0	0	0	0	0	0	0	0	0
OPP. PUNT RET.	39	39	43	29	34	46	44	43	41	37	41	30	39	30
Avg. Ret.	8.1	8.3	10.2	8.1	7.7	9.1	11.7	7.0	7.1	9.1	6.3	7.2	9.0	6.8
OPP. KICKOFF RET.	49	73	55	70	56	68	62	36	65	74	56	66	43	58
Avg. Ret.	16.6	20.5	20.7	17.6	20.2	20.7	21.8	16.3	19.2	19.0	18.9	19.5	24.1	17.4
OPP. PENALTIES	95	84	103	97	108	109	100	86	83	93	96	84	78	88
Yards	809	676	897	796	844	973	787	645	564	701	834	644	607	698
OPP. 3RD DOWN ATT.	197	187	205	221	210	201	207	216	197	217	198	199	205	198
Converted to First Down	68	65	86	105	83	86	71	86	70	67	91	71	93	76
Third Down Efficiency	34.5	34.8	42.0	47.5	39.5	42.8	34.3	39.8	35.5	30.9	46.0	35.7	45.4	38.4
OPP. 4TH DOWN ATT.	14	11	16	16	9	10	11	16	17	18	16	15	13	16

— 265 —

	Atl.	Chi.	Dall.	Det.	G.B.	L.A.Rm	Minn.	N.O.	N.Y.G.	Phil.	Phx.	S.F.	T.B.	Wash.
Converted to First Down	5	6	8	12	3	3	5	11	7	8	8	4	7	7
Fourth Down Efficiency	35.7	54.5	50.0	75.0	33.3	30.0	45.5	68.8	41.2	44.4	50.0	26.7	53.8	43.8
OPP. TOUCHDOWNS	44	31	36	49	40	49	34	30	23	33	50	26	45	35
Rushing	11	10	18	22	16	17	12	8	9	9	20	7	20	8
Passing	31	19	12	21	20	30	20	21	12	23	29	17	22	21
Returns	2	2	6	6	4	2	2	1	2	1	1	2	3	6
OPP. EXTRA POINTS ATT.	44	29	35	48	40	49	34	30	22	33	50	26	45	35
Opp. Extra Points	42	27	35	48	39	46	32	30	22	32	48	26	43	35
OPP. FG/FGA	19/26	22/28	18/26	23/30	24/35	24/32	30/36	21/35	16/22	22/27	16/20	19/23	18/27	18/23

Defense—AFC

	Buff.	Cin.	Clev.	Denv.	Hou.	Ind.	K.C.	L.A.Rd	Mia.	N.E.	N.Y.J.	Pitt.	S.D.	Sea.
OPP. POINTS	263	352	462	374	307	353	257	268	242	446	345	240	281	286
OPP. FIRST DOWNS	288	308	314	306	279	320	268	266	268	307	318	257	268	280
Rushing	105	116	117	110	88	130	85	95	110	151	112	102	92	86
Passing	159	180	169	181	160	176	164	152	145	139	186	130	152	171
Penalty	24	12	28	15	31	14	19	19	13	17	20	25	24	23
OPP. YDS. GAINED	4607	5605	5190	5345	4635	5614	4887	4413	4547	5697	5455	4115	4425	4609
Avg. Per Game	287.9	350.3	324.4	334.1	289.7	350.9	305.4	275.8	284.2	356.1	340.9	257.2	276.6	288.1
RUSHING (NET)	1808	2085	2105	1963	1575	2212	1646	1716	1831	2676	2018	1615	1515	1605
Avg. Per Game	113.0	130.3	131.6	122.7	98.4	138.3	102.9	107.3	114.4	167.3	126.1	100.9	94.7	100.3
PASSING (NET)	2799	3520	3085	3382	3060	3402	3241	2697	2716	3021	3437	2500	2910	3004
Avg. Per Game	174.9	220.0	192.8	211.4	191.3	212.6	202.6	168.6	169.8	188.8	214.8	156.3	181.9	187.8
OPP. RUSHES	483	442	512	456	392	513	373	439	461	565	423	446	424	413
Avg. Yards	3.7	4.7	4.1	4.3	4.0	4.3	4.4	3.9	4.0	4.7	4.8	3.6	3.6	3.9
OPP. PASSES	455	543	444	479	460	492	512	437	462	374	516	460	462	504
Completed	254	300	253	284	267	301	267	246	257	218	311	236	254	300
Pct. Comp.	55.8	55.2	57.0	59.3	58.0	61.2	52.1	56.3	55.6	58.3	60.3	51.3	55.0	59.5
Tackled	43	25	31	34	38	29	60	48	45	33	38	34	45	33
Yards Lost	326	205	211	289	272	203	421	335	348	224	308	228	345	252
Intercepted By	18	15	13	10	21	9	20	13	19	14	18	24	19	12
Yards Ret.	151	146	212	190	295	173	250	102	288	194	205	385	188	182
Ret. for Td	2	1	1	1	1	1	1	1	2	0	0	1	0	0
OPP. PUNTS	66	63	67	62	62	58	73	64	75	56	56	64	70	77
Gross Avg.	38.2	40.4	38.1	41.4	34.9	42.0	40.2	38.2	40.2	40.6	41.4	40.7	41.1	41.8
Touchbacks	5	4	4	5	3	2	4	6	8	5	6	3	5	5
Net Avg.	32.6	33.5	33.8	36.6	30.6	35.5	33.4	34.0	34.5	29.4	33.6	37.6	34.9	37.2
Blocked	3	0	0	1	1	0	5	0	1	1	0	1	0	0
OPP. PUNT RET.	31	36	41	22	23	42	44	24	40	50	35	16	28	29
Avg. Ret.	8.1	9.8	10.4	7.2	8.1	8.0	9.3	6.4	9.9	10.1	7.7	6.6	4.6	8.8
OPP. KICKOFF RET.	72	43	45	69	71	49	81	49	53	38	61	56	62	51
Avg. Ret.	15.8	22.0	17.9	19.1	18.7	19.6	17.2	20.9	20.6	17.2	19.4	22.3	16.9	17.8
OPP. PENALTIES	107	100	96	105	133	104	125	86	91	73	107	88	87	108
Yards	839	819	681	839	1005	781	849	710	749	488	859	714	720	766
OPP. 3RD DOWN ATT.	208	213	211	195	174	204	204	201	206	192	200	204	202	207
Converted to First Down	89	96	103	84	65	88	81	76	79	83	88	80	83	76
Third Down Efficiency	42.8	45.1	48.8	43.1	37.4	43.1	39.7	37.8	38.3	43.2	44.0	39.2	41.1	36.7
OPP. 4TH DOWN ATT.	19	12	3	13	13	14	15	16	19	14	17	14	14	11
Converted to First Down	10	2	2	7	6	7	3	9	7	7	10	6	6	7
Fourth Down Efficiency	52.6	16.7	66.7	53.8	46.2	50.0	20.0	56.3	36.8	53.8	71.4	35.3	42.9	63.6
OPP. TOUCHDOWNS	30	41	59	43	37	36	30	26	26	52	39	26	33	32
Rushing	13	15	21	16	12	12	12	4	11	29	15	13	10	7
Passing	17	24	32	22	18	20	16	20	14	21	23	9	22	19
Returns	0	2	6	5	7	4	2	2	1	2	1	4	1	6
OPP. EXTRA POINTS ATT.	30	41	59	43	37	36	30	26	26	52	38	25	33	32
Opp. Extra Points	29	40	56	38	34	35	29	25	26	52	35	25	33	32
OPP. FG/FGA	19/25	22/28	17/26	26/33	17/21	32/43	16/20	29/33	20/29	27/31	26/33	18/28	16/21	21/27